DRESSING DANGEROUSLY

DRESSING DANGEROUSLY

DYSFUNCTIONAL FASHION IN FILM

| Jonathan Faiers

YALE UNIVERSITY PRESS • NEW HAVEN AND LONDON

FOR DELL AND INEZ WITH LOVE

Designed by Paul Sloman

Printed in China

Library of Congress Cataloging-in-Publication Data

Faiers, Jonathan.
  Dressing dangerously : dysfunctional fashion in film / Jonathan Faiers.
       pages cm
  Includes bibliographical references and index.
  ISBN 978-0-300-18438-9 (cl : alk. paper)
  1. Fashion in motion pictures. 2. Costume–Symbolic aspects. I. Title.
  PN1995.9.C56F35 2013
  791.43'6564–DC23

                    2013004997

FRONTISPIECE: STAGE FRIGHT
1950, dir. Alfred Hitchcock.
Charlotte Innwood presents the stained dress (Photofest).

CONTENTS

INTRODUCTION

'To assemble large-scale constructions out of the smallest and most precisely cut components. Indeed, to discover in the analysis of the small individual moment the crystal of the total event'.[1]

In *Dressing Dangerously: Dysfunctional Fashion in Film* many 'small individual moments' 'precisely cut' from film narratives will be discussed in order not to understand the crystal of the total event, the narrative itself, but to consider other events also reflected in its facets, reflections that are necessarily transitory and illusory, but none the less dazzling and inextricably part of our experience of that crystal. This study will attempt to consider the reflections of clothing in film that glisten alongside its often brighter construction of character and the propulsion of action. Character and plot development are clothing's accepted functions within the narrative of mainstream film. As soon as these clothing-related moments have been precisely cut from their individual narratives, however, and set alongside other moments from other narratives, following Walter Benjamin's 'principle of montage', they are then free to reflect and illumine other spaces both within film and beyond the confines of cinematic representation. Of course an acknowledgement and discussion of how these clothing-related moments occur, their position within the narrative and possible ramifications will be necessary, but what else they might say about our individual experience of dress, similarities and contingencies with other sequences in often widely different productions, and their visual and psychical resonance will be the primary concern of this study. These sequences or moments have been chosen because of their ability to manifest an excess of meaning both visually and textually, beyond their allotted position within the film's plot and mise-en-scène. This excess in turn links them to similar 'surplus' moments and suggests an alternative function, a *dysfunctionality* that, until excised from their narrative, often remains as a momentary oddness, a concentration that seems unwarranted or, as Slavoj Žižek termed it when discussing *The*

Hitchcockian Blot, 'a small supplementary feature, a detail that "does not belong", that sticks out, is "out of place", does not make any sense within the frame of the idyllic scene.'[2] So *Dressing Dangerously* will attempt to understand why raincoats are frequently carried rather than worn and why forgotten jewellery reaps the most violent retribution. Whether it is ever possible to walk in 'dead men's shoes' and to summon up spirits with just the aid of a scarf. Why men should always dress themselves and when it is acceptable to wear an all-white suit. Is yellow the new red and are cowboy suits *de rigueur* for town wear? And why monograms should be avoided and bloodstains removed as quickly as possible.

The clothing and accessories considered in this study occupy alternative spaces in film to that of their more conventional companions which fulfil the fundamentally recognised function of clothing to protect from the elements and preserve modesty, and in addition the specifically cinematic conventions of conferring glamour and acting as vestimentary indicators of character. While many of the items considered in *Dressing Dangerously* fulfil these widely accepted roles, they do this reluctantly if at all, and are noticeable instead for their dysfunctionality; often unworn, non-protective, problematic and transformative. This dysfunctionality, however, is not to be understood as insufficiency or redundancy but rather as a necessary stage in their development from conventional items of film costume into objects of sartorial agency, whose original or popularly understood function is rejected in order to assume significance beyond the parameters determined by the film's narrative. Jean Baudrillard suggested that the material object once it has entered the space of the collection is 'divested of its function, abstracted from any practical context' and 'takes on a strictly subjective status'.[3] Although the clothing considered here may not always entirely lose its original function, it does assume an additional status to that bestowed on it by the formal limitations of film and, just as Baudrillard's objects are liberated from their practical value within the spatial and classificatory boundaries of the collection, so too these garments resist their narrative 'value' within the overall structure of the film.

In *Dressing Dangerously* the garments considered oscillate between their characteristic practical, gendered and fashionable territories – the qualities that many studies of cinematic clothing have investigated – and more uncharted psychological, emotional and meta-cinematic terrains, which are often ignored, or considered only as minor elements of the particular film narrative in which they feature. The responses that these dysfunctional, or perhaps we might refer to them as alternatively functional, garments invoke in the viewer is as insistent as the aspirational or sexualised ones normally accorded clothing in film. The mimetic process of identification with similar moments of discomfort, loss or even trauma in the viewer's everyday experience of clothing triggered by these dysfunctional cinematic garments is surely more comprehensive than the accepted production of (typically gendered) sartorial desire, and yet remains critically under researched. These dysfunctional vestimentary sequences act as fictional reminders of the viewer's personal history and contact with clothing and, in turn, bring to the fore similar fictional representations of dress (for it is impossible to excise one specific example from the sea of stored images that comprise our individual visual memories), establishing the contents of what I have termed a 'negative cinematic wardrobe'. This uncoupling from narrative, brought about by the excessive visual or textual emphasis placed on a garment, or by the personal associations it triggers in the viewer, interrogates the authority of mainstream film's ability to immerse the viewer within the film's action.

Suturing, literally meaning a stitch and most commonly used when referring to the surgical procedure of sewing together a wound, was originally introduced as a term by film theorists such as Jean-Pierre Oudart in the 1970s, who in turn took Jacques Lacan's formulation of the term *suture* describing the relationship between the conscious and unconscious.[4] Meaning in its simplest sense the process by which a spectator is literally 'stitched' into the action of a film, the term seems especially apposite when talking about the film viewer's relationship to on-screen clothing. Most tellingly for this study, it is when the suture or stitch starts to come apart, due to the stress placed on the 'seam' or the immersion within fiction, by the constant oscillation between our lived experience of clothing and the fantasy of cinematic clothing, that it is at its most revealing. This unravelling is assisted by the negative wardrobe of dysfunctional dress. Of course, it could be argued that many such incidences of the intrusion of reality occur when watching film, and indeed much experimental or avant-garde cinema has been constructed round this disjuncture, but within mainstream cinema these moments are comparatively rare and by no means universally experienced. However, the wearing of clothing and the vicissitudes of dress are commonplace experiences; therefore, instances of cinematic dysfunctional dress become an invaluable tool with which to analyse how dress functions both on screen diegetically and off screen.

TERMINOLOGY

Terms such as 'dysfunctional' and 'negative' are vital to this study and therefore require further consideration. It is perhaps surprising that some of the most perceptive comments concerning clothing and its dysfunctionality are to be found in the work of historians writing before the study of clothing had become classified as dress studies or fashion theory. Quentin Bell in 1947 provided a check list of fashionably dysfunctional items of dress. Starting at the top of the body and working downwards, he records hats designed to give no protection to the head or that render the wearer helpless in high wind, and continues down the length of the body noting in passing: strangulating neckwear, constricting corsetry, impeding sleeves, life-endangering skirts and excruciating footwear.[5] Similarly, Doris Langley Moore, the pioneer fashion historian, writer and museum founder, was acutely aware of clothing's or, more accurately, fashion's inherent illogicality.[6] In her groundbreaking television series on the history of dress broadcast by the BBC in the 1950s, she peppers her clipped commentary for the 1956 episode *Sense and Nonsense in Fashion* with comments on the clothes being modelled as 'strikingly unsuitable', 'nonsense', 'demented' and 'crazy'.[7] However, both Bell's and Langley Moore's point was not merely to classify fashion's eccentricities as such but rather to illustrate Thorstein Veblen's argument that in order for fashion to fulfil its true socio-economic function, it needs to be as impractical and expressive of an indolent lifestyle as possible.[8] While Veblen's theories of conspicuous consumption more than a hundred years after they were formulated remain fundamental to the understanding of the development and contemporary importance accorded to fashion, its systems and circuits, a similar but not identical consideration of the necessity for narrative impracticality or dysfunctionality can aid our understanding of cinematic clothing beyond the parameters of glamour and characterisation.

'Dysfunctional' as a term is understandably construed as negative, suggesting that the object to which it is applied has ceased 'working' or become 'unusable' and, although many of the garments considered in this book fail to deliver their original purpose at the most fundamental level, the disproportionate or unexpected emphasis placed on them triggers an automatic and complex series of additional emotional responses in the viewer. These may include references to other film moments where similar examples exist and that are contingent with our own experiences and situations such as wearing inappropriate clothing, clothing that does not fit, gets dirty or is mislaid. The catalogue of dysfunctional clothing is both endless and universally experienced and so when a similar scenario is played out on film we feel an empathetic response. These clothing sequences when liberated from the constraints of conventional cinematic narrative and considered in conjunction with other similarly excised fragments reveal dysfunctionality to be charged with the potential to evoke both personal memories of clothing (real or cinematic) and for them to act as more than straightforward signifiers of class and gender or as records of visual fashion history. As Victor Burgin, discussing the memories of film fragments, suggests:

> The narratives have dropped away like those rockets that disintegrate in the atmosphere once they have placed their small payloads in orbit. Detached from their original settings each scene is now the satellite of the other. Each echoes the other, increasingly merges with the other, and I experience a kind of fascinated incomprehension before the hybrid object they have become.[9]

This hybrid object is the subject of this work, an amalgam of both dress and film studies, rejecting chronologies and remaining receptive to the challenge that the 'image flux', to quote Burgin again, offers. Dysfunctionality becomes a necessary agent of dispersal, displacing the customary spectacular seductions of cinematic clothing and exposing the garments hidden at the back of the negative cinematic wardrobe.

Naturally, clothing in mainstream film must fulfil some, or all, of its accepted functions, and it is often proclaimed that the chief task of clothing in film, and by extension the work of the film costume designer, is that the clothes be 'appropriate', fit the character and in many instances should be 'unnoticeable' for fear that if the viewer's attention is drawn to clothing, it could jeopardise the smooth flow of narrative progression or, as it has been put, 'the "best" costume design may be invisible'. In short, there is a danger of costume's breaking the cinematic frame.[10] *Dressing Dangerously* wilfully breaks those frames in order to allow these disparate dysfunctional objects to abandon their responsibilities and 'act out of character', to consider how they communicate meta-cinematically as well as culturally, politically and philosophically. The concept of dysfunctional dress can be possible only within the parameters of the film itself, and that the examples discussed in this book are scripted and intrinsic to the conventions of plot and narrative goes without saying. As with all interdisciplinary studies, the dangers of becoming complicit in the very structures one is hoping to interrogate, of becoming seduced by the object of study, are ever present but worth risking in order to ascertain the ultimate benefits of attempting to chart seldom visited territory.[11] By analysing the minor imperfections that characterise the dysfunctional wardrobe, the small but significant stains and blemishes, the scuffs, marks and tears, culled from a wide variety of film fragments, a space can be constructed that encompasses and acknowledges our personal interaction with clothing alongside its representation on film, a space where 'the combination of these disparate elements' will activate 'the dissolution of any boundaries between fact and fiction, original and simulation, fixity and movement'.[12]

As with the term 'dysfunctional', 'negative' is to be understood not as prohibitive, absent or lacking but perhaps photographically, as something without which the positive would be unachievable. The negative cinematic wardrobe stocked with items of vestimentary lawlessness exists in tandem with its modish partner, but its contents have been obscured by more fashionable or conventional items, which have long benefited from critical attention centred on areas such as film costume's relationship to fashion, costume and the construction of gender, historical accuracy in the costume film and the skill of the costume maker.[13] Jean Dubuffet suggested that 'It is the nature of culture to cast a spotlight on certain productions. For the benefit of these productions, it drains the light from all others, without worrying about casting them into darkness' and, like a wardrobe in which it is possible to see only those garments hanging at the front, the negative cinematic wardrobe needs critical illumination for the full potential of its contents to be revealed.[14]

The negative cinematic wardrobe is an attempt to establish a space for the various articles of dress considered in this work. It is a storage space that exists alongside our common understanding of a wardrobe as originally a chamber, and then subsequently a piece of furniture where clothes are kept, or 'guarded', as its etymology makes clear, from the French *garderobe*; a space where clothes are 'guarded' or 'warded'. A wardrobe also has a specific theatrical derivation, meaning the range of articles of dress that will be worn during a theatrical production, or in the case of *Dressing Dangerously* a film. If we consider the term negative to mean an opposite or an absence, then when applied to the accepted function of a wardrobe, the implication is that the clothes within it are unguarded, unwatched and unregulated. It is this meaning that is pertinent to the articles studied here; unseen, or perhaps overlooked, these garments occupy a specular storage space, similar to its positive partner, but with certain functions reversed or missing. As if a mirror had been placed in front of its contents and, just as a mirror reverses the order or position of objects reflected in it, so too are the functions of the garments hanging in the negative cinematic wardrobe similarly reversed. Therefore, typically its clothes provide no protection, remain unworn or are not kept safe. The referent of photography earlier served to explain this term, and that understanding of the photographic negative being fundamental to the positive image, of a necessary earlier stage in the production of the recognisable, is equally necessary to the garments under discussion: the possibility of loss, of discomfort, of exposure, makes the security, comfort and admiration of their positive counterparts possible. Conversely, the stripping away of the garments' function effected by its negative reflection, its removal of its 'wards', its normative functions, allows these 'unguarded' garments to be transformed, to become an alternative set of vestimentary signals with a communicative power beyond the confines of film narrative. Stocking this negative wardrobe is, however, prohibited by its utilisation in the construction of film narrative and by its status as one among many garments worn in the same film. So, in order to choose from the negative cinematic wardrobe, its contents must first be selected and then liberated from the grip of the narratives they appear in, as Gaston Bachelard suggested: 'the real wardrobe is not an everyday piece of furniture. It is not opened every day, and so, like a heart that confides in no one, the key is not on the door.'[15]

SELECTION

Just as the terms dysfunctional and negative demand clarification, so too does the term 'mainstream film' which has been used so far to establish the parameters of the films selected for this study. Mainstream film is employed in its broadest sense to mean commercial or popular film as opposed to art, art house, avant-garde, underground, low-budget, independent or any of the other epithets used to describe films made outside the major studio film system. In addition this work confines itself to English-language productions and therefore either American or British film industry productions, with a few exceptions, and those which at some point went on general theatrical release.[16] Susan Hayward provides a useful condensation of the key characteristics of mainstream, or dominant, cinema, as she also terms it, establishing that the primary plot line revolves around order/disorder/order restored, that there are central characters and therefore the plot is character-driven, the continuity of the film is seamless and editing does not draw attention to itself, and that the mise-en-scène, lighting and colour are appropriate to the genre.[17] She also quotes Annette Kuhn who suggests that mainstream or dominant cinema is the result of the synthesis between the economic and the ideological, acknowledging the centrality of the classic studio system of Hollywood film from the 1930s and 40s as central to this process.

The majority of films considered in this study conform to this template; however, their critical reputation varies enormously with productions from universally regarded directors such as Alfred Hitchcock (who figures large in this study and to whom

I shall refer later), alongside obscure, practically forgotten directors and productions. Similarly, the genres most frequently discussed here tend to be grouped round thrillers or film noir, comedies and horror, melodrama and so-called 'women's pictures' of the 1940s and 50s, as well as the occasional foray into what might be termed 'B' or cult film territory, which was felt necessary in order to provide a full range of possibilities for the dysfunctionality under discussion. What is not included is perhaps easier to state: films that typically demand a certain kind of uniform for their principal characters, such as war films and prison films, are not discussed because the imposition of a standardised type of clothing on the main protagonists of the film can be understood as a form of predetermined sartorial dysfunctionality whereby individual clothing choices are not permissible. Yet, what is more important, the audience's experience of wearing uniform (school uniform perhaps being an exception) will be less frequent than that of civilian clothing and this, in addition to the fact that the 'uniformity' of uniform is so much a part of the mise-en-scène of these films – integral to the viewer's suturing into the fictional space of prison or army camp – that the individual emotional responses to the clothing represented are inhibited. It could be argued that when uniforms are stained, or otherwise presented as less than perfect, this marks out their dysfunctionality even more forcefully, but these occurrences are typically heavily scripted (the sergeant berating the sloppily dressed private, for instance) and the example of dysfunctionality so firmly enclosed by the narrative development that it loses the quality of excess, of being surplus and uncontainable within the mise-en-scène. Similarly, costume film (with a few notable exceptions) is not within the remit of this book.[18] Historical costume initially appears to be the quintessential example of dysfunctional fashion, especially when considering its inevitable historical inaccuracies and its tendency to 'historicise' contemporary clothing, so that costumes purported to be 'historical' are refracted through the fashionable lens of the prevailing modes popular at the time the film was made, 1930s 'Rococo', for example. As

Anne Hollander suggests, as long as certain universally agreed vestimentary 'signals' are retained, costume film can invoke a historical period no matter how contemporary its vision of the past may be: 'Bette Davis behaved and dressed quite differently in her two versions of Queen Elizabeth, one in 1939 and one in 1955; both were in "authentic" period dress and naturalistically acted, although neither much resembled the clothes and gestures in Queen Elizabeth's actual portraits. Each looked correctly dressed and naturally behaved for its time.'[19] Above all, though, how historical costume attempts to evoke a specific period, how this is achieved, the prevalence of certain historical periods at specific junctures in cinematic history and how inevitably historical costume comments on contemporary fashions would require an analysis of films that are beyond the remit of this study. This fascinating subject has been explored by writers such as Pam Cook in her *Fashioning the Nation* in which she examines the costuming of Gainsborough Studios productions of the 1940s and its relationship both to British national identity and European fashion; and the costume film's specific 'dysfunctionality' is a fertile area deserving of further research.[20] Independent or avant-garde film is also beyond the remit and scope of this study, since the techniques employed to make the viewer conscious of the formal structure and production of film itself, typical components of these films, often focus the viewer's attention on aspects of the film's construction that may well include the representation of clothing. Therefore, again the 'out of placeness' of the visual or textual emphasis given to clothing is clearly signalled and as such encourages a specific set of associations in the viewer, rather than the individual often unrefined responses triggered by the eruption of dysfunctionality in mainstream film.

This broad selection has both advantages and disadvantages. Many of the films discussed are well known and as such form part of a popular, shared visual cinematic language, and therefore the specific clothing-related sequences, it could be argued, form an important part of our common mediated 'experience' of clothing. Mainstream film's ability to become embedded within the public consciousness assists in the production of what Raphael Samuel termed 'unofficial knowledge', a body of information concerning a wide variety of socio-cultural and historical phenomena.[21] Continuously circulating within the public arenas of cinema, domestic DVD players, television and various digital formats, it is likely that the average viewer will have given certain films repeated viewings, whether intentionally or unintentionally. This repetition of certain productions as well as the constant access to films of a wide chronology, and of different genres being systematically broadcast, downloaded and otherwise accessed, aids the unconscious acquisition by each of us of a personal collection of film and film moments. Allowing for differences of age, geographical location and domestic viewing patterns, these individual experiences of past film viewings, and in this case dress-related sequences, can constitute a collective memory, a cinematic archive of dysfunctional dress. This memory is of course fallible and dependent on individual response and many other contributing factors; these clothing memories might be triggered while watching film, via everyday lived experiences of our own clothing or enter completely unbidden, involuntarily, ushered in by apparently random or inconsequential incidents. Sequences vividly recalled, half forgotten or apparently consigned to oblivion fill the negative cinematic wardrobe. The accuracy of these memories is necessarily unreliable, however, and individual acts of restitution mean that the wardrobe's contents are always in a state of flux, filled with garments whose ownership, purpose and appearance is penetrated by those garments hanging next to it. Burgin again elucidates this integration of fact and film fiction: 'The more the film is distanced in memory, the more the binding effect of the narrative is loosened. The sequence breaks apart. The fragments go adrift and enter into new combinations, more or less transitory, in the eddies of memory: memories of other films, and memories of real events.'[22]

This book attempts to stop momentarily the flow of these achronic fragments, to consider the ultimately impossible task of reconstituting these scattered images into fluctuating, 'recycled' dysfunctional 'shorts', brief ruptured films that dematerialise as soon as they are assembled. The images in *Dressing Dangerously* provide a parallel commentary to the text, contrasting the official 'functional' images often issued by the film studios as publicity material, with smaller, obscure 'dysfunctional' moments that are 'grabbed' before fading again. These 'film strips' of dysfunctionality are of course only made possible with the advent of digital technology, which has 'exponentially expanded the range of possibilities for dismantling and reconfiguring the once inviolable objects offered by narrative cinema.'[23] These brief 'films' are accompanied by commentaries assembled from splinters of film dialogue, passages from literature, lines from song lyrics, with the 'action' taking place in locations featuring critical landmarks relevant to our socio-cultural understanding of dress. Inevitably incomplete and partial, these dysfunctional processions await our own individual responses and memories of clothing, both filmic and real, to join them, lengthening or branching off from the sequence before it loops and plays again. With new additions and new exclusions, the examples used to construct these films are infinitely reinterpretable according to the 'assembler': the examples contained in *Dressing Dangerously* provide a mere glimpse of the richness of film as a source of information once its narrative grip is loosened, as Raymond Bellour identified: 'film never stops saying something other than what one thinks it says, and [that], above all, it says it differently than one, always too easily, would make it say it.'[24]

It is unsurprising that many of the films featured in *Dressing Dangerously* could be categorised as crime films. Clothing and personal possessions as constituting clues, an ability to act as 'witnesses' to a crime, is a firmly established literary and cinematic concept and this study will explore exactly how a model of dysfunctionality can inform our understanding of clothing as clue. The films of Hitchcock can, superficially at least, be similarly categorised as crime films, the majority featuring murder alongside other criminal activities, and his films reoccur at regular intervals throughout this book.[25] Hitchcock's mastery

of the arresting visual image, the psychic charge with which his mise-en-scène is invested and the excessive attention placed on clothing in his films means that the films provide fertile ground for the location of dysfunctionality. This, coupled with the universal popularity of his films, means that at any given time they may be broadcast on television, screened at cinemas either individually or as part of film festivals, available and constantly reissued as DVDs, downloads and other formats. Similarly, fragments of his films are referenced or used in advertising, promotional videos and related commercial media, and stills illustrate a never ending stream of books, journals and magazine articles devoted to his work. All this results in Hitchcock's films, and for the purposes of this study clothing-related sequences from his oeuvre, occupying a prominent position in our popular visual memory and perception of cinematic clothing. Žižek has observed that this concentration on Hitchcock's work, his status as an *auteur* with an immediately recognisable visual and directorial style, 'has taught us to pay attention to the continuum of motifs, visual and others which persist from one film to another irrespective of the changed narrative context'. While Žižek is referring exclusively to Hitchcock's work, this 'continuum of motifs' is traced persistently throughout *Dressing Dangerously*, within Hitchcock's films themselves, as well as across films from different genres, periods and directorial styles.[26]

Hitchcock's meticulous attention to detail, especially concerning the clothing used in his films, is well known. His belief in the style of dress worn by his actors having to be commensurate with the characters they were playing, meant that for example when filming *Psycho* he insisted that the clothes for Janet Leigh playing the secretary Marion Crane, rather than be designed, were bought from a local store and cost no more than a secretary on an average salary would be able to afford. His assertion that the clothes in his films be unobtrusive unless the script called for it meant that costume designer Edith Head, who designed the clothes for a total of eleven Hitchcock films, was familiar with his strictures concering dress. While working on *The Birds*, she recalled, 'He virtually restricted me to two colors, blue and green. We had worked together for so many years that I was well aware of his feeling about garish colors . . . He preferred "nature colors", as he called them: beige, soft greens, and delicate turquoises.'[27] This 'unnoticeable' approach to dress is elsewhere brought to a logical conclusion in his use of items of dress and accessories as McGuffins – the objects that propel the action of the film forward, link leading characters together and yet ultimately are revealed as 'nothing at all', meaningless or 'dysfunctional', as with the raincoat from *Young and Innocent* discussed in the 'Exchange Mechanisms' section of this book. However, for all the examples of the unobtrusiveness or even non-existence of dress in Hitchcock films, there are other examples that emanate an excess, an unwarranted surplus, creating parallel narratives of dysfunctionality, as in the assorted bags featured in *Dial M for Murder* and considered in the 'Criminal Accessories' section here. These 'superfluous' narratives of dysfunctionality are what constitute *Dressing Dangerously* and account for the prevalence of Hitchcock's productions among the other featured films. The clothes and accessories in these sequences build a tension 'between the "official" content of the totality of the work and the surplus that comes forth in its details'.[28] The 'tension' that Žižek locates within Hitchcock's work is discernible in many of the films considered here and, when positioned alongside other similar moments of tension that emanate from the clothing's dysfunction, makes their psychic and emotional connection to the viewer all the more insistent.

Whenever a film is mentioned in the text, an endnote will furnish the date of the film's first theatrical release, the director and the costume designer. This last fact, however, is problematic and needs some clarification. The information concerning the costume designer of a film has been taken, where possible, from the credits of the actual film; in some cases where the costume designer was uncredited and attempts to ascertain who was responsible have failed, this is indicated in the note as 'uncredited'. Elsewhere the commonplace practice of commissioning a famous fashion designer, or utilising their designs for the leading actors while the rest of the cast's clothes were designed by an in-house, studio designer, is indicated by the 'star' designer's name followed by the actor who wore the clothes, for example Hubert de Givenchy (Audrey Hepburn). The use of terms such as 'costume designer', 'wardrobe', 'gowns by' and other variants followed by one or maybe more names has led to a degree of confusion concerning the hierarchy of these specific costume-related roles. Generally speaking, famous film costume designers such as Travis Banton, Adrian or Edith Head, for example, can be assumed to have designed the costumes for the principal, usually female, leads in a film only. Theirs are often the only names credited and therefore the designers of clothes of the subsidiary characters and extras remain largely unknown. Other credits list 'wardrobe supervisor', rather than designer, and this blanket term can encompass a range of activities from designing the actual clothes, buying ready-made clothes, fitting and altering existing costumes or the star's personal items of clothing, directing and allocating teams of other dressers, or simply maintaining the physical condition of the clothes during the production. In addition, many actors, especially leading men, furnished their own wardrobes, certainly up to the 1950s; for example, Cary Grant was well known for selecting his own wardrobe once he became an established star. Likewise prominent female stars would insist on purchasing, or having the studio purchase, Paris fashions as part of their contractual agreement for appearing in certain films. Marlene Dietrich's insistence on being dressed by Christian Dior when she starred in Hitchcock's *Stage Fright* is a case in point and is discussed in detail in the last section, 'Stubborn Stains'. This terminological imprecision concerning the actual designer of a film's costumes means that for the majority of the films listed, certainly from the period before the 1960s, only the named 'star' designer, whether from the worlds of fashion or film, is mentioned. Therefore the information supplied should not be regarded as definitive concerning the costume designer of each film, beyond the well established costumiers and their stars; the identities of those who provided the majority of a film's clothes, especially during the so called 'Golden Age' of Hollywood, remains largely under-researched.

STRUCTURE

The overall structure of *Dressing Dangerously* follows a direction from outer to inner. As the book progresses from overcoats, raincoats and furs, via suits, accessories and finally revealing the body of the wearer by means of rips, tears and stains, so too does the consideration of the filmic examples move from a multiplicity of dysfunctional surfaces to more sustained and penetrating examinations of specific sequences. While generally adhering to this excavatory methodology, as with all exploratory surveys, detours are inevitable, made necessary by the encounter with unexpected structures, alternative routes and unforeseen contingencies. These detours pass through spaces where dysfunctional clothing can be found but which exist beyond the confines of the films under discussion, older spaces found in literature, for example, or the adjacent spaces of popular culture and fashion, as well as the foundational spaces of history and theory. Passing through the layers of dysfunctional clothing (and it is a penetration of layers rather than a process of sequential stripping), there will be encounters with contiguous garments, some dysfunctional, others not. Collectively these encounters, these interruptions, will facilitate a refocusing of clothing's relationship to film and its position within film; this, while pausing briefly at the familiar vistas of dress and gender, fashion and film and clothing and narrative, to gather relevant dysfunctional images, will continue to examine the contents of the negative cinematic wardrobe. It is my intention to relinquish the desire for definition and to realise that the study of dress in film, to paraphrase Foucault's famous announcement, 'is no longer one of tradition, of tracing a line, but one of

division, of limits; it is no longer one of lasting foundations, but one of transformations that serve as new foundations, the rebuilding of foundations.'[29]

Alongside the general movement from outer to inner, the individual sections of this work have an internal rhythm, an alternation between references to a number of brief sequences in rapid succession and longer, sustained examinations of dysfunctionality in a single film. This oscillation between accelerated streams of images and slower reflective pauses is an attempt to emulate that same process of psychic concatenation where visual references link together and hurtle towards a particular image, which we can then choose to refocus via the lens of our personal experiences and memories. The other deciding factor in the establishment of this alternating rhythm is that many of these incidences of dysfunctionality are by nature brief, take place at the margins of the action or in some cases seem purely accidental and therefore appear inconsequential when considered individually. Indeed, the brevity of the sequences often made the establishment of their location within the main narrative body of the film hard to ascertain, momentary dysfunction far outweighed by the time allotted to functionality, a position similar to that of the narrator of Edgar Allan Poe's celebrated tale *The Gold Bug*, who felt 'sorely put out by the absence of all else – of the body to my imagined instrument – of the text for my context.'[30] However, once these often elusive moments were considered alongside each other, a significant alternative representation of cinematic dress started to emerge and, when conjoined with more sustained considerations of longer sequences, the dysfunctional cinematic body took on sartorial flesh.

This book's first chapter considers outerwear in the form of coats and raincoats and other forms of protection. The masculine overcoat is discussed as a symbol of status, repression and a means by which alternative identities are assumed. Its ability to act as a 'cloaking device', to cover and disguise, will be traced and its limitations ascertained. My consideration of raincoats commences with an assessment of the role of the trench coat in mainstream film and whether its military origins make it in the end unsuitable for civilian wear. The raincoat as an 'exchange mechanism' suggests that its appearance in film as an unworn, abandoned or carried object transforms it into a dysfunctional form of protection. Whereas Chapter 1 concerns itself with menswear, Chapter 2 (devoted to furs and jewels) examines the censure which mainstream cinema reserves for women whose desire for fur and jewellery poses a threat to the normative patriarchal acts of gift-giving and procurement centred on these luxury items. 'Trophies' explores fur's historical eroticisation, mink as the livery of shame and the extent to which fur's dysfunctionality adds to its desirability. In 'Talismans', unworn, broken and cursed jewellery is discussed in conjunction with psychological trauma and dysfunctionality. The 'planted' jewel and the disguising jewel suggest an alternatively dysfunctional deployment of these traditional items of conspicuous display. Accessories are the subject of Chapter 3 – the most plentiful articles to be found in the negative cinematic wardrobe. Most easily lost, stolen or misappropriated, the dysfunctional accessory demarcates a cinematic space emoting pain, fear and embarrassment. Hats as representative of the loss of authority, shoes as weapons, gloves as sartorial reminders of the absent body, the tie as a restrictive and restricting accessory, the bag as an insecure receptacle and the scarf as the archaic link to a mythological legacy of supernatural manifestations are some of the dysfunctional qualities explored and which generate an understanding of the accessory's pivotal role in the dysfunctional wardrobe.

Menswear is revisited, with the suit and tie comprising the main garments studied, in Chapter 4. 'Cutting a Dash' looks at the criminal propensity for spectacular tailoring, and the contradictions inherent in sartorial obsessions that cloak hyper-masculinity with a veneer of vestimentary excess. 'Well, as long as the lady's paying . . .' examines the intrinsically dysfunctional act of men being dressed by women, how this contests male hegemony and invariably is accompanied by violence and death. Finally, 'White Lies and the Tailoring of Evil' is devoted to the inadvisable practice of wearing all white, a style repeatedly associated with the personification of evil in the dysfunctional lexicon. Chapter 5 encompasses many of the more universally experienced moments of vestimentary dysfunction. 'Seeing Red' examines the cultural and historical inadvisability of choosing to wear red and how that is manifested in key dysfunctional cinematic outfits. 'It's from Paris!' asks whether being too fashionable is always problematic and how styling tips invariably lead to shame and disappointment. 'Wear and Tear' discusses torn clothing, who is allowed to tear and who is torn, and how tears act as a formal rupture of the visual text. The final chapter positions twentieth-century fashion's advocacy of monogrammed clothing and initialled accessories alongside the contemporary 'brandscape' and in 'The Mark of the Beast' conflates the contemporary obsession with branded luxury goods and the cinematic representation of the dysfunctional monogram. The impossibility of the brand's expectation, coupled with its failure to deliver its promised benefits, inevitably results in trauma for those living under its sign. 'Stubborn Stains' is reserved for that most common of wardrobe malfunctions, the stained garment, but, unlike the everyday stains accrued on one's clothing, this section is reserved for bloodstains and their spectacularly dysfunctional appearance in cinema. As the agent of the deceived gaze, the blood stains considered in this section are invariably not what they purport to be, and act as 'matter out of place'.

PART 1

1 CLOAKING DEVICES

Button up your overcoat
When the wind is free
Take good care of yourself
You belong to me[1]

The overcoat's primary function is as a form of protection against inclement weather, and the donning of coats, raincoats and similar outerwear is customarily featured in film as a means of reinforcing for the viewer that the scene is taking place during cold weather, rainfall or other adverse weather conditions. A warm overcoat or rainproof mackintosh signifies protection and safety, a defence against the elements, a buffer between the wearer and the outside world. The actions commonly associated with putting on a coat such as buttoning up, belting, wrapping and cloaking, unsurprisingly are also terms suggestive of safety, preparation and concealment. If the overcoat's principle function is to provide physical protection for the wearer, a number of its secondary sartorial qualities are also repeatedly used in film to assist in the economic, social and moral construction of the wearer's character. For the male, a smart overcoat signals respectability, formality and often an attendant conservative and reserved manner, a literal covering up of both lighter items of clothing and emotions.

Popular film as a visual record of changing fashions bears witness to the gradual demise through the course of the twentieth century of the overcoat as an essential component of the male wardrobe, and by viewing films set in urban locations, at least, it is possible to trace the changing fashions in men's coats leading to the contemporary dominance of generally shorter, sportswear-derived outerwear for men.[2] During the majority of the twentieth century when a suit was still the staple item of male dress and weather demanded a further layer of protection, the overcoat was obligatory.[3] Styles such as the polo coat typically made of camel-hair, belted and broad-shouldered, and similar coats but made from dark, heavier woollen cloth, double-breasted, waisted and usually cut with peaked lapels, were fashionable for men throughout Europe and North

ANGEL FACE
1952, dir. Otto Preminger.
Diane performs 'voodoo noir' and
draws Frank to her by wearing
his sports jacket.

America during the 1920s and 30s, and films from this period feature a variety of such coats. As the century progressed, lighter topcoat styles such as the single-breasted, velvet-collared Chesterfield and Crombie, and looser fitting, raglan-sleeved lighter cloth variants became the standard item of men's outerwear; films made in the period between the 1940s and the early 1970s reflected this change in men's fashionable outerwear. With the rise in popularity of the trench coat, masculine 'covering up' continued until the socio-political and cultural upheavals that followed in the wake of the Second World War, and which led to a destabilising of the conventions of dress for both men and women from the late 1950s onwards. This manifested itself in a more relaxed attitude to dressing and the lifting of many of the sartorial restrictions that had characterised male dressing throughout the earlier part of the century and, in relation to the subject under discussion, the rise of casual shorter-length jackets and sportswear worn as outerwear. Unlike the jacket, a full-length, traditionally styled man's coat signals sobriety and from the 1960s onwards was increasingly associated with either older sections of society or at least those engaged in professions that demanded a level of sartorial conformity.[4] As these vestimentary shifts became established in reality, cinema was quick to capitalise on this convenient visual means of differentiating character – a shorthand where the traditionally overcoated or 'buttoned-up' character was understood as conservative, while the casually dressed was characterised as socially progressive and liberated.

The 1967 film *Barefoot in the Park* uses a traditional man's overcoat in just such a manner; newly-weds Paul Bratter (Robert Redford, an aspiring lawyer) and Corie (Jane Fonda) move to a tiny, fifth-floor Manhattan apartment with no elevator.[5] Much of the film's comedy is derived from the opposing views that the couple adopt to their new marital home: Corie is the excited, unconventional optimist, while Paul is portrayed as serious, inflexible and conformist. Paul's character is epitomised by his immaculately cut, yet conventional navy blue Chesterfield topcoat with velvet collar. This garment is indivisible from Paul's characterisation and, owing to the freezing temperatures inside the couple's love-nest, he wears the coat throughout the majority of the film, rarely taking it off and even keeping it on in bed in an attempt to keep warm. Paul is as serious as his smartly tailored coat implies and, much to Corie's frustration, seems incapable of spontaneity and lacking in any sense of fun. The couple's emotional polarisation is made explicit when Paul in his ubiquitous Chesterfield, shivering in their tiny bed, is joined by Corie who wears a duffle coat, a garment suggestive of vestimentary radicalism, the coat of choice of the university student, artist and political activist throughout the 1950s and 60s. While Corie may have few intellectual pretensions, their fundamental differences in temperament are effectively signalled by their choices of overcoat. Needless to say, these differences are reconciled by the end of the film and Paul's unconventional streak is revealed once he gets drunk and gives away his restrictive overcoat to a tramp in Washington Square, abandons his shoes and goes 'barefoot in the park'.

The film derives much of its comedy from the gradual stripping away of Paul's 'uptight', slightly pompous attitude, signalled finally by the removal of his coat. In the case of Neil Simon (on whose play the film is based and who wrote the screenplay), the use of clothing as a sartorial indicator of temperament reoccurs in much of his work and, it seems, is universally understood. One only has to recall the marked differences in clothing between the slovenly and brash Walter Matthau and the fastidiously coordinated Jack Lemmon playing Oscar and Felix, the warring apartment sharers in *The Odd Couple* (made a year later than *Barefoot in the Park* and with the director Gene Saks continuing his fruitful alliance with Simon as writer), to see the full comedic potential of this.[6] The cloak of respectability that a smart overcoat can convey, and the moral rectitude that is implied by such garments, can elsewhere be understood as a facade that both protects and deceives but ultimately weighs heavy on its wearers. In the British film *Victim*, Dirk Bogarde plays the successful, married and impeccably dressed lawyer Melville Farr.[7] The film is justifiably regarded for its crusading stance against legislation at the time (it was released in 1961) that criminalised homosexual acts between consenting adults in England and Wales.[8] Farr, unbeknown to his wife and colleagues, is homosexual and is being blackmailed, and the majority of the film's action concentrates on his decision to find and prosecute the blackmailer, thereby exposing himself and ruining his career. He appears in the early scenes of the film fastidiously tailored and top-coated as befits a successful London lawyer, the coat in question a dark wool, raglan-sleeved, velvet-collared Chesterfield topcoat, which Farr accessorises with tightly furled umbrella and gloves, the perfect picture of a sartorially correct and protected member of the British establishment. Later glimpses of Farr's possible non-conformism begin to show in his clothes as more and more is revealed about his private life. The subtleties of cut and dress that had initially suggested Farr's conservatism are contrasted in a later scene with that of two colleagues from his chambers. Farr walks hatless next to his colleague who wears a bowler and Chesterfield of a more traditional fitted cut, while the third lawyer wears a comparatively old-fashioned, double-breasted patelot-style overcoat. Now Farr's more extravagant full-cut coat appears as perhaps a little too fashionable, a little too immaculate, to be quite 'proper'. More clues are revealed when on Sunday Farr changes into an equally stylish tweed topcoat and matching suede gloves, the urbane man about town dressing up as a country squire. Once Farr decides to risk everything by exposing the extortion racket, his normally perfect exterior is disrupted by him appearing in two key scenes with the collar of his coat turned up and, although a comparatively minor sartorial adjustment, this sign suggests the unravelling of his perfect facade (see illus. pp. 22, 23). *Victim* is rich in coat signification: the legal profession and the police are kitted out in discreet formal overcoats and sensible trench coats, while the underworld London homosexual community are dressed in varieties of outerwear that betray their inferior status (donkey jackets, shabby pale raincoats), their flamboyance (loud checks) or marginalisation (leather jackets).[9]

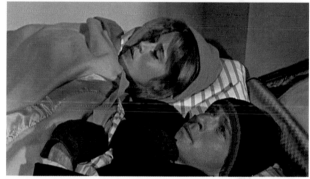

BAREFOOT IN THE PARK
1967, dir. Gene Saks.
[top] Paul keeps his coat on in all situations;
[middle] overcoats at bedtime;
[bottom] Paul abandons overcoat and
formalities in Washington Square.

The vestimentary facade of acceptability and assumed social acceptance projected by Farr's coat is ultimately illusory, and no amount of impeccable tailoring will allow him back into the fold of the British establishment once his private life is exposed. However, if a coat becomes one of the few known attributes of the wearer, and little else is known or revealed concerning its owner, then a coat can also exert an undue influence on the viewer's opinion of the wearer, becoming a locus of speculation and fantasy. The coat worn by Peter Sellers as Chance/Chauncey Gardiner in Hal Ashby's 1979 film *Being There* is one such garment.[10] On the death of his former employer, Chance the gardener is forced to leave the house in which he has apparently lived all his life and outside which he has never ventured. Dressed in the expensive but dated clothes belonging to his deceased employer, Chance ventures out into the streets of contemporary Washington, D.C., wearing a suit, Homburg hat and double-breasted, dark blue heavy wool overcoat thickly padded and waisted, which emphasises the shoulders and upper torso, and is typical of the fashionable male silhouette of the 1920s and 30s. (see illus. p. 24) Through an accidental meeting with his wife, Chance is adopted and taken into the household of a wealthy Washington businessman and confidant of the president. Innocent, sheltered and television-obsessed Chance, with his reserved manner and utterances based on television dialogue he remembers and oblique horticultural references (his only area of expertise) which are mistaken as wise pronouncements, is swiftly regarded as a sagacious political pundit, winning the respect of the president. While his sparse pronouncements are the chief cause of this misattributed wisdom, his clothing also plays a decisive role in the political insiders' assessment of him. His outmoded and reserved tailoring is understood as a mark of breeding and conservative fundamental American values.

Many films have plots based on the assumptions made about a person according to what they wear; this can be unintentionally misleading as in the case of Chance in *Being There*, can conform to the usual attendant social elevation that accompanies the

VICTIM
1961, dir. Basil Dearden.
[facing] The upturned collar as a protective
dismantling of Farr's perfect exterior
(ITV/Rex Features);
[top] the immaculate Melville Farr
(ITV/Rex Features);
[bottom] country tweed for
a weekend in Chelsea.

wearing of new or obviously expensive garments, or intentionally misleading.[11] Worn outside in public and under the gaze of strangers, a coat cannot help but make an impression on passersby, and therefore has occupied a central role in literature and film that deals with clothing as signification, as an indicator of social position and as the garment that can either cloak existing identities (as in Farr's immaculate coats in *Victim*) or assist in the assumption of new ones. 'He returned home in the most happy frame of mind, threw off his coat and hung it carefully on the wall, admiring afresh the cloth and the lining; and then he brought out his old, worn-out coat, for comparison. He looked at it and laughed, so vast was the difference.'[12] In Nikolai Gogol's celebrated short story *The Overcoat* (1842), Akakii Akakievich, the pathetic hero, fleetingly glimpses his life transformed by the acquisition of a sumptuous new overcoat, replacing his old worn-out one, an object of embarrassment for him and amusement and ridicule for his co-workers. His sartorial transformation is short-lived, however, and as Gogol's chilling tale unfolds Akakievich is mugged, his overcoat stolen and his eventual demise hastened by the lack of seriousness with which this vestimentary theft is treated by the St Petersburg authorities. At the climax of the story Akakievich delivers supernatural justice, returning to the scene of the crime in spectral form to steal the coats from the shoulders of the very officials who had refused to take the theft seriously. The concepts of vulnerability and protection, the assumption of new identities, theft and supernatural revenge that are the very fabric of Gogol's coat are also common characteristics of cinematic overcoats, topcoats, raincoats and similar outerwear. So that, for all the coats that conform to their generally accepted function of providing protection and bestowing sartorial respectability, there are as many that provide only momentary protection, much like Akakievich's coat, enjoyed briefly only to be lost, stolen or, in the most extreme cases, cause harm or even death.

The dysfunctional cinematic overcoat's fluctuating status is caused by its intrinsically mutable and peripatetic existence, which is true of both cinematic and actual coats. Coats being

BEING THERE
1979, dir. Hal Ashby.
Chance dressed in the past steps
out into contemporary Washington.

essentially outerwear are doomed to an existence of being put on and taken off, they are the elements of our dress that we shed on entering enclosed spaces; once removed they migrate for a time to the backs of chairs, to lobbies, cloakrooms and other less defined locations, until worn once again. Unlike other clothing that luxuriates in designated locales – chests of drawers and wardrobes, for example – coats endure a nomadic existence, constantly travelling to and from indeterminate corners of domestic and public spaces and on and off bodies, unlike other items of dress which typically stay on the body until the wearer chooses to undress fully. This peripatetic existence combined with the coat's ability to disguise and cover up means that the cinematic overcoat is implicated, often directly, in more than its fair share of criminal activity. It is present as its wearers arrive and leave the scene of the crime, it is forgotten in haste, it is mistaken for similar garments (the trenchcoat, indelibly identified with the on-screen detective, is especially prone to this), it is stained, torn and objects are regularly placed within its pockets or lost from it in the form of belts and buttons.[13]

Coats, even though temporarily worn, become imbued with the personality of the wearer, so much so that on film they assume an almost autonomous identity and when implicated in criminal activity are subject to the same scrutiny and processes of identification and recognition to which the criminal body itself is subject. For example, photographs of the suspect raincoat in Billy Wilder's *Witness for the Prosecution* (1957) are passed round the court like mug shots, while the distinctive bold houndstooth check topcoat with contrasting enlarged check collar-facing is the only form of identification that Frank Bigelow (Edmund O'Brien) can supply to the police concerning his poisoner in *D.O.A.* (1950).[14] So distinctive is this coat that it becomes the perpetrator of the crime itself as the audience never learns its wearer's true identity, and both Bigelow and the viewer have no choice but to equate the coat with the deed. This particular coat's distinctive mid-twentieth-century styling not only registers optically with Bigelow and the viewer but also acts as a form of sartorial psychological profiling; this

WITNESS FOR THE PROSECUTION
1957, dir. Billy Wilder.
[top] The criminalisation of
the suspect raincoat.

D.O.A
1950, dir. Rudolph Maté.
[bottom] The murderer makes a
sartorial spectacle of himself.

is not the coat of a murderer who wishes to fade into the background but rather that of an urbane man about town. The spectacular topcoat matches the anonymous murderer's equally spectacular choice of poison, the 'luminous toxin' with which he laces Bigelow's drink and which courses through his body as he relates to the police in flashback the deadly encounter with his checked assassin. Checks, be they dog-tooth, window-pane or tartan, have long been the favoured pattern of the extrovert, most typically worn by entertainers and those wishing to cut a sartorial dash. Here, however, the murderer's loudly checked overcoat is understood as dysfunctional, drawing attention to the presence of the poisoner and yet diverting attention away from his true identity so that he is known only by his checked livery.[15]

'I see through you, you don't think I see through you? You could wear two wool sweaters and a racoon coat, I'd still see through you.'[16] Mr Corcoran's observation addressed to Lenny

Cantrow (Charles Grodin), the married and socially unaccept-able suitor of his daughter Kelly (Cybill Shepherd) in the 1972 comedy *The Heartbreak Kid*, belies a commonly displayed attri-bute of the cinematic coat and jacket, namely that by donning a coat, particularly one belonging to someone else, the wearer is able to assume an alternative identity and pass as something they are not. Clothes make the man, perhaps, but on screen, clothes, especially coats, disguise one man while projecting the image of another.[17] This projection can be very short-lived, as the unfortunate Akakievich found in Gogol's tale, and literature is full of such aggrandising outerwear. Edith Wharton, a sharply astute commentator on dress and the social invisibility engen-dered by inferior clothing, paints a remarkable picture of such a coat in her concise, melancholic tale of New York on the very cusp of the twentieth century entitled *A Cup of Cold Water*.[18] In the story Wharton details the economic decline and imminent self-imposed exile from New York society of

Woburn, the impeccably dressed but destitute subject of the story. Woburn, in typical Wharton fashion, manages to make some bad investments which eradicate the small amount of money left to him by his equally financially naive father, but not before Woburn has become accustomed to the finer things in life, especially clothes. These material objects allow him to project an image of himself as a man of means and taste, and to foster dreams of courting the eligible Miss Talcott. The story opens with a mistaken coat; on leaving a society ball Woburn is given 'a ready-made overcoat with an imitation astrachan collar in place of his own unimpeachable Poole garment' by an inattentive footmen. Wharton uses this image of Woburn's coat – Savile Row tailored, impeccably cut – as a foreshadowing of how easily outward appearance, and by implication economic security and social position, can be exchanged and lost.[19] Even though 'the fur-lined overcoat with cuffs and collar of Alaska sable had alone cost more than he had spent on his clothes for two or three years previously', its value for Woburn is incalculable; it guarantees his admittance to New York society's balls and allows him to offer his arm encased in its luxurious sleeve to the fair and the privileged.[20] However, as Peter Stallybrass has observed in his essay *Marx's Coat*, 'the fetishism of the commodity inscribes *im*materiality as the defining feature of capitalism' and Wharton underscores this by opening her story with the 'drowsy footman' who is unable to recognise the exchange value of Woburn's coat.[21] The footman in effect disarms the coat's social function, re-inscribing its 'thingliness', as Stallybrass has termed it, rendering it equivalent to all coats (however inferior in terms of cloth or cut), as fundamentally a garment worn over other clothes to keep the wearer warm and nothing more.[22]

No such inattention to detail besets Melvin Purvis (Christian Bale) in *Public Enemies* (2009); however, for him John Dillinger's coat is the personification of its owner.[23] So fundamental to the construction of its wearer's public image is the coat now in Purvis's possession that for him it has assumed the status of vestimentary epidermis, formed from textile DNA that is as unique to Dillinger as his fingerprints. Purvis gathers his men

PUBLIC ENEMIES
2009, dir. Michael Mann.
[facing] 'Windproof – 32 oz. wool'.

FRENZY
1972, dir. Alfred Hitchcock.
[above] Crimes against style make
Blaney the chief suspect.

to show them the coat left behind at the scene of a bank robbery: 'According to the bank teller, Barbara Patske, this is John Dillinger's coat. It's made by Shragge Quality out of St Louis. Price $35.00. Windproof-32 oz. wool. Top stitching.'[24] The belief in a garment's power to act as a direct form of communication, a form of vestimentary tracking device that will reveal the whereabouts of its owner, is an enduring one and appears regularly in literary and cinematic narratives alike. This almost supernatural power of a garment to become imbued with the presence of its wearer when coupled with the contemporary detective and forensic techniques that *Public Enemies* revels in makes the material garment into a talismanic object. Purvis's conviction of the coat's ability to lead him to Dillinger seems unshakeable as he states:

> Agents in our offices across the country are identifying every store in the United States that sold this overcoat. Then, we will cross-reference every Dillinger associate at locales where that coat was sold. He was in a place. He got cold. He bought a coat. Unless he was travelling through, he was being harboured nearby. If he returns we will be there. It is by such methods that our bureau will get John Dillinger.[25]

The forensic formation of dress is central to this study and informs many of the arguments in *Dressing Dangerously*. This cinematic cathexis focused on articles of clothing and accessories fills the drawers and hangers of the negative wardrobe and, conversely, accounts for the unwarranted attention given to the disposal of such clothing. The burnings, burials and shredding of articles of dress that punctuate cinematic history are surely a testament to the belief in the power of clothing to situate the owner in specific spaces at specific times. This conviction accounts for Purvis's certainty that Dillinger will be brought to justice, that the empty coat will lead him to the body of its owner. Purvis views Dillinger's coat with the objective detachment that befits an FBI agent, but just as prevalent both on screen and certainly in our actual experience of clothing is its emotional resonance. Clothing has an irresis-

tible power to evoke the wearer, and we, too, imbue our clothes with our smell, we mark them with the indelible traces of past events; our favourite clothes are special not just because of how they look but because of the memories they evoke. Similarly, the clothes of lovers, family and friends act as textile conduits providing emotional and sensory contact with those who are absent, so that it has become almost obligatory in films that deal with recent bereavement, for example, to include a scene where the surviving partner buries their face in the clothes of the departed in order to revive an olfactory memory of the loved one. This propensity for clothes to narrate lives and experiences is something of which the clothing industry and especially its marketing divisions are fully aware, so that an item of dress as ubiquitous as a pair of denim jeans, for example, becomes the perfect vehicle for this narrative operation: 'You have a close relationship with your jeans. Your jeans are a second skin, faded and ripped and bulged by your experiences. They are lived in. After a party they smell like a party. They are a familiar old friend, a repository of memories, a comfort blanket.'[26]

Forensic descriptions of clothing can of course be misleading and minute details of dress can incriminate the innocent just as effectively as they can deliver the guilty. Monica Barling (Jean Marsh) in Alfred Hitchcock's *Frenzy* (1972) believes she has seen the serial killer terrorising London, but with the detailed description she gives to the police she unwittingly incriminates an innocent man, Richard Blaney (Jon Finch), allowing the true killer to remain at large.[27] Asked whether she can describe what he looked like and what he was wearing, she responds: 'Yes I think I can . . . He was wearing a rather old-fashioned jacket with leather patches on the shoulders and at the elbows, in my opinion it was quite unsuitable for London. He was also carrying a raincoat.'[28] Hitchcock delights in undermining the efficacy of Barling's forensic detail, for the viewer is already aware that she is describing the wrong man, and then throws in a casual aside to crimes against style with the reference to the jacket's unsuitability for London (see illus. p. 27). Such a detailed description is cherished by the police and the jacket in question is transformed from an unsuitable sartorial choice into the embodiment of the killer, its description appearing in the press; in a subsequent scene Blaney's innocent request to have it cleaned by the staff at the hotel where he stays incriminates him still further.

The representation of a garment as the embodiment of its owner is the source of the corporeal discourse that typifies much of the literature of dress; metaphorical descriptions of clothing as a second skin are understandable given that clothing is the barrier between our naked selves and the external world and that, like skin, clothing is protective, encasing and containing the body, defending it against extremes of temperature and infection. Possession of the 'windproof-32 oz. wool' coat is for Purvis as good as having Dillinger's skin: he believes him now to be vulnerable, stripped of his defence. How Dillinger's coat came to be found, however, is indicative of the dysfunctionality of cinematic dress, for while on Dillinger's body the coat fulfils all its practical and fashionable functions, it is at the moment of its removal and the loss of its original function that its potential for harm is unleashed and it becomes an item of dangerous dress. During Dillinger's most recent bank job, he notices that the bank-teller he has taken hostage is shivering, so takes off his coat and wraps it round her body as he pushes her into the getaway car. This act of cloaking that symbolises possession and vestimentary marking out of another's body is a motif that is repeated throughout *Public Enemies* as an adjunct to Dillinger's sensibility to the cult of personality, which he enthusiastically constructs for himself, aided and abetted by a media hungry for exploits of the 'people's' gangster. In order for this cult of personality to be fully endorsed by the American public, a constant stream of information concerning Dillinger's likes and dislikes, his modus operandi, his foibles and so on is required, details that, in short, turn him from public enemy to everyone's favourite personal enemy. His clothes play no small part in this, a factor that Dillinger realises as he gives his cloaked hostage his hat, saying: 'Here doll – something to remember me by.'[29] This particular souvenir is snatched back from her

PUBLIC ENEMIES
2009, dir. Michael Mann.
[top] Dillinger cloaks the hostage;
[bottom] Dillinger cloaks Billie.

head as he leaves her tied to the tree some distance from the scene of the crime, but he can be assured that this act of vestimentary play will be remembered and recounted, adding to the Dillinger folklore. More importantly, he leaves her wrapped in his coat, the coat that will become Purvis's eventual means of tracking him down.

Dillinger's desire to shed his sartorial skin for others is repeated in the scene where he meets his lover Billie Frechette (Marion Cotillard) for the first time. After leaving the club where they first encounter one another, he notices her shaking with cold and again, in a repetition of the earlier scene with the hostage, he cloaks Frechette with another of his overcoats (see illus. p. 29). The coat motif is explored with increasing complexity as Dillinger later goes to the club where Frechette works as a cloakroom attendant. As he talks to her, a customer trying to retrieve his coat interrupts them at which point Dillinger strikes him, forces the cloakroom ticket out of his hand, gets the coat himself, throws it at the customer and then proceeds to hold out Frechette's own coat with the words 'You ain't gettin' other people's hats and coats no more neither.'[30] Following this turning point in their relationship, the couple return to Dillinger's apartment where he presents Frechette with a fur-collared coat, a reference presumably to their first meeting when her old thin coat was unable to protect her from the icy wind, but also as the refinement of the acts of dressing and possession we have seen Dillinger performing up to this moment in the film. Having picked Frechette to be his companion, Dillinger now needs to cloak her permanently and mark her as his own, which he does not by the temporary cloaking of her in his own coat but by buying her an expensive new fur-trimmed coat. While not perhaps of the quality of Woburn's Alaskan sable-lined coat featured in *A Cup of Cold Water*, the presence of fur here is an important detail as this will not only mark Frechette as his but also allow Dillinger publically to demonstrate his wealth – fur being second only to jewellery as the favoured mode of conspicuous consumption displayed on the female body by the economically advantaged male.[31]

Possession by the wearing or being covered by another's clothes is a persistent theme encountered throughout literary and film culture. One need only think of the cinematic incarnations of Dracula commencing with Bela Lugosi's portrayal, where Dracula customarily gathers into his body his intended victims under his cloak, a form of vestimentary prelude to the Count's ultimate possession of them, to realise how powerful and persistent is the correlation between possession and the wearing of another's clothes. More light-hearted and ultimately less deadly than Dracula's possession are the numerous instances of female cinematic protagonists whose romantic possession is expressed by their donning the 'skins' of their lovers. This device seems to persist throughout romantic comedy up to the present day in films such as *Bridget Jones: The Edge of Reason* (2004) where Bridget (Renée Zellweger), after one of the innumerable misunderstandings between herself and Mark Darcy (Colin Firth), storms out of his apartment only to find that she has inadvertently, but inevitably perhaps, put on his coat, signalling her desire for the cloak of security and respectability he will provide for her if only she will allow it.[32]

This act of possession is also a discursive operation, however, in that not only is the wearer possessed by the owner of the garment in question but the wearer can also become the possessor and, in order to feel closer to someone, the protagonist, typically female, will wear the clothes of those she wants to possess. The occupation of another's clothes can range from the light-hearted and cosy romance of Doris Day snuggling down in Rock Hudson's jacket in *Pillow Talk* (1959), to the rarer female possession of another woman's identity, as undertaken by Rosanna Arquette 'becoming' Madonna after purchasing her jacket in a second-hand clothing shop and suffering from amnesia in *Desperately Seeking Susan* (1985).[33] More obsessive still is the ritual marking of Robert Mitchum's jacket by Jean Simmons in *Angel Face* (1952).[34] After murdering her father and stepmother, Simmons, playing the role of the spoilt and increasingly deranged Diane Tremayne, attempts to stop Frank

Jessup (Mitchum) leaving her and starting a new life in Mexico, even though Jessup, who has been falsely implicated in the murders, has married Diane in order to escape conviction. Finding Frank absent from his apartment, Diane prowls around his room fondling his shirts, stroking, smelling and eventually putting on his jacket, spending the whole night curled up in it, marking it with her scent as would an animal, substituting Frank's arms for the tweedy embrace of his sports coat (see illus. p. 18). She tries to draw him back via her occupation of his clothes, a reworking of the belief in the remote manipulation of a subject via their material possessions more commonly associated with the practices of ritual magic, here transposed to the setting of mid-twentieth-century California, with Diane practising a form of 'voodoo noir'. [35] So entrenched is the belief

in the associative power of items, or even portions, of dress to act as both substitutes and agents of transformation for their owners, that the rituals of possession played out by Diane Tremayne in *Angel Face* are understandably even more prominent in horror film, where articles of dress are regularly stolen, cursed and then used to manipulate their owners.

A production of 2009, *Drag Me to Hell*, contains a remarkably relentless example of the coat, or at least parts of the coat, used as a catalyst for danger and conduit for harm. [36] Christine Brown (Alison Lohman), a young mortgage advisor keen to gain promotion, refuses to extend the loan taken out by an old gypsy woman who comes to Brown's bank begging for an extension. Later the gypsy attacks Brown in a car park and in the ensuing fight rips a button from Brown's overcoat, curses it and returns the button to Brown. The audience subsequently learns that this cursed object must be passed on in three days' time to someone else, otherwise the present possessor will die.[37] Much of the rest of the action of the film revolves round the heroine's attempts to get rid of the button and tackle the increasingly violent supernatural manifestations that are a component of the gypsy's curse. The climactic scene consists of Brown forcing an envelope (which she believes contains the button) into the mouth of the now deceased gypsy, thus freeing herself from the curse. With the curse apparently lifted, we see Brown preparing to meet her boyfriend at the railway station to go on a trip, but she is waylaid by the sight of a pale-blue overcoat in the window of a dress shop on the station concourse. On impulse, she persuades the assistant to open up and let her buy the coat and proceeds to meet her fiancé who comments appreciatively on her new purchase. However, he then enquires what had happened to her old coat as he had found the missing button (similar envelopes containing the button and a rare coin got mixed up earlier in the film): as Brown realises with horror her mistake, she steps back off the platform edge and onto the railway tracks as the ground opens up and she is dragged screaming to hell.

While *Drag Me to Hell* is replete with all the lurid CGI effects necessary for a mainstream horror movie in the twenty-first century, its power to shock comes not so much from its visual trickery but from its deliberation on clothing and accessories as conduits for harm. The disappointment and sense of loss commonly felt when one loses a button from a favourite garment is here capitalised on, and the all too common feelings of regret and annoyance experienced when clothes become damaged or spoilt are transformed into the stronger emotions of fear and danger. Similarly, the reaction and chain of events that follow Brown's acquisition of the new overcoat at the end of the film are an amplification of the anxiety and anticipation felt when new garments are worn for the first time. Granted, a film such as *Drag Me to Hell* takes these ubiquitous clothing-related emotional responses to an extreme level, but its use of

DRAG ME TO HELL
2009, dir. Sam Raimi.
[top] The cursed button;
[bottom] the new blue coat for
Christine's trip to Hell.

traditional folk tales concerning cursed garments and possessions is made more believable owing to our shared experiences of the perils that clothes can usher into our lives.

In the negative cinematic wardrobe, coats are prone to infestation and, just as moths infiltrate and wreak havoc in the real wardrobe, the coats in this wardrobe are riddled by the traces of fabricated and cloaked identities. Worn for warmth and protection, other functions lie dormant, embedded in their weave, receptive to the wearer's aspirations, desires and fears; they are emotional triggers that will transform them into coats of repression, coats of vulnerability and coats of obsession. It follows, therefore, that characters for whom clothing, particularly their overcoats, have strong psychologically disruptive potential should be especially careful about where their garments are stored. A wardrobe is perhaps the most obvious space offering security but also the potential for further contamination and additional traumatic infestations. 'I like big closets – easier to keep things in order.'[38] So declares Robert Ryan, playing the psychopathic handyman Howard Wilton in the 1952 production *Beware, My Lovely*, which explores in remarkable detail the coat as bearer of psychosomatic tension and its storage problems. As has been suggested, the overcoat in film is often typified by its apparent homelessness, its nomadic or peripatetic existence, doomed to be flung onto pieces of furniture, damaged or lost. However, *Beware, My Lovely* redresses this apparent disregard for the coat and in its seventy-seven minutes condenses a host of literary and psychoanalytical constructions centred on the wardrobe and its contents that have since migrated into popular consciousness as perhaps the quintessential metaphor for emotional and sexual repression. The wardrobe as a metaphor invokes Gaston Bachelard's seminal study *The Poetics of Space*, an invaluable context for this book's concept of the negative wardrobe, and indeed Bachelard could almost have been assessing Wilton's actions in *Beware, My Lovely* when he writes: 'Only an indigent soul would put just anything in a wardrobe. To put just anything, just any way, in just any piece of furniture, is the mark of unusual weakness in the function of inhabiting.

In the wardrobe there exists a center of order that protects the entire house against uncurbed disorder.'[39]

It is not the intention of this text to attempt to discuss the vast literature available on the imagery of the wardrobe or closet and the processes of repression, especially sexual, associated with this article of furniture. Suffice to say, complex socio-cultural constructions such as the signification of the wardrobe are often unravelled with remarkable visual acuity on film. Once the eye is liberated from the seductive influence of narrative and film is looked at as a sequence of independent informative fragments, then an early production from the Boulting brothers' canon such as *Seven Days to Noon* (1950) can, by the use of a brief but telling visual sequence utilising the wardrobe as a repository of repressed erotic impulses, provide an acerbic commentary on sexual attitudes in post-war Britain.[40] Towards the end of this film, as the police and military conduct a house-to-house search for the missing atomic scientist Professor Willingdon, there occurs a brief scene in which a soldier searching through the drawers of a large wardrobe finds a lady's brassiere, holds it up to his chest, then pulls out a pair of French knickers, holds these also to his body and then proceeds to put them inside the front of his tunic and leave (see illus. p. 34). It forms an eight-second sequence that, although included, no doubt, as a light-hearted interlude in this nuclear-threat drama, manages to refer to highly complex questions concerning deviant sexuality, the law and repression prevalent at this moment in British society.

Harry Horner's *Beware, My Lovely* revisits the same psychologically charged space of the wardrobe and Wilton's vestimentary obsessions are utilised as the early symptoms of the schizophrenia that will subsume him as the film unfolds. At the beginning of the film the viewer witnesses Wilton finishing some repairs and calling to his employer, a Mrs Warren; getting no response, he prepares to leave but not before opening the door of a closet inside which is the body of the murdered woman. Wilton leaves town and we next see Helen Gordon (Ida Lupino), a recently bereaved war widow (the film is set in 1918) and boarding-house keeper, take pity on the itinerant Wilton and employ him as a handyman. On telling him to put his coat in the downstairs closet, the following conversation between the two characters takes place:

> Wilton: 'Mrs Gordon, if you don't mind I'd like to take my coat somewhere else.'
> Gordon: 'Your coat?'
> Wilton: 'Yes, you see I didn't know it was a storage closet. It might get dirty, it's my only coat.'
> Gordon: 'Well I have a cedar closet upstairs; you can put it there if you like.'[41]

From the delivery of this sequence of dialogue onwards, the film is imbued with vestimentary and closet references: Wilton is unable to open the door of the landing closet upstairs and so hides his coat under a sheet in the wardrobe in Gordon's own bedroom instead. As the film's tension mounts, Wilton's behaviour becomes ever more unstable and we see him turn face down a photograph of the deceased Mr Gordon in his army uniform and learn subsequently that he was considered mentally unfit for active service. Further indication of his unpredictable temperament occurs when he reacts angrily to the flirting of Gordon's young niece, who then upsets him more by pointing out the unmanliness of his employment (he is polishing Mrs Gordon's floor at the time, dressed in an apron she has leant him). His behaviour grows increasingly volatile and violent towards Gordon, whom he eventually keeps as a hostage in her own house, while the issue of his coat and its whereabouts form a persistent metaphor for his own fleeting and unstable mental condition. At one point Gordon searches for it and is surprised to find it among her own dresses; after explaining that he put it there because it is 'easier to keep things in order', Wilton notices a military greatcoat, puts it on and attempts to kiss Gordon, a vestimentary visualisation of Wilton attempting to don, along with the army coat, the sign of authority and normative sexual position of the spouse. Proof of Wilton's schizophrenia escalates, with him attacking Gordon with scissors, blacking out, imprisoning her in her basement and then inviting

SEVEN DAYS TO NOON
1950, dir. Roy and John Boulting.
[top] Out of the closet.

BEWARE, MY LOVELY
1952, dir. Harry Horner.
[middle] In the closet;
[bottom] The coat makes the man?

her up to admire the Christmas tree he has decorated for her. Towards the end of the film, when Wilton has apparently calmed down and Gordon has persuaded him to leave (into the arms of the waiting authorities), the extent of his delusional disassociation can be gauged by his apology to Gordon: 'Sorry to have taken so long getting my coat – it was in your bedroom closet with a sheet over it', which suggests that his recent actions have become so deeply repressed that the only object that can fill the resulting temporal and emotional void is his coat, the vestimentary cathexis for his fragmented identity.[42] Shot after shot features the protagonists against wardrobes, holding coats, ordering closets and so forth, making *Beware, My Lovely* a clearly direct representation of the negative cinematic wardrobe – clothes and their problematic care in this instance finally unmaking the man.

2 EXCHANGE MECHANISMS

The trench and other variants of waterproof coat share similar functions of disguise and the assumption of alternative identities to the cloth coats discussed in the previous chapter. However, its often turbulent presence in film suggests that as a garment it has an intrinsic restlessness, traversing both physical and psychological space which is redolent of its complex and contested origins. 'It defies simple classification. Is it to be assessed on its rain-repellent merits? Or is it defined by its militaristic architecture?' are the questions asked in a recent study of the trench coat and, certainly, its transformation from utility to fashionable wear, shedding its elitist military, sporting and aristocratic associations to become the classless ubiquitous garment it is today, can provide a possible explanation for its vestimentary eminence in film, the raincoat being comparable to an actor able to play many parts.[1] Naturally, when considering cinema's utilisation of the trench coat, its most iconic representation comes to mind, that of the private detective's trench coat made famous by Humphrey Bogart and a host of other cinematic gumshoes. The private investigator's coat is his trusted friend, protecting him from the inevitable downpours as he loiters, collar turned up in the shadows, watching and waiting. Raymond Chandler, that essential recorder of the sartorial proclivities of mid-century America's underworld, emphasises the coat's centrality to the private detective's armour in *Farewell, My Lovely* (1940), its omnipresence noted by Philip Marlowe: 'I needed a drink, I needed a lot of life insurance, I needed a vacation, I needed a home in the country. What I had was a coat, a hat and a gun. I put them on and went out of the room.'[2] In this instance, of course, the cinematic and literary raincoat conforms to all its expected functions: it protects, disguises and has pockets capacious enough for revolver, cigarettes and even a blackjack. Marlowe and other celebrated trench-coated sleuths occupy a position that oscillates on the border between legality and illegality, they mistrust and are mistrusted by the police, have more in common and often forge close relationships with criminals and yet have an unerring and often life-endangering moral code.

These hard-boiled characters wear the livery of the trench coat as a sign of the street, protective enough, light enough, anonymous enough for urban warfare. Hailing from the battlefields of the First World War, the trench coat was originally designed for the British Army as an alternative to heavy woollen greatcoats, and as such was an optional item of dress available only to officers, no other ranks being permitted to wear them. Debate surrounds its original manufacture, with the majority of opinion split between the British companies Aquascutum and Burberry, both staking claim to be the garment's originator. Since the coats were optional and privately purchased, veterans returning to civilian life from the war retained and continued to wear them, setting in motion the trench coat's first steps towards becoming a staple of the male twentieth-century wardrobe.[3] Retaining features such as shoulder straps originally designed to display epaulettes and similar insignia, belts with D loops for the attachment of map cases and swords, and large capacious pockets suitable for carrying maps, charts and other documents, the trench, replete with its vestiges of combat, implied tactical know-how and, if necessary, aggression, found its most appropriate resting place on the shoulders of Bogart's assorted cinematic anti-heroes: Sam Spade in *The Maltese Falcon* (1941), Rick Blaine in *Casablanca* (1942) and Philip Marlowe in *The Big Sleep* (1946).[4]

In these productions and others like them the trench coat constructs the character of the private eye as tough, ready for action, yet honourable – a legacy of its original patrician exclusivity transformed into the protective covering of everyman. Bogart was not the only actor regularly seen wearing a trench coat, both on and off screen, and other contenders for the most memorable trench-coat wearing would have to include Dick Powell in *Farewell, My Lovely* (or *Murder, My Sweet* as it was titled at the time of its release) and *Cornered*, Alan Ladd in *The Glass Key*, *The Blue Dahlia* and *This Gun for Hire*, Dana Andrews in *Fallen Angel* and *Laura* and, perhaps the closest contender for Bogart's crown, Robert Mitchum, for *Foreign Intrigue*, *The Big Steal* and the iconic *Out of the Past* (the earliest

[facing] Humphrey Bogart
in trench coat, 1940s
(Everett Collection/Rex Features).

OUT OF THE PAST
1947, dir. Jacques Tourneur.
[above] Robert Mitchum, perhaps
Bogart's greatest contender for most
memorable trench-coat wearing (Moviestore
Collection/Rex Features).

from 1942 to the latest in 1956).[5] Many of these films constitute highpoints in the canon of film noir, where the trench coat takes centre stage as a protagonist, and as such is fulfilling its popularly understood function of both protection from the elements and as shorthand for the character of the private eye and maverick justice seeker. By the 1960s and with the popularisation of shorter, single-breasted styles of raincoat, the trench coat's appearance on screen and off became rarer. This decline was short-lived, however, as the 1970s saw fashion undergoing a succession of nostalgic waves of retro styling for both men and women and the release of a number of ironically nostalgic films. These include the 1975 version of *Farewell My Lovely* starring an older Mitchum suitably trench-coated, referring to his iconic appearances some twenty-five years earlier, the pastiche *Gumshoe* (1971) featuring a trench-coated Albert Finney, *Play it Again Sam* (1972) where Woody Allen's performance is intercut with clips from Humphrey Bogart films and the even more meta-cinematic *Dead Men Don't Wear Plaid* (1982) which paired Steve Martin with a host of trench-coated denizens culled from classic film noir.[6]

When trench coats are worn by more legitimate law enforcers such as policeman, however, or by ordinary members of the public, they can become distinctly more problematic and dysfunctional. It is as if, having migrated from their customary location on the margins of legitimate society when clothing the cynical private investigator, or owing to their martial origins, they are essentially unsuitable for more law-abiding or domestic wear. In *The Pink Panther* (1963), Inspector Clouseau's (Peter Sellers) horror is palpable when he discovers that his police-issue trench coat has been stolen: 'My coat! My Sûreté, Scotland Yard type mackintosh . . . it's gone!'[7] Clouseau's mackintosh taxonomy, emphasising its centrality in the construction of his facade as an officially sanctioned sleuth, suggests that such a powerful, all-purpose, law-enforcing waterproof is too effective to remain covering the shoulders of the bungling inspector and, ironically, as the viewer is made aware, it has in fact been stolen by the far more professional

THIS GUN FOR HIRE
1942, dir. Frank Tuttle.
[facing] Alan Ladd
(SNAP/Rex Features).

A SHOT IN THE DARK
1964, dir. Blake Edwards.
[above] The trench coat becomes
an object of ridicule
(Everett Collection/
Rex Features).

and competent felon, the Phantom (David Niven), who is the master jewel-thief whom Clouseau has been unsuccessfully trailing, and who it could be argued is more entitled to wear such a significant garment. The pop-ularity of Sellers's portrayal of the inept, trench-coated Clouseau in the Pink Panther series did much to dislodge the popular image of the trench coat as the carapace of the effective sleuth established by film noir, transforming it into an object of ridicule.

If American cinema had established the trench coat as the stylish livery of the detective during the 1940s and 50s, British cinema replaced it with single-breasted, unbelted and shorter styles of rainwear. Serious sleuths, spies and assassins in the 1960s favoured less showy and more anonymous garments, indiscernible from those of the average man in the street who wore similar styles. The government agent Harry Palmer (Michael Caine) in a trio of films, *The Ipcress File*, *Funeral in Berlin* and *Billion Dollar*

Brain (1965–67) wears this plain variety of mackintosh, reflecting the sombre, unglamorous, cold-war world of espionage and surveillance.[8] These are raincoats that have none of the swagger and rebelliousness of the trench coat, and are the favourite dress of the civil servant whether a pen-pusher or a spy. It could be argued that after film noir the most memorable wearing of the classic trench was undertaken by women, and Blake Edwards, the director of the Pink Panther films, appears sartorially prophetic when in the rain-soaked climax to his 1961 film *Breakfast at Tiffany's* Holly Golightly (Audrey Hepburn) wears a traditional belted trench, while George Peppard playing her companion Paul Varjak is in a minimal single-breasted, straight-cut rainproof.[9] As they exchange embraces, the couple also exchange their previous identities as kept man and female escort enabled by the protective and transformative power of their raincoats. United under waterproofed cotton, Golightly softens and domesticates the trench coat's former radicalism, while Varjak exchanges his dapper and emasculated status for one of paternal normality, in a raincoat that reeks of suburban conformism.

However, the raincoats featured in *Breakfast at Tiffany's*, whatever their fashionable status and whether they can be interpreted as signs of the couple's acceptance of docile domesticity, also conform to their allotted task of protecting their wearers from the rain. For more problematic, dysfunctional examples of raincoats, two Alfred Hitchcock films – the British production *Young and Innocent* made in 1937 and *Dial M for Murder* made in 1954 – provide contrasting but equally dysfunctional water-proofs.[10] *Young and Innocent* opens with an argument between a man and a woman, and then cuts to a shot of the woman's body being washed ashore followed by the belt from a raincoat. The police who are called to the scene of the crime immediately suspect that the woman has been strangled and that the belt is the murder weapon. Robert Tisdall (Derrick de Marney), a screenwriter who finds the body and who is an ex-lover of the murdered woman, is arrested. In police custody he explains he does indeed own a raincoat but that it was stolen a few days ago from a transport café. The film's plot then centres on Tisdall's attempt to trace the stolen raincoat with the aid of Erica Burgoyne (Nova Pilbeam), the local chief constable's daughter, who is eventually enlisted to help Tisdall prove his innocence. The raincoat in *Young and Innocent* is an example of Hitchcock's famous use of what he termed the McGuffin, in itself 'nothing at all' as he described it, a device that acts as a catalyst for the ensuing action (the pursuit and eventual capture of the raincoat) and also an object that unites the initially reluctant couple. As a raincoat it is useless, it will not be worn, it will in fact only be glimpsed momentarily once in the whole film before vanishing from sight; it is enunciated, it is mythologised, it becomes the mystery, the chase, the unobtainable object, but has renounced its status as a functioning raincoat. Its protective, water-repellent qualities are contested from the outset: the first glimpse of it, or at least the part of it with which the viewer is presented, is its sea-saturated belt, floating ashore, forming the

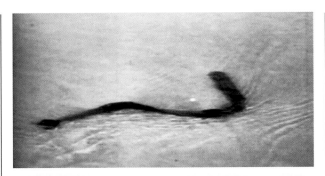

shape of a question mark, forcing us from the very outset to consider its meaning.

As the story unfolds, under interrogation both from the police and the incompetent short-sighted lawyer (his thick glasses are stolen by Tisdall to disguise himself and make his getaway from court, another of example of dysfunctional dress in the film, for without them the lawyer can see nothing and, wearing them, Tisdall is equally disabled), Tisdall confesses that he did have a raincoat and that it was stolen from his car when he stopped at 'Tom's Hat', a carman's shelter. At Tom's Hat, the bizarrely named café (a reminder of the semantic mutability of items of dress, perhaps), the mackintosh is discussed and Erica learns that it is now in the possession of Old Will (Edward Rigby), an itinerant odd-job man, who was given the coat by a stranger. The relaying of this information concerning the coat starts a brawl in the café and the unseen raincoat becomes the instigator of further discord. Will is located and in a remarkable scene of dysfunctional divestment his shabby overcoats are ripped by Towser (Erica's dog), revealing Tisdall's raincoat underneath. It has been suggested that Will's hiding of the raincoat under his shabbier clothing is indicative of his unease at owning such a garment, and the fear that as an odd-job man being in possession of a good-quality raincoat could lead to his being looked on suspiciously by the police: the raincoat is also a 'guilty secret' for Will himself, since people assume that he stole it (see illus. p. 43). Hence he wears it under his outer tramp's clothes, so that his possession of such a 'middle-class' garment cannot be seen.[11] While this is certainly a possible explanation, there is also a more direct economic expediency to Will's dysfunctional attire: the raincoat is one of the many layers of clothing that Will is wearing, worn simultaneously as befitting a nomad with no fixed address. Without wardrobe or chest of drawers in which to keep his clothes, Will must wear all his clothing at once, and protect such a desirable item as a nearly new raincoat under his shabbier coat. The item of clothing worn but not outwardly displayed, the 'guilty secret', however, does have a remarkably persistent presence in the negative cinematic wardrobe. One can find instances from the earliest days of cinema of this dysfunctionality, where clothing is worn neither for the admiration of others nor in its most efficacious and practical manner, and is most likely to confer shame or even retribution on the wearer.

The item of clothing as 'guilty secret' can be traced back to the era of silent cinema, for example in *Orphans of the Storm* directed in 1921.[12] Lillian and Dorothy Gish play the two Girard stepsisters caught up in the turmoil of the French Revolution. They become separated and the blind Louise Girard is abducted and forced to beg by the evil Mother Frochard, who has stripped her of her fine clothes in order to make her new role more believable. Henriette Girard glimpses her sister's velvet cape under the old woman's peasant clothes and accuses her of her sister's kidnapping. The inappropriateness of Will's raincoat in *Young and Innocent* is prefigured in *Orphans of the Storm* as once again fine clothes prove unsuitable for someone trying to make their living begging on the streets, and Louise's cape becomes the 'guilty secret' of Mother Frochard.

Economic inappropriateness is not always, however, the deciding issue in clothing becoming a guilty secret: returning to the subject of raincoats, the 1964 film *Séance on a Wet Afternoon* provides ample demonstration of the mackintosh as guilty secret for far different reasons.[13] Billy Savage (Richard Attenborough), playing the brow-beaten husband of the psychic Myra (Kim Stanley), carries out their plot to kidnap the young daughter of a wealthy couple in order that Myra can, with the help of 'information' passed to her from the spirit world, locate the girl's whereabouts and thus benefit from the inevitable publicity that will follow. Billy changes his persona as subservient spouse to kidnapper, with a succession of mackintoshes becoming the outward symbol of this exchange. Dyeing his hair and changing into an old raincoat, helmet and thick obscuring goggles, Billy travels on his motorbike to kidnap the little girl from outside her school. Once he reaches his destination he changes from his raincoat, reinstating an air of respectability by exposing the suit he wears underneath, and deceives the girl's waiting chauffeur into thinking that he is a teacher and that he has received an urgent message that the chauffeur must hear, leaving Billy free to seize the little girl. Putting his disguise back on, he returns home where the couple hold the child hostage. As part of the plot to bring them into contact with the girl's parents, the Savages issue a ransom demand and Billy once again dons his old raincoat in order to pick up the ransom money. Wearing his light-coloured trench-style raincoat, he directs the girl's father to go to an underground station in order to drop off the money. Billy is then seen on a tube train covering up his kidnapper's/ransom demander's trench coat with a darker lightweight plastic raincoat, or 'pac-a-mac' as it was termed at the time the film was made. With his 'guilty' raincoat covered up, he 'bumps' into the girl's father, grabs the money and then boards another tube train, changing out of the 'pac-a-mac' and using it to hide the ransom money. These raincoats are crucial in the construction of the Savages' successive layers of guilt and their increasingly irrational behaviour as their plot spirals out of control. *Séance on a Wet Afternoon* makes effective use of the raincoat as a symbol, especially in British popular culture, of the sexual deviant, the term the 'dirty mac brigade' being common parlance throughout the 1960s and 70s. The accepted protective associations of the raincoat are exchanged for risk and harm and Billy's repeated acts of cloaking and revelation, the restlessness of his multiple raincoats, accelerate, as do his concerns for his wife's sanity, alongside the realisation that his actions are unbearable, guilty secrets that must eventually be exposed.

In *Young and Innocent*, the fleeting sight of Tisdall's raincoat once it has been removed by Will reveals it to be beltless and therefore useless, confirming his guilt rather than proving his innocence. The raincoat then dematerialises into police custody, never to reappear, but, as typically happens with coats and raincoats in the negative cinematic wardrobe, a clue is found in the pocket. Erica reports how a book of matches from the Grand Hotel, an establishment that Tisdall has never visited, was found in one of the pockets, the fabled mackintosh now being

SÉANCE ON A WET AFTERNOON
1964, dir. Bryan Forbes.
[top] Dressed for kidnapping;
[bottom] disguising the disguise.

able miraculously to provide the last element in the plot which will eventually lead the couple to the identity of the real killer. The discovery of the true murderer and *Young and Innocent's* dénouement commences with the famous aerial shot of the hotel's ballroom and its dancers which slowly closes in on the twitching, blacked-up face of the murdered woman's jealous husband, a drummer in the hotel's minstrel orchestra, who will eventually confess how he committed the murder with the raincoat belt. *Young and Innocent* can be understood as a template for the dysfunctional cinematic raincoat: it is stolen, part of it has become detached, it is used as a murder weapon ('I twisted it round her neck and choked the life out of her'[14]), it is both disguised (under Will's outer layers) and disguising (falsely implicating Tisdall as the murderer), it is the agent for the fulfilment of the Oedipal trajectory uniting Erica and Robert and leads a mythical, immaterial existence throughout the film, both meaningful and meaningless. As with the once seen spectacular check topcoat worn by the poisoner in *D.O.A.* discussed previously, its function is to be the locus of speculation and uncertainty but, unlike Dillinger's coat in *Public Enemies*, the raincoat continuously malfunctions as proof.

In Hitchcock's *Dial M for Murder*, rather than one fabled, insubstantial raincoat there are multiple, tangible raincoats. The raincoats belonging to Tony Wendice (whose elaborate plan to have his wife, Margot, murdered forms the basis of the film's plot) and Chief Inspector Hubbard are to all intents and purposes identical. Unlike the pursued raincoat in *Young and Innocent*, the raincoat in *Dial M for Murder* has become a cipher for entrapment and statelessness; it is multiple, it is specular; it is the 'good' raincoat of Hubbard and the 'bad' raincoat of Wendice. In addition, other identical raincoats are presented throughout the film. The opening scene, for example, consists of a couple walking past the London house where the crime will take place, the man with a raincoat over his arm; later a number of identical raincoats are worn by members of the public gathering round the steps of the Wendice's apartment and, in another scene, a raincoat is worn by Williams, the police

constable, keeping watch on the stairs for Wendice's movement's towards the end of the film. The generic appearance of a man's mid-twentieth-century raincoat (functional, beige, check-lined) is used to full advantage in the film as Hubbard (John Williams) intentionally switches raincoats with Wendice (Ray Milland), so that at the finale Wendice is tricked into revealing his superfluous, incriminating knowledge of the whereabouts of the correct apartment key under the stair carpet and with it the plot to kill his wife. Unlike the raincoat in *Young and Innocent*, the coats in *Dial M for Murder* are not McGuffins; they in fact play a vital role in the mobility and conveyance of the key, the object of exchange that travels between and links the principle protagonists Wendice, Margot and Hubbard.[15]

What is perhaps more revealing than the convenient use of the similar raincoats with similar pockets in which to plant incriminating evidence is their apparently complete loss of any other function than as elements in Hitchcock's baroque 'backtelling' of the crime.[16] These raincoats are hardly ever worn but carried over the arm, incriminating encumbrances that no longer protect, and it is difficult to find homes for them. Karl Marx used the coat as an example of the exchange value of the commodity in the preface to *Capital* and the raincoats in *Dial M for Murder* conform to Marx's definition of the commodity: that is, their useful function has been emptied out in order for their exchange value to be realised. *Dial M for Murder's* coats may no longer be equivalent to Marx's '20 yards of linen', perhaps, but they do represent intangible values related to the wearer's (or carrier's) innocence or guilt, far removed from the practical qualities of wearability, warmth and waterproofed protection.[17] As Stallybrass suggests: 'the coat, any coat, as an exchange-value is emptied out of any useful function. Its physical existence is, as Marx puts it "phantom-like."'[18] *Dial M for Murder's* raincoats assume this phantom-like existence, haunting the film, appearing as doppelgängers, disappearing and re-appearing, commodities that are at once valueless and beyond price.

DIAL M FOR MURDER
1954, dir. Alfred Hitchcock.
[top to bottom]

Initial establishment of the raincoat
as functionless commodity.

Hubbard marks the crime scene with
his raincoat.

Criminal creasing.

Exchange mechanisms.

In a telling sequence, the first actions of Hubbard, the dapper chief inspector, on entering the Wendice's apartment are casually to drop his hat onto the umbrella stand and look about quizzically for somewhere to place his raincoat – he opts for throwing it onto a nearby chair. After the interrogation of Margot (Grace Kelly), Tony Wendice and Margot's old flame Mark Halliday (played by Robert Cummings, who is introduced in the film, raincoat over his arm, disembarking from the *Queen Mary*), the inspector prepares to leave. He picks up his raincoat and looks at it with a pained expression as it has now been crushed into a crumpled bundle, the result of Wendice sitting down on it during the scene, an obvious affront to the apparently vain, self-obsessed inspector. Later in the film, this demarcation of the scene of the crime with raincoats is repeated as we see Wendice enter the apartment and repeat the action performed earlier by Hubbard, throwing his coat on the same chair. Hubbard arrives and the raincoats multiply but, with the chair being taken, this time Hubbard is forced to put his raincoat over the end of a bed, where the testing of the keys and the eventual swapping of the garments take place. The stage is then set for the concluding scene where Wendice returns once again to the apartment, this time with Hubbard's coat on his arm, realises his mistake and eventually reveals his true identity as the author of the plot to kill Margot by locating the correct key under the stair carpet.

The only significant exception to the film's prohibition on the actual wearing of the multiple beige raincoats featured is made by Swann, the man Wendice blackmails into murdering his wife: Swann, atypically, wears, as opposed to carries, his grey raincoat over his rather too loudly checked sports jacket, the sure sign of the petty crook and philanderer. As it is raining on the night of the attempted murder, we see him enter the apartment in his wet, grey raincoat, a garment he is in fact doomed never to remove, as the plan backfires and his intended victim, Margot, ends his life by stabbing him with a pair of scissors. Swann appears to have paid the ultimate penalty for actually wearing his raincoat as it was intended, in order to

provide protection from the rain, and as he lies dead, his coat pierced and bloodied, it seems that raincoats only offer truly effective protection if worn like some talismanic standard over the arm. In *Dial M for Murder*, the raincoat reaches its apogee of dysfunctionality, transformed from the protective carapace of the private detective into a functionless commodity that is carried from location to location like some invalid traveller waiting to be mislaid.

While literature often explores the power of sartorial finery to transform character's lives, as in the coats featured in Gogol's and Wharton's stories, cinema often favours the more ubiquitous raincoat as a unit of exchange. So Guy Holden (Fred Astaire) feels frustrated and short-changed when, having given his raincoat (and calling card) to Mimi Glossop (Ginger Rogers) to cover up her torn dress in *The Gay Divorce* (1934), she refuses to furnish him with her address in exchange (Guy is immediately attracted to her and wants to find out where he can meet her again).[19] Adding insult to injury, Mimi later returns his coat anonymously, neither acknowledging his kindness nor furnishing him with the longed for address, thus breaking the rules of exchange where it is cinematically customary for the owner of a coat to expect payment in return for this ostensible act of charitable protection. Like many others, this raincoat circulates and binds together the protagonists of *The Gay Divorce*, from Guy's arm, to Mimi's shoulders, falling off her body as it is caught, like her dress, on a gate and falls to the ground, returned to her shoulders and then delivered back to Guy in his hotel room. Its travels set in motion a chain of events, as Guy, now in love with Mimi and infuriated by her apparent lack of etiquette, drives through the streets of London in search of her, eventually running into the back of her car and paving the way for the ensuing story of mistaken identities and intentions.

Even more mundane and certainly less stylish than Guy's raincoat is that which features in the British production from 1950, *Seven Days to Noon*. Its central character, Professor Willingdon (Barry Jones), undergoes a political and personal conversion, a conversion that is mirrored in the film by the abandonment of his ubiquitous raincoat and the acquisition of a tweed overcoat and

DIAL M FOR MURDER
1954, dir. Alfred Hitchcock.
The penalty for wearing a raincoat.

with it a new, albeit brief, existence. Willingdon, a British research scientist working on the development of nuclear weapons, steals a bomb, the UR12, and holds the government to ransom, threatening to detonate it in central London unless the current nuclear programme is abandoned. *Seven Days to Noon* is an interesting British example of the nuclear panic film that typified the post-Hiroshima era and which is more usually contextualised with the prevalence of American science fiction films of the 1950s. Unlike American productions which translated the fear of nuclear annihilation from Russia into attacks by aliens from other planets, *Seven Days to Noon* situates the threat as originating much closer to home, from one of its own creators, in fact. As befits a mainstream production of the period, however, Professor Willingdon's anti-nuclear conversion is depicted as mental instability brought on by overwork, rather than a rational rejection of the British, and by extension American, nuclear programme, with his suddenly uncharacteristic behaviour confirmed by his vestimentary impulsiveness.

Before Willingdon first appears on screen the audience is given a verbal portrait of him, or rather his clothes, when Superintendent Folland (André Morell) calls on his family to ask about his movements, recent behaviour and possible whereabouts. On interrogating his wife and daughter, Folland learns that he is wearing a dark grey suit, old grey felt hat and, in the words of Mrs Willingdon, 'And of course his old raincoat, he never goes without that.'[20] As the narrative unfolds, Willingdon journeys to London, rents a room in a seedy lodging house and waits to see if his ransom demands will be met. On seeing a picture of himself in the newspaper, he goes to a barber and has his moustache shaved off, but soon realises that this minor change in his appearance will not allow him to escape detection for long, as a description including what he was last known to have been wearing has been issued. At a point almost exactly half-way through the film, Willingdon avoids a group of policemen who have arrived at his lodgings and runs onto a railway bridge, takes off his old raincoat, bundles it up and throws it over the bridge. The camera follows its trajectory as it flutters

THE GAY DIVORCE
1934, dir. Mark Sandrich.
Services rendered but unpaid for;
Guy receives nothing in exchange for
saving Mimi's embarrassment.

down from the bridge, wrapping itself round the buffers of a stationary train waiting in the railway sidings, a train which, we see in the next scene, has been requisitioned to help evacuate Londoners from their imminent atomic destruction.[21] Divested of his old raincoat and with it his former staid, conventional existence, Willingdon's character and actions from this moment onwards become increasingly impulsive and desperate. The old coat with its connotations of uniformity and compliance acted as a vestimentary buffer against the onslaught of his political and humanitarian convictions and without it they now gain ascendancy over Willingdon during the remainder of London's 'seven days to noon'. In the scene following the disposal of the raincoat, Willingdon enters a pawnbroker's in order to get

himself a replacement. At the shop he meets Goldie (Olive Sloane), a faded actress, and now stripped of his conventional carapace and with it his timidity, Willingdon uncharacteristically converses with this blowsy stranger, who happens to be getting her fur jacket 'out of hock'. As he sifts through the rail of over-coats Goldie suggests to him that the change in the weather will mean that they will 'soon be wearing our coats again I suppose. Horrible thought isn't it?'[22] Willingdon pretends that he has left his own coat somewhere and asks the pawnbroker if he has one that will fit him and the scene closes with the pawnbroker taking Willingdon's measurements (see illus. p. 52).

The pawnbroker's scene in *Seven Days to Noon* is significant for a number of reasons, particularly as it marks the transformation of Willingdon who exchanges his former character, signified by the old coat, for a new one and with it a new identity. The liberation of his repressed desires allows him to socialise with Goldie even before he acquires his new coat, and in the next scene we see Willingdon in his new tweed overcoat waiting outside the stage door of a theatre advertising a review entitled *In the Nude* – a reference to his newly found emotional liberation perhaps (see illus. p. 52). Meeting Goldie again, he takes her for a drink and accepts her invitation to stay at her lodging for the night (Willingdon realises his rented room is now under police surveillance). While there is no possibility of a sexual relationship between Willingdon and Goldie (although she hints at this), his transformation is such that by the closing scenes of the film we will see Willingdon not only staying the night with Goldie but keeping her prisoner, manhandling her when she tries to cry out and creating a vignette of typical domestic disharmony as the manhunt closes in on him.

As a site of exchange, the pawnshop returns us once more to Marx, who, as Stallybrass explores, was only too aware of the exchange value of his own and his family's clothing, which was regularly pawned to supplement his meagre earnings as a journalist while researching the material that would form the basis of *Capital*.[23] Willingdon, divested of his old coat, is now at liberty to select another from the rail and with it will come an exchange value far beyond its original function; Willingdon's new coat will provide warmth but, crucially, a new identity also. As discussed previously, Baudrillard drew on Marx's formulation of the commodity fetish when suggesting that objects liberated from their use value are free to take on a subjective status: while Willingdon's new coat retains its practical function, it could be argued that Willingdon himself is also the object, who has until this point been an object in the British government's system and is understood only as the hard working 'boffin', an absent-minded automaton working round the clock at the defence establishment. Once he decides to leave his family and abscond with the UR12, Willingdon's practical function was divested and this is reconfigured by his jettisoning of his old raincoat on

SEVEN DAYS TO NOON
1950, dir. Roy and John Boulting.
Professor Willingdon's identifying
raincoat is jettisoned.

the railway bridge, and on acquiring his new coat from the pawnshop he at last achieves subjectivity.

Second-hand clothes shops as sites for exchange and coats and jackets as the mechanisms of that exchange figure prominently in a number of films. As mentioned earlier, Rosanna Arquette exchanges her domestic ennui for her fantasy of becoming Susan/Madonna in a second-hand 'vintage' clothes store in *Desperately Seeking Susan*, but these exchanges invariably fall short of their expected outcome or at least are short-lived, as Professor Willingdon discovers. In *Young and Innocent*, Old Will acquires a new set of clothes for his attendance at the Grand Hotel and emerges overdressed in tail coat and striped trousers from what one can only presume to be a second-hand clothing shop, or at least discounted clothing store (for how else would he have afforded the clothes?), observed by a policeman. 'Well if it isn't Cinderella! What's the idea?' the policeman asks, reinforcing the inappropriateness of Will's dress and the immediate suspicion he arouses once out of his customary itinerant's habit.[24] On reaching the hotel, further reinforcement of the inadequacies of Will's recently acquired sartorial elevation is provided by the drummer/murderer, who literally sees through Will's disguise and recognises him as the same tramp to whom he gave his raincoat after the murder of his wife. The audience sees Will from the drummer's perspective and his conspicuously overdressed appearance dissolves into Will the itinerant china-mender in shabby layered clothing, his exchange in fact only part-exchange.

Santelli Brothers is the name of the second-hand clothing shop that takes centre stage in the 1942 portmanteau film *Tales of Manhattan*, consisting of a series of stories featuring a man's evening dress tail coat.[25] The Santelli Brothers sequence forms an entr'acte half-way between the film's more extended stories concerning a magically indestructible tail coat. Only one of the two sequences set in the clothes shop made it into the final version of the film released in 1942, but both provide interesting perspectives on the second-hand clothes shop as a site of identity exchange. In the sequence included in the final version, two thieves break into the shop in the dead of night specifically

SEVEN DAYS TO NOON
1950, dir. Roy and John Boulting.
[top] Willingdon at the site of exchange;
[bottom] a new coat, a new identity.

to steal a set of evening clothes (including the magical tail coat) in order to gain admittance to an illicit gambling house. Wearing his 'monkey tails', the thief is admitted and swiftly sets about holding up the casino and stealing the wealthy gamblers' money. Later, while escaping in an open aircraft to Mexico but still wearing the evening coat, some sparks from the plane's engine blow onto the coat which starts to smoulder, causing the crook hastily to jettison the coat out of the aircraft, with its pockets still stuffed with his ill-gotten gains. As with the raincoat that becomes wrapped round the train buffers in *Seven Days to Noon*, the camera lovingly follows the evening coat's descent from the aeroplane to earth, its apparent indestructibility reinforced by the proximity to technological danger. The sequence that was edited out of the film stars W. C. Fields as a charlatan promoter of the benefits of coconut milk and Phil Silvers as the proprietor of Santelli's. Fields requires an evening coat for a lecture he intends to give at a wealthy sponsor's house and, after rejecting the loud check coat Silvers initially proffers him, he tries on the magical tail coat. It is far too small for Fields, even though Silvers suggests it fits like a glove, prompting the old gag from Fields: 'I don't want it to fit like a glove, I want it to fit like a suit of clothes!'[26] Catching sight of himself in the mirror, however, Fields is surprised by his appearance and, even though the coat is far too tight and the sleeves too short (in fact it is a costume similar to that worn by Fields in perhaps his most famous role as Mr Micawber in George Cukor's 1935 version of *David Copperfield* in which he was memorably dressed in an impossibly tight frock coat), he is momentarily entranced by his own image. On discovering a wallet in the inside pocket, Fields then decides to take the coat, only to discover that it was a ploy by Silvers to make him buy it, and that it contains nothing but paper cut to resemble dollar bills. Second-hand clothes shops on film suggest the possibility of new identities, and with them the promise of wealth, but these alternative visions are invariably short-lived and ultimately prove as illusory as Fields's bogus wallet or Professor Willingdon's belief that he will be able to change the nuclear policies of the British government.

YOUNG AND INNOCENT
1937, dir. Alfred Hitchcock.
[top] Old Will ready for the Grand.

TALES OF MANHATTAN
1942, dir. Julien Duvivier.
[bottom] 'Fits like a glove!' W. C. Fields
is forced into the transforming tail coat.

For the actual garments hanging in these spaces of exchange, their practical function as coats is secondary to their symbolic value as conferrers of status and prestige; ownerless they wait, their fabric thickening with the potential of alternative identities. The unworn coat freed, however momentarily, from covering the body becomes a form of textile screen onto which can be projected the fantasies of both owner and appropriator alike; Howard Wilton in *Beware, My Lovely* can dream of patriarchal ascendancy as long as his beloved coat is safely stowed away, while Melvin Purvis believes he will achieve forensic triumph when inspecting public enemy Dillinger's '$35.00. Windproof–32 oz. wool' and Diane Tremayne, the *Angel Face*, will draw Frank Jessup to her by her nocturnal marking and scenting of his jacket. It is natural that public cloakrooms, like second-hand clothing shops, throb with the cathected fantasies generated by the unworn coat and, though left unworn for only short durations, have the power to induce the most intoxicating of desires. The alcoholic writer Don

Birnam (Ray Milland) in Billy Wilder's *Lost Weekend* (1945), attending a performance of *La Traviata*, checks his raincoat and hat into the busy cloakroom of the opera house, but not before transferring the bottle of whisky he has in his suit jacket to the raincoat's pocket.[27] On reaching the first act containing the famous drinking song, he fantasises that the chorus performing it has been replaced by multiples of his own raincoat on hangers, one of which has a bottle of whisky peeping from its pocket. Unable to resist this tempting vision, he leaves the performance and goes to retrieve his coat, and the bottle, from the cloakroom. However, there has been a mix up with the cloakroom tickets and instead of his mackintosh he is handed a woman's leopard-skin coat. Frustrated by having to wait until the end of the opera for the owner of the leopard coat who will have his ticket, and desperate for a drink, he becomes angry and rude when the owner, Helen St James (Jane Wyman), eventually appears. This flawed exchange of coats, though, acts as an unanticipated mechanism that will eventually lead to his salvation, for Helen will become his saviour, remaining by his side as he fights his battle with alcoholism. From this point onwards these coats, and indeed others, are caught up in an inexorable round of exchanges. Later, in order to escape the hospital's alcoholic ward in which he is detained, he steals a doctor's coat and makes good his escape. Later still Don steals Helen's leopard coat and takes it to a pawn shop, Helen catches up with him and challenges him, and on entering the shop is surprised to learn that he has pawned the coat not for money but for a gun, with which Helen presumes he will try to commit suicide. The persistent Helen continues to remonstrate with him and back at his apartment, as it is raining and having now no coat of her own to wear, she asks to borrow a coat: he cloaks her in the one he was wearing at the opera when they first met, prompting Helen to observe, 'Funny that we should end up after all these years just as we met; I with your raincoat', to which Don responds, 'And I with your leopard coat. I always get the best of the bargain.'[28] This final trading of coats suggests that he is at last willing to relinquish his old self, signified by his alcoholic's raincoat, to the custody of Helen. Shortly after this last exchange the drama reaches its climax, closing with Don resisting taking a drink and beginning to write the story of his lost weekend. The coats featured in *The Lost Weekend* are part of a mechanism or network of exchange sometimes practical – swapped for money or commodities (in this instance a revolver) – or sometimes that can be exchanged for physical and psychological transformation: drunk for sober, disaster for salvation, for example. Finally they can become a mechanism for escape – into fantasy as in the opera scene or from the confines of the hospital; for Don Birnam, coats 'constitute themselves as a *system*, on the basis of which the subject seeks to piece together his world, his personal microcosm.'[29]

THE LOST WEEKEND
1945, dir. Billy Wilder.
[facing] Hallucinatory coats;
[top] Don exchanges identity from
patient to doctor by the theft of a coat;
[bottom] Don gets the "best of the bargain"
in the final trading of overcoats.

PART 2

3 TROPHIES

Bought you a fur coat for Christmas,
A diamond ring,
And a big Cadillac car, and
everything[1]

The brilliance of jewellery and the enveloping softness of fur are the essential textures of countless iconic moments of western cinema. Would Gloria Grahame's appearance, pistol in hand and face bandaged, at the dénouement to *The Big Heat* (1953), be quite so erotically commanding if she were not draped in hard-earned mink, the epitome of dangerous black and white glamour?[2] Or Marilyn Monroe's subsequent deification as the misunderstood sex symbol be quite so rewardingly discussed if not for the glittering Technicolor amalgam of her face surrounded by diamond bracelets in the 'Diamond's Are a Girl's Best Friend' number from *Gentlemen Prefer Blondes* (1953)?[3] In this way both furs and jewellery are entirely functional: they dazzle the viewer, they provide the perfect setting for the star, showcase the talents of the designer and inspire desire and envy as part of the on-screen narrative, as well as in the actual cinema audience. Furs and jewels function as the wages of sin, the golden fleeces of aspiring actresses, models and gangsters' molls, and from Hollywood's infancy kept women are best kept by jewels and furs. Anne Hollander in her seminal work *Seeing Through Clothes* has summed up the special optical symbiosis between cinematic black and white glamour and actual fashions of the period: 'White gold and platinum came into vogue for jewelry and for hair; draped lame and sequined satin offered rivulets of light to the eye as they flowed and slithered over the shifting flanks of Garbo, Dietrich, Harlow and Lombard'.[4] Similarly, the vogue for fox fur in the 1920s and 30s, particularly the silver and white varieties, was partly instigated and certainly maintained by its dazzling snowy gleam when photographed wrapped round the shoulders of film stars of the period.

That such cinematic visions could inspire contemporary fashion is unsurprising given that, historically, jewels and furs have been the most easily recognisable symbols of wealth and

THE BIG HEAT
1953, dir. Fritz Lang
[facing] Deadly mink
(Moviestore Collection/
Rex Features).

GENTLEMEN PREFER BLONDES
[above] 1953, dir. Howard Hawks.

status, particularly when worn by women. Therefore, if the expected function of fur and jewellery on screen to create opulent visual spectacle is unassailable (fur coats are hardly if ever stained or ripped, jewellery is rarely broken or does not fit, as is the dysfunctional lot of many other items of dress considered in this study), so too is the retribution brought to bear on those who either display or covet such items too obsessively. Yet it is precisely this readily accepted function that gives these particular luxury items when not conforming, or at least refusing to remain symbolically fixed as trophies won by faithful wife and available mistress, their multivalency as dysfunctional, or rather alternatively functional, objects on screen. It is as if their cinematic lustre, sheen and brilliance is somehow too excessive to be entirely contained within the narrative frame and a leakage occurs, bestowing on jewellery and fur a polysemic condition that transcends the usual remit of establishing a character's identity or conferring glamour on the actor.

Co-existent with the immediate optical delight provided by cinema's deployment of the goldsmith's and furrier's art, there is an insistence on the fundamental immorality of such creations. This immorality, certainly when a feature of conventional film narrative, must inevitably be punished and while the viewer can wallow in the visual opulence of Marlene Dietrich swathed by Travis Banton in sable, mink and fox, or Elizabeth Taylor radiant with precious stones both on screen and off, there is also an implicit understanding that such excess is dubiously acquired and is inevitably accompanied by unhappiness, even tragedy.[5] Cinematic narrative has seen fit to punish the very characters whose dazzling images provide its raison d'être, and reserves especial castigation for those whose longing for gold, diamonds and furs erodes their innate moral sense. In *Possessed* (1931), Joan Crawford plays Marian Martin who becomes the mistress of a wealthy lawyer, Mark Whitney (Clark Gable).[6] In what is a relatively straightforward and somewhat old-fashioned morality tale, which brought together two of MGM's most bankable and attractive stars, there is a remarkable montage sequence where the viewer sees Martin's years as a kept woman measured out in the diamond bracelets given to her by Whitney, and which accumulate up the length of her arms as the years roll by.[7] These exquisite shackles, needless to say, are eventually seen as poor substitutes for a life of pretence and subterfuge; the married Whitney will not risk public condemnation by seeking a divorce and Martin, in order to carry on their affair, poses as a divorcée. In another scene Whitney classifies the jewels Martin is selecting from her collection, by date, place and occasion given, a private record of their liaison spelt out in precious metals and stones, but which can never be publically declared. This moralising semaphore encoded in jewels is typical of any number of situations, both literary and cinematic, that hammer home the message that money cannot buy happiness or, more precisely, that jewellery, especially too much (Crawford ends up wearing armfuls of bangles Nancy Cunard-style), is incompatible with social acceptance.[8] It is only once Whitney risks everything by divorcing his wife that he can offer her the gift that she most desires – marriage and respectability.

Whitney's habit of showering Martin with expensive items of jewellery and clothing in *Possessed* is the perfect cinematic demonstration of certain aspects of Thorstein Veblen's concept of conspicuous consumption, a cornerstone of consumer theory, and contemporary ideas about fashion, how it is marketed and consumed.[9] However, the more satirical aspects of Veblen's work (*The Theory of the Leisure Class*, as noted earlier, was first published in 1899 as a critique of America's growing materialism) tend to be overlooked and this humorous vein is ignored in favour of the illumination Veblen's work might be able to shed on the contemporary obsession with status and the desire for designer labels. Echoes of his depiction of society's endless pursuit of costly forms of display and, most significantly, how women are used by men as vehicles for such displays of wealth and status, can be heard and seen in many of the memorable, and often humorous, cinematic explorations of conspicuous consumption. Even though Whitney cannot publically display the bejewelled Martin as his trophy, in private among his inner circle there is a tacit understanding of their relationship, and there the conspicuous bangles reflect their aggrandising light back onto Whitney. The montage sequence seems to ridicule the practice of hanging wife or lover with as much gold and fur as possible as the bangles pile up comically one after the other with relentless predictability.

In its use of jewels and particularly fur, cinema reinforces Veblen's deployment of evolutionary and anthropological examples to expose how little society has evolved from what he termed 'predatory culture', via periods of war-like and peaceable barbarism, eventually arriving at a structured society that supports and produces the main topic of his investigation, 'the leisure class'. Animal skins, precious metals and stones remain as desirable and necessary to the maintenance of societal status both to the provider (typically male) and the wearer (typically female) as the hunting, gathering and display of animals and trophies was to the more 'primitive' society member. While Veblen takes pleasure in revealing just how close his contemporary American leisured class was to this more primitive model, so too cinema delights in depicting the primal desire for fur coats and jewels, whether displayed and worn as the sign of the provider's wealth and status or as the goal of the single woman, who will stop at nothing in order to achieve these trophies. As Veblen suggests, 'the requirement of expensiveness is so ingrained into our habits of thought in matters of dress that any other than expensive apparel is instinctively odious to us. Without reflection or analysis, we feel that what is inexpensive is unworthy'.[10]

The equation between expensive garments such as fur coats with worth or merit, as well as being clear material demonstrations of status, motivates the gold-digging show girl and otherwise demure and respectable housewife alike in films where the fur coat, particularly mink, assumes a symbolic resonance well beyond its obvious connotations of luxury and glamour. We can parallel mink's displacement of other fur in ultimate desirability with the classic period of Hollywood cinema from the 1930s to the 50s, surpassing even the earlier craze for fox

POSSESSED
1931, dir. Clarence Brown.
Marian's shackles grow as the years roll by.

fur, as James Laver pointed out in his classic 1937 study *Taste and Fashion*:

> At the end of the War period squirrel was much utilized, and there was a revival in the use of moleskin. Fashion writers lamented that the cost of chinchilla, sable and broadtail had increased to such an extent that they were now unobtainable except by the extremely wealthy. 'Not long ago,' we read, 'the leaders of fashion regarded mink with scorn', a remark which, however natural it may have sounded in 1924, has a very odd ring to-day.[11]

For the show girl, a mink coat, no matter how it has been acquired, marks a transition from the impoverished, hand to mouth existence as a member of the chorus to the demimonde. A form of respectability signalled by the outward display of conspicuous consumption, mink's enveloping luxury possessed the ability to cloak her disreputable occupation, while for the dutiful wife a mink is not just the sign of her husband's economic prowess but a conduit that will lead to a life more glamorous, sexually charged and ultimately liberated.

One of the more detailed and sustained cinematic explorations of the average, respectable woman's desire for mink can be found in the 1953 film *The Lady Wants Mink* where Jim Connors (Dennis O'Keefe), hard-working, harassed and loving husband to Nora (Ruth Hussey), is made to feel inadequate by his wealthier neighbours, the Joneses, because of his inability to provide Nora with a mink coat.[12] This failure is brought home to Jim when, on the occasion of his wife's birthday, he presents her with a fur-collared, camel-hair coat (which has already seriously stretched his budget), little knowing that moments before Gladys Jones (Eve Arden) has been showing off her new 'sapphire blue mink' made from 'eighty-two skins'.[13] Nora tries the mink coat on, fantasising about being rich, noticed and desirable, qualities that her husband's coat fails to give her. Later that same day Jim questions Nora further about her obsession with owning a mink coat, to which she replies: 'It isn't an obsession, it's a very real desire' and tells Jim

in rapturous tones that she has wanted a mink coat ever since she was at school.[14] Jim then points out that women assume a different mode of speaking when referring to mink, with the following observation: 'Well, a man says boat or car, and it's just words, names. When a woman says mink, well . . . it's positively lascivious!'[15] While this exchange is played out within the context and according to the conventions of mid-twentieth-century, American suburban-set film and television comedy, the Connors's engagement with fur coats, and mink especially, touches on psychological and moral issues that resonate far beyond the confines of its cheery garden fence and kitchen settings.

On one level *The Lady Wants Mink* is a literal dramatisation of the ultimate futility of trying to 'keep up with the Joneses' (Gladys and her car-dealing husband Harvey Jones, in this instance) and Jim is made to feel inadequate owing to the fact that he cannot provide for his wife the same degree of luxury that Harvey affords Gladys with her sapphire mink. Veblen's theories, especially his writing in 'Dress as an Expression of the Pecuniary Culture' (chapter 7 of *Theory of the Leisure Class*), is most often cited today to provide a socio-historical and economic context to the persistence of fashion, and provide an explanation as to why fashionable clothes must be expensive, often impractical and constantly changing. The fur coat is subject to all these conditions, always expensive ('seven grand', as Harvey delights in pointing out to Jim in the case of Gladys's mink), totally impractical (a mink coat is hardly necessary in the temperate climes of California, the setting for *The Lady Wants Mink*) and to a degree subject to the vagaries of fashion; Gladys's broad-shouldered sapphire mink is the height of the mid-century furrier's art and makes Nora's humble camel-hair coat look dull and outmoded.[16] However, animal skins used as clothing also have a primal importance and value, far preceding any contemporary notion of fashion, which when used to make fashionable twentieth-century garments render them doubly desirable. Gladys's sapphire mink signifies contemporary status as well as an evocation of the hunter–gatherer providing warmth and protection for his mate. Jim and Nora's blissful domestic situation is unsettled by Gladys's display, reminding Jim of his inability to display his trophy (Nora) in the correct trappings that would demand both respect and envy from his peers. The mid-century American veneer of civilisation is stripped away to be understood, much as Veblen viewed it some fifty years earlier, as not so distant from primitive barbarian societies where 'The original reason for the seizure and appropriation of women seems to have been their usefulness as trophies' and the appropriate care of such trophies, including providing clothing, must be visibly evident.[17]

The matrimonial mink coat as a sign of the husband's economic security is what is at stake in *The Lady Wants Mink* but elsewhere the mink coat can become a substitute for the husband, a decoy and a burden. Max Ophüls explored mink's excessive potential in two films from 1949, *Caught* and *The Reckless Moment*.[18] In the latter film, Lucia Harper (Joan Fontaine) is defined by her mink coat: it is her livery as the wife of a successful but absent architect. Forced to try to extricate her teenage daughter from an unsuitable alliance with an older man and his accidental killing, Lucia becomes enmeshed in murder, blackmail and possible sexual temptation once she meets the dashing blackmailer played by James Mason. In order to raise some immediate cash without alerting suspicion, she pawns her jewellery but will not part with her mink. For Lucia her fur coat is her missing husband in vestimentary form, her moral compass made from mink. Although Lucia will not part with her protective furry carapace, she lends it to her errant daughter in an act of righteous cloaking, a sartorial action which confirms that her daughter has finally seen the light and found her way back into the lustrous folds of middle-class American bourgeois values. As long as she stays on the path of conventional and successful domestic tedium she too will one day inherit the trophy her mother jealously guards. This use of mink to signify moral constancy is the result of its being an example of the 'correct' way to obtain a mink, as a gift from a successful husband to a dutiful trophy wife. In *Caught*, however, the exces-

THE LADY WANTS MINK
1953, dir. William A. Seiter.
[top] Nora tries on the sapphire blue mink;
[middle] Jim's gift does not measure up.

THE RECKLESS MOMENT
1949, dir. Max Ophüls.
[bottom] Maternal mink.

sive allure, constraints and moral turpitude implicit in mink are brought to the fore. The aspiring charm-school graduate Leonora Eames (Barbara Bel Geddes) gets a job modelling fur coats at a department store. At the store two women call her over to inspect the mink coat she is wearing. As they caress and fondle the coat, admiring its 'full back' and declaring 'the skins are divine', one asks the other: 'Wally signed his contract with Metro yet?' 'No, not yet', the other replies, a response that prompts the first to drag her companion away from the inspection with 'Come along, darling, better have the old one glazed', implying that until her husband increases his income she had better get her old coat reconditioned.[19] Later, Leonora is courted and marries the millionaire Smith Ohlrig (Robert Ryan) and finds herself trapped in a loveless, stifling Long Island lifestyle, where every trophy wife, including Leonora herself, displays the necessary sign of conspicuous excess, the obligatory mink coat. Mink is clearly signalled as both intrinsic to the ideal of a successful marriage and simultaneously a decoy leading to boredom.[20] Once 'bought', Leonora finds herself no better off than when she was being pawed by potential customers in the department store. Attempting to escape her luxurious constraints, she leaves Ohlrig and starts work as a nurse where she meets the 'good' doctor Larry Quinada (James Mason). This union is symbolised again by a coat but this time, instead of fur, it is made from practical, hard-wearing and honest wool, a coat not unlike the one that Jim buys for Nora in *The Lady Wants Mink* and found wanting compared to Gladys's sapphire mink.

The latter, and other films that take a light-hearted approach to mink obsessives, makes full use of fur's primitive associations and its role in the establishment of gender identities. Realising that Jim will never be able to get her the mink she desires, Nora usurps the male position by providing, or at least attempting to provide, a mink coat for herself by buying and raising live minks. As part of this process she falls out with the fashionable Gladys – a necessary stage of her 'de-programming' from the cult of mink – relocates, ironically, to a rural setting away from the city where mink-wearing confers most status,

CAUGHT
1949, dir. Max Ophüls.
'The skins are divine!'
Leonora's pelt is pawed.

and eventually becomes self-sufficient as a mink farmer, all of which leads her to the conclusion at the end of the film that she already has her 'mink' in the guise of a healthy, loving family that has opted out of the rat race. So far so morally satisfying but, underneath the 'I Love Lucy' suburban cheeriness of *The Lady Wants Mink*, the significance of the fur coat as perhaps the most practically dysfunctional, yet symbolically functional garment in the negative cinematic wardrobe is never completely obscured or laughed away. In the consumer-driven society of 1950s America of which *The Lady Wants Mink* is certainly a part, and even though apparently advocating the benefits of a simpler, less commercialised way of living, the real meaning of a mink coat is never forgotten, so that when Nora visits the mink breeder she is informed: 'Course, some married women, mostly the reason they have a mink coat is to advertise their husband's business. The business drops off and so does the mink coat.'[21]

In film the function of the fur coat as an item of clothing that will keep the wearer warm is consistently denied, or at least is relegated to an inconsequential level of significance in favour of its symbolic weight as a sign of ownership, status and especially sexuality. The fetishisitic emphasis placed on fur in film is a popularisation of its fundamental position in literature and psychoanalysis. Sacher–Masoch's cruel fur-clad object of desire and provider of pain and Freud's fetishisitic substitution of fur for the *mons Veneris* or, later and more controversially, as the precursor and frame for the fantasised female penis, all feed into the dense amalgam of sex, danger, violence and illegality that condenses round cinematic fur and especially the femme fatale in fur.[22] It is a testament to the erotic power of fur and the persistence of this fetishisitic excess that even in a comedy such as *The Lady Wants Mink* it is alluded to not just when Jim comments on his wife's lascivious tone when talking about mink, but in the breakfast scene the next morning and Gladys's entrance in her mink coat, wearing only a slip beneath her fur. This prompts Jim to display, his carnal nature as he pretends to bite the coat, mimicking a wild animal and exclaiming:

THE LADY WANTS MINK
1953, dir. William A. Seiter.
[top] Gladys's mink brings out
the animal in Jim.

'I thought it was going to bite me!'[23] The now familiar visual trope of an actress wearing nothing but her underwear beneath a fur coat makes a comparatively early appearance in *The Lady Wants Mink* and, while relatively modest by contemporary standards, Gladys in her erotically charged outfit of fur and underwear is only one among a catalogue of cinematic examples of erotically loaded, dysfunctional dressing in fur, which more recently has included Demi Moore as Madison Lee (the 'fallen angel') in full-length fur, bra and knickers brandishing a gun in *Charlie's Angels: Full Throttle* (2003).[24] The 'fur coat no knickers' premise which suggests that a woman in an expensive fur is 'no better than she ought to be' has been a favoured cinematic construction, with the actress clad in fur and little else an enduring visual cliché. Again, while there are many explicit representations of this, it is perhaps at its most perceptive when treated comically, or in the case of the 'Take Back Your Mink' number from the 1955 film version of *Guys and Dolls*, musically.[25] Miss Adelaide and her dancers perform a striptease to the Frank Loesser song, chanting: 'Take back your mink, Take back your pearls, What made you think, That I was one of those girls?'[26] Stripping down to corsets, gloves and heels, the dancers leave the rejected mink stoles on the ground, only to rush back on stage at the end of the number, pick up the minks and in a knowing aside to the audience ask: 'Well? Wouldn't you?' It is a lyrical distillation of the male fetishisation and attempted control of the threatening female by cloaking her in fur and, simultaneously, the apparent impossibility, once caressed by mink, for the woman to resist this objectification.

The growing body of critical material that considers the socio-political significance of wearing fur, especially in the twentieth century, includes many valuable insights into its erotic resonance, and it is not within the scope of this book to attempt to add to that work by exploring fur's various sexually charged cinematic constructions.[27] Indeed, a whole book could be devoted to fur's cinematic 'life': one only has to recall Mrs Danvers auto-erotically caressing Rebecca's fur against her cheek and then forcing her naive young mistress to do the same

CHARLIE'S ANGELS: FULL THROTTLE
[top] 2003, dir. McG.
Madison Lee the 'fallen angel' brandishing her weapon in fur coat, high heels and little else (Columbia/Everett/Rex Features).

GUYS AND DOLLS
1955, dir. Joseph L. Mankiewicz.
[bottom] 'Take Back Your Mink.'

in Hitchcock's film of 1940, or Raquel Welch as 'Loana the Fair One' in her prehistoric fur bikini as the only memorable feature of the 1966 film *One Million Years B.C.*, to realise the erotic resonance that on-screen fur generates.[28] As stated earlier, in some respects fur is possibly the least dysfunctional item of dress in the negative wardrobe, fulfilling its cinematic role of signifying wealth and status while evoking a specifically sexualised glamour, making fur both on screen and off doubly attractive and ensuring that until its recent condemnation, as the result of the powerful lobbying of animal rights campaigners, it has been regarded with equal amounts of desire, envy and suspicion.[29]

That being said, many of the most interesting uses of fur in film are precisely when it is not being worn or is worn dysfunctionally (with nothing underneath, in warm climes, as a bikini and so on), is derided, discarded or disguised. Popular cinema represents fur in a similar manner, as it does the fashion industry itself: that is, it capitalises on the opportunities it affords for visual spectacle, while simultaneously condemning those who wear it (or in the case of the fashion industry, those responsible for its production and consumption – designers, models, journalists and so on) as immoral, vain, cruel or foolish. Fur, the fashion industry and psychological trauma form an extravagant union, an irresistible cinematic opportunity to showcase the photographic allure of fur, voyeuristically take pleasure in revealing the 'hidden secrets' of the fashion industry and sadistically taking delight in depicting its professionals as psychologically disturbed. In the 1944 film version of the musical *Lady in the Dark*, Ginger Rogers plays Liza Elliott, the editor of *Allure* magazine, pathologically unable to make decisions, about her love life, her career and even the cover of the next issue of *Allure*.[30] In the third of the film's three remarkable musical psychoanalytic sequences, Liza sings 'The Saga of Jenny' (the only number from the original Broadway production to survive its migration to the screen intact) wearing a spectacular mink, jewel-encrusted evening dress. Before this fantasy sequence, Liza wears the same outfit to dinner, its

ONE MILLION YEARS B.C.
1966, dir. Don Chaffey.
Fur as prehistoric conspicuous consumption
(Moviestore Collection/Rex Features).

matching jacket cloaking her body completely in mink from top to toe, which must surely be one of the hottest and most impractical dinner dresses in cinematic history. For the fantasy musical sequence, however, Liza dispenses with the jacket and proceeds to unfasten the front of the skirt to reveal a dazzling bejewelled lining to the skirt. She is now transformed into a fetishised object, her fur 'skin' flayed to reveal her blood-red glittering internal organs, an object of supreme conspicuous fashionable consumption, luxurious, impractical and unobtainable. The 'Saga of Jenny' tells the story of a girl who insists on making up her mind, the very opposite of the confused and emotionally stunted Liza, and to the strains of Kurt Weill's insistent melody we hear how 'Jenny made her mind up at twenty-two, to get herself a husband was the thing to do. She got herself all dolled up in her satins and furs and she got herself a husband – but he wasn't hers'[31] This lyrical suggestion that fur is the way to trap a man is convincingly enacted by Liza as she flings back the mink skirt to reveal her legs showcased in scarlet jewel-encrusted satin, the body sectioned, fashioned and possessed. The outfit itself has achieved a degree of fame, reported at the time to be the most expensive film costume ever made (estimated at $35,000), and has since been the subject of intense debate as to who actually designed it, Edith Head usually being credited. However, Mitchell Leisen, the film's director and former costume and set designer, was notorious for the painstaking interest he took in his film's costuming and most probably the outfit was a joint effort by Head, Leisen and the film's other designer, the Broadway costumier Raoul Penc du Bois. Head herself recounts how she and Leisen covered the design studio floor with mink skins in order to select the most cinematic in terms of their lustrous sheen, and that the original version of the dress, studded with faux emeralds and rubies, proved too heavy for Rogers to dance in, so a second version was made embroidered with sequins.[32] The film was widely criticised at the time for its extravagance (it was released in 1944 at the height of the Second World War) and the costume's excess, in terms of its

LADY IN THE DARK
1944, dir. Mitchell Leisen.
[facing] Conspicuous excess? At the time of
the film's release, Ginger Rogers's jewel-
encrusted, mink dress was reputed to be the
most expensive film costume ever made and
was widely criticised for its extravagance
(C. J. Tavin/Everett/Rex Features).

MILDRED PIERCE
1945, dir. Michael Curtiz.
[above] Mildred's hard-earned mink
brings both glamour and misery.

cost, impracticality, controversial provenance and narrative ambiguity, make it one of the more dysfunctional of cinematic garments.

Liza has the means to furnish her own mink and she is able to select her wardrobe from outfits sent to her for approval as the editor of *Allure*, but her unhappiness is the apparent price she must pay for this sartorial independence: her clothes bring her no happiness and it is not fur that 'gets herself a husband'. It is as if popular film's remit is to offer salutary lessons in the dangers that can befall those who clamour for fur; special punishment being meted out to those women who find their own means of acquiring it. So Nora in *The Lady Wants Mink* is made to realise the virtue of family values over stylish mink by losing her house, and nearly her husband, when she attempts to farm her own coat, while self-sacrificing, hard-working Mildred Pierce (Joan Crawford) in the eponymous film of 1945, toils tirelessly for a better life for her daughter and herself, signified by the broad-shouldered mink (and matching hat) that she wears at the film's deadly climax, but at the cost of a string of unsuccessful relationships and the rearing of a spoilt and murderous daughter.[33] The image of Crawford's haunted and glacial bone structure nestled in the limitless contours of mink from the film's later scenes has come to epitomise the sumptuous power of 1940s black and white cinematography, but it is also a defining image of the miseries of mink (see illus. p. 69). Surely one of the more deserved coats in film history, Mildred's mink, however, sits uneasily on her shoulders, too excessive for this hard-working, pie-making mother. For all its noir glamour, it seems to exceed the limits of the scene, looking for a more typical femme fatale. Mink is a trophy, whether that be for mistress or wife; whether intended as reward, compensation or trap, it is bestowed and woe betide those who earn it for themselves.

Less extravagant than the mink featured in *Lady in the Dark*, and less dramatic than Mildred Pierce's mink, are the various coats and other accessories that punctuate the progress of another cinematic fashion doyenne, Lucy Gallant in the 1955 film of that name.[34] Jane Wyman in the title role embarks on her career as a Texan fashion retailer by selling her own wedding trousseau to the inhabitants of a newly oil-rich boom town, including a remarkable mink clutch bag that generates a frenzy of interest among the fashion-starved Texans. As her rise to fashion retailing pre-eminence unfolds, Gallant is dressed in a variety of minks, emphasising her financial independence and status. Gallant has earned her minks and it is this very independence that must be relinquished if she is to find lasting happiness in the arms of Casey Cole (Charlton Heston). As with *Mildred Pierce*, true contentment can never be found by the single, independent career woman and mink, no matter how stylish or in what quantity, can never be a substitute for male presence. It is ironic that in *Lucy Gallant* a mink coat intended as a gift for the mistress of Gus Basserman (the husband of her oldest friend Molly) is diverted by her canny retailing staff to Molly, who accepts it enthusiastically even though its size makes it apparent that it was not intended for her. However, the gift of mink from husband to wife is able to mask any dishonourable intentions and Molly revels in its soft caress, a vestimentary reward for her tolerance of Gus's boorishness and infidelity (see illus. p. 73).

While the acceptance of mink by a woman from any man other than her legally married partner is consistently understood as an indication of moral deficiency, and the woman who by her own industry obtains her mink is similarly censured and punished for her assumption of autonomy, there are exceptions. Whether as a gift from one of her lovers or, as is more likely, as a result of her ill-gotten gains as the accomplice to the master jewel-thief the Phantom, Madame Clouseau (Capucine) wears a spectacular wardrobe including mink in *The Pink Panther*.[35] The unwitting Clouseau (Peter Sellers) is questioned in court as to how she can afford such a wardrobe and asked how much he earns, to which he defers an answer only to have the barrister (John Le Mesurier) reply: 'Enough to buy your wife a $10,000 mink coat?'; Clouseau: 'No, of course not'. Barrister: 'You are aware that your wife spent $7,000 at Yves

Saint Laurent only last month?'; Clouseau: 'What!' Barrister: 'And two months before that $4,000?'; Clouseau: 'Well that's impossible!'. Barrister: 'We know for a fact that your wife spent at least $30,000 on clothes during the last year!'[36] The inference that she must be obtaining these clothes somehow illicitly is clear, even though Clouseau attempts to explain her wardrobe as a result of her assiduously saving up her house-keeping money, to which the court collapses in laughter given that Capucine is indeed sitting in court resplendent in Yves Saint Laurent, who designed her clothes for the film. At the end of the film Madame Clouseau is seen driving away with the Phantom and his nephew, while Clouseau himself is taken into custody wrongly accused of the jewel thefts; this suggests that if a woman is to enjoy mink other than as a gift from husband or lover it is best procured illegally, rather than by her honest toil.

Fur's function to demarcate social division and to confer immorality on those judged to be wearing it inappropriately had been established long before the advent of cinema and its use of fur as a visualisation of narratives of social aspiration, greed and decadence. Historically, fur has been the subject of numerous sumptuary laws which list in remarkable detail the particular hierarchies of prohibition that wearing fur (as well as other materials such as silk, lace and velvet) attracted. Alan Hunt in his seminal work on the subject, *Governance of the Consuming Passions: A History of Sumptuary Law*, includes many examples of sumptuary prohibition among which is this sixteenth-century edict:

> Whereas the common lewd who dwell in the city of London . . . have now of late assumed the fashion of being clad and attired in the manner and dress of good and noble dames and damsels of the realm in unreasonable manner, it is Ordered by the Mayor, Alderman and Commons that no such lewd woman shall be so daring as to be attired either by day or night in any kind of vesture trimmed with fur such as miniver [white squirrel], grey work [badger], squirrel . . . or any other manner of noble budge [lamb's-wool] . . .

nor yet to be clothed either in a coat, surcoat or hood relieved with fur or lining, on pain of forfeiting the said vestments . . .[37]

The association of immorality and the wearing of fur is discussed by Hunt not only as a prohibited form of dress for prostitutes but also how, conforming to Veblen's concepts of conspicuous display and consumption, fur's pre-eminence as a sign of economic superiority is inextricably linked to its sexualisation, suggesting that fur: 'became one of the most immediately recognizable signs of vicarious display of wealth on the backs and shoulders of the wives and mistresses of the wealthy and the powerful. In this role fur signifies the transfer of trophy from male to female and, in turn, provides an opening to understand the eroticization of fur.'[38] So Gladys, wearing nothing but her slip underneath her mink, or indeed Madison Lee only a set of lacy underwear, can be clearly understood not only as the visualisation of the direct link between the fur coat as the 'wages of sin' (presumably Gladys's seven-thousand-dollar coat is her recompense for submitting to the attentions of her boorish, car-dealer husband) but also as a form of tactile auto-eroticisation; the caress of animal fur against flesh is a vestimentary evocation of the human sexual intercourse that has 'paid' for the coat.

'We're sisters under the mink' declares Debby to the corrupt policeman's widow Bertha Duncan in *The Big Heat*, recognising their shared livery of mink as a sign of the woman who will get what she wants by any means necessary (see illus. p. 73).[39] So closely imbricated is mink with immorality as a furry exterior that simultaneously proclaims dissolution and social ascendancy that it has become a vital visual trope of the femme fatale. As Petra Dominková suggests, 'She wants her wealth to be seen and so she embellishes herself with glittering jewellery, luxurious designer dresses and hats. But one fashionable commodity in particular has become synonymous with *film noir's femme fatale*: the mink coat.'[40] Mink-clad molls constitute some highly memorable images in film noir from 1940 to 1950: joining pistol-packing Debby, the formidable mink-coated

BUTTERFIELD 8
1960, dir. Daniel Mann.
Gloria's extra-marital mink
becomes a catalyst for harm
(SNAP/Rex Features).

slayer in *The Big Heat*, is a cast of seductive Venuses in fur including Lana Carlsen (Ida Lupino) in *They Drive by Night*, Verna Jarrett (Virginia Mayo) in *White Heat*, Mary (Ava Gardner) in *Whistle Stop*, Vera Novak (Jeanne Cagney) in *Quicksand* and Cora Lister (Ella Raines) in *Brute Force*.[41] So indispensable is the mink coat displayed on the body of the gangster's moll as a measure of his financial prowess that in a more contemporary dissection of gangster culture such as Martin Scorsese's *Goodfellas* (1990), the irresistibility of this act of conspicuous consumption is emphasised not just in the

wardrobes of the gangsters themselves but in one particular scene of the mistresses also.[42] Two days after a major heist, Jimmy Conway (Robert De Niro) and his gang are celebrating, when one member arrives in the new pink Cadillac he has bought for his wife, incurring Jimmy's wrath given that he has repeatedly told them that they must not buy anything ostentatious for fear of attracting suspicion from the police. Jimmy placated, the party continues until another gang member enters the bar with his mistress clad in a full-length white mink coat. As Jimmy strips the coat from the woman's shoulders, bundles it up and pushes them both outside into the snow, he shouts: 'Didn't I tell you not to attract attention! In two days one gets a fuckin' Cadi, one gets a $20,000 mink! . . . Get it outta here!'[43] This vestimentary echo of the hopelessly outmoded way of life of the mobster is interrogated throughout *Goodfellas* and the Goodfellas' inability to abandon a predilection for conspicuous consumption becomes instrumental in the eventual downfall of Jimmy and his associates.

When not featured in crime film, extra-marital mink is similarly understood as the sign of corruption and immorality. The equation between loose morals and mink is crystallised in the character of Gloria Wandrous (Elizabeth Taylor) and her relationship to the mink coat that she acquires in *BUtterfield 8*.[44] The mink in question is originally taken by Gloria from Weston Liggett's (Laurence Harvey) apartment by way of rec-ompense for her torn dress and as a rejoinder to what she feels is an insulting cash payment for their sexual encounter. Thereafter the coat becomes a symbol of infidelity (it is in fact Liggett's wife's mink) and continues to be represented through-out the film as a form of sartorial branding, the livery of the 'common lewd'.[45] The mink coat is a catalyst for harm wher-ever it is left and proves to be ultimately cursed, as Gloria's apparent inability to reject it, and the life it represents, ends with her death at the wheel of her sports car. In direct contrast to Gloria Wondrous is the hard-working and morally upright Lora Meredith (Lana Turner), the central figure in Douglas Sirk's melodrama *Imitation of Life* (1959).[46] As an aspiring actress at the beginning of the film, Meredith has to negotiate the advances of her lecherous agent Allen Loomis (Robert Alda), who attempts to seduce her with the aid of a mink jacket:

> Loomis: 'Say . . . you're not allergic to mink are you?'
> Lora: 'Mink? No I don't think so.'
> Loomis: 'Good! [Gets mink jacket out of the closet] Try this on for size.'
> Lora: 'But whose is it?'
> Loomis: 'Mine, and I only loan it to very special clients. I want you to wear it tonight.'

LUCY GALLANT
1955, dir. Robert Parrish.
[top] Mink, the fitting (or ill-fitting)
present for the faithful wife.

THE BIG HEAT
1953, dir. Fritz Lang.
[middle] 'Sisters under the mink'.

GOODFELLAS
1990, dir. Martin Scorsese.
[bottom] Too conspicuous consumption.

Lora: 'You want me to wear . . .'
Loomis: 'Please, I've got to think of my reputation. I haven't been seen with a girl without a mink since the heat wave of 1939! Come on . . .' [Puts mink on her shoulders and starts to embrace her][47]

Mink is here clearly signalled as the essential weapon in any self-respecting Lothario's arsenal and Meredith's rejection of this temptation reinforces her fundamental integrity. It is interesting that even though Meredith becomes a highly successful actress, and sumptuously attired and bejewelled, she remains apparently impervious to the seduction of the mink coat, opting only for the occasional trim rather than full-length fur (unlike Mildred Pierce whose character, relationship with her black friend and confidant and filial difficulties are duplicated by Lora in *Imitation of Life*). However, although Lora eschews the glamour of mink, she has no such reservations when it comes to her jewellery, which dazzles throughout the film. Lana Turner's jewellery in the film was reported to have been valued at more than a million dollars, while the outfits created by Jean Louis cost in the region of $78,000 and consisted of thirty-four separate costume changes, making the wardrobe expenditure for *Imitation of Life* one of the highest of the period. If mink is out of the economic reach and aspiration of both suitor and quarry, then occasionally a lesser pelt can be substituted, as Dana Andrews playing the taciturn detective Mark McPherson in *Laura* (1944) suggests.[48] Responding to the acerbic critic Waldo Lydecker's (Clifton Webb) enquiry as to whether he has ever been in love, McPherson responds: 'A doll in Washington Heights once got a fox fur out of me.'[49]

Mink is so firmly embedded in the visual grammar of popular cinema as the essential item in the wardrobe of the decadent, the procurable or those 'on the make', that it is often at its most significant when not being worn. This dysfunctional use of fur can be found in a number of cinematic showbiz party sequences where the coats belonging to the assorted show girls and aspiring actresses at the party are dep-osited in the bedroom, where they lie strewn across beds and satin counterpanes like

IMITATION OF LIFE
1959, dir. Douglas Sirk.
[top] The mink trap.

PARTY GIRL
1958, dir. Nicholas Ray.
[bottom] The mink-laden bed.

so many freshly skinned pelts in trophy rooms dedicated to the sisterhood of mink. These fur-laden scenarios function as atavistic reminders of a time when animal skins were the sign of the hunter's prowess and his ability to provide for his mate. However, the 'hunters' in the next room where the party is in full swing are more likely to be impresarios, film producers or crooks and, rather than a spear and club, the weapons used to capture these furs are a cheque book and an account at Saks of Fifth Avenue or Bergdorf's. In *Party Girl* (1958) the dancer Vicki Gaye (Cyd Charisse) witnesses the ritual tossing of the fur coat onto the bed at the mobster's party she has been persuaded to attend, an indication of the pos-sibilities open to her if she follows the conventional route of the show girl, while Birdie (Thelma Ritter) playing Margot Channing's (Bette Davis) acerbic dresser and confidante in *All About Eve* (1950), comments on the furs accumulating on the bed during the party Margot is hosting.[50] Coming in to collect a coat which a glamorous movie starlet has just deposited, Birdie observes that 'The bed looks like a dead animal act' and, after locating the coat, explains that even though its owner has just got here, now 'She's on her way, with half the men in the joint.'[51] Both these films use the fur-laden bed as a means of signalling the commodification of female sexuality, with the furs occupying the traditional site of sexual intercourse. For those women who have as yet not gained their fur and are still aspiring to the ranks of mink and sable, the apparent disregard for these expensive luxury items, tossed carelessly onto the bed, becomes not only a perfect example of Veblen's concept of conspicuous consumption but also as conspicuous waste. These coats are not used to keep the owner warm, as they invariably travel to the party by car rather than on foot, and are worn purely to make a suitably conspicuous entrance, after which they are immediately discarded, only to be collected at the end of the party and carried out again to a waiting car. Here dysfunctionality is refined to a noticeable degree: the coats serve no practical thermal purpose and function conspicuously only for a fraction of the time that their owners participate in the social ritual of

ALL ABOUT EVE
1950, dir. Joseph L. Mankiewicz.
[top] 'Dead animal act';
[bottom] fur fills the frame
in the party scene.

the party. Yet, as always, the garment's dysfunctionality ushers in alternative functions and the coat becomes an object whose very impracticality becomes its function, as Karen, Margot's friend, observes in the following exchange with Eve, who has entered the bedroom to add a magnificent fur coat to the pile already amassed on the bed: Karen: 'Now who's showed up at this hour? It's time people went home – hold that coat up.' (Eve holds it up; Karen whistles.) 'Whose is it?' Eve: 'Some Hollywood movie star, her plane got in late.' Karen: 'Discouraging, isn't it? Women with furs like that where it never gets cold.'[52]

In other films a mere mention or glimpse of mink is enough to trigger cinematic narratives of chauvinism that rely on the acceptance of the gift of fur from a man to a woman. One sustained utilisation of mink's association with immorality and licentiousness can be found in the Doris Day vehicle *That Touch of Mink* (1962), which in its title alone suggests the persuasive power of fur, even in the smallest of quantities.[53] *That Touch of Mink* is a straightforward morality tale that casts Day as the simple country girl Cathy Timberlake, defending her virginity against the persuasive whiles of the suave businessman Philip Shayne (Cary Grant), whom she first meets when his car drives past her in the pouring rain, drenching and staining her clothes.[54] From this point the 'will she, won't she' comedy of sexual manners proceeds, using the tested romantic Hollywood cliché of whether Philip will ever give Cathy the gift she really desires – marriage.[55] Shayne showers her with gifts, trips abroad, expensive dinners and most significantly a new wardrobe. His neurotic and reluctant assistant Roger (Gig Young) is assigned the task of outfitting Cathy so that she can accompany Shayne on a trip, but Roger is reluctant to carry out this task. Shayne: 'The sparrow's flying south . . . She's gonna need a lot of clothes and stuff. So make all the arrangements.' Roger: 'No! I may have delivered the victim but I will not dress her for the sacrifice!' Shayne: 'Try Bergdorf Goodman. I hear they're showing a new line of sacrificial gowns.'[56] Cathy does indeed go to Bergdorf's and is

[facing] Cristóbal Balenciaga coat in Donegal tweed lined with sable, 1962 (Fundación Cristóbal Balenciaga).

THAT TOUCH OF MINK
1962, dir. Delbert Mann.
[top] The performance of fur at the Bergdorf fashion show.

ROBERTA
1953, dir. William A. Seiter.
[bottom] The fur that comes complete with its own security force.

treated to a fashion show that includes a lime-green brocade coat and trousers hemmed in mink, a black evening dress and stole lined with white mink and a remarkable blue satin mink-lined coat. This last outfit leaves Cathy breathless and gasping with desire as it is first modelled unbuttoned, revealing the mink lining, and then three alternative 'top coats' in green and red satin and beige wool are brought on. In the manner of a conjuring trick, these top coats are held up in front of the model who is guided by a male assistant towards them, emerging each time wearing a differently coloured coat but all with the same mink liner. (see illus. p. 77) Finally the sequence cuts to Cathy back in her apartment wearing the beige mink-lined coat, caressing its luxurious inner softness.

The performance of fur modelling has a particular function in cinematic history, invariably demanding an added layer of performativity including male 'helpers' who reinforce fur's deeply embedded role as a locus of sexual attraction and act as necessary masculine 'protection', signifying its value. An earlier example of this comes in the celebrated fashion-show sequence from *Roberta* (1935) and can be understood as a precursor for many such furry performances.[57] In *Roberta*, as in *That Touch of Mink*, a succession of fur (and feathered) or fur-trimmed outfits are paraded to the strains of 'Lovely to Look At'; with the entrance of a model wearing a full-length sable coat, two liveried footmen step forward to relieve her of the coat (and presumably, to keep watch over it), revealing underneath the model's figure-hugging, bare-shouldered sequinned sheath dress (see illus. p. 77).[58]

The Bergdorf sequence from *That Touch of Mink* sends out a clear message that mink does not necessarily have to be ostentatious but may be more seductive when worn so that its full effect is known and felt only by its wearer, a form not so much of conspicuous consumption, perhaps, but rather 'inconspicuous excess'. One can understand the understated use of fur in *That Touch of Mink* as indicative of the move towards a 1960s minimalism, an aesthetic that even the most luxurious of designers evidenced in their work. For example, an outfit designed by Cristóbal Balenciaga in 1962, the same year as *That Touch of Mink* was released, appears to all intents and purposes to be a simple, immaculately cut, Donegal tweed coat, until on closer inspection its sable-lined bodice is revealed (see illus. p. 76).[59] This traditional use of fur as a provider of warmth, rather than outward show, is a technique to which Balenciaga, that most inconspicuously excessive designer, resorted regularly in his designs, and for Cathy Timberlake makes her dilemma even more perplexing as her mink-lined coat reinforces the proximity of Shayne's primal desires as well as his contemporary good taste and discretion. Mink's power, however, whether floor-length or a mere touch, is indisputable and the audience receives confirmation of this when in a later scene Cathy travels in Shayne's private jet for their romantic rendez-vous in Bermuda. The air stewardess attempts to stow away Cathy's mink, but she hastily grabs it back, its lining now fully exposed, and fondles it lovingly as she settles back in her seat, cradling in her arms the reward for the impending loss of her virginity. Arriving in Bermuda (the perfect climate to render her mink redundant and dysfunctional), Shayne and Cathy enter a lift together with another couple, the woman wearing a more conventional mink coat, the obvious dress of the 'kept' woman, who winks at Cathy knowingly, reinforcing both in Cathy's mind and the audience's that mink is not only the sign of conspicuous consumption but also the livery of shame. Later that same evening Shayne, frustrated by Cathy's various strategies to avoid consummating their liaison, goes for a cigarette by the hotel pool where he meets the man from the earlier lift scene. Recognising Shayne's despondent air, he engages in conversation. Man: 'Havin' trouble too huh?' Shayne: 'Well . . .' Man: 'Before you give 'em the mink coat they all talk a big game. Now the little lady gets headaches. She prefers to be alone.' Shayne: 'What did you do?' Man: 'I belted her – how about you?' Shayne: 'Right across the chops.'[60] While neither the plot nor the viewer's understanding of both the character Philip Shayne and the actor Cary Grant's essential urbanity and chivalry would permit such an act, and the viewer realises that he is merely humouring the stranger, the underlying odour of sexual aggression and chauvinism that clings to mink is brought to the fore in this scene. From this moment on, the mink coat and whether it will be accepted by Cathy or not becomes crucial.

After the disastrous, unconsummated weekend, Cathy decides to return Shayne's gifts and the mink coat is sent back along with the rest of her newly acquired wardrobe. Roger picks up the mink, declaring: 'When she sent this back she became a symbol of hope to all of us who sold out for that touch of mink.'[61] It is an unusual speech for a male character, although throughout the film Roger's sexuality has been interrogated; his subservient role as secretary to Shayne, the repeated slaps he receives from Cathy's indignant room-mate, and the fact that we see him undergoing psychotherapy sessions, all suggest a passive, hysterical condition more commonly constructed as female in mainstream Hollywood cinema. Both in *That Touch of Mink* and *The Lady Wants Mink*, comparatively weak male characters (Roger and Jim Connors) are depicted as psychologically unbalanced. Roger is obviously so by his need for therapy, and Jim in *The Lady Wants Mink* in a remarkable sequence where he undergoes a form of psychological disassociation, wrestling with his double, or subconscious self, a trauma resulting from his inability to provide a mink coat for his wife. This characterisation of fur as somehow psychologically disruptive and its presence a source of mental distress underscores mink's essential cinematic function in reinforcing gender stereotypes, so that only the powerful, financially secure male can handle fur and use it accordingly as a visual sign of his economic prowess. For those men of lesser standing it becomes a threat to their sexual identity. This is taken to its extreme when Roger's analyst mistakenly believes that he is in a homosexual relationship with Shayne, who as the dominant partner is giving Roger expensive clothes, including mink, as an inducement to submit to his sexual advances. While this apparent equivalence between fur, loss of identity and psychological trauma is used for comedic effect in the films under

THAT TOUCH OF MINK
1962, dir. Delbert Mann.
[top] Cathy hangs onto her mink;
[bottom] the livery of the kept woman.

discussion, it relies on the fundamental transformative power of fur. Fur coats, perhaps more than any other item of clothing, allow the wearer to assume alternative identities (as has been seen, Nora immediately enacts being wealthy and famous as soon as she tries on Gladys's mink in *The Lady Wants Mink*), and the assumption of new identities once the 'touch' of mink has been felt resonates throughout cinematic history.

One highly unusual cinematic exploration of fur as masquerade can be found in the British comedy *Make Mine Mink* (1960).[62] In the film, a loose translation of the Robin Hood story, a group of unlikely misfits, including Terry Thomas, Hattie Jacques and Athene Seyler, band together to steal fur coats, sell them on and use the proceeds so that Dame Beatrice Appleby (Seyler), an eccentric aristocrat down on her luck, can continue her philanthropic charity work. While the film itself is certainly not on a par with other British comedies of the period, its condensation of all the functional and dysfunctional characteristics of the fur coat discussed so far is remarkable. The initial catalyst for their subsequent fur felonies is the rejection of 'a thousand quid' mink stole by an angry wife who suspects her philandering husband of giving her 'conscience presents'.[63] This rejected fur is retrieved by Dame Beatrice's eternally grateful maid Lily (Billie Whitelaw), who happens to have a prison record. Lily takes the fur to give to her employer who, once she finds out where it came from, is fearful that Lily will be accused of theft and return to prison. This fear prompts Dame Beatrice's motley crew of lodgers to return the fur without the owners suspecting anything, and it is this minor contact with the handling of stolen goods that excites them to carry out their subsequent string of raids on furriers and fur refrigeration depots. As their thefts increase in success and notoriety, the group adopt a series of ever more elaborate disguises, pretending to be wealthy customers and fur lovers. This reaches a peak in Hattie Jacques's transformation from the masculine tweed-wearing etiquette teacher Nanette Parry into a curvaceous white-mink stole-wearing vamp, a sort of outsize Diana Dors, or precursor to Divine as he appeared

in John Waters's 1972 transgressive comedy *Pink Flamingos*. Subsequent tableaux depict the gang of crooks 'frozen' in their fur coats as a consequence of being trapped in the cold storage section of a fur warehouse – their furs proving ultimately dysfunctional and incapable of keeping them warm – and yet another version of the 'fur-laden bed'. Posing as police, the gang 'raid' an illegal gambling party and make off with the furs in the ensuing mayhem. In an excess of furry masquerade, Elizabeth Pinkerton, the neurotic porcelain-repairing spinster, returns wearing three fur coats over her bogus policeman's uniform – a visual distillation of the intricate relationship between fur, legality and excess.

Such insistent use of fur as masquerade in *Make Mine Mink*, and its recurring theme of deception, suggests an essential quality of dishonesty connected to fur. This dishonesty derives from the actual thefts enacted throughout the film, as well as fur's association with the criminal classes' need for costly vestimentary expression. Phrases such as 'mutton dressed as lamb' and 'a wolf dressed in sheep's clothing', seem apt descriptions of Hattie Jacques and Terry Thomas's fur-clad appearances in the film. Similarly, in fashion history itself, authenticity and fur have had a long and uneasy alliance and, with the advent of synthetic dyes in the nineteenth century, the possibility of disguising one type of fur as another has challenged the integrity of fur, as Laver suggests:

> The new use of synthetic dyes made it possible to employ a variety of furs which would before have been despised – particularly rabbit, which, under the name of cony (generally dyed cony), is now an important part of the fur industry. Marmot could be dyed to represent mink, and musquash to resemble sealskin. A whole new chapter of the fur industry was opened.[64]

The broad and somewhat heavy-handed farce of *Make Mine Mink* can be understood as a transitional example of British film comedy, displaying neither the subtlety in writing of a classic Ealing comedy, for example, nor the knowing sexual innuendo of the *Carry On* films. It is interesting to compare its own cinematic status with its representation of fur, which at this point in fashion history was undergoing an equivalent transformation. Broadly speaking, by the advent of the 1960s the full-length fur coat, little changed in terms of cut and styling since the 1940s, was looking increasingly outdated, the preserve of the wealthy older woman. In the hands of a growing number of radical designers, however, fur was being treated in a less formal way, dyed, faked and used ironically in outfits that belied its essential thermal utility (fur gilets, fur-trimmed mini dresses and coats and so on). Of course, the full-length mink or sable coat remained a quintessentially desirable item of luxury clothing, but the fur as symbol of wealth, prestige and status, and hence also as a symbol of the conservative establishment, meant that the more radical of 1960s designers looked for ways to make fur 'fun', emphasising its fancy-dress, exotic or sexual references. So the peculiar ambivalence with which fur is treated in *Make Mine Mink* with its emphasis on the fur coat as the costume of wealthy dowagers, villains or hyper-sexualised vamps seems entirely appropriate for a film that appears oblivious to the social revolution that will take place in the ensuing decade, and to which fashion made a major contribution.

Returning to the 1940s and the heyday of the fashionable mink coat, Alfred Hitchcock's wartime propaganda film *Lifeboat* (1944) provides an intriguing example of the hard-earned mink as sign of unstable social demarcation.[65] Following the battle between an Allied ship and a German U-Boat, the survivors of the sunken vessels assemble in a lifeboat in the North Atlantic. The opening shot of the lifeboat and the film's star, Tallulah Bankhead, playing the world-weary photo-journalist Connie Porter, sees her cocooned in luxurious mink bemoaning her laddered stockings. In the claustrophobic space of the lifeboat, Porter's possessions (travelling rug, camera, typewriter) and luxurious items of dress (stockings, mink coat, jewellery) are obsolescent symbols: with their status-affirming functions neutralised, they are gradually lost overboard or transformed

MAKE MINE MINK
1960, dir. Robert Asher.
[top] The dysfunctional
fur that fails to warm;
[middle] transforming fur;
[bottom] the 'trophy room'.

from luxury items into practical artefacts. Her mink coat and all its customary connotations of wealth and privilege take centre stage in the initial scenes; it is used as the pivotal object defining the socio-political positions of those occupying the lifeboat, from the proto-Communism of Kovac (John Hodiak), the Allied ship's engineer, who 'hasn't got a mink coat', to the millionaire capitalist, Charles 'Ritt' Rittenhouse (Henry Hull), with Porter at a point between these two polarised positions as the celebrated self-made journalist who has worked hard for her mink. The class distinctions underscored by the wearing of mink are brought to the fore in the scene where an English woman, Mrs Higgins, whose baby dies in her arms after boarding the lifeboat, comes round from her state of deep shock to find that Porter has leant her the mink coat to keep warm: Higgins: 'It's a beautiful coat! Is it real mink?' Porter: 'I hope so!' Higgins: 'It's lovely! I've always admired mink. It's the most . . . lady-like fur there is, I always said. So warm and comfortable. Thank you so much for letting me wear it.'[66] Realising the absence of her dead child, Higgins becomes distraught and attempts to jump overboard, which forces the lifeboat's 'crew' to tie her down to stop further suicide attempts. Later, after falling asleep Porter wakes and, complaining of cold owing to the lack of her mink, notices that Higgins has freed herself and succeeded in throwing herself off the lifeboat wearing the mink coat.

The mink coat in *Lifeboat* distils many of the cinematic functions of fur already discussed: it demarcates class and social status, its inspires envy and yet simultaneously interrogates those demarcations, raising questions concerning the fake and genuine, which, in a tragic turn, can be applied not only to the coat itself but also to those who wear it. While we learn later in the film that Porter was certainly not born with a silver spoon in her mouth or mink coat on her shoulders, at least she has earned her fur. Not so the distraught working-class Higgins, whose momentary transgression and assumption of a higher social status when wearing the 'lady-like fur' must be punished and so plunges to her watery grave wearing it. Hitchcock's positioning

Princess Anne in black-and-white fun fur, 1969 (Ronald Spencer/ Daily Mail/Rex Features).

of the mink coat as a cursed object, which needs to be jettisoned if the protagonists are to survive, is typical of the emphasis the director placed on clothing and its alternative functions. In *Lifeboat* the characteristic light-heartedness with which the desire and acquisition of fur are often treated in film is overturned, and Porter's fur is as much a reminder of the barbarism that will erupt in the lifeboat as it is a trophy of her overcoming her humble origins. Fur, and its indissoluble association with hunting, violence and death is revealed as the fashionable covering of an increasingly contested idea of civilisation in a time of war, when society quickly reverts to an animalistic condition closer to Veblen's conception of predatory culture.

LIFEBOAT
1944, dir. Alfred Hitchcock.
[top] Connie in mink in the North Atlantic
(20th Century Fox/Everett/Rex Features);
[bottom] 'I've always admired mink'.
The curse of fur and those
unentitled to wear it.

4 TALISMANS

As with fur, jewellery is used to denote wealth, power and status but, unlike fur, it can also become a central element in narratives of both psychological and physical violence. This is understandable, given the comparative value of jewellery, added to which the fabled, often violent histories of famous gems have influenced both literary and cinematic accounts of jewellery. Introductions to historical accounts of jewellery typically acknowledge this unhappy association, with bloody stories of deception, theft and murder giving additional lustre to the brilliance of the gems described. This rich heritage is similarly reflected in the history of screen jewellery. Gems and jewellery as the motive for theft, violence and murder take centre stage in heist films from all periods of Hollywood and British cinema: the detailed planning of the robbery, depictions of the jewels' elaborate security, the heist itself and the inevitable disintegration of the tightly knit group of thieves during or after the theft comprises much of the action of many famous heist films. The precious stones that drive the plots of heist films function ironically as unattainable objects so that, once removed from their resting places in bank vaults, museums and jewellery-store safes, they are consigned to a restless existence, transported, lost, fought over until restored to their former positions as spectacular, remote objects. If it is actual pieces of jewellery that are stolen rather than unset gems, then these are invariably 'fenced', broken up or otherwise disposed. Personal items of jewellery, which this section will address, although often far less spectacular than the objects featured in heist films, retain some of those same qualities of remoteness and a resistance to possession, a dysfunctionality that has more affinity with precious stones' essentially inorganic un-naturalness, which Roland Barthes acknowledged in his essay 'From Gemstones to Jewellery':

> As for the quintessential stone, the diamond, it is beyond time: never wearing, incorruptible, its limpidness forms the moral image of the most deadly of virtues – purity; in terms of substance, the diamond is pure, clean, almost aseptic; but whereas there are some purities that are tender, fragile (water for example), there are others that are sterile, cold, steely; for purity is life, but it can also be, by contrast, infertility, and the diamond

is like the sterile son emerging from the deepest point of the earth, non-productive, incapable of rotting down, hence incapable of becoming the source of new life.[1]

Beyond the dominant scenarios of expensive jewellery given either as rewards for the faithful wife or as payment to the kept woman or mistress, rarer pieces exist from the cinematic jeweller's stock, pieces that act as catalysts for change, that function as talismans averting evil and as charms by which extraordinary events are ushered into the story. Cinematic convention tolerates the mistress's desire for glittering jewels so long as she is finally taught to see beyond their brilliance and renounces glamour for respectability, as Marian Martin does in *Possessed*, or as long as she possesses the integrity and naiveté of Marilyn Monroe's Lorelei Lee in *Gentlemen Prefer Blondes*, who finally gets her man and his rocks. Not so the female character whose love of gems surpasses all other emotions or, even worse, bypasses grateful husband or 'sugardaddy' altogether and, like the autonomous mink-obsessives discussed previously, gets her jewels for herself. The punishment for female agency in mainstream Hollywood cinema has been an integral area of critical enquiry for a succession of film critics since the early 1970s and, it could be argued, was a highly fertile ground in which early feminist film theory first flourished and established its centrality to film criticism.[2] While pioneering works considering how women were constructed in mainstream cinema, how they were framed, lit, dressed and so on, made important contributions to the field, it is perhaps the incorporation of psychoanalytic theory that provided early critics with the tools to interrogate how women are represented in mainstream film.[3] Mainstream cinema's deployment of the classic Oedipal trajectory – which typically would have the male protagonist at the beginning of the film in a state of equilibrium, undergoing a series of crises, eventually resolving these and finally 'settling down' with a 'good' woman – was opposed by feminist discussion concerning the role of women in film noir, melodrama and what came to be understood as 'women's pictures'. The

threat posed by female characters in films of these genres (the femme fatale is a classic example) paved the way for more detailed use of psychoanalytic theories centred on notions of voyeurism, fetishisation and, to use the term as Laura Mulvey first applied it to male gendered spectatorship, scopophilia.[4] Although much has been written concerning the clothing of these characters, and how that either assists in their passivity as fetishised objects or, more rarely, resists easy assimilation by the (male) viewer, comparatively little work has been undertaken on the key role that jewellery plays in many of these films. While it is not within the scope of this work to conduct a comprehensive feminist or psychoanalytic reading of the role of jewellery in mainstream cinematic narrative, I note that jewels repeatedly function not as adornment per se but rather as catalysts that create a setting for broader theoretical and socio-cultural reflections, including jewels as signifiers of loss and mental instability, as catalysts for desire and destruction and as conduits for the assumption of alternative identities.

In a number of US and British melodramas produced in the 1940s, such as *The Locket*, *Whirlpool*, *Black Angel*, *Conflict* and the costume dramas *Gaslight* and *Madonna of the Seven Moons*, items of jewellery feature either as direct manifestations of typically female, psychological trauma or as evidence of criminal activity associated with or as a result of emotional instability.[5] This formulation of gems as traumatic lodestones, which facilitate a cinematic representation not only of the mental states of the characters themselves but also in many instances the use of psychoanalysis to understand those states, is entirely in keeping with the emphasis placed on psychiatry in film melodrama of this period. The impact of psychoanalysis on American culture in the 1940s due to the presence of émigré psychiatrists fleeing Nazi Germany was immediate and far-reaching, and Hollywood was swift to reflect this in its productions from the period. Celebrated examples of psychoanalysis on film, such as Hitchcock's *Spellbound* and Fritz Lang's *Secret Beyond the Door* of 1945 and 1947 respectively, have been studied as examples of Hollywood actively promoting the benefits of psychiatry. Yet, while these films and others like them evangelised on behalf of the 'talking cure', Hollywood also reflected a more general, and not always favourable, awareness of the troubled mid-century mind, and often resorted to devices such as jewellery to understand complex conditions such as kleptomania or displacement disorders.[6]

Otto Preminger's *Whirlpool* opens with a sequence that has Ann Sutton (Gene Tierney), the unfulfilled wife of the distinguished psychoanalyst William Sutton (Richard Conte), walking out of a department store, preparing to drive away, only to be stopped by a store detective who searches her purse and finds a brooch with its $300-price tag still attached (see illus. p. 84). The brooch in the shape of a mermaid, an impossible mythical creature, mirrors the unreality of much of Ann's behaviour and presence throughout the film. Accused of shoplifting and brought back into the store she faints and, on regaining consciousness in the manager's office, appears to have no recollection of stealing the brooch, although an assistant had witnessed her doing so in the reflection of a display cabinet. A potential scandal is averted and the store manager advised to drop the charges by the timely intervention of David Korvo (José Ferrer), an alternative therapist whose treatments include hypnotism. He persuades the manager that such a wealthy customer as Mrs Sutton had no financial motive for stealing the brooch but that she is in fact a kleptomaniac. From the moment of the discovery of her theft, Ann Sutton is increasingly constructed as neurotic, prone to sudden changes of mood and paranoid actions (we see her look at the brooch on returning home, put it back in her bag which she then hides under a cushion in her bedroom thus banishing the evidence of her kleptomania from view). Following a hypnotherapy session given by Korvo, Ann inhabits the rest of the film in a semi-trance, a condition Korvo exploits when, still under auto-suggestion, Ann is found, emotionless and silent, at the scene of a murder. The murdered woman has in fact been strangled by Korvo, using Ann's scarf which he had stolen previously. In a re-run of the shoplifting scene, Ann is questioned by police and a psychiatrist who ask whether it is her scarf and in addition how the brooch, the one she shoplifted, but now with a damaged clasp, was found next to the body. 'Question: This pin with a clasp broken was found on the floor near the murdered body. Did you drop it while you were strangling Theresa Randolph? Answer: I don't know'.[7] Ann cannot answer and remains in a comatose state as her husband, now convinced of her mental instability, comes to collect her from the police station.

After a series of implausible plot developments, Ann is cleared of the murder, Korvo dies and she is returned to the loving arms of her husband with the detective advising: 'I'll pass Mrs Sutton over to your custody, Doctor.'[8] The audience is left to assume that Ann will return back to suburban boredom and the possibility of extensive courses of treatment given to her by her husband to correct her kleptomania, which the audience would be forgiven for believing was an attempt to add variety to her unfulfilling, uneventful existence. Ann's characterisation as neurotic, dissatisfied with her role as the doting wife of a successful clinician and her attraction to the charlatan Korvo is typical of films of this period which employed psychoanalysis to find justification under the general heading of 'nervous conditions' for the apparent rejection of mid-century American domestic bliss. The brooch becomes a symbol of her ineffectual life: she steals it but we never see her wear it, even at the scene of the crime, and yet it somehow materialises in the police station. By then, though, it has become doubly dysfunctional in that its clasp is broken and like Ann's mind (or marriage) is damaged and useless. The dominant ideology of popular film of the period is maintained, however, so that by the end of the film the audience can be assured that Ann will eventually be 'cured' by the love of her husband and psychiatry will win the day.

Kleptomania surfaces again but with a much more deadly outcome in *The Locket*, a remarkable cinematic exploration of the trauma of loss leading to full-blown, murderous kleptomania and dissociative disorder, represented by a series of jewellery-related incidents. On the eve of Nancy's wedding, her story is told via a series of flashbacks, or stories within stories, their convoluted layering mimicking the complexities of Nancy's (Laraine Day) mental condition. Her bridegroom, John Willis, receives a visit from Nancy's former husband, the psychiatrist Dr Blair (Brian Aherne), who attempts to warn Willis about Nancy's true mental condition. Once again as in *Whirlpool*, the coupling of a psychiatrist with a mentally unstable woman suggests a belief in the power of psychiatry and, by inference, love to heal the damaged female mind but, unlike that film, *The Locket* is ambiguous concerning psychiatry's effectiveness: the audience later learns that the doctor himself had suffered a complete mental breakdown on discovering the extent of Nancy's illness, a case of 'physician (unable to) heal thyself'. Blair tells Willis how he too, on the eve of his own wedding to Nancy, was paid a visit by a former lover, the artist Norman Clyde played by Robert Mitchum, and it is at this point that Nancy's real or repressed story begins to unfold.

As a child, Nancy is given a heart-shaped locket by the daughter of a wealthy woman in whose home Nancy's mother works as the housekeeper. The locket, however, is almost immediately taken away by the mistress of the house because it is a valuable family heirloom set with a real diamond. Distraught, Nancy is forced to give the locket back, only for it to go missing. Nancy is wrongly accused of stealing it back and, even after the locket is found caught in the rich child's dress, Nancy is nevertheless forced to confess to a crime she did not commit. This traumatic episode scars Nancy emotionally and throughout her adult life and various relationships, first with Clyde and then Blair, she steals valuable items of jewellery in an attempt to compensate for this early childhood loss. The scale of Nancy's crimes escalates from jewel thefts to murder when she kills a wealthy man at a party and steals his wife's collection of jewellery. A butler is blamed and subsequently executed in Nancy's stead, the knowledge of this driving Clyde to suicide after attempting to convince Blair of her guilt. Blair's story takes over and the audience sees the couple attending a country-house party given by Lord and Lady Wyndham, in war-torn England. During a tour of the ancestral home and Lord Wyndham's collection of antique jewellery, Nancy is shown a pendant: 'That little locket there, the heart-shaped locket, belonged to Queen Anne, she wore it at her christening.'[9] Needless to say, this piece of jewellery, so reminiscent of the lost childhood locket, entrances Nancy. Blair, noticing her expression, is concerned, even more so when they later learn from the Wyndhams' driver that Lady Wyndham's diamond necklace worth £12,000 has gone missing. Back in wartime London, the Blairs' apartment is bombed and as Blair frantically searches through the wreckage he comes across a stash of jewellery, including the heart-shaped diamond pendant. Confronting Nancy with the evidence and witnessing first her denying all knowledge of it and then her complete mental dissociation, he realises that what Clyde had tried to convince him of was true and that Nancy is a murderer as well as a kleptomaniac. This realisation in turn traumatises Blair so much that he is confined to an asylum, where his tales about his wife are understood by the attending doctors as fancies of a diseased mind.

Next *The Locket* cuts to the present with Blair (now recovered) trying to convince the new groom of Nancy's guilt. At the dénouement of the film, the wedding ceremony, the final irony of the film's tortuous plot is revealed as the audience realises that Nancy's new mother-in-law, Mrs Willis, is none other than the same wealthy woman who accused her of theft as a child and that Nancy is about to marry her son. As a wedding gift Mrs Willis gives Nancy the original heart-shaped locket. As it is placed round her neck, the restoration of what Nancy felt was wrongly taken from her all those years ago is too much for her troubled mind and, instead of bringing relief, this potentially cathartic moment catapults her back to the scene of her childhood trauma. She collapses at the altar in a state of infantile regression, completely traumatised and unresponsive, much like Ann Sutton in *Whirlpool*, but in *The Locket* the promise of restoration is far from certain as we see both the intended husband and Dr Blair follow Nancy out to

THE LOCKET
1946, dir. John Brahm.
[top to bottom]

The childhood gift.

The ancestral locket that triggers
traumatic memories.

The discovery of Nancy's stash.

The locket as bridal gift becomes a
catalyst for infantile regression.

the waiting ambulance that will transport her to a psychiatric unit. Susan Stewart has suggested that 'the locket is always threatened by loss, for its magic is dependent upon possession' and Nancy's kleptomania is understood as repetitive and ultimately unsuccessful attempts to restore this original item of lost and unattainable jewellery.[10] For Nancy, the locket takes on incantatory power and the audience sees her in flashback as a child lovingly stroke it between thumb and finger, kissing it and declaring: 'Thank you God! I will never ask you for anything again.'[11] To have this precious gift then taken away and in addition wrongly accused of stealing it, sets in motion the chain of events that the audience sees retold in multiple flashbacks. As with many true cases of kleptomania, the stolen objects are often unused and so it is with the jewels that Nancy steals and even commits murder to obtain: they are never worn, remaining functional only as secondary symbols of her primary object of desire and loss. Lord Wyndham's antique diamond locket, being heart-shaped, could perhaps be an appropriate surrogate but even this is no substitute for the original. Finally, when Nancy receives the long-lost object of desire on her wedding day, the primary motivation and purpose of her adult life is removed so she no longer has any meaningful adult existence, and therefore regresses to the moment of the original loss, becoming a child in an adult's body.

Nancy's regression to a moment of childhood trauma brought on by a piece of jewellery is the same process by which Phyllis Calvert in a dual role is transformed from the repressed wife, Maddalena Labardi, into the wild and uninhibited gypsy Rosanna in the Italian-set, 1945 British production *Madonna of the Seven Moons*. As a teenager, convent girl Maddalena is raped while walking through the woods; not long after she becomes betrothed to a wealthy wine merchant, Giuseppe Labardi, and settles down as his pious and reserved wife. When the action switches to the present day, the appearance of their free-spirited and sexually liberated seventeen-year-old daughter Angela (Patricia Roc) unsettles Maddalena and not long after she disappears, taking all her jewellery with her. Giuseppe relates

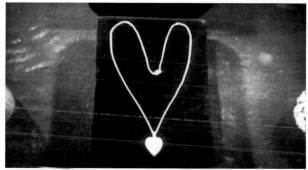

to his daughter that this has happened before, that at traumatic moments Maddalena suffers memory loss and becomes the wild and provocative Rosanna, the mistress of a jewel thief and gypsy brigand, Nino Barucci (Stewart Granger). The catalyst for this transformation is a pair of 'gypsy' earrings in the shape of seven moons: when she wears these, Maddalena's previous identity as the conventional wife and mother is expunged along with the memory of her traumatic rape. Once the earrings are put on, her repressed desires are allowed to surface in the guise of the erotically impulsive Rosanna. As in the American productions discussed previously, a family friend and psychiatrist, Dr Ackroyd, is on hand to legitimise her strange behaviour and declare that she suffers a split personality, the distinctive earrings acting as the mechanism by which her alternative personality manifests itself. 'Gypsy' earrings occupy a notable position in the displays of transformative cinematic jewellery, not always confined to female adornment. At the beginning of *Golden Earrings* of 1947, the receipt of a pair of gold gypsy earrings in the post by the British agent Colonel Ralph Denistoun (Ray Milland) acts as a device by which his story of being disguised as a Hungarian 'gypsy' is related.[12] On the eve of the Second World War and in order to escape from Germany, he is helped by a gypsy woman, Lydia (Marlene Dietrich), who darkens his face, dresses him in gypsy costume, pierces his ears and gives him a pair of golden earrings to wear. Disguised as a gypsy, he successfully manages to make his way back to England. The earrings remind him of his vow to return to her after the war and, summoned back and wearing the earrings once more, he is reunited with Lydia, proving that the assumption of alternative identies via jewellery is permissible when the wearer is a man.

Psychiatry and jewellery, in the shape of that most personal of items, the locket, feature in another film from this period, released in 1945: *Conflict* stars Humphrey Bogart as Richard Mason, trapped in a loveless marriage and besotted by his sister-in-law. Mason murders his wife but is eventually tricked into betraying his guilt and is brought to justice by an elaborate plot devised by a family friend and psychiatrist, Dr Mark Hamilton

GOLDEN EARRINGS
1947, dir. Mitchell Leisen.
[facing] The colonel becomes a gypsy
(SNAP/Rex Features).

MADONNA OF THE SEVEN MOONS
1945, dir. Arthur Crabtree.
[above] Rosanna's earrings
usher in her alter ego.

(Sydney Greenstreet). Hamilton, beginning to suspect Mason of the murder, tricks him into thinking that his wife must still be alive in a series of jewellery-related episodes. Some time after Mason has murdered his wife, a tramp is picked up by the police in possession of his wife's cameo ring, which the tramp says he stole from her after she was supposed to be dead. Later still, Mason receives a pawn ticket in the post, which when he goes to redeem it turns out to be for his wife's locket, again suggesting that she is alive and perhaps in need of money. These and other devices eventually lead Mason back to the scene of his crime (rather than childhood trauma as with Nancy in *The Locket*), to ascertain whether the body of his victim is still there, an act that reveals to the police and the psychiatrist Hamilton that Mason has murdered his wife.

In order for these psychologically charged items of jewellery to register most effectively with cinema audiences, their form is often symbolically loaded, as with the heart-shaped locket or mermaid brooch. Their intrinsic monetary value is not at issue here but rather their recognisability or ability to connect with the cinema audience. Conventionally conspicuous and aspirational luxury items such as diamond bracelets, pearl necklaces and ruby rings are too anonymous and generic to carry such emotional weight. These are items that, having lost their allotted function as typically precious jewellery worn to confer glamour and status, assume other functions and gain symbolic rather than financial value. If they are to be identified as clues, left at the scene of the crime or remembered by eye-witnesses, then it is necessary that they be distinguishable from the usual stock of cinematic jewels. These pieces form a 'special collection' of objects curious and rare because of their form or provenance rather than the costliness of their stones or settings. The gift of a heart-shaped brooch at the beginning of *Black Angel* (1946) is followed swiftly by its recipient's murder, its sweetly romantic shape belying its fatal consequences. Then the brooch disappears, becoming the mythical central item in the unravelling of the identity of the murderer, until the memory of the brooch prompts the perpetrator himself, the

murdered woman's estranged, psychologically traumatised and amnesiac husband, to confess his crime.

In more light-hearted but equally memorable fashion is the scorpion pin used to conceal the coded flight plans of a hundred American bombers in *My Favourite Blonde* (1942), a pastiche of Hitchcock's *The 39 Steps*, starring Bob Hope as Larry Haines, the owner of a vaudeville penguin act, and Madeleine Carroll as the British agent Karen Bentley (Carroll had been the star of Hitchcock's film released seven years earlier).[13] The brooch, seen briefly at the beginning of the film, is used by Bentley to transport the vital wartime information but to avoid detection she plants it unbeknownst to him under Haines's jacket lapel. Thereafter the brooch becomes the object that binds the unlikely couple together, as in *The 39 Steps*, in their battle against fifth columnists. As with the mermaid-shaped brooch in *Whirlpool*, the scorpion brooch registers as both visually memorable and as a culturally significant creature that is both deadly and has a sting in its tail, becoming a fitting symbol for the film's comic plot of mistaken identity and double crossing.

These dysfunctional items of jewellery are regularly planted or secreted about another's clothing: Karen Bentley's furtive pinning of the scorpion brooch behind Haines's lapel in *My Favourite Blonde* is just one example of the concealed jewel which, once planted, is difficult to retrieve, a dilemma that faces Marlene Dietrich playing the glamorous jewel-thief Madeleine de Beaupré in Frank Borzage's 1936 production *Desire*.[14] Posing as the wife of the psychiatrist Dr Maurice Pauquet (Alan Mowbray), in an early example of the intersection of psychiatry, jewellery and deception, she manages to steal a valuable pearl necklace from a Parisian jeweller. On fleeing Paris and heading for the Spanish border, she meets a naive engineer, Tom Bradley (Gary Cooper), and uses him to get the stolen necklace out of France by planting it in his pocket as they cross the border into Spain. However, her subsequent efforts to retrieve the necklace prove difficult and provide ample time and opportunity for the unlikely couple's physical attraction to each other to develop. The pearls, as with the scorpion brooch in the later film, entangle the film's protagonists, metaphorically binding them together. This motif of the planted jewel and its aborted retrieval has continued to be exploited in popular film; *French Kiss*, Lawrence Kasdan's romantic comedy from 1995, reworks *Desire*'s secreted jewel stratagem, with Kevin Kline in the Dietrich role as the jewel-thief Luc Teyssier, who in order to get through French security plants stolen jewellery in Kate's (Meg Ryan) bag as they sit next to each other on the flight to Paris.[15] Kate's bag is stolen, setting in motion the couple's progress through the romantic French countryside in pursuit of the stolen goods, during which they inevitably fall in love.

Jewellery in these films is largely unworn; its significance and newly acquired function is to be stolen, secreted, lost, used as evidence of mental instability or as the catalyst for murder. As stated earlier, this is perhaps unsurprising given real jewellery's often dramatic and violent history, but what is significant is mainstream cinema's almost perverse delight in denying jewellery's readily understood visual function to make glamorously attired stars look even more spectacular, in favour of these negative functions. Jewellery in film often attains the status of Barthes's gems – 'non-productive, incapable of rotting down, hence incapable of becoming the source of new life.'[16] Not only is cinematic jewellery non-productive but it is also often dangerous. In renouncing its function as adornment it nevertheless cannot disappear or 'rot down' entirely, so it acquires a new destructive function, often unseen and in this sense truly magical. Jewellery so often lost and displaced in film reserves a special compartment in the cinematic negative wardrobe, achieving its greatest and invariably most harmful effects when it is absent. Perhaps jewellery's most significant function in film is to be lost, as Stewart points out of the locket it is always threatened by loss. This material loss often runs parallel to a loss borne by the film's protagonists, whether loss of sanity as in *Whirlpool* and *The Locket*, or loss of life.

In *Dressed to Kill* (1980), the married but sexually frustrated Kate Miller (Angie Dickinson) attends regular psychotherapy sessions during which she discusses her innermost secrets and

DESIRE
1936, dir. Frank Borzage.
Madeleine plants the pearls.

fantasies.[17] After one such session we see Miller pay a visit to the Metropolitan Museum in New York, where she gazes distractedly at paintings and couples (more fulfilled than she?) while compiling a shopping list, symbolic of her domestic ennui. So preoccupied is she that on leaving the gallery she forgets her glove, which is picked up by a stranger who eventually lures her with it to a waiting taxi outside and a casual erotic encounter. Following her earlier session with the psychiatrist, the viewer is encouraged to understand that this is something in which Miller indulges in order to create some form of emotional and sexual autonomy separate from her role

as dutiful wife and mother (it is tempting to understand this scene as a more explicit and ultimately deadly re-enactment of Ann Sutton's kleptomania and attraction to Korvo in *Whirlpool*). After an intense sexual scene in the back of the cab, Miller goes to the stranger's apartment and the story then cuts to Miller waking up in his bed, realising that it is late and hurriedly getting dressed. During the elevator ride down from the apartment Miller realises that she has left her diamond wedding ring on the stranger's bedside table and so decides to return to his apartment on the seventh floor. On the elevator doors reopening at this floor, an attacker gets in and proceeds to slash at Miller with a cut-throat razor. As the brutal attack continues, the elevator descends again to a waiting Nancy Allen playing the prostitute Liz Blake, who takes over from Miller at this point as the film's female protagonist. Miller in the final throes of death reaches out a bloody, braceleted arm to Blake to warn her that her attacker is still inside the elevator compartment, and the final shot presented of Miller is her lifeless, slashed left hand, minus the diamond ring, stopping the elevator door from closing.

The inevitable punishment for Miller's marital infidelity signified by the loss of the diamond ring is clearly signalled, and the use of the forgotten ring as a harbinger of death reinforces the moral and physical danger into which Miller has put herself. Without the symbolic and legal protection of her wedding ring, she is not only morally vulnerable but physically also: she has put herself in harm's way, a fact already intimated by her post-coital discovery of the stranger's notification of his having contracted a sexually transmitted disease. Ringless, she is exposed and the bracelets she wears on the other bloodied hand offer no protection either but rather emphasise jewellery's essentially disastrous and unforgiving origin, as Barthes again suggested:

> whether it was diamond or metal, precious stone or gold, it always came from the earth's depths, from that sombre and fiery core, of which we see only the hardened and cooled products; in short, by its very origin, the gemstone was an infernal object that had come through arduous, often bloody journeys, to leave behind those subterranean caverns where humanity's mythic imagination stored its dead, its damned and its treasures in the same place.[18]

If *Dressed to Kill* has been accused of gratuitous violence and misogyny, its amalgam of sex, death and jewellery is merely a typically gory 1980s cinematic translation of a long-standing historical and literary trope. Equally perverse and, it could be argued, gratuitous is Michael Powell's exploration of the subject of misogynistic violence in the 1960 production *Peeping Tom*.[19]

DRESSED TO KILL
1980, dir. Brian De Palma.
[facing] Ill-fated adornment;
[top] the remembered ring.

PEEPING TOM
1960, dir. Michael Powell.
[middle] The voyeur's gift;
[bottom] the brooch as talisman.

While obviously widely different in terms of provenance, directorial style and production values, *Dressed to Kill* and *Peeping Tom* are both explicit (for their respective dates), explorations of voyeurism, impotence, sadism and murder and both feature serial killers, prostitution and psychiatry as central motfis. *Peeping Tom*'s plot concerning the psychologically scarred Mark Lewis (Carl Boehm), a cameraman who murders and films the death throes of his female victims, is well known, but in one scene jewellery becomes the catalyst for a brief but significant moment of erotic fixation. Following her twenty-first birthday, Lewis gives Helen Stephens (Anna Massey), who with her blind mother rents rooms in Lewis's house, a present of a brooch in the shape of a dragonfly. For Lewis, Helen represents potential redemption and normative sexuality: they go on a date (Lewis without his otherwise ever-present camera) and they discuss plans for him to illustrate her children's story of a magic camera. As Lewis watches her hold up the brooch to her breast and heart, then move it to the centre of her chest, he mimics her actions, as though exploring this woman's body for the first time without the desire to record fear and pain – his mirroring of her actions a form of remote tactile communication. When asked which position he prefers, he indicates her heart, an emotional and active response on his part that runs counter to his usual distanced voyeuristic objectification of women. Helen's brooch assumes the function of a talisman in this scene, providing protection and warding off evil, the dragonfly here able to be read as a creature signifying renewal, rebirth and change, a momentary glimpse of normality that cannot last but which is crucial to Helen's survival (see illus. p. 95).

Mainstream cinema seems able to forgive the love of fur and casts women who hanker after mink and sable as either foolish or at the worst misguidedly mercenary, but to lust after gold and lifeless diamonds is deemed unnatural, intrinsically evil and therefore deserves the harshest of punishments. The Biblical daughters of Zion who are accused of 'glancing wantonly with their eyes' and whom the Lord will punish by taking 'away the finery of . . . the pendants, the bracelets . . . the amulets, the signet rings and the nose rings' and whose 'secret parts' the 'Lord will lay bare', are the progenitors of countless (usually female) characters punished for both a love of jewellery and of the flesh.[20] Blood and diamonds, the impossible meeting of the most vital of substances with earth's eternal and hardest matter, seem to be inextricably mixed in history, myth and popular culture. The ability of diamonds and other precious stones to cut and penetrate, their hardness contrasted with the softness of flesh, increases the already powerful erotic charge stimulated by the female body adorned with jewels. From the Bible to pulp fiction, from pioneering cinema to slasher movie, jewellery, sex and death continue to furnish irresistible scenarios that revel in the collision between vulnerability and resistance. This brief extract from a story entitled 'Stick With Me, Kid, and You'll Wear Diamonds', concerning the revenge of a sexually humiliated jeweller and written in 1968, could be the template of any number of cinematic explorations of this brutal convergence:

> Her head hung curiously to one side, unhinged by the dozen slashes he had taken at her throat.
>
> Necklace first, I think, he mused, and selected one from the paper bag. Somehow the congealing blood and the diamonds went well together. Now a tiara, he thought. Oh yes, very pretty. Very pretty. And now a bracelet. Perhaps two. Yes, two. Why not.
>
> He chuckled.
>
> 'My you look nice', he said aloud, when he had finished.
>
> 'My goodness, what diamonds do for a woman.'[21]

In fact, there are a few cinematic examples where the danger implied by the proximity of flesh and gems is not always played out on the female body. Perhaps one of the more celebrated occurs at the climax to *Marathon Man* (1976) in the scene where Babe (Dustin Hoffman) tells the Nazi Szell (Laurence Olivier) that he can keep as many of the diamonds he has extorted from his concentration-camp victims as he can eat.[22] Szell starts to swallow the diamonds but can only manage one, realising that the stones' hardness will lacerate his internal organs, a uniquely direct cinematic exploration of the invasive penetrating power of precious stones. For a male translation of the deadly erotic encounter in *Dressed to Kill*, the more recent Australian co-production *Lantana* (2001) provides a variant on the missing jewel as sign of sexual infidelity.[23] One of the film's early sequences depicts the unhappily married detective Leon (Anthony La Paglia) having sex with a woman called Jane in a motel room. On getting dressed, Jane notes with some distress that she has lost one of her pearl earrings, which were a present from her husband. Driving home to his wife after this illicit sexual encounter, Leon reaches into his crotch and retrieves Jane's earring which had become caught in his underwear, and which he holds up with at first bewilderment followed by wry amusement at the erotic memory this piece of jewellery conjures up. Unlike *Dressed to Kill*, however, neither Jane nor Leon (while both lonely and emotionally confused) are punished with the severity reserved for Angie Dickinson in the former film; instead, the lost earring takes on a significance as one of a number of artefacts (including a woman's shoe in a remarkable sequence) which are either lost or, possibly, discarded. These lost accessories are symbolic of the deeper issues of trust, betrayal and grief central to the film, and the pearl earring is a remarkably explicit visualisation of the misplaced jewel as a metaphor for misplaced or careless sexual activity.

Jewellery given and worn as tokens of love and then lost incriminates the loser and ushers in the potential for retribution by the donor: why was this cherished love-token removed? Why was it found in the possession of someone else? How can such an emotionally significant gift be so casually treated? This is the inference that the sadistic husband uses to hasten his wife's descent into madness in both the British and American versions of *Gaslight*.[24] In both films a cameo brooch given to the wife is then 'stolen' back by the husband in order to provide further evidence of her mental instability, a forgetfulness bordering on psychosis. It is part of his elaborate plan to have her declared insane and committed to an asylum, leaving him free to search

MARATHON MAN
1976, dir. John Schlesinger.
[top] Szell eats a diamond.

GASLIGHT
1940, dir. Thorold Dickinson.
[middle] The 'mislaid' brooch and the
construction of mental instability;
[bottom] the jewel's secret recesses.

for the rubies he was unable to locate after murdering their wealthy owner and which remain hidden in the house the unhappy couple now occupy. The British version starring Diana Wynyard as Bella Mallen, the psychologically tortured wife of Paul Mallen, alias the murderer and bigamist Louis Bauer (Anton Walbrook), adds an extra dimension to the story of the lost jewels. On finding her brooch once again where her husband has hidden it, she notices a compartment in the back of it (the brooch is also a locket) and undoing it finds the missing rubies hidden in specially constructed recesses. As Bauer continues to search frantically for the missing rubies, Bella is aware of their location all the time, 'hidden in plain sight', and in a final irony reveals to Bauer their location in a vase on their mantelpiece. *Gaslight*'s use of the jewel as simultaneously absent and concealing gives the cameo brooch the talismanic power of Stewart's locket, which she compares to a doll's house (*Gaslight*'s cluttered and claustrophobic interiors closely resemble a Victorian doll's house), the disappearing and reappearing jewel and its hidden rubies representing 'the tension between inner and outer spheres, of exteriority and interiority. Occupying a space within an enclosed space', the brooch symbolises for both Bella and Bauer 'the secret recesses of the heart: center within center, within.'[25]

If items of jewellery are not lost but stolen, similar accusations to Bauer's of Bella are likely to be made: Ginger Rogers playing Joan Victor, the long-standing mistress of the financier and counterfeiter Louis Galt (Stanley Baker), in *Beautiful Stranger* (1954), has the diamond bracelet given to her by Louis stolen.[26] When the bracelet later turns up as payment of a debt owed Galt by one of his associates, Galt automatically assumes that Joan is having an affair and has given it away to her new lover to help pay his dues. Galt is enraged because his assumption that Joan has casually given away the cherished object renders it for him now doubly meaningless, no longer valued by Joan and of importance to others only for its monetary value, all its romantic significance and function having been negated.

Misconstrued or misdirected jewels act as catalysts for similar retribution and awakenings to the realisation that the position of faithful spouse or long-standing mistress is no longer able to command the expensive gifts that a new mistress can. The 1941 film *You'll Never Get Rich* capitalises on the mistaken gift of an engraved diamond bracelet intended for the dancer Sheila Winthrop (Rita Hayworth) from a wealthy impresario and serial philanderer, Martin Cortland (Robert Benchley).[27] When Sheila rejects the gift, Cortland mistakenly gives it to his long-suffering wife, who on seeing the inscription realises that it was not meant for her. To cover up his mistake Cortland enlists the help of the dance director Robert Curtis (Fred Astaire) and asks him to pretend to be in love with Sheila and give the gift to her in the presence of his wife. This being the second time that Sheila has been presented with the jewel, she is enraged. The bracelet is then implicated in a number of implausible cases of assumed and mistaken identity, narrative devices used to bring Sheila and Robert together for a number of musical routines and which, as is often the case with items of contested jewellery, becomes the object that links the two protagonists together throughout the film. More mundane than diamonds, but as telling, is the misunderstood Christmas gift of a gold necklace that Karen (Emma Thompson) finds in the pocket of her husband's coat in the British romantic comedy *Love Actually* (2003).[28] Initially assuming this to be a sign of his willingness to reignite their failing marriage, she realises her mistake when unwrapping the expected gift and finds instead a compact disc, the necklace intended for his secretary with whom he fantasises about having a relationship. Confronting him later, Karen asks the perennial question of the patient wife to her gift-giving unfaithful husband: 'Imagine your husband bought a gold necklace and, come Christmas, gave it to somebody else . . . Would you wait around to find out if it's just a necklace or if it's sex and a necklace or if, worst of all, it's a necklace and love? Would you stay? Knowing life would always be a little bit worse? – Or would you cut and run?'[29]

As Alan Hunt discusses, not only is jewellery the perfect medium for the display of conspicuous consumption but its material value is also increased by a concomitant erotic value: 'Nowhere is this more apparent than in the complex coupling of aesthetic and sexual significance associated with the female neck and breast as a site of display, both of precious metals and stones, but also of the body itself, with the valorisation of soft and unblemished skin in close proximity to the breasts themselves as primary signifiers of sexuality.'[30] A forceful and direct cinematic exploration of this valorisation occurs in Martin Scorsese's 1995 film *Casino*.[31] As the prostitute turned trophy wife of the casino boss Sam Rothstein (Robert De Niro), Ginger McKenna (Sharon Stone) is constituted by her love of jewellery; her all-consuming desire for gold and jewels places her alongside such celebrated literary gold-lovers as Volpone and Fagin. Ginger makes no secret of her desire for money and Sam is prepared to shower her with jewellery, clothing and fur in an attempt to buy her love and loyalty. In what could be seen as the defining and prophetic moment of their relationship, Sam pins a diamond and emerald brooch onto Ginger's breast before they embrace, while his voice-over informs the audience: 'I fell in love right there. But in Vegas, for a girl like Ginger, love costs money. Ginger's mission in life was money.'[32] Sam eventually persuades her to be his wife with the promise that she will be set up for life no matter what happens, and proves his word by giving her a guided tour of their new marital home replete with room-sized wardrobes bursting with fur coats and an enormous box of Bulgari jewellery, at which Ginger gasps ecstatically, asking as she pulls on bracelets and necklaces, luxuriating in the touch of precious metal and stones against her flesh: 'So do you think it's too much if I wear these all on the same day?'[33] From this point in the film Ginger positively glistens as she wears a succession of dazzling outfits accessorised with jewels from the besotted Sam.

Barthes's description could equally be applied to the glittering Ginger when he writes that the diamond is a 'paradoxical substance, both lit up and stone cold: it is nothing but fire and

CASINO
1995, dir. Martin Scorsese.
Ginger the living jewel
(Universal/Everett/Rex Features).

yet nothing but ice. This cold fire, this sharp, shining object which is nevertheless silent, what a symbol for the whole world of vanities, of seduction devoid of content, of pleasures devoid of sincerity!'[34] The audience sees the true extent of her pathological relationship with jewellery played out in a remarkable sequence that renders Ginger first as a piece of animated jewellery and then attempting to inculcate her daughter into her obsession. Opening with the blinding flare of flash-bulbs and to the accompaniment of the tune 'Stella by Starlight', Ginger dazzles the guests at the Las Vegas country club, gliding gleaming-haired, encased in a shimmering beaded dress and accessorised with diamond and gold earclips. She is a moving jewel and, as she makes her dazzling progress through the club, once again Sam's voice-over informs us of the pleasure he receives watching her work the room, but that 'they didn't really know what moved her', at which the scene cuts to a bank vault with Ginger displaying her growing collection of jewellery to her infant daughter in a pushchair. 'Do you want to see this one?' Ginger asks, caressing a selection of bangles and, while opening another box, tells the child: 'Daddy gave me all this jewellery because he loves me so much'. Trying a bracelet on the child, she declares it to be 'Fabulous!' and holds up rows of jewelled necklaces in front of the toddler while intoning hypnotically 'Look at this! Look at this!'[35] Ginger is at her most animated and, it could be argued, her most sexually aroused when luxuriating in her jewellery collection. In the true tradition of the hoarder, her gold and jewels are not to be worn or spent, rather they are to be retrieved from their secure hiding place, caressed, fondled, 'made love to' and then locked away again. Ginger's love of jewellery is as all-encompassing as any of the great literary misers and her scene in the vault is comparable with that from Frank Norris's celebrated novel of greed, *McTeague* (1899), where Trina, McTeague's wife, derives a similar erotic pleasure from her collection of gold coins:

> She polished the gold pieces with a mixture of soap and ashes until they shone, wiping them carefully on her apron. Or, again, she would draw the heap lovingly toward her and

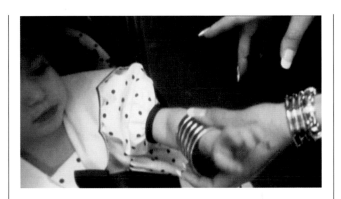

CASINO
1995, dir. Martin Scorsese.
[facing] Ginger luxuriates
(Universal/Everett/Rex Features);
[above] Ginger introduces her
daughter to the pleasures of jewellery.

bury her face in it, delighted at the smell of it and the feel of the smooth, cold metal on her cheeks. She even put the smaller gold pieces in her mouth, and jingled them there. She loved her money with an intensity she could hardly express. She would plunge her small fingers into the pile with little murmurs of affection, her long, narrow eyes half closed and shining, her breath coming in long sighs.[36]

Ultimately, just as Volpone's, Fagin's or indeed Trina's riches provide no lasting security, so too Ginger's addictive personality leads only to her death from a drug overdose and 'In the end all she had left was 36 hundred in mint condition coins', a glittering remnant of her dysfunctional need for gold.[37]

> DIAMONDS: The time will come when man will manufacture them! To think that they're nothing but coal; if we came across one in its natural state, we wouldn't bother to pick it up![38]

For the duration of the time that the protagonists in *Lifeboat* are forced to spend in proximity to one another, Connie Porter's diamond bracelet is a source of comment for the other passengers, and indeed conflict between herself and the proto-Communist Kovac. Porter tells him at one point that they share similar humble origins, both being born into poverty in Chicago, but that her diamond bracelet has been her 'passport from the stockyards to the gold coast. It got me everything I wanted.'[39] The diamond bracelet becomes an obstacle to the couple's growing physical attraction and prompts an exchange between Porter and Willi, the German seaman, who attests to its geological, rather than its symbolic worth, and who identifies it as an impediment to Porter's relationship with Kovac. Willi: 'They're really nothing but a few pieces of carbon, crystallised under high pressure at great heat . . . He likes you, but he hates the bracelet. You'll have to get rid of it.' Porter: 'The bracelet? I've worn it for fifteen years, it's brought me nothing but good luck.' Willi: 'He hates it!' Porter: 'I wouldn't take it off for anything or anybody in the world.'[40] It is interesting that it is the Nazi, who is plotting to lead the lifeboat's passengers into German captivity, who is least distracted by the jewel's economic

and social significance; like Barthes, he is able to recognise the diamond bracelet as an object that 'represents the inert, the stubbornness of the thing to be nothing but itself . . . infinitely unchanging.'[41]

As with many items in the dysfunctional cinematic wardrobe, however, Porter's diamonds undergo a significant transformation: they are rendered dysfunctional (in this case both as an effective status symbol – what use are they within the severely limited social circle of the lifeboat and its passengers? – and as an item of erotic value – Kovac is revolted by Porter's diamonds) in order for a new value to be revealed. Near starvation, and having almost given up hope of ever being rescued, Porter decides to give Kovac her bracelet to use as bait to catch a fish, prompting Rittenhouse to declare: 'There never yet was a poor fish that wouldn't bite on one of those', as we see the bracelet attached to a line, dropped overboard and then murkily glinting underwater.[42] Eventually a passing fish takes the bait and swallows the bracelet, at exactly the same moment as a ship is sighted, causing them to drop the line, fish, bracelet and all. Porter's Cartier bracelet now joins the rest of her possessions on the ocean bed, her diamonds refashioned as essentially 'worthless' are returned to 'the earth's depths, from that sombre and fiery core, of which we see only the hardened and cooled products.'[43] The bracelet's earthly, monetary value vanishes as it sinks to join the other rocks on the ocean bed and, like many other dysfunctional cinematic luxury items, is stripped of its social, economic or fashionable significance in order to return to its primary state.

LIFEBOAT
1944, dir. Alfred Hitchcock.
The Cartier bracelet
transformed into bait.

PART 3

5 CRIMINAL ACCESSORIES

I put my shoe on my head,
My hat on my feet,
Forgetful the whole day through,
I can't think of
Nothin' but love,
Concentratin' on you![1]

Accessories feature prominently both in the cinematic and actual wardrobe: shoes, hats, scarves, ties, gloves and bags are the most plentiful, disposable and often replaced sartorial additions and yet, conversely, are often the most treasured. The perennial advice given in countless guides that 'correct' accessorising is the key to true style, or that accessories provide an easy way to 'dress up or down', 'update' or 'tie together' an outfit, suggests an interesting duality at once fashionably ephemeral and simultaneously indispensable. Certainly, up to the twentieth century's acceleration of fashion, these small additions to the wardrobe offer the most reliable clues as to the date of a particular style of dress. When the principal articles of clothing remained relatively unchanged for long periods, the height of a heel, the way a stock or cravat was knotted or the embellishment, colour and fabric of a glove provide important clues as to the specific period of an outfit. Accessories' ability to act as chronological sartorial evidence remains true today, even in the constantly changing and proliferating world of contemporary fashion. The modern obsession with the latest designer bag or shoe has constructed a clichéd landscape peopled by self-confessed 'shoe fetishists' and 'handbag junkies', an environment where the once sacrosanct 'timeless classic' is seasonally modified or 're-imagined' and where last season's accessory is a far greater sartorial misdemeanour than last season's dress. Leaving aside the accessory's primary function in the maintenance of the contemporary fashion industry, this section will attempt to understand the key position that such items hold in the dysfunctional cinematic wardrobe, where their reliability as forensic evidence of crime is far less dependable than the real life accessory's ability to prove the date or provenance of a wardrobe. Mainstream cinema is rich in dysfunctional accessories; it would be possible to devote an entire book to just one category of accessory, shoes or bags for example, so frequently do they feature as objects that defy or resist their commonly understood sartorial and physical functions. Therefore, this section will necessarily take the form of a vestimentary 'trailer', momentarily spotlighting a succession of familiar and less well-known cinematic accessories, and pausing to look more closely at the dysfunctional potential demonstrated by bags in *Dial M for Murder*, ties in *Frenzy* and the scarf in *Drag Me to Hell*.

On screen, the imprecise position occupied by the accessory, both superfluous and necessary, is translated as a symbolic latency, where articles such as shoes, hats and scarves are able to display their potential to become something else, whether that be evidence, a weapon or a motive. The semantic link between the vestimentary accessory and the legal understanding of the term as someone who aids and abets a criminal act, or conceals a crime, is inescapable and, while acknowledging fashion journalism's delight in appropriating juridical discourse with expressions such as 'the fashion police', 'fashion victims', 'crimes against fashion' and so on, the 'criminal accessory' can be a surprisingly accurate term when exploring the negative cinematic wardrobe. An accessory, as a literal addition to a subject's wardrobe, is fundamentally secondary to the main garment or garments. These items, therefore, constantly teeter on the precipice of being discarded, abandoned, replaced and lost. This fate is typical of many of the garments studied in this book but accessories' separateness from the primary garment, their portability, the comparative ease with which they can be taken off (shoes slipped out of, scarves and ties unknotted, for example), make them acutely vulnerable, often neglected and prone to theft. The same could perhaps be said of jewellery but, given its typically greater value, more notice is taken of its absence than say a bag or a hat and, unlike these accessories, jewellery is rarely removed or put down until the wearer returns to the safety of their domestic environment. Accessories occupy an indeterminate hinterland somewhere between the ornamental and economic symbolism of jewellery and the

primary function of preserving warmth and modesty provided by the principle items of dress. Although they have specific functions – bags to carry things in, gloves and hats to protect the hands and head – they are fundamentally inessential. Shoes here are an exception, as in most societies and certainly in many climates and terrains shoes are necessary to preserve the wearer's feet from harm. However, in their fashionable elaboration and inappropriateness, certainly when considering shoes for women, they are typically dysfunctional, and cinematic footwear is characterised by broken or trapped heels, squeaky or noisy soles and, Cinderella-like, are too tight and regularly characterised in film as impediments to walking.

> [Juror no. 8 is talking on a payphone; Beverley Sutphin comes up behind her and grabs the phone from her]
> Sutphin: 'You can't wear white after Labor Day!'
> Juror: 'That's not true anymore.'
> Sutphin: 'Yes it is! Didn't your mother tell you? Now you know.'
> [Sutphin starts to beat the juror over the head with the phone]
> Juror: 'No! Please! Fashion has changed!'
> Sutphin: 'No it hasn't!'
> [Sutphin continues the beating until the juror is left lifeless on the floor, her white, summer shoes now dyed red with her blood][2]

In John Waters's 1994 film *Serial Mom*, the conflation between criminal behaviour and crimes against fashion is clearly demonstrated, with the fashion faux pas of wearing white shoes becoming the motive for the most merciless killing of Beverley Sutphin's (Kathleen Turner), the eponymous serial mom.[3] If the flouting of an outmoded American sartorial proscription can be the catalyst for a brutal murder, there is further cinematic evidence that shoes themselves can be refashioned as murder weapons: for example, in *Single White Female* (1992), the worlds of fashion and crime are interwoven, with shoes playing a central and deadly role.[4] In the film, the fashionable Manhattanite Allison Jones (Bridget Fonda) places an advertisement to find someone with whom to share her apartment and takes in Hedra Carlson (Jennifer Jason Leigh). Hedra is not all she seems and the film charts her progress from admiring 'out of towner' to identity-stealing, murderous sociopath. In the obligatory 'show me how to dress like you' sequence, Allison and Hedra go shopping and we see Allison try on a pair of metal-heeled suede court shoes, the very same pair that Hedra emerges from the changing room wearing. After each insists that the other buy the shoes, Hedra finally persuades Allison to purchase them by saying that she can always borrow them whenever she wants. This early intimation of sartorial symbiosis becomes central to the film's plot of assumed identities and multiple personalities as Hedra duplicates Allison's wardrobe, cuts her hair to look like her and eventually impersonates her. Dressed as Allison, Hedra tricks Sam (Allison's boyfriend) into thinking that she is Allison and under cover of darkness steals into his apartment and performs fellatio on him. On discovering her true identity, Sam argues with Hedra during which she throws one of the metal-heeled shoes at his head, causing him to turn and rush at her. At this she then stabs him through the eye with the other shoe's heel and kills him. Hedra then leaves the building wearing the same shoes, one with a still-bloodied heel.

Identity theft achieved by the stealing, or in this case the duplication, of another's wardrobe, is central to the plot of *Single White Female*, and the familiar expressions of walking or stepping into another person's shoes take on special significance as Hedra becomes Allison, 'trying on' both her identity and her boyfriend. Peter Wollen has suggested that films featuring fashionable transformations, albeit usually without the criminal intentions of Hedra's, are 'makeover movies' and lists among others perhaps the most potent cinematic example of this – Bette Davis's transformation from dowdy spinster to style icon in *Now Voyager*.[5] The adoption of a new wardrobe and with it a new personality has provided cinema with an opportunity to exploit the spectacular capabilities of the costume and make up

SINGLE WHITE FEMALE
1992, dir. Barbet Schroeder.
[top] Identity theft;
[bottom] the shoe as weapon.

department to maximum effect (Fonda's and Leigh's similarity is at times uncanny). Nevertheless, Allison's profession as a fashion software designer in the film appears prophetic, since in an earlier scene the viewer observes Allison demonstrating a software programme that allows clothes to be remodelled digitally without the necessity of making up actual samples. While in 1992 this kind of programme was still in its infancy, it was not long before the facility to redress and 'remake' oneself virtually became a familiar component of both online and actual fashion retailing.[6]

The phallic symbolism of the shoe exploited in *Single White Female* and the heel's mimetic re-enactment of sexual penetration when piercing Sam's skull is unmistakeable. Less obvious but more perversely, a shoe, specifically a satin mule, is implicated in an act of masochistic revenge underscoring Gene Tierney's traumatic regression from lover and mother to daughter in *Leave Her to Heaven* (1945).[7] The scene of Ellen

Berent Harland's (Gene Tierney) 'accidental' near-immolation and auto-abortion is carefully constructed before-hand by her placing the toe of her slipper under a piece of loose stair carpet. We see in close-up the offending footwear, before Ellen throws herself headlong down the stairs, knowing in advance that her shoe will become 'false evidence' and be labelled as the apparent cause of her headlong fall and the loss of her baby. This act is imperative for the father-obsessed Ellen who must rid herself of the unwanted child in order to maintain her principal identity as the virgin daughter: the offending shoe is transformed into the guilty phallus, the cause of her unwanted maternity. A stiletto-heeled court shoe rather than bedroom mule is implicated in the revenge for sexual violation enacted by Elizabeth Taylor playing the sometime model and prostitute Gloria Wandrous in *BUtterfield* 8. Gloria uses her stilettos to excruciatingly painful effect as she stamps and grinds her heel into the foot of her lover Weston Liggett (Laurence Harvey) after he suggests she should charge more for her 'services'. Her stilettos, which help construct her identity as the glamorous prostitute (along with the contested mink coat previously discussed in 'Trophies'), and which fetishised her as Liggett's erotic object of desire, are redeployed to mark and punish her disrespectful client.

In the negative cinematic wardrobe, the single shoe is the typical condition, which is understandable given that one shoe is useless and cannot be conventionally worn; so, divested of its traditional function, it is free to take on wider significance. As in *Leave Her to Heaven* and *BUtterfield 8*, it is a single shoe that acts as the catalyst for a particularly explicit visual juxtaposition of footwear and violent sexual imagery in the British 'teen slasher' film *The Haunted House of Horror* (1969).[8] The film, an unsettling mix of 1960s psychedelia, 'swinging London' and haunted-house mystery, stars an improbably cast Frankie Avalon as Chris, a member of a group of 'teenagers' who decide to spend the night in a house reputed to have been the home of a homicidal maniac, and which was the scene of a series of grisly murders. The homicidal maniac is eventually revealed to be one of the group's own members, who proceeds to relate the story of his tortured childhood to Chris before emasculating him by stabbing him in the groin with the same large blade he has used previously to murder another member of the group. While the plot and acting are typical of the genre and period of the film, what is of interest is the remarkable camera work that cuts together shots of the murder with that of one of the group's female members, Sheila (Jill Haworth), who has been exploring the house and managed to get the heel of her shoe stuck in the rotten treads of an old wooden staircase. Trapped on the stairs, she witnesses the gruesome scene and, in a series of jump cuts, the audience witnesses the knife penetrate Chris as Sheila struggles with the heel of her shoe, eventually leaving it behind to flee barefooted from the slasher. Close-ups on the shoe's heel trapped in the rotten wood, Sheila's struggle to free it and even closer shots of the shoe's inner lining stamped with the brand Norvic (a major British shoe manufacturer and

LEAVE HER TO HEAVEN
1945, dir. John M. Stahl.
[facing] False evidence.

HAUNTED HOUSE OF HORROR
1969, dir. Michael Armstrong.
[above] The shoe as witness.

[top to bottom]

LANTANA
2001, dir. Ray Lawrence.
The shoe as fetish.

NIAGARA
1953, dir. Henry Hathaway.
Lover's loafers

Dead man's shoes.

MARNIE
1964, dir. Alfred Hitchcock.
The shoe as false alarm.

retailer of the period) are fetishistically intercut with sequences of the knife piercing the victim's body. *Lantana* (previously discussed in the 'Talismans' section) utilises an equally fetishised image of a woman's shoe that may or may not be evidence of murder. Opening shots reveal a woman's body, wearing only one shoe, caught in the branches of a lantana bush; later, one of the possible murder suspects is seen at night throwing an object into the bushes. The next day a neighbour who has witnessed this act searches and finds a shoe in the branches. Retrieving it, she takes it back to her home, where subsequently the police identify it as belonging to the missing woman, whose body featured at the beginning of the film; the shoe is then bagged and tagged ready for forensic analysis. It transpires that the woman's death was accidental and the disposal of the shoe innocent, as it had been left behind by accident rather than foul play, challenging once again the expected role of the accessory as proof of crime. The forensic procedures are in place but prove ineffectual and what had potential as evidence reverts to its primary status as a dysfunctional single shoe. What is particularly noticeable, however, is the fetishistic camera work that lingers over the shoe caught, as if in a surreal window display, in the branches of the lantana bush and then taking centre stage as the police discuss its significance before it is finally enclosed in forensic plastic. The viewer is directed towards the shoe in these scenes, a mundane object that seems to exude a profligate resonance that is then revealed at the end of the film as superfluous and indeed meaningless.

'Killer' shoes abound in the dysfunctional cinematic wardrobe; a contender for the most stylish and most incriminating shoes must surely be the brown and white men's loafers worn initially by the lover of Rose Loomis (Marilyn Monroe) in *Niagara* (1953).[9] As Rose and her lover, Patrick, plot to dispatch her jealous husband, George (Joseph Cotton), the loafers become his defining feature, foregrounded as he sprawls on his rooming-house bed, and tracked in a later scene set in the tunnel under Niagara Falls where he plans to kill George. The plot is unsuccessful and it is George who kills Patrick and

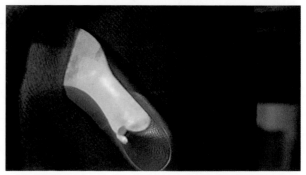

disposes of his body in the water. Reclaiming Patrick's distinctive footwear rather than his own in order to fool the authorities into thinking that it is his own body that will be found, George plans his revenge on the treacherous Rose. He will for the remainder of the film literally 'walk in dead man's shoes', as first he strangles Rose and then finally kills himself as he plunges over the Falls in a stolen motor boat. The loafers in *Niagara* are both definitive and cursed: those who wear them are fated and their distinctive, extrovert styling marks out those who dare to wear them as duplicitous and homicidal.

More distinctive footwear is the only feature that identifies the ringleader of the gunmen whom the saxophonist Danny (Stephen Rea) witnesses murder his band manager and a deaf mute girl in *Angel* (1982).[10] All he can recall being able to see of the murderers when later questioned by the police is the orthopaedic footwear worn by their leader. The equivalence of extraordinary footwear and dysfunctionality featured in *Niagara* is in *Angel* unequivocal, where the physical dys-functionality symbolised by the orthopaedic footwear matches the wearer's ruthless and dysfunctional psychological state. If the shooting of the deaf mute girl is employed as a device by which the audience is able to gauge the degree of cruelty and disregard for human life of the gunmen in *Angel*, deafness or at least impaired hearing is featured in another celebrated example of criminally implicated footwear. In order to escape detection by the office cleaner, Marnie (Tippi Hedren) in Hitchcock's eponymous film of 1964, takes off her chestnut-brown court shoes and puts them in her coat pocket, so that she can tiptoe from Rutland & Co. with the money she has just stolen from the safe.[11] As she progresses stealthily towards the stairs, one of the shoes begins to slip from her pocket, eventually clattering to the ground but without alerting the cleaner who continues mopping the floor. Marnie makes good her escape and the audience is then offered an explanation of the cleaner's non-responsiveness when a security guard arriving on his shift walks up behind her and has to shout in her ear in order to make himself understood, her impaired hearing

made manifest. Marnie, shoeless, stockinged feet barely touching the ground, tiptoes away from the scene of her crime, encumbered by the shoes in her pockets; she thus performs a physical representation of her unstable mental condition, her contact with solid ground, and by implication reality, fleeting and dysfunctional.

Robert Stevenson's *Walk Softly, Stranger* (1950) is set in the town of Ashton, home to the Corelli Shoe Factory, and opens with the arrival of gambler and ne'er-do-well Chris Hale (Joseph Cotton).[12] Hale secures a job at the factory and soon starts a relationship with the company's wealthy heiress, Elaine Corelli (Alida Valli). The plot, involving robbery, murder, retribution and finally redemption, follows late film noir conventions, but what is of singular interest is that Elaine is crippled and confined to a wheelchair, visually accentuating the irony implied in the film's title and the source of her wealth derived from footwear in which she will never be able to walk. Her anxieties and insecurities and Hale's battle to shake off his dubious past and reform are framed within a visual discourse of shoes, feet and walking, shots of Elaine being carried by Hale and the Corelli shoe factory as a locus of dysfunctionality.

Shoe shops and factories are utilised cinematically as spaces of commercial exploitation, failing industrial enterprise and unrewarded labour. Shoe-shop assistants dream of escape from daily toil, are beset by autocratic or ineffectual managers and undergo ritual humiliation from pompous customers. These sites of industrial misery are populated by loyal but ultimately betrayed workforces and, understandably, also become the location of nascent trade unionisation. Demeaned by days spent kneeling at strangers' feet, shop assistants dream of elevation, reminders of the disregard in which feet are held and which Bataille discussed: 'But whatever the role played in the erection by his foot, man, who has a light head, in other words a head raised to the heavens and heavenly things, sees it [the big toe] as spit, on the pretext that he has this foot in the mud'. Disgruntled and ambitious shoe salesmen with 'heads raised to heaven' populate cinema's shoe trade.[13] In the 1930 film *Feet*

First, Harold Lloyd as the aspiring and self-aggrandising assistant Harold Horne pretends that he is a leather tycoon in order to impress his boss's daughter, and spends the remainder of the film extricating himself from the awkward situations this imposture brings about.[14] Horne sets the template for many luckless assistants to come, who dream of better conditions or better lives. A shoe department is the central location for the 1941 production *The Devil and Miss Jones*: the film's plot concerning worker's rights and unionisation in a large department store is a typical post-Depression narrative extolling the virtues of the simple life and the basic humanity of everyday folk.[15] The attempts by the tycoon Merrick (Charles Coburn), who owns the store, to discover who the agitators are by going undercover as a salesman provide the film's comedy, and Merrick's inherent compassion and sense of justice is gradually re-awakened as he works alongside and socialises with Mary Jones (Jean Arthur) and her co-workers. Perhaps it is only fitting that it should be in the shoe department that the basic rights of the worker are championed, shoes being the one truly indispensable accessory and receiving the most wear and tear. Shoes as weapons picked up to threaten, shoes as accidental bringers of harm falling off shelves and causing concussion, and the various struggles to fit reluctant children and pernickety adults into unwanted footwear, are the typical occurrences in this dys-functional shoe department. It is a department identified by Merrick's private detectives as the 'hot-bed' of political dissent, bestowing on footwear a politically subversive dimension. On the subject of political resistance and footwear, a thought needs to be spared for perhaps the most luckless shoe worker of all, the unfortunate shoe repairman Harry Buttle in Terry Gilliam's dystopian fantasy *Brazil* (1985).[16] Buttle, owing to a bureaucratic glitch, is mistaken for the illegal freelance heating engineer Harry Tuttle and dragged away by the Big Brother-like author-ities who control Brazil's society; they torture him to death, the ultimate subjugation of the lowly shoe worker.

If shoe retailing is littered with unachieved dreams, then those engaged in shoe manufacture and shoe design fare little

THE DEVIL AND MISS JONES
1941, dir. Sam Wood.
[top] Accidental weapon;
[middle] heavy duty weapon;
[bottom] awkward customer.

better.[17] Failing shoe businesses prove burdens to their heirs and shoe designers' aspirations end in redundancy and retribution. Two films released in 2005 – one British, *Kinky Boots*; the other American, *Elizabethtown* – tackle the shoe industry's shortcomings and use failure as a catalyst for change, both corporate and personal.[18] *Kinky Boots* concerns the fate of the shoe manufacturers Price & Sons. Charlie Price (Joel Edgerton), inheriting his father's company, tries to reverse its ailing fortunes. A chance encounter with a transvestite performer, Lola (Chiwetel Ejiofor), leads to Price & Sons successfully repositioning themselves in the shoe market as producers of women's shoes in larger sizes and fetish wear for transvestites. *Elizabethtown* opens with the failure of the shoe designer Drew Baylor's (Orlando Bloom) new line, causing Mercury Shoes, his employers, to lose nearly a billion dollars. His spectacularly dysfunctional and uncommercial designs and their detrimental financial consequences force Baylor to contemplate suicide. However, this act is averted and the realisation of his shortcomings as a designer becomes the deciding moment in a personal reassessment of his goals and ambitions.

While it has enormous commercial potential, the formula for the shoe deodoriser that Stanley Yelnats III (Henry Winkler) searches for in *Holes* (2003) eludes him.[19] His son (Shia LaBeouf), meanwhile, is wrongfully accused of stealing a pair of baseball boots donated to a charity by the baseball legend Clyde 'Sweetfeet' Livingstone, when they descend unexpectedly from the skies, striking Yelnats junior on the head. Not realising that the shoes have been stolen, he decides to keep them and when later found in his possession is sent to a mysterious desert labour camp. The complex tale consisting of stolen treasure and gypsy curses ends with the vindication of Stanley and his father's successful marketing of the deodoriser 'Sploosh', which is seen advertised on television by Sweetfeet Livingstone at the end of the film. Sports shoes, or at least the counterfeit brand 'Pumma', feature bizarrely in *Knock Off* (1998), starring Jean-Claude Van Damme as the Hong Kong-based fashion designer and fake clothing brand importer Marcus Ray.[20] Once again, the sales

KINKY BOOTS
2005, dir. Julian Jarrold.
[top] Introducing the new line.

HOLES
2003, dir. Andrew Davis.
[middle] Shoes from heaven.

KNOCK OFF
1998, dir. Hark Tsui.
[bottom] Brand identification.

failure of his spectacularly unconvincing versions of genuine Puma shoes sets in motion a plot that revolves round the handover of Hong Kong's sovereignty to China in 1997, denim fashion shows and Russian micro-bombs.

Certain films provide what amounts to a checklist of the most common and less deadly aspects of dysfunctional footwear. *The Out of Towners* (1970) George and Gwen Kellerman (Jack Lemon and Sandy Dennis) encounter a succession of sartorial mishaps on their visit to New York, but it is their footwear that is the cause of their greatest distress.[21] In their progressively more unfortunate and frantic visit with only the clothes they have on their backs (their luggage was lost in transit), Gwen first breaks the heel of one of her shoes only to have the other one run over by a car, forcing her to negotiate Central Park barefoot and consequently cut her foot. After sleeping rough, George wakes to find himself shoeless and, fearing the worst, suspects that he has been mugged for them. His anxiety is only slightly relieved, however, by the appearance of his wife who is wearing his shoes clown-like as the final accessory to her now completely dishevelled and comic appearance.

Elsewhere the all too common experience of ill-fitting, new or tight shoes causing sore feet reoccurs throughout popular cinema in a reworking of the Cinderella motif. 'We must have walked 150 miles already!' declares Joe Allen (Robert Walker) to Alice Mayberry (Judy Garland) in *The Clock* (1945) when, after spending all afternoon touring a museum, the couple stop by an Egyptian sphinx and lift themselves up to sit on the pedestal in front of the statue.[22] Alice takes off her shoes and begins to massage her aching feet but, on hearing the footsteps of the approaching guard, jumps back down to earth momentarily shoeless. On the guard's departure Alice sits back up on the pedestal and continues to massage her feet, eventually donning her shoes again with the camera framing her act between the paws of the sphinx, making a visual analogy of permissible barefootedness as long as it is elevated to the status of art, as opposed to her transgressive act of shoelessness. Old Will, the china-mender who features in the previously discussed

Young and Innocent, voices the discomfort that his new boots (recently purchased to allow him access to the Grand Hotel) cause him and complains to Erica, adopting the role of an ugly sister who suffers in order to attend the ball: 'These boots pinch a bit, I 'aven't had time to slit 'em for me corns!'[23]

Compulsive acquisition of shoes has recently been identified as a growing cause for concern, a result due in part to the representation of shoe-buying as a permissible psychological disorder. In a relatively short space of time, a figure such as Imelda Marcos (the wife of the long-ruling president of the Philippines), whose vast collection of shoes was widely held up in the 1980s as proof of her lack of a firm grip on reality and sense of social justice, has been supplanted by fictional characters such as Carrie in the hugely popular American television series *Sex and the City*, a character whose celebrated shoe obsession, especially with the designs of Manolo Blahnik, is seen not so much as evidence of an unaffordable profligacy but rather a prerequisite of stylish women, unable to resist the allure of a new pair of shoes and who reward emotional upset and disappointment in life with new footwear whenever possible. That this 'symptom' has now gained a degree of social prestige can be judged by its popular manifestations alongside the commonplace experiences of footwear, and more recent films such as *In Her Shoes* celebrate this disorder.[24] Rose (Toni Collette) and Maggie (Cameron Diaz) are sisters who both compensate in different ways for their lack of emotional stability and the dysfunctional relationships they have with their surviving parent and stepmother. Rose, a successful attorney, compulsively buys shoes and hoards them in her wardrobe in order to cope with her anxieties. While the film's plot moves towards a normative resolution with Rose finding the love of a good man and marrying him, an act which will presumably cure her of her shoe compulsion, it simultaneously relishes her obsession.

The ability of shoes to act as transformative accessories can partly explain the obsessions of characters such as Rose. Shoes promise their wearer's alternative identities and, mistaken or otherwise, are regularly accessed on film in that way: so, as has been discussed, in *Niagara* George's appropriation of the murdered man's brown and white loafers suggests that he can now assume his previously denied status of fulfilling lover to his wife, but instead they confer on him the unexpected role of wife-murderer. As a result of Richard Drew's (Tom Hanks) distinctively dysfunctional choice of footwear – one red trainer, one ox-blood loafer – he is randomly targeted as the subject of a CIA surveillance operation in the film *The Man With One Red Shoe* (1985).[25] His unwitting involvement in an elaborate plot concerning a government power struggle is sparked by his unconventional choice of footwear, and his mismatched shoes echo the ill-fitting identity as a Soviet spy placed on him by the surveillance team. In *Accidental Hero* (1992) a single shoe left at the scene of an aeroplane crash by the pickpocket Bernie LaPlante (Dustin Hoffman) is refigured as the identifying trace of the mysterious hero who helped rescue the survivors.[26] Yet it is not LaPlante who ultimately benefits from this new identity but the opportunist Vietnam veteran John Bubber (Andy Garcia), to whom LaPlante gave his other shoe: when the media clamours for the hero of the crash to come forward it is Bubber, armed with the shoe as 'evidence', who is celebrated as the 'accidental' hero. The attempted assumption of a new identity as a tramp by the screen director John L. Sullivan (Joel McCrea) in *Sullivan's Travels* is the film's central plot, but it is the theft of his shoes which finally robs him of his true 'self'. After spending the night in a shelter for the homeless he awakes to find his shoes have been stolen and along with them a piece of paper hidden in them stating his true identity, and he is forced to don the decrepit pair of boots left behind by the thief (see illus. p. 119). When the thief is later killed, he is identified as Sullivan because of the note in the shoes. Sullivan meanwhile suffers from memory loss and is convicted of assault and sent to prison, where he is unable to reclaim his true identity, until his memory gradually returns and he is able eventually to prove his innocence. With more time to spend perfecting his new identity, the inmate Andy Defresne (Tim Robbins) in *The*

THE OUT OF TOWNERS
1970, dir. Arthur Hiller.
[top] Making an impression.

THE CLOCK
1945, dir. Vincente Minnelli.
[middle] "We must have walked 150 miles already!"

THE MAN WITH ONE RED SHOE
1985, dir. Stan Dragoti.
[bottom] Mismatched shoes and ill-fitting identity.

Shawshank Redemption (1994) spends his days in prison plotting his escape.[27] As part of his duties as prison accountant and the brains behind the warden's money-laundering schemes, Andy also acts as the warden's servant, polishing his shoes being one of his duties. As his fellow inmate Ellis 'Red' Redding (Morgan Freeman) narrates: 'Andy did like he was told, buffed those shoes to a high mirror shine. The guard simply didn't notice. Neither did I . . . I mean, seriously, how often do you really look at a man's shoes?'[28] It is in the warden's shoes, which he has substituted for his old prison-issue ones, that Andy makes his escape, his transformation from lifer to successful escapee complete with the addition of the lustrous footwear and new identity as 'Randall Stephens', the fictitious alias that he created as part of the money-laundering scam.

The transformative power of shoes is borne out by their prominence as objects in folklore and fairy tales: Cinderella, the Twelve Dancing Princesses, the Elves and the Shoemaker and of course the Red Shoes – and no account of dysfunctional and harmful cinematic footwear would be complete without acknowledging the supernatural strength of Vicky Page's (Moira Shearer) ballet shoes in Powell and Pressburger's celebrated 1948 production *The Red Shoes*.[29] Loosely based on the original Hans Christian Andersen story of the demonic shoemaker and his deadly creation, the fairy story provided the inspiration for the film's central ballet sequence: the red shoes lead Vicky in a double dance of death both on stage and off, and this literary heritage provides a blueprint for cinema's representation of the shoe, at once deadly and bewitching. While *The Red Shoes* is steeped in literary tradition, more recent cinematic production has been assiduously constructing its own footwear mythology. In the *Candyman* films, the successful horror franchise of the 1990s, the supernatural hook-handed avenger has his ancestry, and presumably his financial status, explained by Professor Philip Purcell, who relates that the Candyman's father 'amassed a considerable fortune from designing a device for the mass-producing of shoes after the Civil War'.[30] More innocently but equally fantastic is the town of Spectre featured in *Big Fish*

(2003) where visitors are encouraged to remove their shoes and hurl them over a high wire suspended far out of reach above the entrance to the town so as to prevent people from leaving (see illus. p. 119). Spectre's citizens remain forever shoeless and apparently carefree, a mythological reassignment of the common American ado-lescent practice of forcibly removing a victim's shoes and throwing them over telephone wires.[31] Even the rather more prosaic profession of shoe design can acquire supernatural agency, as in the ghostly romance of *P.S. I Love You* (2007) featuring Holly (Hilary Swank), the grieving partner of her recently deceased lover Gerry (Gerard Butler), who hurls a shoe in a fit of grief which knocks over a small 'shrine' dedicated to Gerry.[32] This display contains a clip from a pair of Gerry's braces, a memento of one of their sexual exploits, and which miraculously falls onto the shoe as a decorative buckle in an act of supernatural cobbling. This message from the grave prompts Holly to undertake a course in shoe design and forges a new productive career for her by the close of the film. The power of shoes in film seems unassailable, and their very dysfunctionality in many productions can be seen as the means for them to take on other meaning and significance, as Boris Lermontov (Anton Walbrook), the Svengali-like impresario from *The Red Shoes* explains: "Time rushes by, love rushes by, life rushes by, but the Red Shoes go on.'[33]

'Is this the handbag, Miss Prism? Examine it carefully before you speak. The happiness of more than one life depends on your answer.'[34]

Oscar Wilde's *The Importance of Being Earnest* (1895) famously uses a handbag mistakenly issued from the left-luggage depart-ment at Victoria Station in London as the place where the baby Ernest of the play's title is discovered. While this highly unlikely occurrence is central to the play's themes of assumed identities, coincidence and the instability of social conventions, looked at specifically in terms of what it suggests concerning the func-tion of bags, it becomes a model for how this particular acces-sory has since been commonly utilised in cinematic narrative. Surprising, missing or completely inappropriate contents, the habitual switching or mistaking of one similar-looking bag for another, bags stolen or returned to the wrong owner and abandoned in left-luggage departments are the typical fates of the cinematic bag. Generally unconcerned with the illusory fashionable identities desired by the contem-porary devotee of the luxury branded bag, the cinematic bag is often generic: what is at stake is not its styling but its contents and the desta-bilisation of its security. In *Dial M for Murder* Hitchcock appears to be referring to Wilde when the audience learns that Victoria Station was the location for the apparent theft of Margot Wendice's handbag by her attempted murderer, Swann. As it turns out, this 'theft' had been carried out by Tony Wendice, Margot's husband, as part of his plan to frame Swann. The convolutions of the film's plot, and its narrative of marital infidelity and retribution, are dazzling enough but, as has already been explored in the section on coats, *Dial M for Murder* layers further, specifically clothing-related, narratives under-neath its primary dramatic one; like the narrative of the unworn and displaced coat, the 'unsafe', sexually ambivalent bag is a subtle yet insistent visual motif that recurs throughout the film.

Early in the film we hear Wendice telling Swann how Margot had burned all the letters from her lover, Mark Hal-liday — 'all except one. That one she transferred from handbag to handbag, it was always with her'[35] — but in the next breath he goes on to explain how he stole the letter and (as is later revealed) the bag also, thereby instantly interrogating its status as a safe and secure receptacle. The scene continues with Wendice plotting the fake burglary, part of which involves him displaying a suitcase, complete with luggage labels, and inform-ing Swann that it contains clothes of his 'for the cleaners', and that during the burglary Swann is to tip the clothes out onto the floor and fill the suitcase with valuables. As with the inse-cure bag, this sequence introduces dysfunctional variants: the bag of unexpected and unsuitable contents; clothes to be dry-cleaned, cigarette boxes and tennis trophies and, later, absent or 'wrong' latch-keys. Other bags are constantly mentioned in the film such as the small attaché case in a check-room 'somewhere in London', which contains the thousand pounds Swann will receive once he has committed the murder.

On the evening of the arranged murder, the taking and replacing of keys from Margot's bag commences and we see her check the key that she keeps in a purse inside her bag, which later Tony snatches up and pretends to rifle through looking for money, his real intention, however, being to steal the key. The camera lingers over Tony deftly opening bag and purse behind his back and taking the key. This shot marks the beginning of the bag's transformation from understated elegant woman's accessory to an object that is literally man-handled and used as a device to undermine conventional gender roles. From now on the bag will be carried more frequently by men than by Margot herself and is converted into a locus of insecurity for its contents and the sexuality of its bearers alike. Immediately after the bungled murder attempt, Tony replaces the key in the bag and, to underscore its elevated status in the film, the viewer sees it positioned on a pile of expensive art books: the simple brown bag is placed on a 'pedestal' surmounting the French Impressionists, Giovanni Bellini and Leonardo da Vinci (see illus. p. 122). The bag assumes importance as a nomadic object that links the characters together as it is passed among them; it is now destined to be ownerless, its secret, the key, vanished from sight within its recesses. At the close of this scene Margot is taken to the police station for questioning but forgets her bag; this time it is her lover, Mark Halliday, who picks it up and carries it to her: the bag, just like a work of art, has now become public property. It will re-appear towards the climax of the film but for now the persistent visual discourse of the bag shifts emphasis onto the traditionally male varieties of attaché and briefcases.

After Margot's conviction for the murder of Swann, we see Tony Wendice return to the apartment with the blue attaché case that contained Swann's un-needed payment for the murder. He is interrupted by Halliday and swiftly hides the case under

DIAL M FOR MURDER
1954, dir. Alfred Hitchcock.
[top] The insecure receptacle;
[middle] hidden in plain sight
[bottom] 'You can't walk down
the street like that!'

DIAL M FOR MURDER
1954, dir. Alfred Hitchcock.
The bag as a work of art.

a dressing-gown on the bed. Chief Inspector Hubbard arrives briefcase in hand, which he promptly dumps on the makeshift bed Wendice has been sleeping on in the living room, while Mark hides in the bedroom. Wendice is questioned by Hubbard about the case with which he has been spotted and says that it has been stolen, which along with the theft of Margot's bag from Victoria Station emphasises the motif of the stolen bag. Mark, sitting down on the bed in the next room, discovers the attaché case hidden under the gown and, as the inspector proceeds with his interrogation, forces open the locks to reveal the used pound notes with which Wendice was going to pay Swann and which instead he has been systematically spending. The lie is revealed but Wendice apparently convinces Hubbard and Halliday that in fact he has been covering for Margot, who

was being blackmailed by Swann, hence the money. The functions of both brief and attaché case in this scene are questionable: Hubbard's case is apparently empty and has no function other than to be carelessly dumped on a bed, or perhaps to provide him with an appropriate business-like air, while the attaché case takes on a mythical status as an object identified by witnesses all over London, purportedly stolen, hidden and revealed and filled with either winnings from the dog track, hush or blood money, according to which of Wendice's stories is to be believed.

The final scenes of *Dial M for Murder* bring the various motifs of the unsafe, sexually ambivalent and surprisingly filled bag together. Margot is brought to the apartment under police custody and finds to her confusion that the key in her bag does not fit the lock; the contents of her bag can no longer be relied on and she relinquishes the bag to Hubbard, who now takes possession of it and verifies that Margot is unaware that the keys to her apartment have been switched. Margot appears dazed and bewildered and her detachment from reality is given form by her incomprehension not only at what is in her own handbag but also when the inspector shows her the now empty blue attaché case and questions her about it; all she can reply in robotic fashion is: 'What is it? I don't understand', bags having now become enigmatic, unreliable objects for Margot.[36] Hubbard gives the handbag to Detective Pearson to take back to the station and become part of the bait that will trap Tony into revealing himself as the person responsible for switching the keys. Pearson promptly puts the bag over his wrist in an overtly feminine manner, causing Hubbard to declare: 'Oh wait a minute you clot! You can't walk down the street like that! You... you'll be arrested! Here put it in this.'[37] Hubbard then grabs his apparently empty briefcase and he and Pearson put the handbag, containing the inner purse with the key, inside the briefcase, an act that can be read as the containment of feminine transgression within a carapace of male respectability or as an interrogation of the bag's accepted function as a secure receptacle (see illus. p. 121). Although Hubbard fears that his detective's sexual identity may not be secure enough to brook the carrying of a woman's handbag in public, no such strictures hamper Tony Wendice. We see the failed wife-killer brazenly holding his wife's bag as he finally returns to the apartment and reveals that he knows the whereabouts of the correct door-key – not in the bag but under the stair carpet where Swann had replaced it. The bag is finally discarded on a chair, de-sexed and unreliable, a useless receptacle that can only offer up unwanted contents, as the film ends.

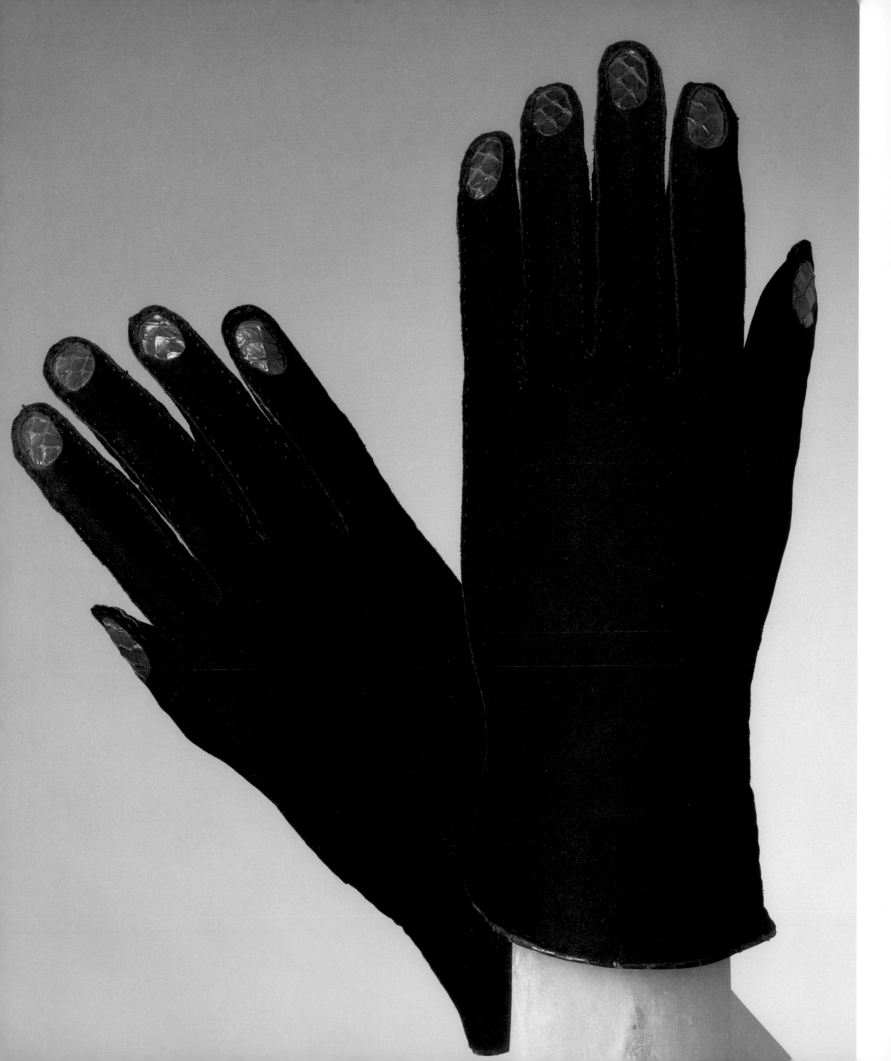

The glove, as the accessory that most closely resembles in shape the body part it is used to cover, is consequently also the item in the cinematic wardrobe that most often signifies the owner. Whether mislaid, stolen or planted, the glove is repeatedly perceived as the disembodied textile substitute for the subject, a material part for the whole. The cinematic glove insistently demands of the viewer an act of imaginative reincarnation of the owner's hand, which 'empty' shoes or hats cannot equal. While these items are undoubtedly strongly associated with their owners, it is only the glove that schematically places the wearer directly at the scene of a crime, because of the glove's intimate and anthropomorphic connection to its owner's hand. It is this visual bond between hand and glove that has made the latter a powerful symbol in art practice, especially in Surrealism whose exponents, greatly influenced by Max Klinger's celebrated cycle of nineteenth-century etchings, *Paraphrases on the Finding of a Glove*, made it their pre-eminent accessory.[1] This fact that did not escape the Surrealist proclivities of Elsa Schiaparelli who, alongside her celebrated shoe, hat and buttons in the shape of lips, created in the 1930s gloves replete with red snakeskin fingernails, evening gloves with metallic claws at their tips and a 'reptilian' pair with gilded kid fins running along the backs of the fingers, making her the doyenne of the dysfunctionally fashionable accessory. The animism that Schiaparelli's gloves playfully celebrates is central to the cinematic glove also, and its ability to represent in cloth or leather the actual flesh and blood hand, coupled with its fundamental protective and concealing function, makes its dysfunctionality all the more potent. Philippe Perrot in *Fashioning the Bourgeoisie* has suggested that in the nineteenth century gloves 'illustrate the dialectic of conformism and distinction inherent in clothing behaviour in mobile societies. Casting an egalitarian veil over 'chirographic' defects, over the original stigmata graven on the hands, gloves became also an indispensable accessory of social demarcation.'[2] The fundamental dichotomy that Perrot detects in the historical glove, of facilitating the masking of manual defects while simultaneously exposing the wearer's class and economic position by its colour and fabric, is translated in film into the glove as an accessory that has the potential to deceive, implicate and endanger.

Gloves, black suede and red snakeskin, by Elsa Schiaparelli, 1936–7 (Philadelphia Museum of Art. Gift of Mme. Elsa Schiaparelli, 1969).

As early as 1929 Hitchcock realised the potential of the glove when in *Blackmail* he has Alice White (Anny Ondra) leave her gloves behind after she has stabbed to death the artist who attempted to rape her.[3] Subsequently investigating the crime, Detective Frank Webber, Alice's boyfriend, finds and recognises one of her gloves at the scene and later confronts her with it. The couple are interrupted by the criminal Tracy, who has witnessed the crime and has Alice's other glove in his possession. This new function of the pair of incriminating gloves gives the film its title, as Tracy then proceeds to blackmail the couple with the forgotten glove. Just over ten years later in *Rebecca*, Hitchcock again exploits the glove's suspenseful potential, as the nervous new bride of Maxim de Winter fumbles and drops her gloves in embarrassed panic at her first meeting with the formidable Mrs Danvers. Her gloves are an awkward accessory that, rather than confirm style or status, betray her humble origins and become the sign of the imposter. More deadly still are the gloves featured in the previously discussed *Dressed to Kill*, where Kate Miller's fashionable Isotoner gloves embellished with chevrons of white brogued leather are used initially to signal her frustrated distraction in the Metropolitan Museum when she absentmindedly leaves one on a gallery bench. This same glove is picked up by her mysterious admirer and is later used to lure her to what will eventually be her grisly death. Exiting the museum, Kate disappointedly casts aside her remaining glove, only to notice a few moments later the other one being dangled enticingly out of a waiting taxi cab, its limp fingers, lifeless and twitching in a vestimentary foreshadowing of her own death throes, which the audience will shortly witness. As she hastens to her erotic encounter and her doom, the figure of her transvestite avenger is glimpsed for a split second and, as Kate steps into the cab, the scene cuts to a close-up of a black-gloved hand slowly dragging the abandoned glove from the Metropolitan's steps. This symbolic grasping of Kate's 'hand' by her assassin is a mimetic rehearsal of the subsequent 'possession' of her flesh and blood hand by the slasher's blade.

DRESSED TO KILL
1980, dir. Brian De Palma.
The glove as lure.

The cinematic glove as a form of sartorial calling card, a sign of its owner, refers to its historical significance; just as one's status and fashionabliity could be 'read' through the cut and colour of one's gloves, so too do cinematic gloves function as criminal calling cards. Perrot is again invaluable here: 'The glove hid the hand, but its form, material, color, and uses regulated by a meticulous code were revelatory . . . At balls gloves had to be brilliant white; at the theater or in a drawing room, straw or buttercup yellow were preferred. These were the basic precepts, but color could also indicate social, moral or political predispositions.'[4] One of the more insistent examples of the glove as calling card is that used by the 'Phantom', the alias of Lord Lytton (David Niven), the master jewel-thief in *The Pink Panther*, whose felonious trademark is to leave a man's white evening glove embroidered in gold with the letter P at the scenes of his crimes. Here the Phantom, an incorporeal figure, elusive and unseen, is made teasingly manifest to Inspector Clouseau, yet the Phantom's absence is underscored by the presence of the glove, and the Inspector's inept attempts to apprehend the thief are mocked by the omnipresent white accessory.

In popular perception the glove as a means to escape detection, to avoid leaving fingerprints at the scene of the crime, routinely donned by felon and forensic examiner alike, is interrogated in film. The glove in *The House on Telegraph Hill* (1951), which should leave no trace of its wearer's presence, becomes paradoxically a piece of potentially incriminating evidence.[5] Victoria Kowelska (Valentina Cortese) suspects her husband of trying to murder her for her inheritance, and after a near-fatal car crash she discovers that her car's brake cable has been cut and the fluid leaking out has caused the brakes to fail. Later that same night she discovers a suspicious patch on the garage floor and a pair of her husband's gloves stained with what appears to be brake fluid. A close-up of the stained glove, the camera fetishistically lingering over its two soiled finger tips, the other fingers lost in atmospheric darkness, prompts the viewer to equate stain with crime, so strongly embedded is the

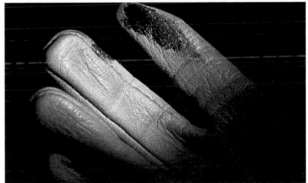

THE PINK PANTHER
1963, dir. Blake Edwards.
[top] The glove as calling card.

THE HOUSE ON TELEGRAPH HILL
1951, dir. Robert Wise.
[bottom] Unreliable evidence.

function of gloves to protect the wearer from soiling, criminal or otherwise. Gloves and car accidents, or rather arranged accidents, feature again in Otto Preminger's *Angel Face* (released a year after *The House on Telegraph Hill*, in 1952), with the offending accessories evincing an almost supernatural proclivity for evil. Diane Tremayne (Jean Simmons) offers a pair of new gloves to her despised stepmother who is unable to locate any of her own. However, this uncharacteristically endearing gesture on the part of Diane provides no stylish accessorising of her stepmother's outfit but instead ushers in her fate. As she dons the gloves, she asks Diane to wish her good luck, before turning the ignition key to her car which has been tampered with by Diane, so that it automatically lurches backwards in reverse at full throttle, plunging over a cliff. Diane's plan backfires, though, killing not only her stepmother but her beloved father also, making these particular driving gloves possibly the unluckiest pair in cinema history. The dysfunctionality of cinematic gloves is inescapable and they are typified as mislaid, planted, stolen and stained, unworn, unprotective and exposing, the antithesis of functional gloves. Yet their very dysfunctionality makes these gloves fecund with alternative meaning and significance.

The glove as a destructive accessory features regularly in horror film, shielding the wearer while wreaking death and destruction on others. Film is littered with 'killing' gloves and, beyond those donned for simple strangulation, or fingerprint-less shooting, a special collection of 'limited edition' gloves has been periodically released. *A Nightmare on Elm Street*'s Freddy Krueger (Robert Englund), with his razor-clawed glove, became a cinematic icon of the 1980s, the prosthetic surrealism of his fingers extended by eviscerating metallic 'nails', forming the stuff of childhood nightmares and swiftly passing into the visual lexicon of contemporary cinematic horror.[6] The clawed glove was subsequently historicised by Martin Scorsese in *Gangs of New York* (2002) where in the first of the set-piece gang fights the viewer sees Hell-Cat Maggie donning a pair of taloned gloves (not perhaps as stylish, but reminiscent of Schiaparelli's) in order to make her blows more lethal, and then later Amsterdam

Vallon (Leonardo DiCaprio) wears a nineteenth-century version of the Roman *cestus*, a spiked leather combat glove worn by gladiators to equally deadly effect.[7] A modernised version of the *cestus* appears again in *The Glove*, a cult horror film from 1979 which has John Saxon as the bounty hunter Sam Kellogg, paid $20,000 to track down and capture Victor Hale, an ex-convict who is seeking out and killing former prison guards with a laced leather, metal-plated riot glove.[8] This particular glove makes a just instrument of revenge, given that it had been used by the guards to torture former inmates and now extracts gruesome reprisals on an illustrious cast of victims including Aldo Ray, Keenan Wynn and Joan Blondell. The killing glove can trace its cinematic lineage through a number of prosthetic or otherwise modified killing hands, with extended nails, hooks or similar deadly attachments, from the 1930s with Boris Karloff's unforgettable bronze nails in *The Mask of Fu Manchu*, and an assortment of hooked undesirables such as the wooden-armed Inspector Krogh (Lionel Atwill) in *Son of Frankenstein*, on to full-blown prosthetic weapons of manual destruction, including the knife-thrower's hands grafted onto Stephen Orlac (Colin Clive) by Dr Gogol (Peter Lorre), the possessor of his own spectacular pair of customised killing hands in *Mad Love* (see illus. p. 130), to the black cybernetic metal-crushing prosthetics in *Dr No* (Frederick Wiseman; 1962) and the previously discussed, mercilessly hooked hand in *Candyman*.[9] The inconvenience and everyday dysfunctionality of these deadly accessories has most recently been ameliorated by characters such as Wolverine (Hugh Jackman) in the *X Men* series of films (2000–13), whose adamantium scalpel-sharp retractable claws spring out but conveniently retract back into his modified skeleton, making shaking hands less of a liability. All these variants on the dysfunctional hand, whether simple glove or elaborate prosthetic, construct a popular visual trope that equates the modified hand with evil, the normative organ of touch traduced into an instrument of dysfunctional harm.

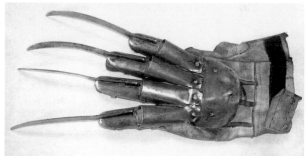

A NIGHTMARE ON ELM STREET
1984, dir. Wes Craven.
[top] The stuff of nightmares
(Moviestore Collection/Rex Features).

[bottom] Home-made Freddy Krueger glove used by Jason Moore in the attempted murder of his sleeping friend in 2006 (Mark St George/Rex Features).

You know how long I've been on ya?
Since Prince was on Apollonia
Since OJ had isotoners
Don't act like I never told ya[10]

Among the wealth of fashionable allusions to Christian Dior, Kate Moss, Louis Vuitton and clothing brand A Bathing Ape in Kanye West's 2007 hit song 'Stronger', the reference to the American football player O. J. Simpson's 'Isotoners' is used as an insistent refrain and recounts the role that the pair of gloves (allegedly bought for Simpson by his wife) played in what has been dubbed the trial of the century and 'the most publicized murder case in history'.[11] A key dramatic moment occurred when OJ, sports star turned film actor, accused of the murders of his wife Nicole Brown Simpson and her friend Ronald Goldman, demonstrated Cinderella-like that the pair of dark brown leather (rather than the cream variant favoured by Kate Miller and featured in *Dressed to Kill*), cashmere-lined Isotoner gloves found at the crime scenes were too small and that he could not fit his hand into them. Eventually acquitted and the evidence of the gloves dismissed as inconclusive, the gloves, nevertheless, remain indelibly associated with the murder trial, so that some ten years later West used them as a sartorially damning reference. Simpson's Isotoners assumed mythical, shape-shifting proportions during the trial, a real-life echo of the multi-valency and visual persistence of the cinematic glove as accessory to crime and vestimentary trace of the criminal.

The way you wear your hat
The way you sip your tea
The memory of all that
No, no they can't take that away from me[12]

Unlike gloves, hats in film are rarely deadly; instead their primary dysfunction is to render the wearer ridiculous. Women's hats are typically described as 'silly' while men's are regularly crushed or thrown away. Oddjob's (Harold Sakata) razor-sharp, steel-rimmed bowler hat, used to deadly effect in *Goldfinger* (1964) is, of course, a notable exception and joins the arsenal of specially

MAD LOVE
1935, dir. Karl Freund.
[facing] Dr Gogol's customised prosthetics
(Everett Collection/Rex Features).

[above] O. J. Simpson tries on a pair of
gloves in court, Los Angeles, 1995
(Sipa Press/Rex Features).

designed killer accessories sported by James Bond's foes.[13] These custom-made accessories are if anything 'superfunctional' rather than dysfunctional, fulfilling their primary functions as weapons admirably. Yet even these alternative uses are ultimately interrogated, for Oddjob's bowler acts as a conductor, leading to his fatal electrocution. Perhaps the most celebrated 'silly' hat is that which stops Garbo in her tracks in *Ninotchka*, causing her

to observe: 'How can such a civilisation survive which permits their women to put things like that on their heads? It won't be long now comrades!'[14] Although Ninotchka outwardly condemns the decadent millinery, she purchases the hat and secretes it in a drawer, periodically taking it out and admiring it before she decides to wear it, the hat becoming the catalyst for the abandonment of her political convictions. Other ridiculous hats can have more lasting and harmful repercussions, however, such as that featured in *Witness for the Prosecution*. Tyrone Power playing the murderer Leonard Vole first makes the acquaintance of the widowed Mrs French (Norma Varden) when he sees her trying on hats in a milliner's. He persuades her against the more conservative models she has picked out and eventually flatters her into taking an extravagant creation with an oversized bow, a style he later refers to when talking to Charles Laughton playing the barrister Sir Wilfred Robarts: 'Actually it was quite a ridiculous hat. Silly thing with ribbons and flowers.' Robarts: 'I'm constantly surprised that women's hats do not provoke more murders . . .'[15]

The hat figures again in another chance meeting between Vole and Mrs French, when she sits in front of him at a cinema wearing the same hat, prompting him to ask if she might remove it. This second accidental meeting cements their relationship and paves the way for Vole eventually to bludgeon the wealthy Mrs French to death. She should perhaps have trusted her initial judgement concerning headwear and not have been fooled into taking the frivolous style that leads to her death.

Men's hats fare little better but, unlike female headwear which often symbolises frivolity and foolishness, it is the abandonment or ruination, rather than the wearing, of the male hat that is most significant cinematically. Men's hats impart gravitas and status, they protect and cover the head; therefore it follows that any loss or destruction of this accessory implies an attack on male formality, intellect and superiority. As Bataille observed, the censure associated with the foot and earthly matters concerning shoes, as noted earlier, is made more forceful by the approbation heaped on elevated subjects: 'with their feet in the mud but their heads more or less in light, men obstinately imagine a tide that will permanently elevate them, never to return, into pure space.'[16] The dismantling of male patriarchy symbolised by the loss or destruction of the hat is often set in motion by the arrival of the female love interest, ushering in acts of capital dysfunction. In the early scene between Cary

NINOTCHKA
1939, dir. Ernst Lubitsch.
[facing] Ninotchka is seduced
by decadent millinery
(Everett Collection/Rex Features).

WITNESS FOR THE PROSECUTION
1957, dir. Billy Wilder.
[top] 'I'm constantly surprised that women's
hats do not provoke more murders . . .'

BRINGING UP BABY
1938, dir. Howard Hawks.
[bottom] Capital dysfunction.

Grant and Katharine Hepburn in *Bringing Up Baby* (1938) we see these diametrically opposed, and yet equally dysfunctional, depictions of headwear deployed to maximum comic effect.[17] The sheltered academic palaeontologist David Huxley (Cary Grant), seeking a donation for his museum from the wealthy Mrs Random, encounters her scatter-brained and unconventional niece Susan Vance (Hepburn) at a smart restaurant. Vance is dressed in a dazzling lamé gown and remarkable and highly dysfunctional matching veil which, rather than covering her face, doubles back on itself to form a kind of animated lamé outline to her neck and shoulders. The veil, rather than lending the face the customary mysterious glamour, is used as a comic accent quivering with amusement at every exaggerated gesture Susan makes, a vestimentary visualisation of laughter. Huxley is in full evening dress of top hat and tails, a uniform that would normally confer elegant poise and control on its wearer, but in *Bringing Up Baby*, a veritable feast of dysfunctional costuming, Huxley's evening dress is reduced to the comic attire of the circus clown.[18] Even before meeting Vance, he fumbles and drops his hat as the cloakroom attendant asks if she can take it, and as he stoops to pick it up knocks heads with the bemused hat-check girl. Rather than entrusting it to her, he decides to keep it with him, so that when he slips on an olive dropped by Vance he falls over and crushes his hat completely (see illus. p. 133). His crushed hat widens the crack in his academic facade and from this moment onwards Huxley begins his transformation under the tutelage of Susan from museum fossil into screwball exhibitionist. The restaurant scene closes with the pair exiting the restaurant hat crushed, clothes ripped, waddling like a vaudeville act performing a comic turn.

Abandonment of male sobriety in the presence of female allure symbolised by the loss of headwear is even more directly signalled in *Bell, Book and Candle* (1958).[19] James Stewart playing the bewitched publisher Shep Henderson embraces Gil Holroyd (Kim Novak), a Greenwich Village witch, on top of the Flatiron Building on the morning of his impending nuptials to his long-suffering fiancée. With the declaration 'I'm gonna mush

BELL, BOOK AND CANDLE
1958, dir. Richard Quine.
[top] 'I'm gonna mush your nose';
[bottom] throwing caution to the wind.

your nose', he tosses off his hat and we watch it drift and circle in the wintry light from the top of the famous New York landmark, in a cinematic homage to Edward Steichen and Alfred Stieglitz's iconic photographs of the same building, eventually coming to rest in a slushy 5th Avenue.[20] The hat's trajectory symbolises Shep's journey from cynical publisher to enchanted lover as, descending to earth, all loftier pretensions are abandoned as he falls under the spell of the elemental and 'earthy' witch. Another hat as the symbol of male sovereignty, of order triumphing over chaos, is used in the title sequence to *Miller's Crossing* which, although made some thirty years after *Bell, Book and Candle*, employs the same visual metaphor of a hat, buffeted by the breeze.[21] Liberated from its owner's head, the hat becomes a free-floating vestimentary evocation of the vulnerability of masculine identity, a function that Stella Bruzzi discusses at length in *Undressing Cinema*:

> In the title sequence an immaculate fedora carried by gusts of wind, wafts through an autumnal wood and comes to rest, in close-up, amongst the leaves. The Fedora, associated throughout Miller's Crossing with Tom (Gabriel Byrne), becomes an insistent symbol of his masculinity and integrity, thus his only moments of vulnerability are when he is temporarily separated from his headwear.[22]

> 'The neck, to be sure, was no longer imprisoned all the way to the lower lip, but the silk, satin or starched velvet cloth was wound around it several times, hugging it tightly with an even more refined knot.'[23]

The act of tying a tie or a scarf round the neck mimics strangulation: the knotting and drawing tight of tie, cravat and scarf is a dress rehearsal for asphyxiation. Unlike all other articles of dress, neckwear must always recall the act of strangulation, a decapitation of head from body by means of the most exquisite materials. The symbolism of these acts of vestimentary harm reverberate throughout myth and reality, from Antigone hanging herself with her own scarf, to Isadora Duncan's death as a result of the collision between fashion and modernity, to

MILLER'S CROSSING
1990, dir. Joel and Ethan Coen.
The Fedora in the forest.

the British serial killer Dennis Nilsen's use of a tie attached to a piece of twine as his preferred method of execution.[24] It comes as some surprise, therefore, that ties and scarves used as murder weapons are comparatively rare on film. There are, however, as always, the exceptions that prove the rule, and one of the memorable examples of the tie as murder weapon can be found in Hitchcock's 1972 film *Frenzy*, a sartorial tour de force with not only the use of neckties as murder weapons but also the forensic detailing of a suspect's sports jacket, and

a classic Hitchcockian scene involving the murderer prizing open and breaking the fingers of the woman he has just raped and strangled in order to retrieve his tie-pin.[25] 'I say, that's not my club tie is it?' exclaims one of the onlookers as the naked body of a woman, striped tie knotted round her neck, is dragged from the River Thames at the beginning of the film.[26] This flippant sartorial insistence contrasted with graphic violence characterises the film, and the onlooker's enquiry can be understood as an indication of how the ensuing action will interrogate the tie as a sign of masculine authority, respectability and normality. The tie as a textile equivalent of the phallus, both in its general shape and its ability to be read as a directional sign connecting the head downwards to the genital region, is one of the most insistent indicators of gender difference in the male wardrobe. Additionally, the tie's historical antecedence in the stock and cravat and the particular attention paid to this article of dress and how it should be tied and worn lend *Frenzy*'s use of the relatively conventional 1970s examples as murder weapons especial significance. This powerful combination of the schematic rendering of virility, established conformity (the reference to club ties makes clear the tie's ability to be 'read' as a sign of male exclusivity) and a legacy of male narcissism informed by historical figures such as Beau Brummell, fabricates the tie as a method of strangulation simultaneously ironic, effective and perverse. Only a relatively smartly dressed and respectable man would have a number of ties at his disposal to choose from as murder weapons, but this construction of the fastidious and sartorially conscious figure is challenged by the necessary action of removing the tie, thus spoiling the ensemble, and using it to commit murder, which indicates a personality that derives pleasure from this vestimentary paradox.

In *Frenzy*, the 'necktie murderer', who quite soon is revealed to the viewer as Robert Rusk (Barry Foster), a dapper, Covent Garden fruit importer, makes his first appearance wearing a plain green silk tie with an ornate diamond-set tie-pin in the shape of the letter 'R'. His overly fastidious dress seems somewhat inappropriate for his trade, and as the film unfolds his spruce 'man about town' facade is revealed as masking a sociopathic, sexually motivated hatred of women. After being struck off the books of a dating agency because of his sadistic requirements, we see him violently rape and then strangle the proprietor of the agency. The audience is left in no doubt as to the sexual gratification Rusk derives from the act of removing his tie (a tweed check, complementing his suede jacket) and strangling his victim with it, greater than that obtained from the rape itself; his post-asphyxiation panting is a measure of the degree

ISADORA
1968, dir. Karel Reisz.
[facing] 'Affectations can be dangerous'
(Everett Collection/Rex Features).

FRENZY
1972, dir. Alfred Hitchcock.
[top] 'I say, that's not my club tie is it?'
[bottom] Tied neck.

of sexual satisfaction gained from the act of releasing the constriction round his own neck and using the same cause of that constriction – his tie – to choke the life out of his victim. After the murder, Rusk, satiated, undoes the top button of his shirt, either in search of further release or perhaps simply to correct his appearance, for a buttoned collar with no tie would be unthinkable for such a well turned-out serial killer. Rusk seems to be following the advice of those nineteenth-century neckwear obsessives who furnished guides as to the correct protocol concerning the cravat, figures such as one H. Le Blanc who in 1828 published *The Art of Tying the Cravat* and suggested under the heading 'Important and Necessary Observations' that 'In case of apoplexy, or illness . . . it is requisite to loosen or even remove the cravat immediately' and that the cravat should also be loosened before sleeping, study or important business, as 'It is universally allowed that the least constraint of the body has a corresponding effect in the mind, and . . . a tight cravat will cramp the imagination.'[27] Neither Rusk's sartorial nor psychopathic imagination is 'cramped', and as viewer's we are guided to associate his ever changing displays of neckwear with the rapidly increasing body count. It appears that plain silk ties are for everyday 'normal' use, whereas patterns are reserved for Rusk's 'special occasions'; the body floating in the Thames at the beginning of the film has a broad, striped tie round the neck and for the murder of Mrs Blaney at the dating agency he chooses a checked tweed, while for his next victim, Babs (Anna Massey), he selects lilac silk with a darker diagonal background stripe. It is ironic that Rusk only breaks this self-imposed stylistic regime at the dénouement of the film, as he is caught by Chief Inspector Oxford (Alec McCowen), who observes: 'Mr Rusk, you're not wearing your tie', the tie in question being of un-patterned rust silk knotted round the throat of the naked woman lying dead in his bed.[28]

Both visual and textual puns relating to ties and neckwear abound in *Frenzy* and in typically Hitchcockian fashion the anti-hero, Richard Blaney (Jon Finch), who is falsely accused of the murders, spends the majority of the film tieless and

FRENZY
1972, dir. Alfred Hitchcock.
Tie-necks.

declares to his girlfriend Babs, prior to her own rape and murder: 'Do I look like a sex murderer? Can you imagine me creeping around London strangling all those women with ties? That's ridiculous! For a start, I only own two!'[29] Similarly, in the first half of the film, a number of female protagonists wear feminised versions of the masculine tie, in the form of tie-neck, or 'pussy bow', blouses. Mrs Blaney wears such a blouse, accessorised by a bar brooch that resembles a man's tie-pin in the scene where she is raped and murdered (punishment for assuming masculine costume?), and Monica Barling (Jean Marsh), the agency secretary, wears a tie-neck blouse, while Gladys, the receptionist at the Coburg Hotel where Blaney stays the night, clutches her bow-tied throat as she reads a newspaper account of the latest victim of the Necktie Murderer. All these women are caricatured as sexually undesirable and are dressed accordingly in a parody of male attire: Mrs Blaney the successful businesswoman who could not make 'a go' of her own marriage, the prim and spinsterish Monica Barling and the 'blousy' Gladys past her prime who spends her time gossiping with the effeminate hotel porter. It seems that only the young and desirable female protagonists such as Babs are 'tieless' and yet, once killed, will also wear a tie, one from Robert Rusk's personal wardrobe.

With ties occurring only rarely as a means of strangulation, film has called into service an assortment of other accessories to commit this particular crime. Loosely based on 'true' events, the 1968 film *The Boston Strangler*, has Tony Curtis playing the mass-murderer Albert DeSalvo notoriously using women's nylon stockings to dispatch his victims.[30] Another more recent cinematic account of an equally notorious, but fictional, killer, Tom Ripley, 'extends' Patricia Highsmith's original novel to include a heard, but not witnessed, strangulation scene carried out with a belt from a dressing gown. In the concluding scenes of *The Talented Mr Ripley* (1999) Matt Damon playing Tom Ripley, realising that his theft of the murdered Dickie Greenleaf's identity will be discovered by his current lover Peter Smith-Kingsley, prepares to strangle him, draping the dressing-gown belt round his own neck and pulling it tight in a form of dress rehearsal for the actual deed. Later we see Ripley standing in his cabin and as the camera closes in on his face the audience hears the dialogue from the previous scene continue until Smith-Kingsley's words are choked into silence.[31]

As stated earlier, given the tie's practicality as a means of strangulation, its use as a murder weapon is comparatively rare in mainstream cinema. More typically, the tie's dysfunctionality centres on its reluctance to be knotted correctly (especially when it is a bow tie), its inappropriateness or flashiness, its tightness (indicating its destructive potential) and its tendency to attract stains. Iconic images such as Oliver Hardy fiddling with his tie as a sign of his mounting panic or in sheer frustration at Stan Laurel's ineptitude remind the viewer that from its infancy film's representation of neckwear has provided equal measures of embarrassment and discomfort for a succession of leading men. In *Holiday* (1938), for example, Cary Grant as the self-made, socially conscious Johnny Case meets and falls in love with the wealthy, privileged banker's daughter Julia Seton (Doris Nolan).[32] References to ties occur throughout the early part of the film and act as signifiers of social mobility. On arriving at the family mansion on New York's Park Avenue to meet Julia's father Edward Seton (Henry Kolker), Case is wearing a somewhat old-fashioned and, by inference, working-class bow tie (he is in his own assessment 'a plain man of the people' who 'began life with these two bare hands'), which Julia has warned him not to wear and which she insists he changes.[33] His growing awareness of the strict social codes and snobbishness of his fiancée's world is brought into sharp relief when he encounters Julia's sister Linda (Katharine Hepburn), whose free-spirited rejection of her family background and unconventionality captivate Case, preparing the ground for the film's 'which sister will he choose' plot.[34] Linda's contrasting attitude to the Seton family heritage is expressed using the tie motif again, as she points out to Case that the mansion is haunted by 'frightful ghosts all wearing stuffed shirts and mink-lined ties'.[35] Having exchanged his bow tie for one of Edward Seton's own ties in readiness for his meeting with the head of the family, Case's neckwear becomes comic material as the solemnity of Seton's formal interview with his prospective son-in-law is undermined as he is unable to take his eyes off Case's chest, eventually prompting him to declare: 'Interesting neck-tie you have. I have a haberdasher who's made my ties for many years and that pattern I seem to recognize', to which Case responds: 'Perhaps, sir, because this happens to be your neck-tie.'[36] The inference being that no matter how much he might try to disguise his working-class origins, in matters of dress Case will always betray himself.

In Samuel Fuller's *Pick Up on South Street* (1953), Thelma Ritter plays the police informant and tie-peddler Moe Williams, who is first seen selling information about the identity of a particular 'cannon' – a pickpocket who targets women – whom the police are anxious to question.[37] Moe, complete with attaché case full of neckties, sells one of the detectives a tie for a dollar, before proceeding to strike a bargain for the information they seek. As the broadly anti-communist tale unfolds, where even among 'stoolies' and 'cannons' there is a code of honour that will not allow them to stoop so low as to helping a 'commie', we see Moe selling ties (presumably stolen) in the street as well as in her tie-festooned room in the Bowery, a retail cover operation masking her true occupation of selling information to the highest bidder. She persuades Candy (Jean Peters), the girl who has been pickpocketed by Skip McCoy (Richard Widmark), and who is also an unwitting Communist 'mule', to buy one of her ties before revealing the whereabouts of McCoy, informing her: 'I happen to carry a complete line of personality neckwear. Bargain prices!' This particular tie then becomes the bond between Candy and McCoy, even though at their first meeting McCoy calls it a 'crummy tie' and rejects Candy's advances by pretending to throttle her with it. Moe eventually meets her fate at the hands of the Communist spy and, as she slowly delivers her world-weary, anti-Communist swansong, the camera closes in on her head behind which hang

HOLIDAY
1938, dir. George Cukor.
[top] 'That pattern I seem to recognise'.

PICK UP ON SOUTH STREET
1953, dir. Samuel Fuller.
[middle] Moe selling ties and information;
[bottom] Saint Moe.

the assorted ties that act as a nimbus fabricated from flashy 1950s neckwear for the 'saintly' stoolie's martyrdom.

When not causing social embarrassment because of their style, or even becoming the backdrop to a life of petty crime, ties tend to cause sartorial distress – dropping into food, getting caught in machinery and generally taking on a dysfunctional life of their own. As discussed in the last section of this work, 'Stubborn Stains', Jack Vincenne's tie becomes spattered with blood as an ominous foreshadowing of the massacre to come in *L.A. Confidential* (1997) and, while not always so menacing, ties on film tend to act magnetically, attracting dirt and shame in equal proportions.[38] Witness Walter Matthau's pre-occupation with his stained tie in the 1963 film *Charade*.[39] Matthau plays the bogus CIA agent Hamilton Bartholomew, from whom Regina Lampert (Audrey Hepburn) seeks help after the murder of her husband. Bartholomew's entrance on screen has him interviewing Lampert in his office at the American Embassy, while desperately sponging a grease stain from his tie, forcing him to confess dourly. 'Excuse me for a moment, Mrs Lampert. Stubborn little devil! Dry cleaning wise things are all fouled up . . . Last time I sent out a tie only the spot came back!'[40] This declaration then prompts a lengthy speech on spying and espionage utilising a discourse full of cleaning and staining metaphors. *Charade* follows *Bringing Up Baby* in featuring Cary Grant once again grappling with the vicissitudes of clothing in another dysfunctional dress-rich vehicle, the later film including a tie-related scene where he sets a trap using his tie-pin as a nail round which he stretches a thread unravelled from his sock in order to tell him if Lampert leaves her hotel room. Cinematic ties as acceptable decorative details in otherwise sober masculine outfits rest uncomfortably on their wearers' chests, stubbornly refusing to remain clean, tied and of the correct pattern. They confound the typical male protagonist and if worn by those more conversant in matters of dress become the sign of psychological aberrations, which can lead even to murder.

CHARADE
1963, dir. Stanley Donen.
Sponger Bartholomew.

As with ties, scarves are rarely encountered cinematically as murder weapons, although eminently suitable. *Dial M for Murder*, however, features a scarf as an unsuccessful, or dysfunctional, murder weapon. On the night of the planned murder, Swann secretes himself behind some curtains and selects his own evening scarf as the weapon with which to dispatch Margot Wendice when summoned by the pre-arranged phone call. Amid the folds of the curtains, Swann knots the scarf in preparation and, owing to the shadowy darkness of the room and the curtains, the white scarf takes on an autonomous, almost ectoplasmic appearance, writhing and appearing to knot itself, while Swann's gloved hands remain indistinct. In the ensuing struggle Swann fails to strangle Margot and is stabbed to death with a pair of scissors. Tony Wendice, on his return, hastily re-arranges the crime scene, dousing the scarf with lighter fuel and burning it and planting a pair of Margot's stockings so that they will be mistaken for Swann's attempted murder weapon; it would appear that, cinematically at least, as in *The Boston Strangler*, stockings are more acceptable than scarves as asphyxiating agents.[1] A notably bizarre example of the scarf as a successful murder weapon can be found in Roger Corman's 1959 film *Bucket of Blood*, a delirious collage of beatnik drug culture, performance art and horror film.[2] Walter Paisley (Dick Miller), a waiter at the Yellow Door Café, becomes a sculptor manqué, enjoying momentary celebrity among the 'in crowd'. The reason for his newly found talent is that his lifelike 'sculptures' are in fact Walter's murder victims whom he covers in clay. Alice, a part-time model, becomes Walter's latest work of art, a 'lifelike' representation of a naked woman's struggle with asphyxiation, deriving its authenticity from the fact that earlier Walter dispatched Alice by strangling her with her own scarf as she posed for him.

Scarves, unlike the various accessories discussed so far, have what might be understood as an autonomous existence, an independence from the human body that makes them unique in the negative cinematic wardrobe. Unlike gloves, shoes and even hats, which to a greater or lesser degree echo the form of the body part on which they are worn, scarves are fundamentally

DIAL M FOR MURDER
[facing] 1954, dir. Alfred Hitchcock.

BUCKET OF BLOOD
1959, dir. Roger Corman.
[above] Walter creates another artwork.

flat, untailored pieces of cloth, their unspecified form allowing them to assume proportionately diverse functions. It could be argued that as a component of western fashionable dress, scarves and shawls act as textile conduits between the ancient, non-western draped tradition and modern western, tailored clothing, 'humanity sewn and humanity draped', as Perrot expresses it.[3] Scarves suggest a more fundamental approach to dressing, where the form is simply wrapped without additional shaping achieved through cutting and darting. Given this ancient antecedence, it is not surprising that in film scarves are often imbued with a mythical, supernatural power, are animated and mysterious. As this work has attempted to argue, much cinematic clothing is at its most significant when unworn, abandoned or divested; it is only then, in a state of dysfunction, that it can function alternatively. Jean Baudrillard, discussing the collected object, made this process clear when he observed that an object in a collection is freed from its normative functional state and is able to assume a meaning given to it by the collector; cinematic clothing often operates accordingly but, unlike the collected object, scarves in film function autonomously, unfettered by the dictates of the wearer.[4]

In *Killer's Kiss*, Stanley Kubrick's second feature film made in 1955, Davey Gordon (Jamie Smith), a welterweight boxer past his prime, meets and plans to run away with Gloria (Irene Kane), a 'taxi' dancer trapped in an abusive relationship with her boss, Vincent Rapallo (Frank Silvera).[5] As Davey walks to meet Gloria he encounters two inebriated conventioneers dressed in fezzes similar to those worn by members of the American Shriner organisation. They accost Davey, steal his scarf and proceed to perform a dance with it causing him to run after them and making him late for his assignation. This inconsequential incident has unexpected ramifications, becoming the narrative catalyst when, waiting for Davey, his manager is beaten up by the jealous Rapallo's henchmen, who mistake him for the boxer, setting up a chain of events that escalates into murder. While relatively brief, the scarf sequence has a visual resonance that seems excessive when considering its duration and incidental nature, the scarf 'dance' that the Shriners perform has a captivating Diane Arbus quality as we see the two fez-wearing drunks cavort with the scarf against a backdrop of illuminated New York dance halls and bars.

The visual significance afforded the scarf in *Killer's Kiss* is typical of this particular accessory's treatment in a number of films from different genres and periods. *Breakfast at Tiffany's* is one of the most extensively analysed films, central to debates concerning the status of the fashion designer versus the costume designer.[6] Holly Golightly's (Audrey Hepburn) relationship to clothing is central to the film, as is well known, and the audience is made aware from the outset that her elegant appearance is in fact arrived at chaotically. Following the iconic opening title sequence in which we see Golightly, immaculate after a night on the town, window-shopping at Tiffany's in the Manhattan dawn, she encounters Paul Varjak (George Peppard) in a scene that allows the audience to see behind her glamorous facade. She wears an oversized man's dress shirt doubling as a nightgown, keeps a pair of ballet pumps in the fridge, retrieves one of her black alligator shoes from a pannier carried on the back of a large stuffed toy donkey, spends a few seconds on hair and make-up and emerges in the famous ensemble of little black dress, wide-brimmed hat and flowing chiffon scarf. To her question: 'How do I look?' Varjak provides the response which the audience has been formulating: 'Very good. I must say I'm amazed!'[7] Her apparently dysfunctional toilet belies this immaculate soigné entrance and, to emphasise her chaotic sartorial artifice, we see her make final front-door adjustments to her image with the help of a makeshift dressing table formed from her letter-box which has a mirrored flap and safeguards her lipstick and perfume.

This haphazard elegance, or 'hangover chic' as it has been described, is a part of the film's characterisation of Golightly as chaotic, confused and vulnerable but, in addition to this carefully scripted nonchalance, Golightly's scarf performs a truly dysfunctional role that tends to be overlooked among the celebration of 'effortless style' which has become part of the film's continuing perception.[8] As she emerges in the outfit described and walks to the kitchen to retrieve her dark glasses, her scarf becomes wrapped round her face, obscuring her completely and, masked and sightless, she exits her apartment with Varjak. This fleeting moment of dysfunctionality seems to jar against the sequence's studied artifice; presumably too inconsequential to re-shoot, these few seconds are, it could be argued, as effective a deconstruction of Hepburn's fashionable cinematic image as is much of the critical commentary that has proliferated since the film's release. Her gamine beauty is hidden from the audience and the elaborate production is temporarily swept away, the scarf's wayward tendencies escaping set-dresser and cinematographer alike, and performing the function requested by Ferdinand in Webster's *The Duchess of Malfi* of 1612–13 on seeing his dead sister, to 'Cover her face. Mine eyes dazzle.'[9] When looked at in isolation, the image has a surreal, disturbing quality, reminiscent of an earlier moment of fashionable image-making and the work of Erwin Blumenfeld and his obsession with veiled, draped and masked female forms.[10] Alternatively, perhaps this hiding of Golightly's face is a subtle reminder of her character in Truman Capote's original novel as a paid escort or, as he described her, an 'American geisha': shame compels her face to be hidden and, as implausible as this might at first sound, it is reinforced later in the same scene when she encounters the wealthy older 'interior decorator', Emily Eustace Failenson, or '2E' as she is known (Patricia Neal).[11] Varjak is in reality a kept man, a male prostitute and 2E is reversing the traditional roles of the man installing his mistress in a convenient love-nest, the interior of which she has also decorated. The awkwardness of the encounter is again underscored by Golightly's wayward scarf and, as the two women are introduced to each other, the scarf again completely obscures Golightly's face, rendering her anonymous, faceless and a *persona non grata* in the company of the older, wealthier and 'respectable' woman.

A far more prosaic and less sophisticated example of the dysfunctional scarf is that of the suffocatingly long, home-made,

usually knitted variety. In fact, there is a link between the chic world of Holly Golightly and the cosy domesticity of the amateur knitter, as in a later scene from *Breakfast at Tiffany's* we see Holly knitting a strange, formless red object. This piece of knitting seems to have a life of its own and, typically, Holly has no idea what she is creating, suspecting that her knitting pattern may have got mixed up with an architectural blueprint. This out of control approach to the knitted scarf is a recurring motif in film, perhaps its most recent manifestation being the extravagantly long 'house' scarves worn in the *Harry Potter* films. The overlong, invariably striped, knitted scarf has long been established as a form of visual shorthand to denote the wearer possessing above-average intelligence, deriving in part from its academic associations and also from its inclusion in the wardrobe of elderly characters who need to protect themselves from inclement weather. As such the scarves become a vestimentary signal of the wisdom that comes with age. Harry Potter's scarves are merely the most recent in a long line of cinematic professorial scarves, filtered through the wardrobe department of the British television character Dr Who, whose fourth and lengthiest incarnation portrayed by Tom Baker sported an impossibly long scarf. A somewhat more stylish illustration of the endless knitted scarf is that given by Katharine Hepburn as a present to Spencer Tracy in the 1957 film *Desk Set*.[12] Bunny Watson (Hepburn) runs the reference department of a television company, which comes under threat of automation by the engineer and efficiency expert Richard Sumner (Tracy). Appealing perhaps to his more traditional academic sensibilities, she presents him with a knitted scarf in his college colours, declaring to the bemused Sumner: 'This is six feet long' and, informing him how long it took her to find, adds: 'There doesn't seem to be much demand for that kind of thing', a reference to her own department and their obsolete, human-centred research methods about to be swept away by computerisation.[13] The scarf, incongruous on the immaculately dressed Sumner, then takes centre stage in the following office Christmas party scene, as he wears it while playing the bongos and Watson even at one point using it as a skipping rope.

DESK SET
1957, dir. Walter Lang.
The college scarf as
symbol of academic authority.

Silk scarves in film retain some of the specialised, sage-like qualities detected in the knitted college scarf, but add to these a greater degree of sophistication and other-worldliness. As befits the silk square, which in fashion history has provided the ground for some spectacular liaisons between artists and accessory designers, the silk scarf is regularly visualised as an object imbued with its own sense of purpose, regarded with equal proportions of reverence and astonishment.[14] The simple act of a scarf blowing in the wind, for example, depicted in Todd Haynes's 2002 film *Far from Heaven* becomes melodramatically symbolic.[15] As the apparently happily married Cathy Whittaker's (Julianne Moore) reputation as an unconventional college student is discussed by her friends, her lilac scarf is suddenly caught up by the wind, curls round her shoulders then takes to the air, sailing over the roof of her perfect suburban house, seemingly lost. Later her friends laughingly discuss the sexual demands of their husbands over lunch and the viewer is compelled to share Cathy's discomfort as, prior to this scene, her attempt to make love to her husband has been rejected. Lunch and awkwardness over, she looks for her scarf and is startled by Raymond Deagan (Dennis Haysbert), the black gardener, who has retrieved the scarf and on returning it to her states: 'I had a feeling it might be yours . . . it's the colour, it just seemed right.'[16] This innocent exchange marks the beginning of Cathy's growing attraction to Deagan, and simultaneously her estrangement from her husband, the scarf becoming a magical textile that has brought the two protagonists together. It has 'found' Deagan and even prompts him prophetically to raise the question of 'colour' which will be central to Cathy's ostracisation from Connecticut society. The scarf scene also precedes the sequence where Cathy stumbles on her husband kissing another man, when her carefully constructed picture of Connecticut domestic bliss begins to crumble. The motif of illicit sexuality, both her husband's and, more shockingly perhaps to the local community, that of her own attraction as a white woman to her black gardener, is initiated by the liberation of the scarf from her neck, enabling both it and Cathy to 'fly free'.

FAR FROM HEAVEN
2002, dir. Todd Haynes.
[top] Cathy loses her inhibitions;
[bottom] 'I had a feeling it might be yours.'

This symbolic giving up, intentional or otherwise, of articles of dress is a regular motif in romantic melodramas of this period, and can be understood in the same context as the sequence from the previously discussed *Bell, Book and Candle*, which transforms the scarf as an apparently simple accessory into an object of mystery and wonder, its earthly beauty defying even the special abilities of the Manhattan witches whose story the film tells. It is Christmas and Gil Holroyd is giving presents to her brother and aunt, all modern-day witches. To her brother, the jazz buff, she gives records and to her Aunt Queenie (Elsa Lanchester) she gives a purple, sequinned lace-edged scarf. As Queenie takes it out of its box and holds it up in front of her face she exclaims: 'Oh! This is lovely, Gillian! What does it do?' Gillian: Makes you look beautiful.' Suspecting that it has magical properties, Queenie asks: 'You mean . . . ?' Gillian: 'No, Auntie, it has no powers. I just thought it was pretty.' Queenie (obviously disappointed): 'Oh . . . it . . . it is. Eh, it's very pretty . . . I . . . I love it'[17] While ultimately disappointing to a fully committed witch, to Gil Holroyd who is caught between mortal and supernatural attractions throughout the film, the scarf's earthly beauty is equal to any more otherworldly gift, acquiring the same status afforded scarves as 'works of art' by fashionable mortals.

The scarf as a harbinger or catalyst for harm might well have been what Queenie had in mind when unwrapping her present but it is in a later, much less magical (unless one attributes the fashion industry supernatural powers) but equally style-centred production that scarves seem to unleash their full potential for mayhem. In *The Devil Wears Prada* (2006), the much put-upon new junior assistant, Andy Sachs (Anne Hathaway), is charged with collecting, among numerous other tasks, some twenty-five scarves from Hermès for the formidable editor of *Runway* magazine, Miranda Priestley (Meryl Streep).[18] Some time later, Andy's fortunes have changed to the extent that she is now Priestley's favourite, supplanting her former assistant Emily (Emily Blunt), and Andy is forced to tell Emily that it is she who will be going to Paris, not Emily, to cover the season's

[facing] The scarf as a work of art. Printed Scarf, 'Standing Figures' designed by Henry Moore for Ascher Ltd, 1946, silk (Philaldelphia Museum of Art. Purchased with funds contributed by an anonymous donor, 1989).

BELL, BOOK AND CANDLE
1958, dir. Richard Quine.
[top] Supernaturally beautiful.

THE DEVIL WEARS PRADA
2006, dir. David Frankel.
[bottom] Airborne Hermès.

collections, a piece of news that Andy knows will devastate Emily. Andy contacts Emily who, in a reversal of the previous scene, is now the junior laden down with the distinctive orange Hermès bags and, distracted by Andy's phone call, Emily is knocked down by a car. The collision sends the bags hurtling into the air, releasing a flurry of multi-coloured silk scarves that flutter to earth as the scene cuts to Emily hospitalised, wounded and unable to go to Paris, her fashionable life apparently terminated.

While the presence of the Hermès scarves is perhaps co-incidental to Emily's misfortunes, certain scarves display genuinely magical properties in film. For example, in William Dieterle's rapturous fantasy *Portrait of Jennie* (1948), the ghostly Jennie of the title is summoned up when the struggling artist Eben Adams (Joseph Cotton) finds a newspaper-wrapped parcel on a bench in Central Park.[19] On his discovery of the parcel, Jennie (Jennifer Jones) magically materialises and declares it to be hers. After spending the afternoon together, which includes Adams sketching the young girl, he returns home and unwraps the parcel to find a silk scarf. This scarf, it appears, has not only summoned up the ghostly Jennie but also become the catalyst for his future fame and success as a painter, as he sells the sketch he made of Jennie and then embarks on the portrait that gives the film its title. At his next meeting with Jennie, she has mysteriously aged and when Adams returns the scarf to her she cannot recall having left it. She then suggests: 'I'll tell you what, why don't you keep it for me until I grow up, then I'll have one more reason to grow up fast', which she does at an extraordinary pace, becoming significantly older each time they meet.[20] The scarf acts as Adams's link between his mortal world and the timeless, or at least time-accelerated, world of the spectral Jennie; if mortal scarves can be understood as textile remnants of more ancient forms of dress, then, similarly, the scarf in *Portrait of Jennie* ties together Adams's post-war New York and Jennie's timeless topography.

A more direct link between this world and the next is forged by the scarf featured in the séance sequences in David Lean's

PORTRAIT OF JENNIE
1948, dir. William Dieterle.
[top] The timeless scarf

BLITHE SPIRIT
1945, dir. David Lean.
[bottom] Setting the scene.

1945 film of the Noël Coward play *Blithe Spirit*.[21] Madame Arcati's (Margaret Rutherford) burnt-orange scarf inscribed with the signs of the zodiac recalls in its decoration the vogue for artists' scarves mentioned earlier, and can be understood aesthetically as an early example of the desire for fantasy that informed post-war fashions, culminating in the excesses of Dior and the return of luxurious embellishment of clothing and accessories. As a successful part of the exorcist's paraphernalia, however, the scarf is ultimately unsuccessful: although introducing a note of chic occultism into the decorative scheme of the drawing room when Madame Arcati throws it over a table lamp, the ghosts of Richard Condomine's (Rex Harrison) two wives remain stubbornly present. More effective, but equally comedic, is the 'magical' scarf that is bequeathed to Vince Vaughan playing Peter LaFleur, the coach of the Average Joes in *DodgeBall* (2004).[22] The scarf in question belongs to the legendary dodgeball champion Patches O'Houlihan (Rip Torn) who, now elderly and wheelchair-bound, becomes the Average Joes' sadistic, no-holds-barred coach. After Patches' bizarre death, it is up to LaFleur to bring his side to victory and finding himself in the final of the championship pitted against the odious White Goodman (Ben Stiller), he calls on the power of Patches' scarf. Retrieving it from inside his shorts, LaFleur holds it reverentially in front of him and asks it for guidance. Magically, Patches' face materialises in the centre of the stained scarf, a comedic hybrid between the Turin Shroud and St Veronica's veil which, according to Christian legend, retained the image of Jesus after she used it to wipe his forehead on the road to Calvary. The apparition of Patches instructs LaFleur to trust his instincts, before mysteriously disappearing again; LaFleur then proceeds to tie the scarf across his eyes and thus blindfolded miraculously dodges the ball hurled at him by Goodman (see illus. p. 152). The still blindfolded LaFleur then swiftly returns a shot, hitting Goodman right between the eyes and winning the tournament for the Average Joes. Relic, veil, weapon, blindfold, airborne harbinger, the scarf in film is all and none of these things. Inert material that undulates with a life of its

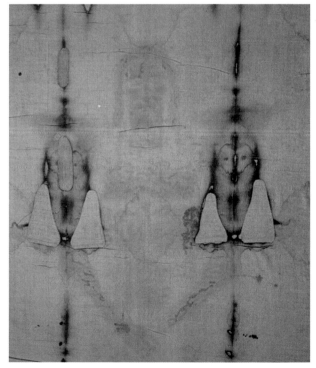

own, a flat plane that is transformed by a simple knot or convulsion into a thing of beauty and evil, it seems that the scarf has an indeterminacy, a statelessness absent from other accessories, the precise form of the hat or shoe, for example. This formlessness, to call up Bataille's famous condition, is what lends the scarf its visual power, whether momentarily playing across and obscuring Audrey Hepburn's face or escaping from Julianne Moore's neck to sail free for an instant above the rooftops only to disappear again from sight.[23] The scarf's fluid, amorphous movement across the screen dematerialises all else in the frame, if only for a split second. Looked at as stills, these often inconsequential passages make the viewer aware of the fundamental artifice of film, for they resist being 'still' and remain a blur.

The scarf's multivalency has more recently been exploited in the 2009 horror film *Drag Me to Hell* previously discussed in 'Cloaking Devices'. There the scarf or kerchief is a small square edged with lace and decorated with rosebuds. It is first seen when Christine Brown (Alison Lohman) refuses to grant a loan extension to the formidable gypsy, Mrs Ganush (Lorna Raver), who coughs into it and then places her false teeth on

it. The square next appears as a deceptively innocent herald drifting hypnotically like a butterfly in an underground car park as Brown prepares to drive home. She watches the scarf flutter then loom up in front of her windscreen, only to float on by, and as she tracks its progress into the distance behind her, she is confronted by the face of Mrs Ganush who has materialised in the back seat of her car. The scarf appears to be acting as a form of textile familiar, conjuring up and preceding its owner, but unlike the romantic materialisations of Raymond Deagan in *Far From Heaven* or Jennie in *Portrait of Jennie*, this scarf has summoned up harm, its beguiling flower-sprigged flutterings being the overture to the bloody struggle that takes place between the gypsy and Brown. Later as Brown journeys to the cemetery in order to lift the curse that has been placed on her, the scarf re-materialises. As it flies towards her windscreen, the grimacing face of the gypsy woman becomes visible within the folds of the scarf, almost causing Brown to lose control of the car, but as quickly as the terrifying face presses against her windshield it is caught up by the wipers and dragged back and forth like an old rag. The attempt to make Brown crash the car having failed, the scarf revives and is sucked inside the car via the radiator grille, penetrates the interior of the car and emerges from the dashboard, shooting towards Brown's face, blinding and suffocating her. As with the raincoat ensnared round the buffer of the train in *Seven Days to Noon* discussed in Part 1's 'Exchange Mechanisms' or Isadora Duncan's strangulation, the collision between textiles and automated transport, whether fictional or actual, is always a portent of destruction. From the materialisation of the gypsy's face, evoking Patches O'Houlihan's magical apparition, to the obliteration of Holly Golightly's face discussed in *Breakfast at Tiffany's*, this scarf explores every dysfunctional possibility. Now suckered onto Brown's face, its printed rosebuds become her eyes and mouth, taking on an eerie death's-head formation, which is gone as soon as registered, a vision that can neither be fully comprehended nor captured but acts as a portent of her own eventual death. As Georges Didi-Huberman proposed concerning the stains on the Turin Shroud: 'It seems only to exist in tonal variations, only as an effect of its support . . . the tonal variations of the fabric have no precise limits, sequence or articulation', a description befitting the amorphous com-position of the scarf in *Drag Me to Hell*.[24]

Brown manages to stop the car and gets out clawing the scarf away from her face, eventually casting it onto the ground. No sooner does it touch the ground, however, than it rises up again and flies straight towards Brown's mouth and down into her throat, in an attempt at internal throttling where external suffocation has failed. The avenging scarf catalogues and enacts every variety of asphyxiation and if not for Brown managing to hang on to its tip, its mission at this point would have been successful. Brown's struggle to pull the scarf back up from her windpipe is graphically realised and, even when once finally expelled and torn in two, it attempts to re-form itself before finally expiring under Brown's boot. The religious symbolism is inescapable, as Brown performs a horror-movie translation of Jerusalem's Temple veil rent apart at the moment of Christ's death on the Cross: 'And, behold, the veil of the temple was rent in twain from the top to the bottom; and the earth did quake, and the rocks rent'.[25]

DODGEBALL
2004, dir. Rawson Marshall Thurber.
[facing] Second sight.

DRAG ME TO HELL
2009, dir. Sam Raimi.
[top] The scarf as familiar;
[middle] becoming scarf;
[bottom] internalisation.

PART 4

He wears the finest clothes
The best designers, heaven knows
Oooh, from his head down to his toes
Halston Gucci, Fiorucci
He looks like a still
That man is dressed to kill[1]

The relationship between an excessive attention to stylish and conspicuous forms of dress and criminal activity is a recurrent visual narrative 'shorthand' throughout cinematic history. Studied, immaculate, exceedingly fashionable or flashy tailoring is the hallmark of the cinematic and literary gangster alike, and provides the perfect counterpoint to the destruction and carnage wrought by its wearers. It is as if spectacular tailoring provides, if not completely effective camouflage, certainly a sartorial deflection or veneer for the gangster, a flawless disguise that cloaks a dysfunctional and chaotic disposition.

A felon's desire for the admiration and acceptance that accompanies good tailoring is so central to many of the earliest cinematic incarnations of the gangster that it can almost become the raison d'être for his criminal activities and ascendancy. Paul Muni, playing the mobster Tony Camonte in *Scarface*, directed in 1932 by Howard Hawks and Richard Rosson, is a case in point; as we chart Tony's violent rise to criminal stardom we also witness him buying increasingly ostentatious suits, jewellery and expensive handmade shirts.[2] Yet, no matter how flashily or expensively dressed, Camonte's psychopathic tendencies must surface and, while his tailoring becomes increasingly flamboyant, his scarred face remains an insistent indicator of his equally disfigured psyche. Films including *Scarface*, *The Public Enemy* and *Little Caesar* established a cinematic template that both reflected organised criminal activity during prohibition America and also helped to construct the public image of what the typical gangster looked like and aspired to. Indeed, it is rumoured that Al Capone himself liked *Scarface* so much that he had his own copy of the film.[3]

SCARFACE
1932, dir. Howard Hawks and Richard Rosson.
[facing] Tony's sartorial ascendancy
(Everett Collection/Rex Features).

THE PUBLIC ENEMY
1931, dir. William A. Wellman.
[above] The trappings of success
(Moviestore Collection/Rex Features).

This symbiosis between the fictional Hollywood gangster of the 1930s and the media-conscious leaders of actual organised crime in America at the time is a potent example of cinema's influence on men's fashion during the Depression years, and as profound as the more widely acknowledged influence that Hollywood musicals and so-called 'women's pictures' had on female dress in the same period.[4] For all the moral lessons clearly signposted in these films – that crime and its trappings such as expensive clothes do not pay – the aspirational signals sent out by screen villains and indeed by the actors who regularly played them are undeniable. For example, George Raft, one of the memorable screen gangsters from the period, is indicative of this sartorial blurring between on-screen characterisation and off-screen personal style and history. Raft's biography could easily be that of one of the characters he later found fame playing in the early 1930s. Born in a ten-family tenement building in the Hell's Kitchen district of Manhattan, Raft had by the 1920s progressed from amateur boxing, pool-hall hustling, working as a gigolo and driving bootleg liquor trucks for his friend the racketeer Owney 'The Killer' Madden into a celebrated dancer headlining at a number of popular New York nightspots as well as on Broadway. He swiftly established a reputation as one of the sharper and more fashionable dressers of his circle, noted for being an early wearer of dark shirts with a pale tie, and reputedly using a full jar of Vaseline to achieve his signature 'patent leather' pomaded hairstyle. His progression to leading cinematic gangster, as celebrated as Edward G. Robinson and James Cagney at the time, was kick-started when he took the role of the coin-tossing sidekick Guino Rinaldo to Muni's Camonte in *Scarface*. Raft's increasingly flamboyant appearance both on and off screen, as well as his acquaintance with Madden and a number of other notorious underworld figures such as Bugsy Siegel and Meyer Lansky, the 'mob's accountant', increased his reputation and helped perfect his construction as the spectacularly tailored hood-cum-actor. A measure of Raft's widespread recognition as a sartorial leader can be judged by his appearance in the July

1936 edition of the English bespoke tailoring magazine *The Tailor and Cutter*, where an image of the strikingly dressed Raft appears under the heading 'Clothes on the Screen' whose text details his wardrobe, including 'loose weave Shetland of brown and white . . . tan and white sport shoes, dark brown shirt with matching pocket handkerchief and a light tie.'[5]

This heightened, overly fashionable clothing of the classic Hollywood gangster acts as a form of sartorial defence, tailored armour perhaps, that distinguishes the mobster as an extra-ordinary being, beyond the bourgeois conventions of correct and acceptable dressing. The criminal's spectacular clothing, however, is simultaneously suggestive of a fundamental flaw, for throughout history the male who pays too much attention to personal appearance and clothing has always been depicted as 'other', deviant, unhealthily particular and ultimately 'worthless', as the essayist William Hazlitt made clear when he suggested (in 1819) that 'Those who make their dress a principal part of themselves, will, in general, become of no more value than their dress'.[6] A fastidious man who dresses to be noticed is represented as suspect, untrustworthy, often effeminate and homosexual. This equation of obsessive appearance, criminality and homosexuality is a persistent undercurrent in many of the classic Hollywood mob films of the 1930s, when any more explicit reference to male sexuality would have been strictly taboo. The previously mentioned *Little Caesar* of 1931 is one such example, where Edward G. Robinson playing Rico Bandello (obviously modelled on Al Capone) is seen, once his criminal ascendancy has been established, immaculately if flashily tailored complete with diamond studs and tie-pins. Rico, a paranoid petty criminal with a superman complex who rises through the criminal ranks, displays a rampant misogyny and incredulity towards romantic heterosexual relationships, while simultaneously maintaining an equally strong, and at times thinly veiled, attraction to his long-time male buddy Joe.

Baldassare Castiglione writing in Venice in 1528 notes in his *Book of the Courtier* that the ideal nobleman should pay less attention to his appearance and have a countenance

July 3, 1936   835   THE TAILOR AND CUTTER

Clothes on the Screen

FOR SUMMER COOLNESS.—When not appearing in his current Paramount picture, "Yours for the Asking," George Raft cools off in a loose weave Shetland of brown and white mixture. With it he wears tan and white sport shoes, dark brown shirt with matching pocket handkerchief and a light tie. The Panama completes the outfit.

LITTLE CAESAR
1931, dir. Mervyn LeRoy.
[above] Rico and Joe, partners in style
(SNAP/Rex Features).

[left] George Raft as he appeared in
The Tailor and Cutter in 1936.

not so soft and womanish as many procure to have, that doe not onely courle the haire, and picke the browes, but also pamper them selves in everie point like the most wanton and dishonest women in the world: and a man would thinke them in going, in standing, and in all their gestures so tender and faint, that their members were readie to flee one from an other . . .[7]

Given the censure that has long surrounded the narcissistic male, it is perhaps ironic that such an overtly masculine construction as the cinematic gangster should be so often characterised as foppish and self-obsessed. However, it is precisely through this excessive attention to personal appearance that the criminal distinguishes and elevates himself from the crowd. He has the means, self-regard and arrogance to defy convention and court the approbation of the law-abiding status quo in matters sartorial. Stella Bruzzi in her *Undressing Cinema: Clothing and Identity in the Movies* suggests: 'When considering the costumes of the screen gangster the spectator is struck by this ambivalence, that here are characters who have both cultivated an aggressively masculine image and are immensely vain, and whose sartorial flamboyance, far from intimating femininity or effeminacy, is the most important sign of their masculine social and material success.'[8]

Bruzzi here identifies a number of fundamental characteristics pertaining to the flashily dressed gangster, including the obvious function of noticeably fashionable or expensive clothes to signify economic superiority and success. The gangster demonstrates not only his ability to afford (or at least procure) expensive clothes but also, in their very luxuriousness and impracticality, suggests that the wearer either does not have to work for a living or at least is involved in a profession that does not involve manual labour or physical exertion and therefore the risk of soiling his clothes. As Veblen noted in his *Theory of the Leisure Class*, 'Our dress, therefore, in order to serve its purpose effectually, should not only be expensive, but it should also make plain to all observers that the wearer is not engaged

in any kind of productive labour.'[9] His correlation holds true today as much as it did when written in 1899, and in our contemporary technologised society that has seen the erosion of traditional manual labour, the necessity to appear not merely white-collar but apparently leading a life consisting solely of leisure activities and formal social engagements has become the norm for many, regardless of their actual economic status.

One of the clearly defined examples of this 'conspicuous consumption', to use the term first formulated by Veblen, can be found in the obsession with clothing that characterises the lifestyle, aspiration and indeed the lyrical content of many of today's hip hop and, for want of a better term, gangsta rap artists, who can be considered as the natural successors of the sartorially distinguished cinematic gangster. This discussion started with a consideration of the 1932 film *Scarface* but it is Brian De Palma's 1983 remake of the film, starring Al Pacino as Tony Montana, which has had an enormous impact on contemporary rap artists.[10] Leaving aside the obvious criminal career trajectory shared by both the character and many contemporary 'foot soldiers', the look of the film, Pacino's wardrobe, his hedonistic and violent lifestyle and so on have been the inspiration and template for those artists responsible for the offshoot of rap sometimes dubbed Mafioso rap, whose lyrical content typically celebrates organised crime, mobsters, designer clothes, violence, champagne, prostitution and drugs. Sections of dialogue and the original score from the film have been sampled for countless tunes and provided the titles for any number of tracks, while artists such as Jay-Z and Brad Terrence Jordan (who changed his name to Scarface) have publicly expressed their obsession with the film. *Scarface*'s iconic status within rap has even spawned a documentary entitled *Scarface: Origins of a Hip Hop Classic* which features a roll-call of rap luminaries testifying to the influence of the film.[11] This suggests that the distinction, as with George Raft's career in the 1920s and 30s, between fictional cinematic gangster and a contemporary commercialised and mediated gangster lifestyle has become increasingly blurred. As William

Jelani Cobb states in his 2007 book *To the Break of Dawn*, 'The hip hop narrative is the unrequited step-child of the American crime epic; the music takes as its primary concerns those same themes expressed in this country's primordial folklore . . . themes projected onto the screen of the mind by Coppola, Scorsese, and De Palma.'[12]

In both the film, as worn by Pacino, and in the appearance of today's rap stars, immaculate and expensive tailoring fulfils the true function of spectacle as defined by Guy Debord in his *Society of the Spectacle*, where apart from the obvious signalling of the power and success of the wearer, it also unites its audiences in a spectacle of aspiration that masks the true separation and disadvantage of the group to whom it appeals. As Debord suggests: 'The spectacle presents itself as something enormously positive, indisputable and inaccessible. It says nothing more than "that which appears is good, that which is good appears". The attitude which it demands in principle is passive acceptance which in fact it already obtained by its manner of appearing without reply, by its monopoly of appearance.'[13] Again, the promotion of a lifestyle of excess, where the acquisition of material goods at any cost and the subsequent display of those same goods is essential, has its origins in the construction of the avaricious, sharply dressed cinematic gangster, so that we have now arrived at a moment where the media actively promotes Tony Montana's dictum: 'The world is yours!'[14] A spectacular construction of excess has emerged whose components are drawn from the increasingly interrelated worlds of celebrity culture, popular music and fashion, which in its seemingly relentless exhortation to consume would perhaps have startled even Veblen, and conforms more to a concept of invidious consumption, that is, consumption expressly undertaken to induce envy, rather than the relatively straightforward processes of consumption designed to express the consumer's status.

One of the most effective figureheads of this assemblage of aspirational desire is the singer Kanye West (the Louis Vuitton Don), whose lyrics are littered with the labels of a designer lifestyle and who has previously worked with Marc Jacobs on

SCARFACE
1983, dir. Brian De Palma.
[top] Before, and [bottom], after.

Kanye West front row at Philip Lim,
Autumn/Winter 2009, New York
(Startraks Photo/Rex Features).

a shoe line for Louis Vuitton in 2009. He commissioned Ricardo Tisci, the head designer at Givenchy, to design the album artwork for his 2011 release with Jay-Z entitled *Watch the Throne* including the track 'Niggas in Paris' which contains the lines: 'What's Gucci, my nigga? What's Louis, my nigga? What's drugs, my dealer? What's that jacket, Margiela?' These lines West contextualised, in an interview given to *XXL Magazine*, by explaining: 'I am where art meets commercial. The sweet spot between the hood and Hollywood. Having a conversation with Karl Lagerfeld and Jay-Z within the same hour. When we're in Paris dressing all crazy at fashion shows, we listening to Jeezy. Jeezy in Paris, that's what it is.'[15] He continued his obsession with the world of high fashion by launching his debut women's-wear label DW Kanye West in 2011, which was met with a mixed critical reception by the fashion press.[16] West's consuming desire to achieve both cultural and fashionable ascendancy provides a contemporary translation of the 1930s film gangster's rise to power publicised by ever more expensive clothes and trappings. His acute understanding of the relationship between the worlds of fashion and popular culture and the social esteem that the ability to consume their related products can confer echoes Pierre Bourdieu's findings:

> If among all these fields of possibles, none is more obviously predisposed to express social differences than the world of luxury goods, and, more particularly, cultural goods, this is because the relationship of distinction is objectively inscribed within it, and is reactivated, intentionally or not, in each act of consumption, through the instruments of economic and cultural appropriation which it requires.[17]

Of course, Prada dinner jackets and front-row seats at couture fashion shows are well out of reach of the average West fan, but this is precisely the point: as Debord suggested, in order to function properly the spectacle must be 'inaccessible'.[18] The shedding of more conventional streetwear in favour of tuxedos and cashmere that many of West's contemporaries have affected returns us once more to the sartorial aspirations of the cinematic

gangster. In the 1930s mob films previously discussed, the main protagonists undergo a similar transformation and as soon as their ill-gotten gains allow, dress more and more expensively. What many of these films also depict is the chief protagonist's love of flashy clothes contrasted with a more successful – for which we can read more violent – criminal, who has given up the need for ostentatious display and conspicuous consumption, in favour of a more refined and understated and, by implication, higher-class form of dressing. For these high-achieving criminals, 'displaying wealth was no longer equated with displaying worth. Manliness and sobriety were thus means of claiming social as well as political authority. Social leadership for men was determined by renouncing the effeminating world of fashion'.[19] These characters form a benchmark that the gangster on the make hopes one day to emulate but, as is often pointed out, these impeccably and tastefully dressed characters consider themselves businessmen rather than criminals, and so until the 'hands on' approach to violence has been left behind and they have achieved sufficient power so that others can do their dirty work, our cinematic gangster's clothes must always echo in their dubious taste their similarly questionable criminal activities. In the film version of 1947 of Graham Greene's celebrated novel *Brighton Rock* (entitled *Young Scarface* when originally released in America), Richard Attenborough plays Pinkie Brown, the seventeen-year-old razor-wielding psychopath and small-time hoodlum running a protection racket on Brighton's racecourse.[20] Pinkie's clothes and those of his gang members will be returned to shortly but in the scene where he has a meeting with Colleoni, the crime boss on whose territory Pinkie is ineffectually trying to muscle in, the aspiration of the fledgling gangster for the more established criminal's lifestyle is made apparent. We see Pinkie covering his obvious feelings of inadequacy as he confronts Colleoni, resplendent in discreetly cut suit, carnation and silk handkerchief, in the sumptuous surroundings of the hotel from which he runs his criminal empire. Pinkie suggests a further meeting at the racecourse, to which Colleoni replies that he has not been on a racecourse for twenty years and that he is now a businessman, nothing he can try with his men would affect him; he ends his speech with the reassertion that 'No, you can't damage a business man', to which Pinkie replies, in a forerunner of Tony Montana's famous speech in *Scarface*: 'You think you're all the world, don't ya?'[21]

An overtly showy dress sense is understood as the inevitable accompaniment to a lack of sophistication, refinement and taste, the sort of characterisation that Raymond Chandler constructs via his clothing for Moose Malloy in *Farewell, My Lovely* (1940):

> He wore a shaggy Borsalino hat, a rough grey sports coat with white golf balls on it for buttons, a brown shirt, a yellow tie, pleated grey flannel slacks and alligator shoes with white explosions on the toes. From his outer breast pocket cascaded a show handkerchief of the same brilliant yellow as his tie. There were a couple of coloured feathers tucked into the band of his hat, but he didn't really need them. Even on Central Avenue, not the quietest-dressed street in the world, he looked about as inconspicuous as a tarantula on a slice of angel food.[22]

The predilection for attention-grabbing outfits is regarded as proof of criminal tendencies by cinematic sleuths and felons alike. In *Gideon's Day* (1958) the corrupt detective Eric Kirby (Derek Bond) sports a distinctive blue windowpane checked waistcoat on the same day that he is exposed for taking bribes by his superior, Chief Inspector Gideon (Jack Hawkins). After suspending Kirby from duty, Gideon asks the doughty Sergeant Golightly what he thinks of him, eliciting the response: 'I never did trust a man who wears that kind of waistcoat, sir!', proof enough, it seems, of Kirby's disreputable character.[23] However, it is not just the law-abiding who find flashy gangster 'threads' problematic: Pearly Gates (Peter Sellers) is the criminal leader of a gang forced to cooperate with the police in order to thwart the activities of a rival gang in *The Wrong Arm of the Law* (1961).[24] As part of the plan to expose the gang and bring them to justice, Gates agrees that Chief Inspector 'Nosey' Parker (Lionel Jeffries) will go undercover and pose as one of Gates's

BRIGHTON ROCK
1947, dir. John Boulting.
[top] Pinkie is challenged by
Colleoni's tailoring.

GIDEON'S DAY
1958, dir. John Ford.
[bottom] 'That kind of waistcoat.'

gang, but in order to do this will need a new wardrobe, one that will not immediately proclaim his true profession. Gates hands Parker two hundred pounds suggesting: 'Get yourself kitted out with some decent clobber, not too flash. I like my boys to look smart, you know: single weight worsted, two button, no turn ups.'[25] This precise wardrobe specification is ignored; however, as Parker transforms himself into 'Big Time' Parker resplendent in bow tie and brocade smoking jacket, it suggests that it may not be just the criminal fraternity who likes to cut a dash. If Pearly Gates can understand and tolerate Parker's sartorial splendour, no such leniency is granted J. Edgar Hoover's (Leonardo DiCaprio) fledgling agents in the first days of his heading up the nascent Federal Bureau of Investigation. In an early scene in *J. Edgar* (2009) Hoover is enlightening his first four agents as to the Bureau's anti-Communist mission but is challenged by Agent Stokes, who in his broad chalk-stripe suit and burnt-orange tie stands out among his colleagues' more discreet beige and brown outfits.[26] Hoover turns on Stokes, ordering him to 'expose Miss Goldman's sham marriage and you will change that suit of yours.' 'Pardon me, John?' responds the astonished Stokes, to which Hoover replies: 'Your suit sir, your suit! This isn't a saloon. You have some respect for yourself, and more importantly have respect for this department.' The equivalence of an attention to matters of fashion with a liberal ideology is made plain, and this sartorial encounter signals the demise of Stokes, who in a later scene is summarily dismissed by Hoover.[27]

Obsessive colour co-ordination such as Moose Malloy's insistent grey and yellow combination is not merely the sign of the fastidiously flashy gangster but can be indicative of a deeper psychological disorder. The desire to match or contrast every item of clothing down to the most insignificant detail of the smallest accessory suggests a desire for control that borders on the sociopathic. Construction of a pristine and obsessively matched surface for the body acts as a form of sartorial armour, its chromatic perfection relaying a vestimentary message that here is a person who is in control, who will brook no deviation

WRONG ARM OF THE LAW
1961, dir. Cliff Owen.
[top] 'Nosey' Parker enjoys the
trappings of a life of crime.

J. EDGAR
2009, dir. Clint Eastwood.
[bottom] 'This isn't a saloon, sir!'

and derives pleasure in finding the perfect 'match', but only of a sartorial variety, as emotional or sexual 'matches' are invariably too unpredictable for these obsessive co-ordinators. These dazzling carapaces deflect and defend from harm, making their wearers simultaneously conspicuous and untouchable; shielded by silk and cashmere, the criminal retreats momentarily at least into a world where 'making it' is measured out in hand-made shoes and made-to-measure shirts.

One of the more impassioned speeches concerning the difference expressed sartorially between the nouveau riche mobster who favours flashy clothes over subtle tailoring is delivered by Harry Pendel (Geoffrey Rush), the 'Savile Row' tailor in *The Tailor of Panama* (2001).[28] The film uses a tailoring discourse throughout to tell its story of corrupt politicians and mobsters in Panama, the activities of the equally dubious Pendel, who in fact learnt his tailoring 'in the slammer', and Andrew Osward, a British government agent seconded to Panama where he can do as little damage as possible.[29] The pair's first meeting takes place in Pendel & Braithwaite, the tailors, and as Osward is measured up by Pendel for some new suits, the tailoring/political espionage discourse proliferates. This includes references to which way Osward dresses, to the 'left or right, as a means of ascertaining political affiliations, and Osward's suggestion to Pendel that he is after his 'Rock of Eye', the legendary unquantifiable expertise and instinctive affinity with the cutting of cloth that master tailors are meant to possess and which is used in the film as a metaphor for Pendel's criminal and political know-how in Panama. Later in the film, Pendel, enraged by an enquiry from one of the mobsters whom he is fitting for a suit as to why he cannot make him one like Armani, responds furiously: 'Do you think Armani could make a suit like Harry Pendel?' One of the other gangsters asks 'Why not?' prompting a further impassioned outburst from Pendel:

OK. Get out! Fuck off! Go down the road and buy an Armani. Save yourself a thousand dollars. See if I care! At Pendel & Braithwaite you get Savile Row bespoke tailoring with four hundred years of tradition behind it. Down the road you get an Italian gent's outfitter and if you don't understand the difference, then save your money![30]

The clear inference here is that mobsters are only impressed by the most fashionable or the most spectacular styling and that it takes a true 'gent' or perhaps an older, more established criminal, like Pendel himself, to appreciate traditional tailoring. Otherwise they just end up being the butt of fellow criminals' disdain, as demonstrated in *The Dark Corner* (1946), when the henchman Stauffer (William Bendix) describes the crooked lawyer Tony Jardine as 'Tall, yellow hair, fancy dresser – thinks he's class on a stick!'[31]

As stated earlier, many cinematic gangsters embark on an accelerated course of sartorial refinement, so one of the first things Tony Camonte in the original *Scarface* makes is a bulk purchase of luxury shirts of which, he declares to his girlfriend Poppy, he intends to wear one each day. However, as the gangster on the make is invariably an interloper into the world of sartorial refinement, there is the constant doubt as to whether the clothes being purchased and so conspicuously flaunted are the genuine article; the lack of familiarity with fine cloth will always leave a little room for vestimentary insecurity. John Shaft (Samuel L. Jackson) in the 2000 film *Shaft* exploits just such criminal insecurities in his response to People Hernandez (Jeffrey Wright), the drug dealer whose shirt Shaft has just grabbed.[32] Hernandez: 'This is Egyptian cotton motherfucker . . . twenty-two thread. That's like half your shitty-ass pay check, OK?' Shaft: 'You wouldn't know Egyptian cotton if the Pharaoh himself sent it to you, you knockoff-wearing motherfucker!'[33] There are, however, certain shadowy figures whose ability to recognise good-quality clothing is indisputable. In the 1976 film version of *The Great Gatsby*, no matter how much Gatsby spends on his clothes and mansion, and even though he confesses 'I've got a man in London who buys all my clothes', he is persistently dogged by speculation from his Long Island neighbours as to his background and the possibility that his fortune might be derived from bootlegging.[34] In order to impress Daisy Buchanan (Mia Farrow), Gatsby (Robert Redford) provides her with a tour of his mansion that includes the celebrated shirt scene in which he shows off his collection of hand-made English shirts. This reduces Daisy to tears in a cloud of multi-coloured cottons and silks, a perfect visualisation of a character attempting to establish himself as a man of taste and breeding via a spectacular act of sartorial exhibitionism. Yet it appears that no amount of Jermyn Street linen (the shirts for the film version were supplied by the bespoke British shirtmakers Turnbull & Asser, whose boxes are clearly seen in shot, even though the rest of the men's clothes were provided by Ralph Lauren) can ever provide effective protection for characters like Jay Gatsby who is never properly accepted into Long Island society, or both of the Scarfaces Muni and Pacino, alongside Peoples Hernandez, who for all their finery meet violent ends befitting their violent careers.

Returning to *Brighton Rock*, Pinkie Brown's clothes, though 'spivvy' in appearance, pale into the background when compared to his older gang members Dallow and Cubitt.[35] Dallow (William Hartnell) wears an exaggeratedly cut, dog-tooth checked suit that signals his criminal status as effectively as would a sign round his neck, while Cubitt (Nigel Stock) in loud stripes, trilby hat and moustache is the perfect incarnation of the spiv or petty criminal and black marketeer. Their spectacular appearance next to Pinkie, the truly vicious criminal and gang leader, acts as a form of distraction (see illus. p. 168). This use of subservient gang members as a form of sartorial deflection is seen in one of the film's early scenes in which the three men enter a pub where a woman is singing. Pinkie's very first words in the film – 'Won't anybody shut that brass's mouth' – establish his violent temper from the outset and cut through the almost cartoon-like swagger of Dallow and Cubitt in their extravagant outfits.[36] His simmering hatred boils over and he exits, smashing a stack of glasses on the counter, while Dallow and Cubitt's outré style, which at the beginning of the scene acts as a form of vestimentary

THE TAILOR OF PANAMA
2001, dir. John Boorman.
[top] Harry Pendel, the 'Savile Row'
tailor lectures the mobsters on the
shortcomings of Armani.

THE GREAT GATSBY
1976, dir. Jack Clayton.
[bottom] Gatsby's linen fails
to confer respect.

BRIGHTON ROCK
1947, dir. John Boulting.
Dallow and Cubitt provide
sartorial distraction.

comedy, is transformed into a sartorially dysfunctional counter-point to Pinkie's mounting psychosis.

Pinkie's obvious misogyny is hinted at in his distaste for the singer. Again, the correlation between possible homosexuality, or at least sexual naiveté in Pinkie's case, and sadism as essential traits for the crime boss (established as far back cinematically as *Little Caesar*) is further developed in British gangster films. However, there is an essential difference, in that no longer does the criminal sadist take centre stage in terms of dress but rather leaves the possible charge of effeminacy or at least conspicu-ously inappropriate dress to his henchmen, who invariably wear the more extreme outfits. In *Villain* (1971) Richard Burton plays the sadistic and psychopathic Vic Dakin, a character based on Ronnie Kray, one of the two notorious Kray twins who dominated London's criminal underworld in the 1950s and 60s who, as well as their criminal activities, became celebrities who appeared on television, mixing with film stars and entertainers and being photographed by the leading fashion photographer David Bailey.[37] The Krays, always immaculately dressed, assumed the sartorial mantle of their sharply dressed American mobster forerunners, and in turn influenced subsequent film and televi-sion constructions, particularly British, of the narcissistic criminal. In the opening scenes of *Villain* the audience wit-nesses Dakin rise from his bed, study himself in the mirror, splash water on his eyes and lingeringly apply cologne. While his dress is relatively reserved, the scene's attention to his per-sonal appearance and grooming, and the emphasis placed on it, establish from the outset that here is someone with an unhealthy interest in his personal appearance. It is interesting that the first glimpse the viewer is afforded of Pinkie in *Brighton Rock* is also of him lying down in bed. The dressed but prone mob boss is an enduring visual construct that equates power with outward shows of indolence, a manifestation of Veblen's observation that those in positions of power and economic superiority must demonstrate that they are 'not engaged in any kind of produc-tive labour'.[38] Later in *Villain*, in a scene set in a pub, and again reminiscent of the one previously discussed in *Brighton Rock*,

[top] The Kray Twins with their mother Violet, London, 1965 (Associated Newspapers/ Rex Features).

VILLAIN
1971, dir. Michael Tuchner.
[middle] Dakin's ablutions;
[bottom] vestimentary punishment.

which fulfils much the same function, we see Dakin's appearance contrasted against his more fashionably and, in the case of his driver Terry (John Hallam), decidedly effeminately dressed gang members. Unlike *Brighton Rock*, however, the viewer has already been made aware of Dakin's true character, as prior to the pub scene he has become sadistically excited while lacerating an assumed betrayer with a cut-throat razor. As befits a true English gang-land boss with a distorted sense of national pride and tradition, Dakin remains comparatively sombrely dressed throughout the film, adhering to the maxim proposed in the highly influential nineteenth-century English novel by Edward Bulwer-Lytton, *Pelham, Or the Adventures of a Gentleman*, 'Dress so that it may never be said of you, "What a well-dressed man!" – but, "What a gentleman-like man!"'[39] *Pelham* became the bible for the well dressed Englishman; the

preoccupation with not being over-dressed or considered flashy that characterised the nineteenth century, finds ironic inheritors in the equally preoccupied but far from gentle men that populate British crime films.

As *Villain* progresses, elements of Dakin's true personality are revealed: he is psychologically unstable, extremely violent and maintains a sadistic homosexual relationship with Wolfe (Ian McShane), a pimp and small-time drug dealer. Perhaps the most telling scene concerning Dakin's distorted relationships both sexually and with reality occurs as we see him prepare to have sex with Wolfe. After partially undressing, Wolfe is subjected to a series of vicious body blows from Dakin, which winds him and leaves him collapsed and prone on the bed (see illus. p. 169). As Dakin resumes undressing, he whispers tenderly in his ear: 'Take you up town tomorrow – get you some good suits.'[40] This is a remarkably explicit scene for the time the film was made but, more importantly, the perfect distillation in one small scene of the enduring cinematic imbrications of criminality, narcissism, sexual deviance and tailoring. Not only is Dakin offering good tailoring as a form of compensation for the pain inflicted on his submissive partner, but also as a form of sartorial conscience-salving and, presumably, as an attempt to dress his object of desire in a manner that ironically conforms to his sense of propriety and good taste. A relatively brief scene such as this manages to summarise much larger complex issues concerning the construction of criminal identities on screen via their clothing and the vestimentary signals given off by screen felons; it has assisted audiences in the recognition that 'clothing put power in plain view; it shaped the way in which power was thought, enacted, and reformulated.'[41]

> *Normally I would've belted them, but I didn't wanna muss myself all up.*[42]

If Vic Dakin can mask his true nature under a veneer of sartorial sobriety, other cinematic 'bad guys' manifest a more obvious schizophrenic relationship to their clothing, a Jekyll and Hyde tendency where their 'good' side dresses unremarkably and with a disregard for fashion that borders on the shabby, while the 'bad' side revels in spectacular displays of modishness. Although not of the psychopathic order of Vic Dakin, Buddy Love, the Hyde to Professor Julius Kelp's Jekyll in *The Nutty Professor* (1963) broadcasts his chemically induced psychological transformations with ever increasing displays of mid-century rakishness. Following Kelp's (Jerry Lewis) taking of the potion, we see him transformed in true Jekyll and Hyde fashion into a hideous monster; this scene then cuts to Kelp's new persona, Buddy Love (who remains unseen at this point, with the viewer 'becoming' Love via the use of subjective camera work), eliciting astonished reactions from his tailor, passersby and the customers of the Purple Pit, a jazz club that will become the

THE NUTTY PROFESSOR
1963, dir. Jerry Lewis.
[facing] Buddy Love in powder blue mohair;
[top] Buddy Love in enlarged Prince of Wales check.

RESERVOIR DOGS
1992, dir. Quentin Tarantino.
[bottom] The great masculine renunciation.

AMERICAN PSYCHO
2000, dir. Mary Harron.
[top] Power dressing;
[bottom] be prepared.

setting for his subsequent manifestations. However, when the camera finally reveals Love, he is not the expected monster but instead a cool hipster with brilliantined DA and a spectacular wardrobe to match. Love's signature style is suits consisting of tight trousers and 'bum freezer', cut-away jackets in a variety of fabrics ranging from powder-blue wool, purple tartan, enlarged Prince of Wales check and bronze slubbed silk, all with contrasting revers and facings, complemented by vividly coloured shirts with exaggerated cuffs and oversized buttons and completed by a variety of silk ties (see illus. pp. 170, 171). *The Nutty Professor* is fundamentally a production showcasing Jerry Lewis's comedic talents but even in this context the equation between flashy dressing, narcissism and latent sadism is played out. During Love's first appearance at the Purple Pit he is challenged by a student who objects to how he has treated the bartender, at which Love punches him to the ground and then proceeds to take out a large hand-mirror from his inside pocket and check that his coiffure is still in place. The message is clear: stylish clothes do not make the gentleman. It is the dishevelled Professor Kelp who eventually wins the affections and hand of the film's love interest, Stella (Stella Stevens).

Many other films utilise a form of sartorial deflection, subverting the established notion that flashy, noticeable clothing manifests itself in strict equivalence to the criminal disposition of the wearer. Dakin and his more soberly dressed sociopaths are a subversion of the accepted understanding that reserved dress is an indication of a similarly reserved and by extension conformist disposition. One of the extreme examples of this inverse operation can be found in *Reservoir Dogs* (1992), where the great masculine renunciation of the nineteenth century, during which men voluntarily gave up any form of sartorial excess in order to plunge themselves into sombre, business-like and most importantly, moralising black clothes, is perverted so that in the film the criminal's uniform black acts as deflection and camouflage.[43] It is ironic that, after the emphasis on anonymous criminal affiliation painstakingly set up by the film's initial scenes, which is primarily achieved by the unifying black suits and adoption of pseudonyms, this same attire also acts as a sartorial cover for Mr Orange, the undercover cop, emphasising the essentially flawed adoption of what was thought of as a safe disguise. It comes as no surprise that John Harvey in his *Men in Black*, the seminal work on the history and significance of black in men's clothing, should choose to use a line of dialogue from *Reservoir Dogs* as the frontispiece to his book, such was the visual impact of the six black-suited felons when it first hit cinema screens.[44] Here is crime as business made manifest, their black suits more typical of mercantile or religious environments or, given that they were designed by agnès b. who is noted for her minimal, relaxed fashion aesthetic, perhaps architects or graphic designers. In any case, their abstinence en masse from the traditional gangster's more outré styling renders them ultimately ineffectual as criminals, and the painstakingly detailed heist descends into fiasco (see illus. p. 171).

Whether ostentatious or reserved, aspirational or every-day, attracting or deflecting attention, the cinematic criminal's dress is now indistinguishable from the average, upright member of society. Rather than gangsters aspiring to be bankers or aristocrats via their wardrobes, the most effective and deadly of today's fictional criminals are those who have attained economic prowess and social status and the dress sense to go with it but who choose, or are psychologically compelled, to commit random acts of violence. Cinema's current love affair with the serial killer who moves among society undetected is a far cry from the machine-gunning Scarface in his gangster threads. For the contemporary psychopath, the risk of ruining one's clothes is as unthinkable as a bungled bank job would have been for his criminal predecessors. Patrick Bateman, the central figure in Bret Easton Ellis's *American Psycho*, the sociopathic investment banker, serial killer and sexual sadist, is observed at the beginning of both the novel (1991) and its cinematic treatment (2000) going through his morning beauty and exercise regime, an echo of Dakin's morning ablutions from *Villain* but carried to excess, complete with iced eye-mask and an array of skin creams and treatments.[45] As the body count mounts so too does Bateman's clothing obsession and, though he takes the precaution of donning plastic overalls before wielding his chainsaw and other assorted power tools, some blood will inevitably stain his impeccable wardrobe. The defilement of Bateman's stylish designer labels is the only situation that solicits any true emotion, and the search for an effective dry cleaner one of his major preoccupations. More than his horrific crimes or complete disregard for humanity, it is his sartorial obsessions that reverberate cinematically from those earlier but equally obsessed and over-dressed mobsters in his chilling soliloquy, part brand roll-call, part consumer complaint and completely remorseless: 'The Chinese dry cleaners I usually send my bloody clothes to delivered back to me yesterday a Soprani jacket, two white Brooks Brothers shirts and a tie from Agnes B. still covered in blood. I have a lunch appointment at noon – in forty minutes – and beforehand I decide to stop by the cleaners and complain.'[46]

If the flashily dressed criminal is an anachronism dating from a more innocent age of cinema when gangsters dressed to impress, and more recently the criminal ineptitude of the Reservoir Dogs and systematic sadism of Patrick Bateman are camouflaged behind an impeccably bland facade provided by agnès b. and Soprani, then perhaps it is time to reconsider just who among the cinematic criminal fraternity still enjoys the sartorial satisfaction of spectacular suiting. Buffalo Bill (Ted Levine) in *The Silence of the Lambs* (1991) eschews off-the-peg or designer finery and trusts instead his own tailoring skills acquired while confined to psychiatric facilities.[47] Bill's limited-edition skin suits made from the flayed flesh of his overweight, exclusively female, victims attain the status of haute couture, one-offs requiring hours of dedicated needlework and exclusive 'fabrics'. His flesh outfits can be understood as the ultimate in criminal suiting, combining in one garment all the sartorial

needs of the modern-day sociopath: the necessary styling to attract attention (even if that attention is limited to his victims and himself), the ability to confer status and power on the wearer, and the means to resolve any of the latent sexual identification issues that commonly beset his dapper cinematic predecessors, allowing him to 'dress' as female. Buffalo Bill's suits are perhaps the ultimate in vestimentary consumption, startling displays of sartorial obsession, allowing the wearer truly to 'cut a dash'.

In sharp contrast to the meticulously dressed criminal, whose megalomania finds a sartorial outlet in an obsessive attention to the finer details of personal presentation, stands the cinematic construction of the good guy, the 'honest Joe' whose lack of interest in clothes is a measure of his integrity. There are, of course, numerous examples in film of the typical male who, when perplexed by the finer points of dressing, turns to wife, lover or mother for guidance, but what is of more interest here is the specific re-dressing, or makeover (to use a more contemporary term), of a subservient male character in order that he will 'look the part' by a socially and economically superior female. These remodelling scenarios typically centre on the male figures of the 'kept man' and the bodyguard and, in order for the relinquishing of male sexual dominance expressed through the act of being dressed to be legitimated, the female dresser is portrayed as illegal, transgressive or at least in proximity to criminality. As discussed previously, obsessive male interest in clothing is understood as unlawful and therefore the imposition of this sartorial concentration on a lawful man can only logically be initiated at the behest of a 'dishonest' woman.

These re-dressings can be as minor as the change of tie featured in the 1987 film *Someone to Watch over Me*, where Claire Bradley (Mimi Rogers), the Manhattan society hostess, decides that Mike Keegan (Tom Berenger), the detective assigned to protect her after she witnesses a murder, needs a 'more conservative' tie if he is going to accompany her to a benefit being held at the Guggenheim Museum.[2] As has already been noticed when discussing the neckwear scenes in *Holiday*, ties are frequently employed as social markers: for Bradley, the elegant Park Avenue socialite, Keegan's loud tie speaks too stridently of Queens and his working-class origins.[3] However, as luck would have it, before partying at the Guggenheim, Bradley needs to collect a gift from Bergdorf's and while there selects and purchases a more suitable tie for her chaperone, adding that 'if we had more time we'd work on the suit too.'[4] Bradley's aesthetic sensibility is offended by Keegan's tie; the simple cop's brash taste springs from the same social and economic aspirations as that of the

SUNSET BOULEVARD
1950, dir. Billy Wilder.
[facing] Platinum shackles.

SOMEONE TO WATCH OVER ME
1987, dir. Ridley Scott.
[top] Queens tie;
[bottom] Manhattan tie.

flashily dressed gangster but the path of lawfulness means that a policeman with a family residing in Queens will never achieve the dizzy vestimentary heights of a Scarface, and his desire for sartorial self-expression must be contented with a cheap showy tie. Bradley as the socialite sexually attracted to her unrefined minder is the obverse of Dakin in *Villain*, who is compelled to dress his sexual conquests in 'good suits'. She is less deadly, perhaps, and limits herself to neckwear but is ultimately as destructive. This re-styling, albeit minor, seems to act as a catalyst for the destabilisation and emasculation of Keegan who, on arriving at the Guggenheim, is first ridiculed by his police colleagues who suggest that he has become a gigolo, then treated as an object of erotic curiosity by Bradley's wealthy female friends and finally allows Joey Venza, the mobster whom Bradley has witnessed commit the murder, to threaten her, thus negating his role as her protector. The dismantling of Keegan as the honest cop and loving family man continues as we see him increasingly attracted to both Bradley and her way of life and start an affair with her. This affair compromises him professionally, splits up his marriage and eventually puts his whole family in danger when they are taken hostage by Venza.

The act of dressing those in less powerful positions is often a vital component in the construction of the erotic object, and is a commonplace scenario when it is a man choosing clothes for a woman but when the roles are reversed or, as in the case of *Villain*, it forms part of a homo-erotic relationship, this process has a deeper resonance. As has been discussed, male attention to clothing and elaborate display forms part of the construction of hyper-masculinity essential to the cinematic gangster, but when overseen by a woman the resultant effect is to emasculate and the man expensively dressed by a woman is viewed with as much suspicion as the flashily dressed gangster. *Someone to Watch Over Me* plays with the sartorial status quo, so when Claire Bradley buys and makes Keegan wear a more suitable tie she affirms her position as a privileged woman who has everything in life except an ordinary cop whose family she is prepared to wreck for the sexual frisson it offers, borne out by

her obvious enjoyment at the attention they receive from her peers at the Guggenheim party.

John Harvey has suggested that male clothing has 'tended to double entendres, playing on ideas of outer and inner and open and closed', that men's suits in particular 'positively play with closure and aperture' and it is this sexual play, or perhaps tension, that is most noticeable in these male re-modelling sequences.[5] As can be seen in *Someone to Watch Over Me*, it need only be the purchase of a tie that sets in motion an erotic relationship based on who has access, and therefore the right, to dress the male body, a right made even more suggestive if occurring within the re-configured context of the mistress–servant dynamic. The erotic potential of the male surrendering his right to dress himself is central to the blossoming relationship between the ex-con turned chauffeur George (Bob Hoskins) and the high-class prostitute Simone (Cathy Tyson) in *Mona Lisa* (1986).[6] Simone needs a driver who will look inconspicuous and appropriately dressed while he waits for her in the lobbies of the various hotels where she calls on her clients. Initially she gives him some money to buy himself a more appropriate wardrobe but she soon realises that he needs sartorial re-education when he meets her in a gaudy Hawaiian shirt and cheap leather jacket, accessorised by a chestful of gold medallions. George attempts to defend his wardrobe choice – 'See I'm cheap . . . can't help it, God made me that way!' – but to no avail as Simone swiftly responds: 'Being cheap is one thing. Looking cheap is another . . . that really takes talent!'[7] Again the equivalence of lowly background with poor taste in clothes is underscored, leading to the inevitable re-dressing scene, during which the themes of deceptive appearances and the body as a commodified object for sale that underpin the film are played out.

Simone meets George in the Burlington Arcade and proceeds to take him to Savile Row and into Tommy Nutter's.[8] As with *Someone to Watch Over Me*, George is at first captivated by the real silk ties, the ultimate masculine accessory, and follows Simone awestruck as she proceeds to choose shirts and suits, thinking that she is selecting them for herself, possibly to fulfil a particular client's sexual fantasy. On realising that she is choosing them for him, he recoils in anger shouting: 'You can't dress me!' to which Simone replies 'Yes I can . . . try it!', an apparently simple exchange that disguises the more complex narratives of role-play, dressing and undressing and masquerade that are the stock in trade of Simone's profession.[9] The viewer has already been alerted to the film's insistent motif of disguise and 'covering up' as Simone emerges from the various clients' hotels and apartments apparently modestly dressed in full-length overcoat but which invariably falls open to reveal that she is dressed only in her underwear. This theme of sartorial subterfuge is maintained in George's re-dressing scene. Once persuaded to try on the new clothes, George emerges transformed in a well-cut suit, admiring himself with uncharacteristic pleasure in the mirror, a suggestive display of auto-eroticism to which Simone the expert in such matters has introduced him. They then cement their sartorial/sexual relationship as she tenderly drapes an overcoat over his shoulders and he declares breathlessly 'Lovely!', referring both to his awakened narcissism and the mounting desire he feels for Simone. Yet, as unlikely and touching as their relationship appears to be, their criminal backgrounds will not allow the pair to achieve lasting happiness: as always, the act of usurping the male right to dress himself has ramifications, particularly when the dresser is a prostitute who according to cinematic convention must always be punished. George realises in the bloody climax to the film that Simone is irredeemable and is prepared to kill him alongside the pornographer and pimp who demarcate her world. It is ironic that George 'comes to his senses' still dressed in the Savile Row suit but wearing it with his gaudy Hawaiian shirt, thus indicating his return to morality, leaving the worlds of tasteful dressing, good taste and high-class prostitution behind.

For George and Mike Keegan, there is ultimate redemption from the ignominy of allowing themselves to be dressed by a woman and atonement comes with the realisation that both Simone and Claire offered a glimpse of an unobtainable way of

MONA LISA
1986, dir. Neil Jordan.
[top] 'See, I'm cheap . . .';
[middle] Simone takes George shopping;
[bottom] 'Lovely'.

life beyond their own prosaic existence. No such redemption is available to one of cinema's highly invidious 'dressed' men, Joe Gillis (William Holden), the 'kept man' of the faded silent-movie star Norma Desmond (Gloria Swanson) in *Sunset Boulevard* (1950). As the celebrated opening of the film informs us, Joe our narrator is dead, and how he came to be shot in the back, floating face down in Norma's swimming pool, is told in flashback. Among the film's piercing dissections of the transience of fame, beauty and the hollowness of the film industry itself, is perhaps the most devastating portrayal of the kept man or what would probably now be termed as a 'toy boy' on film. We follow the screenwriter Joe, down on his luck, and accidentally meeting with Norma; this soon develops

into a classic addictive relationship with Norma increasingly dependent on the illusion of youth that Joe's presence bestows. For Joe, of course, his moribund existence in Norma's mansion is made bearable by a lifestyle to which he quickly becomes accustomed and which is manifested in the gifts showered on him by his keeper. Joe becomes Norma's male concubine and his escalating loss of self-esteem and increasing detachment from the world beyond Sunset Boulevard is defined by his adoption of the Desmond livery, a gigolo's livery that Joe itemises for Betty Schaefer, the young script-reader who is attracted to him and who offers him his one chance of salvation: 'All my things? All my eighteen suits and all my custom made shoes and the six dozen shirts and the cuff-links and the platinum key chains and the cigarette cases?'[10] As with *Someone to Watch Over Me* and *Mona Lisa*, there is the obligatory protestation scene when the proposal to be re-dressed is first made and Norma, after listing her disapproval of Joe's wardrobe, suggests that she re-style him. He half-heartedly declares: 'I don't need any clothes, and I certainly don't want you buying them for me!'[11] However, his objections are unsuccessful and the destabilisation of Joe's former identity is set in motion in the following scene that takes place in the men's outfitters. With Norma directing Joe's makeover with the authority that befits a movie star used to overseeing her wardrobe, he is transformed into her vision of a leading man resplendent in blue flannel, camel hair and tuxedo. Just how swiftly and completely Joe's re-orientation from self-assured, wise-cracking hack into paid male escort is achieved is hammered home by the worldly sales assistant's knowing looks and the comment that 'as long as the lady's paying for it, why not take the vicuna?'[12] Further intimations of Joe's emasculation are suggested by Norma's threat that if he is not careful she will buy him a 'cutaway', referring to an old-fashioned style of men's tuxedo where the genital area is both exposed and emphasised, the semantic threat of cutting linking directly to Joe's impending symbolic castration as Norma's kept man.[13]

> Desmond: 'Perfect! Wonderful shoulders! And I love that line!'
> Gillis: 'It's all padding, don't let it fool ya. You know, to me getting dressed up was always just putting on my dark blue suit.'
> Desmond: 'I don't like the studs they sent. I want you to have a pearl, a big luscious pearl!'
> Gillis: 'Well I'm not going to wear earrings, I can tell you that!'
> Desmond: 'Ha, ha, cute!'[14]

The scene where Joe makes his entrance in exaggeratedly tailored evening-dress tail coat and white tie at Norma's New Year's Eve party functions as a vestimentary translation of the

SUNSET BOULEVARD
1950, dir. Billy Wilder.
[facing] New Year's Eve.
[top] Norma makes Joe over;
[bottom] 'Why not take the vicuna?'

pair's dysfunctional relationship. She admires his broad shoulders and trim waist achieved via the outmoded tailoring she has bought for him, a double deterioration of his masculinity (his physique is an illusion achieved with cutting and padding) and his contemporaneousness (his silhouette is likened to Rudolph Valentino, the silent matinee idol). He has become her creation, something to be embellished with pearls, a caricature of masculinity which he is now doomed to perform, a role he attempts to refuse when he protests that he has a life of his own and leaves the party. Grabbing his vicuna coat he makes his exit, but not before catching his platinum key-chain on the door handle, a literal reminder of the costly shackles that bind him to Norma. He seeks refuge at a friend's lively party, where his appearance causes comment, the soft touch of his vicuna compared to mink, the archetypal symbol of the kept woman, and his evening dress to that of Adolphe Menjou, the film star most noted for his appearance alongside Valentino in *The Sheik* (1921).[15] Enjoying the company of his contemporaries and a growing attraction for Betty Schaefer, Joe resolves to leave Norma and rings the mansion to have his clothes, 'my old clothes, the ones I came with', packed ready for him to collect. However, he learns from Max (Erich von Stroheim), Norma's faithful retainer, that she has attempted suicide, a cry for help that brings Joe running back to his eventual demise face down in the swimming pool. Joe's inability to renounce his role as Norma's dressing-up doll and his immaculately tailored costumes of vicuna and platinum mean that he must pay the ultimate penalty, and his violent end makes plain to the audience the moral of the film: better dead than kept and dressed.

Such an intimate act as being dressed by another will invariably lead to the dresser and the dressed becoming lovers, or at least to an erotic excursion for the dresser. A somewhat more moralistic variant on this narrative can be found in *Curly Sue* (1991).[16] The wealthy and successful Chicago lawyer Grey Ellison (Kelly Lynch) encounters the homeless, minor conman Bill Dancer (James Belushi) and Curly Sue, his young companion. After a failed attempt to con Ellison, the scene is set for a classic tale of

CURLY SUE
1991, dir. James Hughes.
[top] Choosing the new wardrobe;
[middle] Paisley is preferable;
[bottom] 'Feel like a Goddam fool!'

the lovable orphan who finds a life of comfort and ease difficult to adjust to after her life on the road with Dancer: it follows the cinematic tradition of a number of Shirley Temple vehicles from the 1930s such as *Bright Eyes* and *Curly Top*. Ellison and Dancer are attracted to each other and the rogue is the perfect antidote to Ellison's snobbish, yuppie fiancé. Ellison decides that both Dancer and the young girl need more respectable clothes and, in an extended shopping scene, Ellison accompanied by her assistant go on a spending spree in Marshall Field & Co. This provides a motive for a dialogue-free montage of scenes involving stereotypically effeminate assistants modelling the wardrobe she is choosing for Dancer and in addition the obligatory tie selection scene.

Resplendent in his new clothes, Dancer is taken by Ellison to dinner at a high-class restaurant. As she comes into his room, Dancer has his back towards her and, on turning round, elicits a gasp of admiration from Ellison at his transformed appearance. As with *Mona Lisa*, the remodelled male initially declares his discomfort with the situation, Dancer announcing 'Feel like a Goddam fool', and his unfamiliarity with sartorial niceties needs one last pointer from his mentor as she motions discreetly that he still has a label hanging from the cuff of his new suit. Dancer overcoming this *faux pas* is then swiftly seduced by his new appearance, as Ellison tells him breathlessly 'You look great!'[17] Once suitably attired, their romance can continue apace, setting the scene for the final happily ever after outcome which sees the reformed hobos taking up permanent residence with Ellison.

As stated earlier, the re-styling of a culturally or economically inferior woman by a superior man is far more common in film, and much has been written concerning such transformation scenes. Scottie's remodelling of Judy Barton (the 'second' Madeleine) in *Vertigo* (1958) is perhaps one of the more discussed examples, while Waldo Lydecker's Svengali-like cultivation of Laura Hunt in *Laura* (1944) is made perfectly clear in Lydecker's confession that: 'Laura had innate breeding. But she deferred to my judgement and taste. I selected a more attractive hairdress for her. I taught her what clothes were more becoming to her.'[18] More recently, Richard Gere's re-dressing of Julia Roberts in *Pretty Woman* (1990) has stimulated a wealth of critical analysis, with Stella Bruzzi's comparison of Roberts's makeover with that of Audrey Hepburn's in *Sabrina* remaining perhaps the most thought-provoking.[19] While not necessarily under the aegis of a male benefactor, a number of neglected examples of the transformation sequence form the basis of Tamar Jeffers McDonald's valuable addition to the field, *Hollywood Catwalk*.[20] Of particular interest here are the examples she includes of male transformations and, though none are effected by women, with the exception of Kathy Bates's provision of Leonardo DiCaprio's evening clothes in *Titanic*, they are nevertheless important for what they suggest about the construction of the aspirational and fashionable male body.[21]

An interesting departure from the binary opposition of the usual male/female makeover scene can be found in the 2006 version of *Casino Royale*, which provides a cinematic 'two for one' re-dressing sequence.[22] There, Daniel Craig as James Bond brings a low-cut evening gown to Vesper Lynd's (Eva Green) bathroom in the hotel where the pair are staying, posing as man and wife, in order for Bond to take part in a poker game and win against the world-terrorism financier, le Chiffre. In the following exchange the typical scenario of the dominant male dressing the inferior female is revisited:

> Bond: 'For you.'
> Lynd: 'Something you expect me to wear?'
> Bond: 'I need you looking fabulous. So that when you walk up behind me and kiss me on the neck the players across from me will be thinking about your neckline and not about their cards. Do you think you can do that for me?'
> Lynd: 'I'll do my best.'
> Bond: 'Thank you.'[23]

However, this formula is reversed in the next scene in which Bond, on returning to his bedroom, finds a dinner jacket on the bed which he returns to Lynd's bathroom, declaring:

Bond: 'I have a dinner jacket.'
Lynd: 'There are dinner jackets and dinner jackets. This is the latter. I need you looking like a man who belongs at that table.'
Bond: 'How the . . .? It's tailored' (referring to its fit).
Lynd: 'I sized you up the moment we met.'[24]

Lynd's superior taste and judgement, accompanied by the scopophiliac inference that she has been sizing up Bond's body with enough concentration and thoroughness to allow her to order his immaculately fitting jacket, adds an erotic intensity to Bond's usual encounters with his female adversaries. Lynd gains the upper sartorial hand in this scene, as she observes Bond in the customary auto-eroticisation scene admiring his reflection in Lynd's choice of jacket accompanied by Monty Norman's famous Bond theme, a musical meta-cinematic reference to previous incarnations of Bond and the importance of his tailoring.[25] He is, with the help of Lynd and Brioni, back to his former glory, sartorially armed to take on le Chiffre at the gaming tables.

The concomitant emasculation of the male subject when he permits himself to be dressed by a woman in the re-styling scenes is a testament to the deeply entrenched visual imbrication that exists in film of masculinity and spectacular dressing. As has been seen, a love of flashy, sometimes gaudy and outré tailoring is the sign of that most masculine of cinematic constructions, the gangster. It is noticeable therefore that when dressed by a woman, male characters are persuaded to dress more conservatively, with sobriety and 'good taste', following Hardy Amies's maxim that 'A man should look as if he had bought his clothes with intelligence, put them on with care, and then forgotten all about them' – although feminine taste can sometimes be questionably outmoded, as in the example from *Sunset Boulevard*.[26] It is as if the desire to be tastefully and, most important, discreetly dressed acts as a form of denunciation of the naturally showy male sensibility, the peacock betrayed, perhaps. Women dressers in film are concerned that

CASINO ROYALE
2006, dir. Martin Campbell.
'There are dinner jackets and dinner jackets.'

their men do not stand out in the crowd but remain confident in the knowledge that their wardrobe has been selected with the utmost care, judgement and expense.

It is ironic that this state of almost unnoticeable perfection is what the true dandy aspired to; rather than stand out in the crowd, he remained comfortable in the knowledge that he was dressed with quiet good taste. As Barthes understood, the dandy

> takes distinction that bit further: its essence is no longer social for him, but metaphysical; the dandy stands in opposition not at all to the upper class and the lower class, but only in absolute terms to the individual and the banal; so the individual is not a generalized idea for him; it is him alone, purified of all recourse to comparison, to the extent that, like Narcissus, it is to himself and him alone that he offers a reading of his clothing.[27]

Although the dandy's obsession with clothing seems at first glance to be similar to the sartorial displays of the sharp-suited gangster discussed previously, the essential difference is that unnatural effort and time is spent for precisely the opposite reason, to be unnoticeable to the masses, and the expense and care lavished on appearance registered only by a select minority. His costume is not to cut a dash but to go unnoticed, a self-effacement and denial of what is typically seen as the masculine desire to 'show out', to receive attention. In film, overly tasteful dressers, when not kitted out by women but who dress themselves, are, by extension, treated with sexual suspicion, and the equation of homosexuality and extremely refined dress sense is made even more explicit when a man dresses another man.

As already seen, Dakin's object of sadistic erotic desire, Wolfe, will become even more alluring for him once he takes him uptown to get some 'good suits' to replace his showy 1970s gear. A more recent example from the opposite side of the legal fence occurs in *J. Edgar*, which tells the story of J. Edgar Hoover and his life-long relationship with Clyde Tolson, his assistant, companion and possible lover, although the film is at pains to

J. EDGAR
2009, dir. Clint Eastwood.
More directorial.

avoid suggesting this explicitly. Once Tolson has been hired and rapidly promoted through the ranks, partly as a result of Hoover reading a letter of recommendation for him which lists that he has no 'particular interest in women', we see Hoover taken to Tolson's outfitters; it is a department store where the familiar re-dressing scene is enacted, only this time it is Tolson who styles Hoover (see illus. p. 185). In a reworking of the *Sunset Boulevard* scene, the audience sees Hoover being fitted and fussed around by tailors and assistants while Tolson selects ties (the archetypal masculine vestimentary symbol, becoming once again the focus of this re-dressing sequence) that will best match Hoover's new suit:

> Tolson: 'All right sir, I've found you two tie options, this one is a bit more fashion forward, a little bit louder, but I think it would complement this suit and cut and fabric.'
> Hoover: 'I think it's a bit too loud, don't you think?'
> Tolson: 'Too loud? OK, which is why I found this one, it's a bit more . . . bit more directorial.'
> Hoover: 'A little bit more reserved, I agree.'
> Tolson: 'More powerful.'[28]

We can only assume that, once he has allowed himself to be dressed by Tolson, Hoover's relationship with his companion will inevitably develop into a sexual one, as has been seen in the heterosexual re-dressings. Tolson has styled Hoover to fulfil both their fantasies of Hoover as a powerful figure – a necessarily discreet, one might say, covert force, as befits the head of an institution dedicated to clandestine surveillance, and which reinforces their relationship, played out with lingering glances and moments of intense wordless scrutiny.

Whether it is by women or men, the male who submits to being dressed relinquishes individualism, becoming a projection of the fantasies of the dresser which, as has been seen, are typically fuelled by cultural parameters such as taste, discretion, sobriety and quality. Even when the fantasy is less constrained by social convention, such as Norma Desmond's projection of Rudolph Valentino onto the body of the decidedly mid-century modern Joe Gillis, it is so complete that his body literally conforms to her image of another: the padding of the tuxedo she buys for him delivers him to her on New Year's Eve as Valentino. Once having appropriately styled their vestimentary objects, it becomes much easier for these dressers to move the contact forward into a sexual relationship, which, ironically, will be accompanied by a movement away from dressing and towards divesting. Those highly charged sequences where the new, idealised male body is remodelled act as erotic stimuli: the touching of cloth, matching of ties, tracing the line of a shoulder, draping a new topcoat over the perfect jacket are all suggestive of future disrobing, and bear out Harvey's consideration of the male wardrobe as having an 'inclination to pretend to show the insides of their clothing. Both jackets and coats have frequently had large lapels, which purport to show the inside of the garment turning outwards. Sleeves for many years turned back in big cuffs, and when breeches stretched to trousers, they in time turned up in turn-ups.'[29]

The construction of male identity via dress is something that is understood as a rite of passage once the age of school uniforms and the maternal choice of clothes is left behind. In later life to have no control over one's clothing is something that marks out the wearer as either engaged in menial or servile occupations where uniforms or liveries are required or, perhaps more pertinently to this text, as an unsuccessful criminal who as a prisoner is forced into the anonymity and discipline of the prison uniform. Taking away male identity by removing his clothes is the most effective route to subjugation and these re-dressed objects are some of mainstream cinema's most dysfunctionally fashionable victims. As has been explored throughout this book, dysfunctionality is a state that makes way for new significance, new meaning, new consequences, and the dressed man stripped of his identity is re-clad as an accessory, the dresser's bodyguard or companion. The dearth of cinematic examples of this particular aspect of male dressing is a testament to how deeply this touches the male psyche. It can be gauged by an example drawn from dress history in the resistance to post-war British utility clothing, especially the male 'demob' (demobilisation) suit. British ex-servicemen were issued with a full set of civilian clothes including a three-piece suit, and there was considerable debate at the time concerning its necessarily standardised, economical and unstylish cut.[30] Yet it could be argued that objections stemmed more from the perceived loss of identity than from any specific sartorial issues.[31] Our cinematic makeovers, of course, have no such concerns because their suits are only ever of the highest quality but, nevertheless, the imposition of clothing whether skimped or luxurious must inevitably provoke an intense response. J. B. Priestley used the demob suit as a narrative motif in his novel *Three Men in New Suits*, written in 1945 at the height of popular reaction in the UK to utility clothing and the demob suit; while far removed from Mike Keegan, George, Bill Dancer and even Joe Gillis, his three men share the same palpable loss of identity displayed by those on screen:

> Then it was all different. Three young men in new suits came in. The suits were blue, grey and brown; but were alike in being severely, even skimpily, cut, and in being very new. The young men who wore them – and wore them newly too – were not alike, for one was tallish, fair, good-looking, another was of similar height but dark and beaky, and the third was burly and battered; yet there was a distinct likeness between them, as if all three had come from the same place and had been doing the same things there.[32]

This property of whiteness, to be everything and nothing, is the source of its representational power.[1]

To leave those law-abiding, but emasculated, citizens who allow themselves to be dressed by women and return to the sartorially obsessive gangster, the archetypal garment that perfectly expresses the equation between tailoring and the sociopath, the basting together of cloth and cruelty, is the white suit. Notwithstanding that when found in other forms of clothing – wedding dresses, clerical vestments and baby clothes, for example – white is equated with purity, sanctity and innocence, when used for a man's suit the wearer is inevitably viewed with distrust and condescension. The aforementioned Jay Gatsby, for all his wealth, is regarded as somehow never quite 'right' for Long Island society, due in no small part to his predilection for white suits, while Tony Manero's self-centred arrogance is indivisible from his love of the white suit in *Saturday Night Fever* (1977).[2] The difficulty of keeping all white clothing in pristine condition is another pitfall facing those who opt for this palette: witness the inappropriateness of Rico Rizzo's choice of white lounge jacket and off-white trousers for his first appearance in *Midnight Cowboy* (1969).[3] For Rico, the terminally sick, crippled, small-time crook and would-be pimp, white seems both the aspirational choice for a petty thief who wants to make the big time, and yet is doomed to live out his fantasies of an all-white lifestyle in Miami while languishing in squalor in New York (see illus. p. 191). Even Sidney Stratton's spotless character and lofty intentions of revolutionising post-war British textile manufacturing that comprise the central plot of *The Man in the White Suit* (1951) are transformed into a threat to the economic security of the worker once his cloth is perfected and he dons his miraculous white suit.[4] Stratton's (Alec Guinness) intentions are honourable and, as an idealistic and visionary chemist, he can see only the benefits of developing an indestructible, per-manently immaculate cloth. However, with the typically short-sighted understanding of society characteristic of cinema's representation of the scientist, he is taken aback by

THE UNTOUCHABLES
1987, dir. Brian De Palma.
[facing] Nitti the immaculate assassin
(Photofest).

THE GREAT GATSBY
1976, dir. Jack Clayton.
[top] Not quite right white.

SATURDAY NIGHT FEVER
1977, dir. John Badham.
[bottom] White Narcissus
(Moviestore Collection/Rex Features).

the textile industry and its workers' hostile reaction to his invention. His white suit changes from being the symbol of intellectual and scientific brilliance to that of a livery of shame, marking Stratton out as the enemy of the people and whose dazzling appearance offers him no chance of escape.

The otherworldliness of Stratton's miraculous white suit is taken to its logical conclusion in the comedy science fiction film *Meet Dave* (2008), where Eddie Murphy plays the captain of a group of miniature aliens whose spacecraft takes the form of a full-sized human being (also played by Eddie Murphy) who becomes known as Dave.[5] When deciding how their 'craft' should be dressed, the aliens take their cues from popular American culture and, after viewing Ricardo Montalban's appearance in the television series *Fantasy Island*, decide to dress Dave/the spacecraft in a dazzling, white three-piece suit and matching white brogues.[6] While the original reference might have been *Fantasy Island*, Dave's first appearance on the streets of New York is accompanied by a soundtrack consisting of the Bee Gees' 'Staying Alive' in a direct reference to Tony Manero/John Travolta's famous white suit worn in *Saturday Night Fever*. The references to his appearance and the 1970s continue when, during a conversation with Gina (Elizabeth Banks), he attempts to justify his odd behaviour by declaring: 'Yes, of course I am just a regular person from right here on earth, just like you . . . I just don't get out that much', to which Gina replies: 'Yeah, judging from your suit I'd say since about 1978!' At this point the scene cuts to Dave's interior and the miniature aliens controlling their human-form space ship and Eddie Murphy, this time as the captain, suggesting to his crew: 'Note . . . All white apparel is not as standardized as we thought.'[7] Not standardised, perhaps, but certainly impregnable, as both the suit and Dave survive unharmed and unmarked after being hurtled into the air when Gina crashes into him with her car. The white suit as a form of otherworldly armour will be returned to shortly, but it is interesting to note that Montalban's character in *Fantasy Island*, Mr Roarke, was also apparently immortal and, similarly, his white suit remains unchanged and immaculate throughout the various adventures acted out on the island.

These relatively innocuous and unwitting examples of the inadvisability of donning white provide a range of possible points of entry to a deeper understanding of the correlation between wearing white and social unacceptability, white and egocentricity, white and disability and white and hubris, for example. Yet Sidney Stratton and his sartorial comrades mentioned earlier pale by comparison to the vestimentary sleight of hand adopted by another order of white-suit wearers hell-bent on cinematic destruction. These snowy psychopaths know only too well the saintly camouflage that white can provide and they use to deadly effect the outré distraction they generate, as Stella Bruzzi has asserted:

THE MAN IN THE WHITE SUIT
1951, dir. Alexander Mackendrick.
[facing] Dressing for industrial demise (Photofest).
[top] Sidney dazzled by his genius.

MIDNIGHT COWBOY
1969, dir. John Schlesinger.
[middle] Aspirational white for Rico.

MEET DAVE
2008, dir. Brian Robbins.
[bottom] Not so standardised.

The use of white or off-white ensembles to denote extreme brutality probably derives directly from Al Capone. Both the real and the fictionalised gangster, therefore, occupy a paradoxical position in relation to fashion: while they appropriate the styles of high fashion, they do not ultimately want to blend in or be lost in it, so they cultivate 'an identifiable school of stylishness that, far from operating as camouflage, ultimately functioned like warrior dress'.[8]

Before studying three key examples of the cinematic white suit, a distinction needs to be made from the previously discussed tendency of the mobster towards flashy modes of dressing and the specific case of the completely white wardrobe. As Bruzzi identifies, the use of off-white ensembles by the psychopathic mobster has its origins in Al Capone's predilection for pale tailoring: in many cinematic demonstrations of this phenomenon from the 1930s onwards we see a variety of pale greys and off-whites clothing the bodies of assorted mobsters and megalomaniacs from 'Hood' Stacey in *Each Dawn I Die* (1939) to *Dr No* (1962).[9] Many of James Bond's celebrated villains have favoured an all-white wardrobe: Joseph Wiseman as Dr No appears in a white two-piece suit with high-necked stiff-collared jacket, part Chinese 'mandarin' collar part nineteenth-century Prussian uniform, a double sartorial referent to the 'foreigner' and his tailoring as intrinsically evil, and the outfit is completed by a pair of white glacé kid loafers. Later in the Bond series, Christopher Lee as the international assassin Scaramanga, *The Man with the Golden Gun* (1974), favours a typical mid-70s shirt-jacketed white suit, an outré style befitting the flashy killer who dispatches his victims with golden gun and bullets and which contrasts with Bond's reserved stylishness.[10] A number of the screen's memorable crime bosses have favoured pure white in the form of a tuxedo for evening and formal occasions, such as Tony Camonte in *Scarface*, and while James Bond himself occasionally sports a white tuxedo, these perhaps can be understood as sartorial misdemeanours given how closely associated the white tuxedo has become with the Italian

mobster. In *Thunderball* (1965), for example, Largo (Adolfo Celi) SPECTRE's one-eyed Italian number 2 agent, sports a variety of stylish outfits as befits his mobster origins, including the obligatory white tuxedo.[11] A variation on the white-suited Italian mobster can be found more recently in the *Transporter* series of films starring Jason Statham as Frank Martin, who will transport and deliver anything for a price. In *Transporter 2* (2005) he is pitched against an Italian mercenary, Gianni Chellini (Alessandro Gassman), whose extensive wardrobe is pure white throughout the film.[12] He is first seen wearing an all-white kendo suit and then a variety of white shirts, nearly white linen suits and towels, the one exception being a black silk robe worn after a sex scene with his assassin Lola, played by Amber Valetta.

One of the more direct demonstrations of an all-white ensemble and concomitant lack of integrity on the part of the wearer is that of White Goodman (Ben Stiller), the odious and narcissistic owner of the rival gym to Peter La Fleur's in *DodgeBall* (2004; considered in the 'Gift-wrapped' section earlier for its 'magical' scarf). White Goodman, whose name signals the film's ideological critique of physical fitness, normative sexuality and racial homogeny, appears at the house of Kate (Christine Taylor), the accountant working for his gym, and attempts to persuade her to go out with him. Having informed her that she has been sacked, Goodman suggests that she is now free to have a relationship with him and this, in addition to the manner in which Whiteman is dressed for the prospective date, hardly endears him to her. He wears a completely white leather suit and matching white shoes relieved only by a purple neckerchief. The obvious punning ensues based on his name and appearance as, when answering her enquiry as to who is knocking at her door, Goodman replies: 'It's White . . . Surprise!' to which the astonished Kate, looking him up and down, can only reply: 'White!'[13] When he attempts to kiss her, Kate ends their brief encounter by smashing Goodman's face into the wall, causing his lip to bleed, and he retreats in gleaming white from his unsuccessful tryst on the back of a lilac scooter driven by his personal trainer. Nevertheless, these examples are what might be considered fair-weather or special-occasion white wearers; in the discussion of films that follows, dazzling white is compulsory for the entirety of these sartorial sadists' appearances on screen. For Frank Nitti, Al Capone's ruthless henchman in *The Untouchables* (1987), the genocidal Nazi Dr Josef Mengele in *The Boys from Brazil* (1978) and Adam Cramer, the hate-mongering racist in *The Intruder* (1961), the all-white suit is *de rigueur* for their charted courses of annihilation, white being the non-colour that bleaches and atomises all those who come into contact with it.[14]

The viewer's first sight of Mengele, the Angel of Death (*Todesengel*) or White Angel (*weiße Engel*, so-called from the concentration camps) in *The Boys from Brazil*, is truly divine. We see Mengele (Gregory Peck) arriving by seaplane in Paraguay in the dead of night and, as he steps ashore, lights from the waiting cars dispel the darkness and illuminate Mengele, dazzling his expectant Nazi entourage. His brilliant appearance is due to his wearing a pure white suit and shirt; while the costume designer Anthony Mendleson was obviously referring to the name Mengele had earned in the Second World War, this bravura display of sartorial attention-seeking can be seen as representative of a persistent multi-valency that characterises the cinematic white suit. On the most fundamental level, dressing evil characters in white subverts the universally accepted cinematic convention of white signifying good and black bad, established ever since pioneering silent-cinema directors used white and black cowboy hats to assist in the narrative progression of the early western film. The contrast between these characters' dazzling outward appearance and their inner depravity is irresistible, of course, and as Jean Baudrillard suggested, 'Everything is metamorphosed into its inverse in order to be perpetuated in its purged form. Every form of power, every situation speaks of itself by denial, in order to escape, by simulation of death, its real agony.'[15] The paradox of Mengele wearing white, the colour of purity, juxtaposed with the experiments in racial 'purification' which we see him conducting later in the film is reinforced throughout *The Boys from Brazil*. Whether it be his choice of white lounge

DR. NO
1962, dir. Terence Young.
[top] Part Mandarin, part Prussian,
all white.

TRANSPORTER 2
2005, dir. Louis Leterrier.
[middle] Any colour as long as it's white.

DODGEBALL
2004, dir. Rawson Marshall Thurber.
[bottom] White Goodman.

suit in which to outline his Aryan cloning plan, or the all-white safari suit for experiments on Paraguayan children in his jungle laboratory, or white tuxedo for the Nazi dinner and dance, white is 'the new black' for Mengele. Yet, returning to his first radiant entrance, his white suit becomes more than merely another example of the criminal predilection for ostentatious tailoring: it exudes the quality of whiteness that is historically associated with divine, ineffable sanctity. Mengele's white and that of the other examples discussed shortly signifies not just goodness but inviolability, a whiteness beyond the understanding of mere mortals. John Gage traces this incomprehensible whiteness back to the concept of divine light as formulated by theologians such as Pseudo-Dionysius in the early Middle Ages who suggested: 'we posit intangible and invisible darkness of that Light which is unapproachable because it so far exceeds the visible light'.[16] Mengele's manifestation is both visually unintelligible because of its blinding whiteness and incomprehensible in terms of what he is attempting to carry out – the cloning of ninety-four Hitlers.

Unlike Mengele's dazzling entrance, Frank Nitti's (Billy Drago) in *The Untouchables* is, initially at least, so low-key as to be almost overlooked. We first encounter Al Capone's most deadly assassin, white-suited and accessorised in white matching gloves and hat, sitting against a backdrop of newly washed shirts in the laundry-cum-drugstore that he is planning to blow up if the owner refuses to pay the required protection money. As the owner serves the little neighbourhood girl who is running errands for her mother, we see him in the background rise silently from his bar stool and leave the briefcase containing the bomb and walk out. Seeing this, the girl picks up the bag and starts to catch up with him to return it, at which moment the case explodes, annihilating the drugstore and the little girl, as simultaneously Nitti the White Angel of 1930s Chicago disappears from sight. Nitti as a character is even more inexplicable than Mengele, silent for most of the film, spectral, even supernatural, in his apparent indestructibility and speed. For example, in the scene where he slaughters Jim Malone (Sean Connery), the honest cop and mentor to Eliot Ness, we first

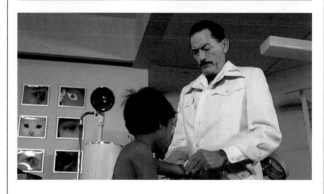

THE BOYS FROM BRAZIL
1978, dir. Franklin J. Schaffner.
[top] Todesengel;
[middle] white for the dinner and dance;
[bottom] medical whites.

see him outside Malone's apartment, a street-lit, pale phantom casing the joint, and then after luring Malone outside Nitti perches like some snowy bird of prey on the fire escape from which vantage point he guns Malone down. In the time it takes Malone to crawl back inside, Nitti appears with supernatural speed as a phantom presence in Al Capone's box at the opera, a pallid angel of death reporting back to his master, his otherworldliness echoed on stage by the white-faced Pagliacci. Gaston Bachelard, remarking on the effect that snowfall has on the environment, observed: 'As a result of this universal whiteness, we feel a form of cosmic negation in action'.[17] Nitti's as well as Mengele's and Cramer's whites create a similar pall of negation over the films in which they feature.

For the ultimate in dazzling whiteness as 'invisible darkness' we need the sharp contrast of black and white film and the polarisation of colour not only in terms of the film's production but also as an ideological position.[18] Roger Corman's remarkable 1962 indictment of racial hatred *The Intruder* returns us once again to notions of racial purity signified by the use of white clothing for the main protagonist, Adam Cramer (William Shatner). In the shimmering heat of the small southern town of Caxton, Cramer arrives to incite racial hatred and unrest on the eve of the town's integration of black and white school children. The opening titles present the tableaux of the white-suited Cramer, in dark glasses (to shield his eyes from his own radiance perhaps?) looking out from a train window at a group of cotton pickers, a visual distillation of the themes of racial segregation, intolerance and injustice that will be played out to masterly effect in the film. On Cramer's arrival in Caxton we see his progress through the town, a white-suited redeemer smiling beatifically, helping a little girl off the bus (both Nitti and Cramer are contrasted by the innocence of children, as indeed is Mengele who ironically seems at his most human while experimenting on his Paraguayan infant subject). He appears to all intents and purposes as a white knight in shining armour, or at least white seersucker. Cramer's triumphant progress through Caxton, charming all those he comes into contact

THE UNTOUCHABLES
1987, dir. Brian De Palma.
[top] Terrorist whites;
[bottom] spectral whites.

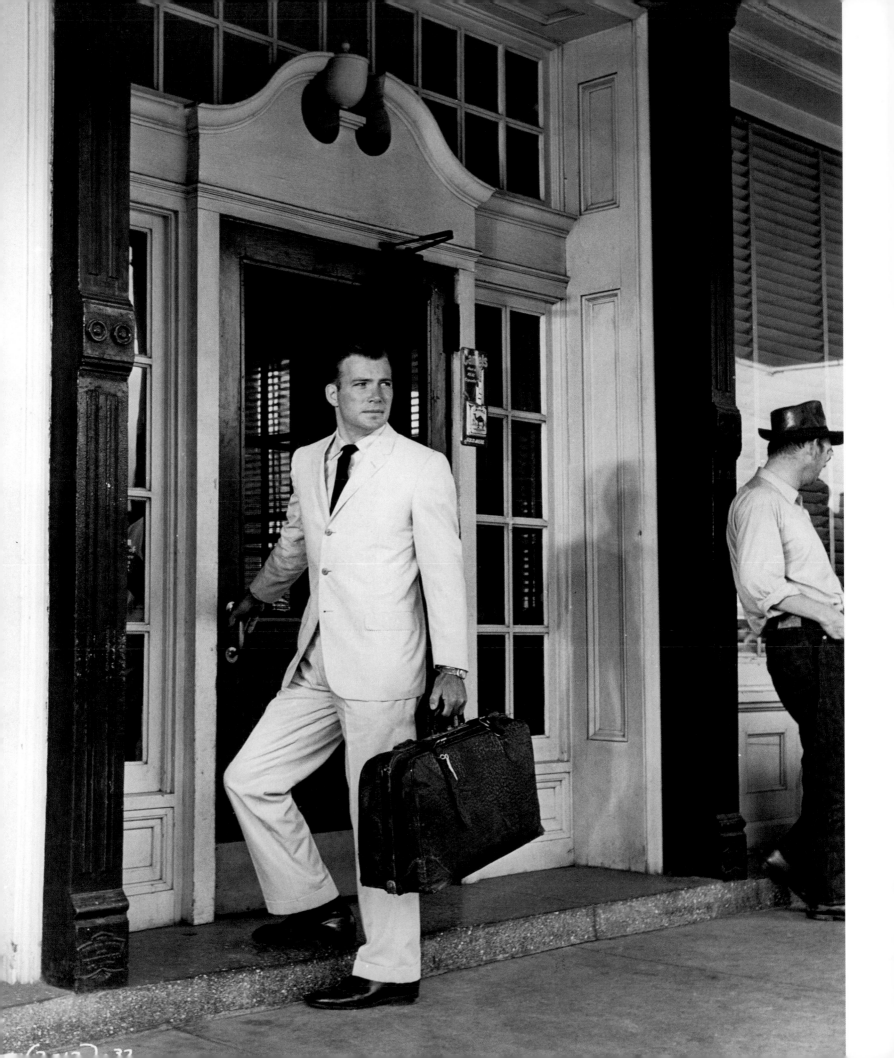

with, is helped in no small degree by the dazzling whiteness of his suit, a vestimentary testament to his saintliness. Only when he checks into the boarding house does the viewer realise that his intentions are far from virtuous: on being asked by the landlady what brings him to town he replies: 'You might say I'm a social worker. I've come to do what I can for the town . . . The integration problem.'[19] From this point onwards the film makes explicit Cramer's true identity as a megalomaniac consumed by prejudice, his ideological 'whiteness' radiating outwards, solarising the town and its inhabitants. 'White expresses a certain corporeality', observes Mark Wigley in *White Walls, Designer Dresses* and, due to the consummate cinematography of Taylor Byars, Cramer's whiteness throughout *The Intruder* is similarly positively tangible.[20] This whiteness is whiter than the midday sun in Caxton, whiter even than the robes of the Ku Klux Klan with whom he rides, and in the supremely super-natural moment where he appears almost as an apparition in Ella's bedroom (the underage daughter of the town journalist whom the viewer has seen Cramer systematically seduce and manipulate to incite further racial hatred), he is transfigured by the light piercing the gloom of her small-town teenage environ-ment. In this scene Cramer's brilliance is of the order that the classical scholar Origen recorded: 'since there are even degrees among white things, his garments became as white as the brightest and purest of all white things, that is light'.[21] Cramer has *become* light and it is perhaps fitting that this most iniquitous and mortal instance of reason blinded by light should be the most effective. For all the Technicolor brilliance of De Palma's contrasting of Nitti's razor-sharp whiteness against the blood-red decor of Al Capone's hotel room and opera box, or the exotic whiteness of Mengele's Paraguayan medico-safari ensembles, it is the ubiquitous white suit of a small-town hate-monger that is ultimately the most chilling.

Most commentators on men's fashion when discussing the modern-day suit liken it to a form of sartorial armour, an immaculately tailored carapace that renders those inside imper-vious to insults, invulnerable to attack and ready for any occa-

sion. With its provenance coming partly from sporting and military dress, and developed and refined with the additions of subtle padding and shaping that transforms the male body into an idealised set of masculine physical proportions, the well cut contemporary suit is to a certain degree metal made cloth. Cramer's suit seems equally indestructible, remaining brilliantly pristine and resistant to fights, cross-burnings, nights spent in jail and the ever present heat of Caxton. His protective whiteness is most effectively displayed in the scene where he incites the 'good folks' of Caxton to racial violence by delivering a rabble-rousing night-time speech, illuminated on the courthouse steps (see illus. p. 197). During his increasingly fanatical oratory, Cramer becomes incandescent both with rage and successive displays of the layering of his whiteness, unbuttoning his jacket, exposing his white shirt, taking the jacket completely off, bundling it up and casting it aside, then finally rolling up his shirt sleeves as he becomes more and more hysterical. He is in fact performing a kind of ideological striptease, for no matter how much he takes off he remains outwardly white, demonstrating that he is white-skinned as well as white thinking. This form of 'Non-Strip Tease' has been discussed by John Harvey who, as has been noted, suggests that even though the male suit plays with notions of exposure (the turning back of a lapel, obsolete buttons that are never fastened and so on), the wearer remains unexposed.[22] So it is with Cramer but ideologically, as well as sartorially, the more he exposes of himself the more his fundamental bigotry is made manifest, cocooned in his protective white-cotton armour; at the end of his speech, one of his converts hastens to return his jacket to him, an action that is repeated in similar 'preaching' scenes throughout the film.

Having established that the white suits in *The Boys from Brazil*, *The Untouchables* and *The Intruder* are fundamental to the almost supernatural propensity for evil of the films' central criminal figures, it follows therefore that these same garments must also provide the means for their eventual destruction. Like all mythical beings whether good or evil, an Achilles heel is as vital to their construction as is their apparent invincibility. From Samson's hair to Superman's costume (whether fashioned on Krypton itself or by Martha Kent out of the blanket he was found wrapped in as an infant), male style equates to male prowess. So it is only when Mengele abandons his love of the all-white outfit that he meets his demise. With his eugenic master-plan in peril, he decides that he himself will secure the safety of his remaining cloned Hitler, Bobby Wheelock (the last of the 'boys from Brazil') and murder his adopted father. It could be argued that Mengele's addiction to sartorial consumption is the cause of his ultimate downfall, as he chooses autumnal-shaded tweeds for his trip to Pennsylvania, blending in with the American landscape, where presumably he thought all white was somehow too outré even for his megalomaniac fashion sense. It is while dressed for the country in reserved green and brown that he meets his grisly and bloody end, savaged to death by Bobby's obedient pack of Dobermans.

Similarly, Nitti meets his fate only after Eliot Ness (Kevin Costner) puts a bullet through his immaculate white hat, knocking it off his head; Ness then proceeds to grab Nitti, pulling off his jacket in the process, a further stripping away of his tailored defences. This act leaves Nitti vulnerable and as he walks away combing his hair in an attempt to restore sartorial order, and presumably immortality, Ness pushes him off the roof of the court-house building which has been the scene of their struggle. As he plummets to earth, De Palma presents the audience with a typical cinematic tour de force when we see the flailing white body of Nitti crash through the roof of a car below. In the concluding shot of the scene, the audience sees his body sprawled and bloodied across the car's seats, his immaculate snow-white tailoring now fatally ruined, along with Nitti himself, the fallen Angel of Death fallen to earth for the final time.

Lastly, what of Adam Cramer, simultaneously the least 'supernatural' of the white-suited psychopaths and, it could be argued, the most effective and ultimately deadly 'white angel'? Not for him the stripping of his protective suit, rather another

[top to bottom]

THE BOYS FROM BRAZIL
1978, dir. Franklin J. Schaffner.
Vulnerable tweed.

THE UNTOUCHABLES
1987, dir. Brian De Palma.
Stripping the armour;
Falling angel.

THE INTRUDER
1961, dir. Roger Corman.
'Boy, you gonna get grass stains
all over those trousers'.

form of sartorial humiliation. At the scene of an abortive lynching he has attempted to engineer, he is struck to the ground by his erstwhile supporter, the local 'big shot' Verne Shipman, and he remains on his hands and knees, his white suit now incongruously pristine in the cold light of morning flooding the school playground where the scene takes place. It is perhaps the final humiliation for Cramer and a testament to the necessity for a villain's whites to remain in perfect order that he is advised to get up off the ground by Sam Carter, his nemesis and to a degree his conscience throughout the film, with the words: 'Boy, you gonna get grass stains all over those trousers if you don't get up', on one level an apparently, and one could argue, inappropriately flippant conclusion to the film.[23] However, this comment on sartorial cleanliness can also be understood as a way of emphasising how fragile the construction of masculinity is, as has been discussed in the previous section concerning male re dressings, and that someone whose destructive tendencies are reliant on the spectacle of immaculate tailoring can all too easily be brought down by the slightest of imperfections. As Debord suggested, once the inevitability of the spectacle is challenged it can no longer demand complete acceptance. Similarly, once the white suit's perfection is disputed, whether by choosing another colour, having it stripped from the body or staining, the spectacle of whiteness is destroyed and along with it the tailoring of evil.

PART 5

11 SEEING RED

'Put on your red dress, baby
Lord, we're goin' out tonight
Put on your red dress, baby
Well, we're goin' out tonight'[1]

If all over white is the favourite colour scheme for the male sociopath in film, then red must surely be its female equivalent. Red, and its socio-cultural construction as the colour of passion, immorality and exhibitionism, has meant that film teems with scarlet women of varying degrees of wickedness and licentiousness. Films such as *Jezebel* (1938) and *The Bride Wore Red* (1937) have been the subject of detailed investigations into the symbolism and power of red, even when as with these two examples the film is in black and white.[2] Richard Dyer in his essay on whiteness in cinema discusses Julie's (Bette Davis) decision to wear a red satin dress to the Olympus Ball in *Jezebel*, a ball where unmarried women were expected to wear white.[3] Dyer suggests that 'The immediate scandal is not just the refusal to conform and uphold the celebration of virginity that the white dress represents but the sexual connotations of the dress itself, satin and red, connotations made explicit in a scene at the dressmaker's ("Saucy, isn't it?" says Julie; "And vulgar", says her aunt, with which Julie enthusiastically concurs).' Dyer suggests that her red dress is not only intended to shock and provoke but also to imply that it is in fact 'ethnically specific'. He positions Julie emotionally and possibly ideologically with the black characters in Jezebel, who are represented as possessing a vitality and rebelliousness undesirable in white women in nineteenth-century, antebellum New Orleans, the setting of the film.[4]

Similarly, Joan Crawford's celebrated red beaded evening gown designed by Adrian for *The Bride Wore Red* has generated considerable critical appraisal. The film is ostensibly yet another variant on the 'clothes maketh man' paradigm, this time with Crawford playing Anni Pavlovich, a singer in a waterfront bar becoming an experiment for the wealthy Count Armalia (George Zucco), who attempts to prove that with the correct

PRETTY WOMAN
1990, dir. Garry Marshall.
Unremarkable red
(Buena Vista/Everett/Rex Features).

clothes and pointers she can pass herself off as a woman of means and breeding at a high-class resort. A variant of the makeover scenes previously discussed in 'Well, as long as the lady's paying . . .' provides a showcase for Adrian's dazzling creations when Anni, armed with the Count's money and letter of introduction, goes to 'Galli: Casa de Moda' to select her wardrobe for the experiment, and among other garments orders the famous red dress. Left to her own devices, unlike the compliant men who allow themselves to be dressed by women, Anni makes an inevitable mistake, and her outré taste epitomised by the dazzling red dress proves to be her undoing, even though the chambermaid and her ally at the resort has previously warned her: 'Not this dress, not here. You may as well wear a sign!'[5] Needless to say, Anni's true qualities outshine the glitter of red bugle beads in the end, and much has been written concerning the film's reinforcement of the need for Depression-era sobriety and the association of beads and similar embellishments with the costumes of easy virtue worn by the cinematic constructions of the gold-digger and the show girl. Most interesting, perhaps, is Jane M. Gaines's account of Adrian's sequinned dress for this film and for another Crawford vehicle, *Sadie McKee* (1934), which she suggests operate on an additional visual register, Adrian's dazzling (and extremely heavy) creations becoming 'a sheet of light that can be seen to be worn – not worn, but seen to be worn, that is not exactly seen as wearable in the practical, translatable sense, but only worn insofar as it is seen.'[6]

It is a testament to the skill of early Hollywood costume designers, working alongside lighting and set designers, that while both *Jezebel* and *The Bride Wore Red* are shot in black and white they manage to convey a palpable sense of the inappropriateness of the famous red dresses that are central to their plots.[7] With the advent of colour, the irresistible spectacle of clothing 'scarlet women' in scarlet continued via costumes including Cyd Charisse's sensational red jewelled dress in the 'Girl Hunt' sequence from *The Band Wagon* (1953), or the

JEZEBEL
1938, dir. William Wyler.
[facing] She will go to the ball
(Everett Collection/Rex Features).

THE BRIDE WORE RED
1937, dir. Dorothy Arzner.
[above] 'You may as well wear a sign!'
(Moviestore Collection/Rex Features).

recently widowed Jane Wyman's inappropriate red dress worn to the country club party in *All That Heaven Allows* (1955), to more recent designs such as Julia Robert's triumphant red gown in *Pretty Woman* (1990).[8] Of course, Roberts playing the prostitute Vivian would redress the effect that both Crawford and Davis produced by wearing red dresses at formal occasions. It is left to Vivian, the hooker with innate breeding and taste, to carry off her red gown when she accompanies Edward Lewis (Richard Gere), who like Count Armalia in *The Bride Wore Red*, has provided Vivian with the means to select her new wardrobe in the Rodeo Drive makeover sequence. However, unlike Adrian's jaw-dropping gown for Crawford, created at a period when Hollywood designers were instrumental in establishing the market for American fashion, with Hollywood providing its inspiration as well as its most effective marketing tool, the designs that Roberts wears in *Pretty Woman* are, as Stella Bruzzi observes, 'not particularly "special", but rather function as a symbolic visual shorthand for desirable femininity'.[9] Bruzzi goes on to list in detail the fashionable derivations for Vivian's red chiffon dress (Yves Saint Laurent, Bruce Oldfield and others), emphasising the officially accepted view that film costume should not be too directional, too 'fashionable' and therefore noticeable, a view given wide currency by the celebrated costume designer Edith Head who repeatedly suggested that clothes should never dominate but rather assist the characterisation of the role.[10] This remains the accepted understanding of the function of film costume today, which would perhaps have seemed incomprehensible to earlier designers such as Adrian or Travis Banton, who designed clothes that, while certainly adding visual richness to a character, also functioned independently from the wearer.[11] As Gaines points out, 'Adrian organized his own sartorial discourse within and sometimes against the mise-en-scène, and sometimes against the characters', an important point that echoes Bruzzi's discussion concerning the relationship between haute couture and film, and how the work of renowned fashion designers when designing for film transcends film costume's usual remit.[12]

It is perhaps ironic that the clothes in a film such as *Pretty Woman* from the late twentieth century domesticate and make anodyne the 'scarlet women' who inhabit 1930s film. The 'fear of fashion', which Head and many of the designers who emulated her betray in espousing clothing's subordinate role in the mise-en-scène, has become the norm and the acceptance of this 'truism' makes even more pressing the need to understand film clothing as more than just the reinforcement or augmentation of character. Clothing can, and indeed often does, function and register independently from the film narrative and part of that independence is derived from the viewer's emotional responses to the clothing on screen, responses that remain present regardless of how remote from our everyday experience elements of the film's plot may become. This emotional response is at its most powerful when clothing operates dysfunctionally. For an ultimately conservative, 'feel good' film such as *Pretty Woman*, it is unsurprising, therefore, that the tasteful red dress worn to accompany Edward on a visit to the opera should generate approval and admiration, a far cry from that worn by Lily Bart (Gillian Anderson) in the film version of *The House of Mirth* (2000) based on the 1905 novel by Edith Wharton, perhaps the most acute literary recorder of the social vicissitudes and economic complexities of dressing fashionably.[13] Lily accompanies Gus Trenor (Dan Ackroyd), her financial backer, to the opera and is so pleased with her own dazzling image that she is 'undisturbed by the base thought that her gown and opera cloak has been indirectly paid for by Gus Trenor'.[14] Terence Davies emphasises the notion of the kept woman by costuming Lily in head-turning red amid a sea of black and white and drives the point home when, on returning home, her aunt declares that she does not like her colour, referring both to the dress and Lily's temperament: it is as unsuitable a shade in 1900s New York as we have seen it was for Julie in nineteenth-century New Orleans in *Jezebel*. For red to retain its shock value, or at least to retain its connotations of immorality, contemporary productions must look to the past and so, like Lily's scandalous appearance in turn of the century New York, *Public Enemies* returns to the era of prohibition (both of alcohol and dress codes, it seems) where Billie Frechette, dressed in a cheap scarlet dress and coat, is taken to a high-class restaurant by John Dillinger. Conscious of the other patrons' glances, Billie stands out, as does Lily, among tables of blue- and black-clad diners and observes: 'They're looking at me because they're not used to having a girl in their restaurant in a three-dollar dress.' While the price of her outfit seems of paramount importance to Billie, it is certainly its garish red that acts as the spur for their disapproval.[15]

Lily's 'colour' recalls Dyer's formulation of the 'ethnically specific' red, which is finally resolved, it could be argued, in *Last Holiday*, where Queen Latifah plays the terminally ill (or so she believes) department-store worker Georgia Bird, who treats herself to a holiday at the hotel where her culinary hero, Chef Didier (Gerard Depardieu), is head chef.[16] *Last Holiday* is a reworking of *The Bride Wore Red*, with race replacing class as the social 'disadvantage' that clothing, including a red chiffon dress, may or may not overcome. In the customary makeover scene, Georgia visits an upmarket dress shop and asks the assistants to 'Make me international', referring perhaps to the necessary worldliness she wishes her wardrobe to achieve, as well as a less American and perhaps more European chic.[17] This demand, along with Julia Roberts's quietly tasteful red in *Pretty Woman*, counteracts the decidedly American show-stopping glamour that Adrian designed for Joan Crawford's European sojourn. Needless to say, Georgia's red is approved by one and all, so much so that she soon has a string of wealthy and important guests clamouring for her attention and, ironically, her perceived business acumen. Depardieu plays a similar role to Crawford's chambermaid, being the only one in on the secret, and watches over her triumphant progress like a culinary guardian angel. It appears that some seventy years after Bette Davis's and Joan Crawford's problematic reds, sexual and racial inequalities have been resolved in mainstream cinema and re-dressed in conservative crimson chiffon.

THE HOUSE OF MIRTH
2000, dir. Terence Davies.
[top] Lily at the opera.

PUBLIC ENEMIES
2009, dir. Michael Mann.
[middle] The three-dollar dress.

LAST HOLIDAY
2006, dir. Wayne Wang.
[bottom] Georgia is made 'international'.

If red may have lost its power to shock, and its inherent social dysfunctionality can only be revealed in black and white, then perhaps it is cut and colour that still have the power to disturb, as long as the wearer is even further beyond the confines of polite society and sartorial convention than any of the aforementioned red dressers. Kim Basinger as the alien Celeste Martin in *My Stepmother is an Alien* (1988) chooses an all-red outfit for her arrival on Earth and her appearance at the party where she meets Steven Mills (Dan Ackroyd).[18] However, this is no ordinary outfit and with its hooped skirt in stretch jersey, matching red gloves and saucer-shaped hat, it resembles an extraterrestrial Claude Montana 'knock off' in its exaggerated sculptural silhouette. Realising her mistake, Martin throws away her hat and starts undressing, much to the consternation of Mills, and returns to the party in a draped floral gown. This newly feminised Celeste is obviously more to his taste, as he droolingly nods his approval and takes her back to his house, the promise of erotic pastel domestic bliss having erased the memory of her strident red entrance.

Red dresses appear to be the particular garments that have most excited cinematic condemnation and latterly approbation, but so deeply embedded is the Western socio-cultural response to red, especially its perception as the hue that means danger, that it regularly seeps across other items of cinematic clothing. Red and its significance on screen could easily be the subject of a whole book, with garments taking prime position as the object of study, but is beyond the scope of this text. Yet, in any work devoted to red clothing in film, the image of the scarlet PVC raincoat worn by the murderous dwarf furtively appearing and disappearing into the gloom of night-time Venice in *Don't Look Now* (1973) must surely be counted as one of the more powerful uses of red in film.[19] Similarly memorable are the previously discussed *Red Shoes* and it is perhaps pertinent to ask whether the murderous shoes that dance their wearer to death both in Hans Christian Anderson's tale and the Powell and Pressburger film would be quite so deadly in another shade. Less persistent, perhaps, but none the less chilling is red's oscil-

lation between a colour that protects and one that harms, as demonstrated in the red snow-jacket featured in *Fargo* (1996).[20] In the snowy landscape of North Dakota, the location for the film, red is used on clothing as a colour that can easily be spotted by those rescuing travellers lost in this colourless environment. In *Fargo*, though, the same potentially life-preserving red jacket becomes the method of targeting its wearer. Inadvertently witnessing the murder of a traffic cop, a red-clad motorist is pursued by the hit man and in his attempt to get away, flips his car over on the icy road. As the murderer pulls up alongside, the driver gets out of the car and starts to run across the snowy wastes. His scarlet snow-jacket illuminated by the hit man's headlights becomes an easy target in dysfunctional red, and he is shot and killed (see illus. p. 209).[21] With the break of dawn, the brightly coloured jacket resumes its original function, pinpointing the exact location of its wearer's body, which forms a red locating scar on the snowy perfection of the landscape.

'What do you mean, let it go! I'm stood up here lookin' like a bottle of dish washing liquid, a summer squash, a stick of butter, somebody's cracked teeth and you want me to let it go!?' So says Cedric the Entertainer playing Ralph Kramden the bus driver, as he enters a benefit dinner dressed in a canary yellow suit in the out-takes played at the end of *The Honeymooners* (2005).[22] Ralph dons the yellow 'designer suit' under sufferance instead of his bus driver's uniform so that he can gain admittance to the dinner being held at the start of the New Jersey greyhound racing season. His attendance at this function is necessary for him to enter the dog that he has spent his life savings on, a stray he believes has the pedigree to be a winner. As a remake of the much loved 1950s American television sitcom of the same name, the film received lukewarm reviews but, as an example of dysfunctional cinematic colour, Ralph's ridiculed yellow provides a possible alternative to red as the shade guaranteed to make its wearer stand out from the discerning crowd. The comparisons pile up – 'sunflower . . . rubber ducky . . . piece of flan' – until Ralph is mistaken for the entertainment and forced on stage by the party's organiser, who registers his extrovert colour choice as the mark of the showman and exhibitionist. Of course, it is entirely possible that embarrassment can be generated from all shades but yellow seems to come close to red in the reaction it causes in film. Like red, yellow has distinct, negative socio-historical significance, associated with cowardice, sensational journalism, the cuckold and, in terms of sumptuary law, yellow was the colour Jews were forced to wear in the form of a piece of cloth or badge of various shapes attached to the breast throughout medieval Europe, and revived in the form of a star by the Nazis in the twentieth century.[23]

Residues of these 'badges of shame' appear to have migrated into popular culture as yellow becomes a colour redolent of humiliation. It is perhaps fitting that one of contemporary popular literature and film's regularly embarrassed heroines, Bridget Jones, opts for golden yellow satin for her setpiece of social mortification, the Law Society dinner scene that takes place in the second Jones film, *Bridget Jones: The Edge of Reason* (2004).[24] Even before this sequence, Bridget (Renée Zellweger) is depicted skydiving in a canary yellow jumpsuit as the roving reporter for *Sit-Up Britain*, her crash-landing into a pigsty captured for national television. On the eve of the Law Society dinner, in a sequence reminiscent of Crawford's in *The Bride Wore Red*, she ignores the advice, 'whatever you do, not the gold!' referring to the less than flattering golden yellow satin draped evening dress, and arrives at the dinner, overly made up and conspicuously yellow amid the more chicly attired guests.[25] Her shame is magnified when at the conclusion to the scene she manages to lose the quiz, assuring an expectantly hushed room that she knows the answer to the final question, which of course she does not, leaving all eyes focused on her embarrassed reddened face offset by the gown of humiliating yellow.

BRIDGET JONES: THE EDGE OF REASON
2004, dir. Beeban Kidron.
[facing] The colour of shame.

THE HONEYMOONERS
2005, dir. John Schultz.
[above] The new red.

Gimme eastern trimmin' where women are women
In high silk hose and peek-a-boo clothes
And French perfume that rocks the room
And I'm all yours in buttons and bows[1]

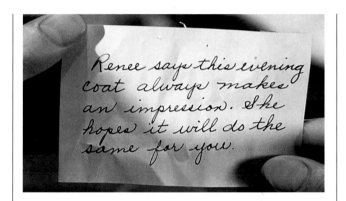

Bridget Jones could have avoided her 'wardrobe malfunctions' if only she had received the same helpful styling tips of which Bette Davis as Charlotte Vale takes advantage in the classic film of ugly duckling to swan, *Now, Voyager* (1942).[2] Charlotte's butterfly-like emergence from her dowdy spinsterish carapace is due to the advice (and wardrobe) she has received from her friend. Her first transformed appearance on the cruise which attracts the attention of her future lover, Jerry Durance (Paul Heinreid), is, as the viewer later finds out, scripted. With the aid of helpful labels pinned to each outfit, with pointers such as 'Silver slippers and silver evening bag will be found in the accessory closet' and 'Renee says this evening coat always makes an impression. She hopes it will do the same for you', Charlotte never puts a sartorial foot wrong and captivates all her fellow passengers.[3] Charlotte's sartorial triumph, however, is mirrored cinematically by numerous dysfunctional and ill-advised outfits – the too stylish, the regrettable and the distinctly bizarre.

This motive [motif] of foreignness, which fashion employs in its socializing endeavors, is restricted to higher civilization, because novelty, which foreign origin guarantees in extreme form, is often regarded by primitive races as an evil. This is certainly one of the reasons why primitive conditions of life favour a correspondingly infrequent change of fashions. The savage is afraid of strange appearances; the difficulties and dangers that beset his career cause him to scent danger in anything new which he does not understand and which he cannot assign to a familiar category. Civilization, however, transforms this affectation into its very opposite. Whatever is exceptional, bizarre, or conspicuous, or whatever departs from the customary norm, exercises a peculiar charm up-on the man of culture, entirely independent of its material justification.[4]

Georg Simmel's investigation of fashion written in 1904 can still provide a valuable context for the representation of the fashion industry and its products in popular film. The figures directly responsible for fashion, whether it be designers, models, promoters or even those who consciously follow and wear the latest styles, are invariably met with distrust, scorn or fear by those beyond fashion's profligate borders. Most productions deal with what happens when an outsider ventures into fashion's orbit, utilising the rational foreigner as a means to throw into sharp relief the shallow, wasteful and ultimately unfulfilling pursuit of fashion and this forms the narrative core of many of the most celebrated films about the fashion industry.[5] Less common is the depiction of the fashionable

figure in everyday or, to paraphrase Simmel, 'primitive conditions' and such sequences can be understood as depicting fashionable dress rendered dysfunctional. Beyond the centres of Paris, New York or Milan, the latest styles appear incongruous, affected and often unintelligible to the provincial gaze. Unlike the gangster's show-stopping suits, or the libertine's shocking reds, these embodiments of what previously has only been experienced as mediated imagery are viewed with mistrust.

Robert Siodmak's 1945 drama *The Strange Affair of Uncle Harry* utilises the conservative and jealous mistrust of metropolitan fashionableness as a way of exploring the oppressive and dysfunctional relationship between George Sanders playing Harry Quincey, the head designer of a New Hampshire textile mill, and his possessive sister, Lettie (Geraldine Fitzgerald).[6] Using a visual discourse of textile design, Harry's stifled existence, represented by his safe domestic designs for cloth (Harry's 'rosebuds' are constantly referred to) and his inveterate star-gazing at worlds far removed from his own, is suddenly galvanised by the arrival of Deborah Brown (Ella Raines), a fashion expert seconded to New Hampshire from the firm's head office in New York. A junior worker at the Warren mill is excited about her arrival and suggests to Harry: 'Now maybe we'll have puppy dogs and palm tree patterns and snazzy colours!'[7] Under Deborah's influence, Harry's designs, his amateur painting and his love for her all blossom; all that is left to cement their romantic partnership is the approval of the neurotic hypochondriac Lettie. While the unfolding plot involving poisonings, broken engagements and hinted incestuous relationships collapses under the weight of its implausibility, the *leitmotiv* of liberal urbanity as opposed to provincial repression is realised by the contrast between Deborah's and Lettie's outfits. Travis Banton's costumes for the film, though certainly augmenting the characterisation of Deborah and Lettie, also form an independent visual narrative. As the film progresses, Deborah is positioned as a succession of sophisticated fashion images – in satin lounge suit against a background of fashion drawings, curled seductively in a Victorian armchair and dressed top to toe in modern tailoring – while Lettie is increasingly constructed as the central figure in religious tableaux, gowned in lacy ethereal whites or preacher-like black and white. Their first meeting sees Lettie in ecclesiastical black velvet with white ruff, while Deborah is the height of New York chic in smartly tailored suit with cropped jacket, alligator purse and playful, knitted striped silk man's tie (Banton was famous for referring to men's dress in his designs for many of his female stars). Deborah's outfit prompts Lettie to exclaim: 'Hello! You're Miss Brown, of course. What a lovely suit! . . . We don't see fashions like that in Corinth!' Her disapproval thinly disguised as admiration is unmistakable and is typical of many such cinematic encounters between metropolitan chic and small-town censure.

THE STRANGE AFFAIR OF UNCLE HARRY
1945, dir. Robert Siodmak.
[facing] 'We don't see fashions like that in Corinth!'

RAISING HELEN
2004, dir. Garry Marshall.
[above] New York v. New Jersey.

This censure remains cinematically undiminished, so that even with the contemporary global dissemination of the most 'directional' of designs, when the fashion stranger comes to town she will always be met with hostility. Reese Witherspoon playing the successful New York fashion designer Melanie Carmichael (née Smooter) in *Sweet Home Alabama* (2002) is constantly reminded that even though she has changed her name, and now looks like 'sex on a stick' in all-black, when she returns home to her roots in Alabama she will necessarily undergo a series of ritual humiliations in order to rid her of her big-city chic pretentiousness.[8] Simmel proposed that differing fashions could be adopted by groups that to all intents and purposes were close to each other in geography or social class: 'Among primitive peoples we often find that closely connected groups living under exactly similar conditions develop sharply differentiated fashions, by means of which each group establishes uniformity within, as well as difference without, the prescribed set.' Transferring his anthropological observations to film can provide an explanation for the effect Kate Hudson's sparkling black mini dress has on her family in *Raising Helen* (2004).[9] Another recent example of the contemporary morality tale teaching that fashion does not equal happiness, *Raising Helen* tells the story of Helen Harris (Hudson) who ends up forsaking her fashionable Manhattan lifestyle as a talent scout at a successful modelling agency to look after her recently deceased sister's children. This of course provides ample opportunity to spell out that motherhood, even surrogate, and fashion do not mix but, prior to her sister's demise, Helen visits the family home in New Jersey for a birthday celebration (see illus. p. 215). Although the geographical distance between New York and New Jersey is negligible (and certainly less than Melanie realised existed between New York and Alabama, for example), the social and psychological distances are apparently insurmountable, at least until Helen forgoes her career. This divide is emphasised when Helen, on leaving the family party to return to New York and her model boyfriend, changes into an extremely short, glittering black dress while protesting: 'It's like they've never seen a dress before!' to which her reserved older sister Jenny replies: 'Um . . . they just haven't seen a . . . half of a dress.'[10]

The majority of mainstream American productions that feature the world of fashion as a substantial part of their plot can be understood as 'propaganda' films, sending out to audiences the clear message that while European fashion (which invariably means Paris fashion) is unassailable in terms of its history and prestige, it is American fashion that will breathe new life into what is regularly characterised in film as dysfunctionally chic, effete and decadent. This process gathered momentum after the Second World War when, with the demise of French fashion production under Nazi occupation, the burgeoning American industry (due in no small degree to Hollywood's promotion of domestic designers and the looks worn by the actors they dressed) took full advantage of the shifting balance of economic power. From the middle of the century American consumers and designers played an increasingly vital role in world fashion. While European fashion regained its influence post-war, American fashion's unique combination of a more relaxed attitude to dressing overlaid with Hollywood glamour ensured the lasting importance of transatlantic style. The glut of films made after the war that promoted the new wealthy American consumer travelling to the Continent depicted European culture, of which fashion was an integral part, as something that was available to experience and buy, but was also made necessarily elitist and 'foreign': it was fine for a vacation and to bring back home in the form of a souvenir, or perhaps a new wardrobe, but it would never replace plain-speaking, democratic American idealism. *National Lampoon's European Vacation* (1985) presents a late example of this fashion 'jingoism' when the Griswold family as part of their tour arrive in Rome and head straight to the designer clothes shops.[11] In an accelerated 'family fashion show' the Griswolds, parents and obnoxious teenagers, try on a number of 'looks' caricatured as typically Italian by comprising clashing colours, ridiculously padded shoulders and plenty of animal print.

Perhaps no more complete representation of the impact that fashionable dress can make on those who have as yet been untouched by its power, and indeed how what is initially characterised as hopelessly dysfunctional, is transformed, becomes supremely practical and then indispensable to that same community, can be traced than in *Lucy Gallant*.[12] Released in 1955, two years before *Funny Face* (perhaps still the most celebrated film about fashion), *Lucy Gallant* remains under-researched and yet its story of the American designer who rises to fashionable glory, overcoming a variety of trials and tribulations, echoes the actual rise to international prominence of post-war American fashion. What is especially interesting about the film is that it tells a familiar American fashion story, but without resorting to the customary device found in other fashion films such as *Roberta*, *Funny Face* and *The Devil Wears Prada*, that of contrasting good, honest American fashion people against the decadent Europeans. Lucy Gallant (Jane Wyman) is American through and through, knows it and is perfectly content to build her empire of fashion untainted by any European influence. It is fitting therefore that Edith Head, the film's costume designer, makes a rare cameo appearance as herself, narrating the fashion show climax to the film. Head's speech suggests an alternative understanding of her work, one that she herself professed should not be considered as fashion but as a kind of timeless *film* fashion. She formed this opinion, it seems, as a result of a costly lesson learnt early in her career when, owing to changes in European fashion trends, her film work looked suddenly out of step with the prevailing styles. However, her designs for *Lucy Gallant* and the speech with which she introduces them suggest, rather, that they were a specifically American rejoinder to European domination. She opens Lucy Gallant's fashion show with the following: 'As all of you know, there is no one permanent fashion centre. It could be in Paris, it could be in Rome, New York or in London. However, after seeing this collection I'm sure you'll agree with me that today, the real fashion centre of the world is right here in Texas'; it is tempting to speculate that Head herself, rather than screenwriters, wrote this particular paean to fashion in the USA.[13]

Her championing of 'home grown' style is especially ironic in this scene because the global theme of the fashion show which details the provenance of the various fabrics used – velvet from France, organdie from Switzerland, scarlet and white Italian satin and so on – features designs by Head herself, a satisfying reprisal for the frustration she had regularly felt earlier in her career when although the designer for a particular film, clothes for the leading lady or specific scenes would be bought in from Parisian fashion houses. As noted in the recent history of Head's career, 'Buying clothes from Paris to populate a film wardrobe was a practice nearly as old as the movies themselves. Silent film stars like Gloria Swanson would wear gowns from designers such as Paul Poiret, which were shipped to the studio, or just purchased by the actresses themselves while in Paris.'[14] *Lucy Gallant*'s dedicated espousal of American fashion, and advanced retailing techniques, distinguishes it as seminal in this respect, and its role in providing a model of uniquely American fashionable enterprise makes its relative obscurity all the more surprising.

After a storm has washed out the tracks, the train Lucy Gallant is taking from New York to Mexico is forced to make a stop at 'New Town', Texas, an emerging boom town in the throes of an oil rush. As the train brakes suddenly, the viewer's first sight of Lucy is through the window of her carriage with her set of white luggage and a large hatbox cascading down all around her after being dislodged from the luggage rack. In this image, she is both constituted by her possessions (the luggage is later revealed as containing an extensive and now unwanted trousseau) and in danger from the falling cases. This ambivalent relationship to dress is something that runs throughout the film's moralistic tale of Lucy's choice between domestic happiness versus a career in fashion. Charlton Heston playing the rancher Casey Cole sweeps the *Fashion* magazine-reading, mink-coated Lucy, and her extensive set of impractically white luggage, off the train and carries her (so as to avoid her elegant New York heels sinking into the mud) to his truck and onwards into the narrative that will see the couple falling in love, Gallant becoming the successful head of a chain of fashion outlets and

Cole striking it rich when he discovers oil on his ranch. Gallant's attire is established from this opening scene as completely impractical for the rough and ready oil town. Even the galoshes she dons for her walk to the boarding house that Casey recommends are no ordinary overshoes, but are in impractical white like her luggage; they might keep her feet dry, but seem more suited for a light Manhattan shower than the quagmire of rain-soaked un-built Texan roads. The practical/impractical paradigm that is Lucy's complex character is revealed throughout the film by this protean construction of dress which, like her own presence in the film, is simultaneously decorative and pragmatic.

The following morning Lucy's landlady Molly (Thelma Ritter) reports on the strikingly dressed stranger's arrival to her friends: 'A real nice girl, friend of Casey's, you know. Clothes like right out of a fashion magazine, and her luggage, it's white, all white! I don't see how she gets to clean it, let alone use it!'[15] Lucy appears in an immaculately tailored suit, the same white galoshes and mink clutch bag and trimmed hat. Molly's friends Irma Wilson and her daughter Laura are introduced and immediately entranced by Lucy's fashionable appearance; Laura: 'What a beautiful suit, and . . . and that purse!' Irma: 'Where'd ya get 'em?', Lucy: 'Well, they're from New York, they're Paris originals.' Irma: 'Paris, France?'[16] Lucy's morning walk through the unbuilt streets of New Town draws amazed glances from the town's womenfolk, a mixture of admiration, mistrust and incomprehension at this stranger in their midst, similar to the outlaw's progress through countless Hollywood western frontier towns. As she proceeds and collects more and more envious glances at her clothes, including from one little girl who, after staring in disbelief at Lucy's mink purse, runs after her mother declaring 'It's made outta fur, Mama!', Lucy takes advantage of the closure of a temporary real estate office and holds an impromptu sale of all her clothing – the unworn trousseau – which we later learn is the result of her being left in the lurch in New York. This remarkable scene, in which Lucy in a single afternoon educates the fashion Philistines of New Town into the esoteric mysteries of Parisian and

Manhattan style and its concomitant price tags, sets Lucy on the career path that is the subject of the rest of the film, and which will see her open a successful Texan fashion retail business. Yet, Lucy's first 'pop-up' shop is pivotal in that it not only establishes the need for American fashion outside the accepted centre of Manhattan (as the women fight over $495 silk organza day dresses, lace and chiffon negligees and high-heeled gold kid sandals) but is also a fine example of the dysfunctionality of fashionable clothing in the context of 'primitive conditions' transformed into a desirable and profitable (Lucy makes $4,865 after a morning's retailing) commodity.[17] The only requirement is that the transformer must be sufficiently stylish for, as Simmel suggested,

> The reason why even aesthetically impossible styles seem *distinguée*, elegant, and artistically tolerable when affected by persons who carry them to the extreme, is that the persons who do this are generally the most elegant and pay the greatest attention to their personal appearance, so that under any circumstance we would get the impression of something *distinguée* and aesthetically cultivated.[18]

This impression Lucy achieves even amid the unlikely circumstances of New Town, Texas.

The impact of being too fashionably dressed, too 'distinguée', as Simmel expressed it, among those beyond fashion's orbit is usually caused by those already working within the fashion industry or who, as in the case of Lucy Gallant, soon will be. Reaction to these chicly dressed denizens of the world of fashion is employed not only to demarcate the gulf between the fashionable and the 'unfashionable' but also to demonstrate that fastidiousness in dress is invariably accessorised by a proportionately inadequate social or emotional sensibility: in short, the fashionable are shallow, irresponsible and selfish. These encounters between fashion's emissaries and the 'real' world usually take place within the rarefied domain of the fashion industry itself and it is only when these impeccably dressed creatures venture beyond fashion's reach that the 'latest thing' becomes ridiculous.

LUCY GALLANT
1955, dir. Robert Parrish.
[top] Edith Head extolling
Texan fashion design;
[bottom] Lucy's 'pop-up' shop.

Even those who, while not directly connected to the world of fashion, consider themselves to be *au courant* in matters of taste can be undone by intentional misdirection from a fashion 'expert'; in this instance even the supremely chic can be transformed into the supremely dysfunctional. A number of examples of sartorial misdirection exists on film: one directly expressive of the precariousness of taste is found in the 1935 fashion-set musical *Roberta*, an early, yet explicit, example of Hollywood's promotion of the domestic American fashion industry.[19] Ostensibly set in Paris, although the audience would not know this as the film remains resolutely studio-bound with the action taking place in an imagined topography, it tells the story of the unlikely American 'takeover' by Randolph Scott, playing the college football star John Kent, of Roberta's, a successful 'French' fashion house. Roberta's is in fact owned by Kent's elderly aunt Minnie, who plays 'Madame Roberta' complete with thick, fake French accent. On her death, the business passes to Kent, who of course knows nothing about fashion, but has fallen in love with Roberta's assistant and the real design talent behind the house, Princess Stephanie, an exiled White Russian (Irene Dunne). The reappearance of Kent's girlfriend, Sophie Teale, jeopardises Stephanie and John's blossoming romance and, in order to push them apart again, Stephanie in collusion with Fred Astaire, playing the entertainer Huck Haines, carry out an elaborate act of sartorial sabotage. Stephanie: 'The more I think of it, the more I'm sure the dress will bring out something elegantly alluring in you.'[20] So says Stephanie to Sophie when showing her a revealing, low-backed black satin evening gown, entitled 'La Sirène Noir'. Little does Sophie know that this particular gown has been cut from Roberta's latest collection at the specific request of her fiancé John Kent, the new owner of the fashion house. On its first showing Kent tells Stephanie: 'I don't like that one' and later, after she has attempted to modify it, continues: 'If you don't mind I'd like that dress out.'[21] This is a surprisingly adamant request from someone with no interest in fashion, who has until the showing of this particular model been quietly acquiescent in matters of couture and personal taste.

While Kent's disapproval seems to stem from a rather prudish distaste for the amount of naked flesh exposed by the gown, Huck, typically, is not so restrained in his opinion, declaring it to be: 'Marvellous! Like a peeled eel!'[22] The dress is soon forgotten until the arrival of the condescending and snobbish Sophie, when, knowing that Kent will disapprove of the dress, Stephanie and Huck set about coercing Sophie to buy it, suggesting first that it has been discarded, then reserved for someone else and finally that it will not suit her, knowing full well that this 'negative selling' technique will only encourage her to buy it. Needless to say, when she reveals the dress later to Kent, throwing off her evening coat and asking 'How do you like it? Isn't it a knockout?' Kent astonishes her by replying: 'It's the worst looking thing I ever saw.'[23]

This sartorial subterfuge is particularly effective as a demonstration of the ephemeral status of taste, dependent as it is on indefinable qualities that often have nothing to do with the actual design of a garment, given that 'La Sirène Noir' is no more or less stylish than many of Roberta's other creations. Instead, its transformation from chic to *déclassé* is entirely dependent on the wearer and the viewer, as Bourdieu famously stated: 'Taste classifies, and it classifies the classifier.'[24] The reaction to the gown can be seen as a convoluted comment on wholesome American clothes versus immoral European fashion. Kent, the all-American jock, dislikes the dress, which has been created by Stephanie, the exiled Russian princess, who has not only been offered shelter and employment by an American-owned Paris fashion house but is also now becoming emotionally involved with Kent; he, from here onwards, will act as a corrective to her old-world European excess. The revolutionary model of working practice that is the House of Roberta, with Huck, Kent, Stephanie and Lizzie, alias 'Comtesse Scharwenka' (Ginger Rogers), working collectively on the new collection, while individually pretending to be something they are not (whether that be aristocratic, fashion savvy, or not in love), is destabilised by the arrival of Sophie who, although American, is representative of an outmoded class-consciousness. It is entirely fitting, therefore, that she chooses a gown reflective of her dissipated, patrician character.

Echoes of *Roberta* can be seen in a later and more infamous example of sartorial misdirection, again from an 'insider', but this time aimed at an interloper from the lower ranks, and certainly a stranger to the world of sophisticated elegance. Mrs Danvers (Judith Anderson), the formidable housekeeper in *Rebecca*, 'assists' the new Mrs de Winter (Joan Fontaine) in her choice of costume for the fancy dress party that will mark her arrival as the new mistress of Manderley.[25] As Sophie is tricked into choosing 'La Sirène Noir', so too is the new Mrs de Winter tricked into wearing a recreation of the very same costume that the deceased but ever present Rebecca, famously and much more stylishly wore. She is easy prey for Danvers's unhelpful fashion tips, having been established from the outset as sartorially naive when she confesses to Maxim during their whirlwind romance in Monte Carlo: 'Oh, I wish I were a woman of thirty-six, dressed in black satin with a string of pearls', little realising that this is the antithesis of what Maxim desires.[26] Once at Manderley and on learning more about Rebecca's unobtainable style, she scans fashion magazines, stopping at an image of a sophisticated evening dress and then in a later scene appearing for dinner in the very same garment, causing, not so much the distaste reserved for Sophie dressed in black satin at the Café Russe, but amusement as Maxim dismisses her attempts at chic: 'Well, what on earth have you done to yourself?' and 'do you think that sort of thing is right for you? It doesn't seem your type at all ... [Laughing] And what have you done to your hair?'[27] His most vehement disapproval, however, is reserved for the costume party scene and her disastrous descent of Manderley's grand staircase (a travesty of the traditional mannequin's descent in a fashion show, here taking place at the 'House of Rebecca'), dressed in the carbon copy of his deceased wife's costume: 'Go and take it off! It doesn't matter what you put on. Anything will do!' To cement her appearance's intrinsic dysfunctionality, Mrs Danvers adds: 'Even in the same dress you couldn't compare!'[28]

Elle Woods (Reese Witherspoon) in *Legally Blonde* (2001) is both too fashionably dressed and the victim of sartorial misdirection.[29] As the sorority president, elected 'Miss June', and

ROBERTA
1935, dir. William A. Seiter.
[top] The 'peeled eel'.

REBECCA
1940, dir. Alfred Hitchcock.
[bottom] 'Do you think that sort of
thing is right for you?'

a fashion merchandising major, Elle has an understandably heightened preoccupation with her appearance but, while a fondness for top-to-toe pink outfits accessorised by a similarly attired chihuahua might be *de rigueur* in southern California, it causes equal amounts of derision and dismay once she enrols at Harvard Law School. Her struggle to assert the rights of the hyper-feminised to be taken seriously by the legal profession comprises most of the comedic setpieces of the film. The apparent impossibility of her task is hammered home soon after her arrival at Harvard when she is intentionally misdirected by her former boyfriend's current fiancée to attend a college party dressed as a Playboy Bunny Girl, a contemporary updating of Mrs Danvers's malicious costume advice. Needless to say, Elle wins the day and strikes a blow for pink Chanel-suited blondes everywhere, suggesting that fashion need not always be the sign of the brainless (see illus. p. 212).

Feeling out of place, whether due to being too fashionable, bad advice or what can only be understood as distinctly bizarre clothing choices, constitutes many of the most significant instances of dysfunctional dressing. Similarly, attempts to 'fit in' or 'pass' by the adoption of what is invariably erroneously understood as the 'local' dress is always risky and ill-advised. Dressing up or down is fraught with danger and embarrassment; in Dickens's *Great Expectations* (1861), for example, Joe Gargery, the blacksmith, visits Pip in his London chambers and dresses, as he thinks, accordingly. This famous scene of sartorial angst sees Joe in his 'utterly preposterous' cravat and collars, supremely perplexed by the unaccustomed hat he wears, and ends with Joe himself declaring 'I'm wrong in these clothes' before departing.[30] Gargery at least has the perspicacity to realise that he is out of place in fashionable London, an ability entirely lacking in many similar cinematic dressers. In many respects, 'dressing down' or trying to fit in with one's supposed 'inferiors' is even more problematic than dressing up, a fact made clear to Walter Wade Jnr. (Christian Bale), the privileged, bespoke-suited sociopath and murderer in John Singleton's 2000 version of *Shaft*.[31] Wade enlists the aid of the drug-dealer Peoples Hernadez (Jeffrey Wright) to find and kill the only witness to Wade's

crime. He wears what he thinks will allow him to blend into Hernandez's Hispanic neighbourhood, an attempt Hernadez questions: 'You tryin' to blend in or something? You look like a fucking duck hunter!'[32] This was, in fact, the second time in 2000 that Christian Bale played a clothes-obsessed sociopath, having completed the role of Patrick Bateman in *American Psycho* in the same year. In an earlier scene in *Shaft*, Wade is held in a police cell with an assortment of villains, one of whom tries to take Wade's shoes: a fight ensues, with Wade beating the other inmate and stamping on his face with the self-same shoes, a typical moment of Bateman-like, clothing-initiated sadism.

Some outfits defy all comprehension and are accordingly dysfunctional, on aesthetic as well as other grounds. For example, the garment that Lee Remick playing Katherine Thorn, the 'adopted' mother of the anti-Christ in *The Omen* (1976), wears in hospital defies categorisation; it is part dressing-gown, part overall, part ceremonial robe.[33] Already disabled by the plaster casts she has been put in following Damien's, the re-born anti-Christ's, murderous attempt on her which leaves her fractured, internally bleeding and no longer pregnant, she attempts to dress herself and leave the hospital. The diaphanous floor-length robe, with no apparent front or back fastenings, proves especially difficult to remove with one arm in a cast and gets caught over her shoulders and face, leaving her veiled and completely disabled. Enter Billie Whitelaw playing Mrs Baylock, Damien's protector, who despatches the defenceless Katherine, by pushing her to her death out of the hospital window, with the offending garment still wrapped round her face and arms. Thorn's bizarre nightwear is reminiscent of the distinctly clerical and spectacularly flounced negligee worn by Gene Tierney in *Leave Her to Heaven* (1945) for the scene where she accidentally 'trips' down the stairs (rather than 'falling' over the banisters as in Thorn's 'accident') and also loses her unborn child, suggesting that only the most outlandish of garments can clothe the miscarriage-prone mother.[34]

Returning to the theme explored earlier, concerning how forms of dress that are acceptable or the norm in one situation become immediately problematic if relocated to a space where their vestimentary signification is either unintelligible or otherwise dysfunctional, the cinematic 'urban cowboy suit' is another specific example of this sartorial shift. Mary Douglas observed: 'There are several ways of treating anomalies. Negatively, we can ignore, just not perceive them, or perceiving we can condemn. Positively, we can deliberately confront the anomaly and try to create a new pattern of reality in which it has a place.'[35] This comment accompanies her larger exploration of how societies construct ritual responses to 'matter out of place', and the examples of urban cowboys found in productions such as *Coogan's Bluff* (1968), *Midnight Cowboy* (1969) and *Blazing Saddles* (1974) can justifiably be considered as cinematic 'matter out of place'.[36] There are numerous other instances of urban cowboys on film (Robert Redford as the faded rodeo star in *The Electric Horseman*, 1979, or John Travolta in *Urban Cowboy*, 1980, spring to mind) but, while these productions interrogate the anachronism of the cowboy code in contemporary society, the films considered shortly explore both moral dislocation and a sense of being geographically 'out of place' to a significant degree via their leading character's dysfunctional dress. The typical sartorial elements of the cinematic cowboy – Stetson, leather fringed jackets, boots and bootlace neckties – have been consolidated to produce the dress code for desert, canyon and prairie, regardless of the film's period. When transposed to the urban landscape, these essential items of dress become anomalous and what formerly provided cover, protection and respect for the wearer, now only receive derision and hostility. In *Coogan's Bluff* Clint Eastwood, playing the Arizona deputy sheriff Walt Coogan dressed in western-styled suit, Stetson, bootlace tie and cowboy boots, is sent to New York to extradite an escaped killer. His outfit immediately becomes a locus of unwanted attention and comment from what Coogan regards as the ineffectual Manhattanite police force and nearly everyone else he meets in the big city. Automatically assumed to be from Texas, Coogan has to deal simultaneously with the sartorial bigotry and his own frustration at 'not getting his man' (the killer escapes) that his appearance promises. The film can be seen as a transitional moment in Eastwood's career and both his character and

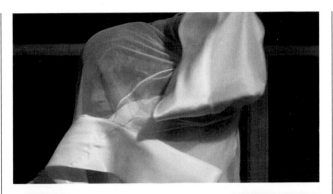

THE OMEN
1976, dir. Richard Donner.
[top] Satanic nightwear.

LEAVE HER TO HEAVEN
1945, dir. John M. Stahl.
[bottom] Ellen chooses lace
for immolation.

COOGAN'S BLUFF
[top] 1968, dir. Don Siegel.
Urban cowboy (Moviestore Collection/
Rex Features).

MIDNIGHT COWBOY
1969, dir. John Schlesinger.
[middle] Urban cowboy.

BLAZING SADDLES
1974, dir. Mel Brooks.
[bottom] Urbane cowboy.

costume position him midway between the cigar-chewing, poncho-wearing, plains-riding 'Man With No Name' and the 1970s-suited Harry Callahan. *Coogan's Bluff* has been referred to as an 'eastern western', and the personal and public reactions to his vestimentary dislocation is the chief expression of the film's generic hybridity.[37]

The cowboy outfit Jon Voight wears as Joe Buck in *Midnight Cowboy* is intrinsic to his persona as a big-city hustler. Leaving his traumatic Texan past behind, dishwasher Joe purposely constructs a new identity for himself as Joe Buck the cowboy gigolo, and the film's opening scenes detail this assembly. Joe showers, deodorises and then proceeds to don a black Stetson, a lucky horseshoe embroidered shirt, western pants, gold-stitched cowboy boots, fringed suede jacket and neckerchief. After admiring his reflection in the mirror, Joe leaves his apartment to say goodbye to his colleagues at the diner, carrying a spectacular cow-skin suitcase, which is later revealed to contain more new, elaborately embroidered cowboy shirts, pin-ups of naked women and a torn cinema poster of Paul Newman as Hud, his fictitious cowboy role-model. As a depiction of the construction of male identity through the act of dressing, the opening of *Midnight Cowboy* pre-dates the similar but more critically considered male dressing sequences of Tony Manero in *Saturday Night Fever* and Julian in *American Gigolo*, yet Joe Buck's innocent appreciation of his own image seems somehow more poignant than Julian's and Manero's auto-eroticisation and his appearance's subsequent deterioration all the more affecting. It is another of Joe's spectacular shirts, embroidered with bluebirds, that initiates his first encounter with Rico Rizzo (Dustin Hoffman), the consumptive petty conman who will become Joe's mentor, companion and, ultimately, dependant. Joe's immaculate appearance at the beginning of the film gradually deteriorates, becoming more and more shabby and stained, equalling his own descent into the grimy underbelly of New York society consisting of pimps, transvestites and rent boys, a far cry from Joe's idealistic and pristine fantasy of himself as the feted hustler kept by a series of wealthy Manhattan

society women. As with Coogan's wardrobe in *Coogan's Bluff*, Joe's cowboy clothing loses its ability to protect and earn respect once it is worn in the big city, and delivers none of the imagined sexual and economic advantages for which Joe longs. However, unlike Coogan's clothes, Joe Buck's outfit is never more than a costume which in his naiveté he imagines will perfect his role as the big-city hustler, so it is entirely fitting that in the film's dénouement we see him discard his soiled cowboy outfit for cheap resort clothing, a new costume for a new role as the nurse who will assist the dying Rizzo in his dream (as ultimately fantasmatic as Joe's dreams of New York) of ending his days luxuriating in the Miami sun.

'If I could find a sheriff who so offends the citizens of Rock Ridge that his very appearance would drive them out of town.'[38] So conjectures the corrupt politician Hedley Lamarr (Harvey Korman) in the 1974 comedy *Blazing Saddles*, who soon after hits on the idea of appointing a black man to be the sheriff of Rock Ridge, as part of his plot to seize control of the town and profit from the sale of its land to a railroad company. Lamarr selects Bart (Cleavon Little) for the post, a convict whom he saves from the gallows to assume the unenviable position of being the first black sheriff, which he assumes will be a short-lived post. To the strains of the Count Basic Orchestra (in situ in the desert), the scene depicting the arrival of the new sheriff opens with a close-up of a Gucci saddle-bag and, panning upwards, the camera lovingly lingers over a coffee-coloured leather belt and holster, piped in cream and finished with silver buckles, travels on past the finest suede trousers and shirt, again piped in contrasting cream, and eventually comes to rest on Bart's face with its effortlessly cool expression, shadowed by the brim of his perfect cream Stetson finished with silver hat-band. Riding over on his matching Palomino stallion, Bart receives acknowledgement from Count Basie before proceeding to Rock Ridge, where as a black man riding into town as their new sheriff he is met by the townsfolk with the predictable mixture of horror and disbelief. This subversion of the typical western mise-en-scène is in strict accordance with *Blazing Saddles'* meta-cinematic, genre-parodying humour, and Bart's appearance as the 'stranger who comes to town' is typical of the film's destabilisation of the western and its established characterisations and plot devices. The sheriff being black provides many of the film's most acerbic gags both visual and dialogical, but it is perhaps Bart's urbanity, his suave sophistication, his 'out of towness' that ultimately generate the most telling indictment of the townsfolk's moribund bigotry. Unlike Joe Buck and Coogan, Bart's outfit is ostensibly perfectly suited to his new role as sheriff – he is after all in the Midwest, not in a big city – but of course he is also the urban cowboy par excellence, and his outsider status is as much due to his fondness for matching accessories and designer labels as to his ethnic background. The double anomaly of their new sheriff being both black and superbly dressed means that Bart is doubly condemned since it is beyond the power of the townsfolk to 'create a new pattern of reality' for this anomaly.[39] That task is left in the end to the unreality of the film itself: a comedy western that eventually collapses as the result of the accelerating dismantling of its structure, with the action spilling onto other film sets, its leading characters escaping to watch the end of their own film in an actual cinema and Bart riding off into the sunset not on his trusty speed but in a chauffeur-driven limousine. As an urban cowboy, sporting Gucci in a Midwestern town in what at one point in the film we learn is supposed to be the year 1874, the film refocuses, parodies and refers to those cinematic moments discussed previously concerning the encounter between the too-fashionably dressed whose Parisian style inspires both envy and suspicion. Indeed, towards the end of *Blazing Saddles* the actors crash into a Fred Astaire-type musical set in 1930s Paris. Bart voices feelings about not only his own situation but, it could be argued, of all those stylish cinematic cosmopolitans who discover themselves among unsophisticated rustics, when after his first disastrous encounter with the good people of Rock Ridge, he finds himself alone: 'Oh baby! You're so talented! And they're so dumb!'[40]

13 WEAR AND TEAR

Me shirt dem a-tear up, me trousers a gone,
Don't wanna end up like Bonnie and Clyde[1]

A man's suit is often likened to armour, providing practical and emotional protection, as well as the perfect site for the display of vestimentary economic superiority. As has been discussed previously, when the suit becomes too showy and elaborated, or when the choosing and purchase of the suit is relinquished to women, its protective status is destabilised and, like the excesses of Renaissance suits of armour, the cinematic suit in these situations is rendered decoratively dysfunctional.[2] The majority of suits on screen function fairly simply, connoting respectability, authority and conservatism, but there are certain sets of clothing that transcend this expected function and assume a super-functional existence as 'armour-plated' suits which bestow a mythical status on their wearers. One of the more notable of these super-suits is that worn by Cary Grant playing the beleaguered Roger Thornhill in *North by Northwest* (1959).[3] Thornhill's lightweight grey wool two-piece is possibly the most widely discussed man's suit in cinematic history and, whether it was actually made by the Savile Row tailors Kilgour French and Stanbury (reputed to be one of Grant's favoured outfitters) or how many of the suits were actually made (six or sixteen appear to be the most commonly accepted figures), the suit has excited film and dress historians alike. Overriding these particular production details, however, is the suit's apparent indestructibility; for the most sustained investigation of this aspect of the suit, Ulrich Lehmann's semiotic reading of it in his essay 'Language of the PurSuit' is invaluable.[4] Lehmann applies Barthes's linguistic concept of *langue* and *parole* to Thornhill/Grant's suit, initially establishing the conventional and superficially unremarkable grey suit as *langue*, that is, a suit that conforms to society's understanding of a suit, a 'structural institution', and Grant/Thornhill's idiosyncratic wearing and habitation of his particular suit as *parole*, 'a subtle but clearly expressed deviation from the norm'.[5] Lehmann also explores the conflation between the character of Roger Thornhill and that of Cary Grant himself, suggesting that the star's characteristic debonair appearance simultaneously facilitates and resists a reading of Thornhill as anything more than his wardrobe 'because he [Grant] essentially plays himself and not a character'.[6]

Cary Grant was not alone, of course, in maintaining a highly successful movie career by 'playing himself' and, certainly under the early to mid-twentieth century studio system, stars noted for playing sophisticated, elegant and relaxed characters tended to appear in public dressed as and 'acting their part'. What is pertinent to this study, however, is not that Grant's suit in *North by Northwest* was of a style and cut that Grant himself favoured and wore but, rather, that meta-cinematically his suit and its indestructibility can be seen as a sartorial nexus that links earlier and later films in which Grant's characters seem to question the condition of sartorial perfection and flawless dysfunctionality. As is well known, Thornhill's suit in *North by Northwest* undergoes a succession of textile traumas, constantly creased, crushed, soiled, shot at, and yet remains unmarked; a quick hotel sponging is all that is needed to restore it to its immaculate condition. Lehmann points out that after the famous crop-dusting sequence, 'The beholder notices no tears or rents in the cloth': it is truly a miraculous garment that can comfortably hang next to the garments worn by the Israelites during their exodus in the wilde rness, whose 'raiment waxed not old upon thee, neither did thy foot swell, these forty years'.[7] This phenomenal suit is discarded at the climax to the film, its perfect surface exchanged for ill-fitting off-the-peg shirt and trousers once Thornhill has been inculcated into the world of espionage that he has accidentally entered; with this change of clothes comes a new-found seriousness, his perfect tailoring along with his glib Madison Avenue cynicism abandoned in readiness for his new role as the hero of Mount Rushmore and saviour of the double agent Eve Kendall (Eva Marie Saint).

Four years later we find Grant immaculately attired as ever playing himself, or perhaps a variant of Roger Thornhill, in *Charade* (1963), a film often described by its fans as the best

Hitchcock film that Hitchcock never made or, as David Thomson put it somewhat more reservedly, 'a modest bow to Hitchcock'.[8] Grant plays Peter Joshua (at least occasionally, for his character assumes multiple identities and names throughout the film) who becomes emotionally involved with Audrey Hepburn playing the recently widowed Regina 'Reggie' Lampert. The complex plot, involving gold stolen by a group of Second World War soldiers, subsequent attempts to relocate the gold by a variety of picturesque criminals and US government agents (one of whom Joshua is eventually revealed as), is played with comic élan by its cast. *Charade* is perhaps most memorable for the relationship between its two elegant stars, Hepburn impeccably dressed by Givenchy, as was customary by this point in her career, and Grant equally stylish in a series of flawlessly cut suits. In an intriguing series of meta-cinematic sartorial references, Joshua in *Charade* deconstructs the supernatural suiting worn in *North by Northwest*, re-dressing Thornhill's impossibly impervious apparel. Joshua's appearance is systematically dismantled throughout *Charade* which, if considered in the light of Grant's off-stage persona (a biographical reading of his film's narratives is difficult to avoid, as Lehmann among others have noted), is a final (Grant would make only two further films after *Charade*, retiring in 1967) undoing of his perfect surface.[9] Reggie tarnishes Joshua's appearance by smearing ice cream on his suit, prompting him to request later as they prepare to go to dinner, 'Let me know what you want to eat so that I can pick out a suit that matches', referring to this earlier soiling of his facade which, unlike the magical grey two-piece worn in *North by Northwest*, is not quite as 'wipe clean'. Joshua then proceeds to enact a sequence that appears to refer directly to his celebrated *North by Northwest* suit and its remarkable properties. In an attempt to distract Reggie from her increasingly endangered situation, Joshua takes a shower in his suit, declaring it to be 'Drip dry!', and tells Reggie that he goes through this ritual 'every day – the manufacturer recommends it'; as he lathers his 'second skin', he reads the label's supposed washing instructions: 'Wearing this suit during washing helps protect its shape.'[10]

CHARADE
1963, dir. Stanley Donen.
[top to bottom]
Initial dismantling with ice cream.
'Drip dry!'
Piercing of the armour.
'Did you hear something?'

Joshua/Grant seems to be offering a slapstick explanation of not just this but his other suits (including Thornhill's) that miraculously keep their shape no matter what befalls them. Before this incident, Joshua has begun the unravelling of his perfect facade when he pulls a thread from his sock (discussed earlier in Part Three's 'One size fits all?') to set a trap. However, this relatively minor dismantling is swiftly superseded in the later scene where his tailoring is torn from his back. Joshua has a rooftop fight with Scobie (George Kennedy), one of the crooks who is chasing the stolen gold and who happens to wear a metal claw prosthesis in place of his right hand (another undesirable who can join the ranks of the prosthetically challenged listed in 'One size fits all?' dealing with gloves and other substitutes for the hand). In the ensuing skirmish Joshua's back is flayed by Scobie's claw and, after his adversary falls to his death, we see Joshua make his way back to Reggie's hotel room, his suit slashed and revealing through the lengthy cut his bloodied shirt and torn skin. Joshua's tailored carapace is pulled apart, a counterpoint to Thornhill's impregnable armour-plated suiting in *North by Northwest*, which needs to be physically removed and replaced by 'normal' clothing in order for his vulnerability to be revealed in a similarly edgy fight sequence – *Charade's* Parisian rooftops replacing the heights of Mount Rushmore. In *North by Northwest*, however, even in his new 'casual' guise, Thornhill's clothes remain impenetrable, his over-large, untailored button-down shirt showing only the merest discolouration after his cliff-top fight: no cuts, no tears. Momentarily, at the very end of the film as Thornhill and Eve are united in the train's sleeping compartment, the viewer is made aware that Thornhill is back wearing his immaculate, double-cuffed white dress shirt: so the much discussed re-dressing of Thornhill and the jettisoning of his superficiality is in fact restored by the end of the film. In the case of *Charade*, however, Joshua appears, tattered jacket in hand, to be nursed by Reggie after his fight, who tears apart his elegant 'skin' still further. In order to disinfect his wounds more effectively, she rips the back of his shirt completely open, making a loud tearing sound, prompting

Joshua to ask: 'Did you hear something?' to which Reggie replies 'No', Joshua returning 'That's odd.'[11] Leaving aside the decidedly erotic implications of a woman ripping open a man's shirt, this 'rupture' resonates far beyond the couple's blossoming diagetic romance, ushering in a process of referential un-suturing, where Reggie/Hepburn and Joshua/Grant's actions wrench the viewer from *Charade*'s fiction by re-enacting a similar scene with identical actors (almost) from some twenty-five years earlier.[12]

'Oh! You've torn your coat!' says Susan Vance (Katharine Hepburn) as she rips the back of Dr David Huxley's (Cary Grant) tail coat in *Bringing Up Baby*.[13] The apparent straightforwardness of this simple statement is belied by the fact that it is she, rather than Huxley who has torn his coat by

holding onto it as he attempts to walk away from her. Her irresponsibility and lack of care is entirely in keeping with her characterisation as the scatterbrained and capricious heiress. Her attempt to explain what happened rejected by Huxley, she walks away affronted, leading to the next instance of sartorial destruction as the back of her gown is torn away as a result of Huxley standing on its hem. The distinctly audible rents in the sartorially splendid surfaces of Hepburn and Grant can be understood as the distant pre-echoes of an equally audible ripping of Grant's shirt in *Charade*, caused by that other supremely stylish Hepburn, Audrey. It is as if Grant's occupancy of the cinema screen as its most elegantly tailored tenant is being ripped away from the fabric of cinematic sartorial legend; *Bringing Up Baby* and *Charade* act as the filmic boundaries that demarcate his domination as Hollywood's most urbane leading man.[14]

The tearing of men's clothing on film acts as a form of *Verfremdungseffekt* where the sudden ripping of the costume jolts the spectator out of their comfortable immersion in the narrative and facilitates a more critical awareness of film as a construction and, of particular interest to this study, by means of the destruction of the film costume itself.[15] In the Cary Grant films these 'tears' in the films' narratives encourage an understanding of his elegantly constructed image, while in *The Seven Year Itch* (1953) the ripping of Richard Sherman's (Tom Ewell) shirt is the act that escalates the film's meta-cinematic development.[16] Sherman, left alone in New York for the summer, fantasises to an apparition of his absent wife a series of melodramatic erotic encounters, including one involving his secretary Miss Morris. Unable to resist his sexual attraction, Morris throws Sherman across his desk and he, on extricating himself from her embrace, stands up to reveal the back of his shirt torn completely open. Turning to his imagined wife, he suggests: 'You remember that torn shirt don't ya Helen? Well now you know how it happened!' His wife replies: 'It got torn at the Chinese laundry – that's how it happened!'[17] The sudden evaporation of his sexual 'other life' suggests that the film's principal comedic strength will lie in the deflation of Sherwood's over-active imagination, yet as the film progresses this is abandoned in favour of increasingly meta-cinematic references that 'rip' holes in the narrative structure. With the appearance of Marilyn Monroe as the impossibly attractive, temporary upstairs tenant, who is nameless and therefore can only be Monroe (much in the same way that Cary Grant can only ever be Cary Grant), the blurring of reality and fiction increases, not only in terms of Sherwood's fantasy life but also the spectator's own cinematic references. Sherwood suggests at one point to Monroe that girls only fall for Gregory Peck and in one of the film's concluding scenes attempts to defend his increasingly paranoid behaviour to Tom Mackenzie, his wife's friend: 'I can explain everything; the stairs, the cinnamon toast, the blonde in the kitchen', to which

THE SEVEN YEAR ITCH
1953, dir. Billy Wilder.
[facing] Richard's torn fantasy.

BRINGING UP BABY
1938, dir. Howard Hawks.
[top] 'Oh! You've torn your coat!'

TALES OF MANHATTAN
1942, dir. Julien Duvivier.
[bottom] Bacchanale moderne.

Mackenzie responds: 'Now wait a minute, Dickey boy, let's just take it easy. What blonde in the kitchen?' Sherman replies: 'Well, wouldn't ya like to know! Maybe it's Marilyn Monroe!'[18]

In another of the stories from the film *Tales of Manhattan* (1942; referred to in Part One's 'Exchange Mechanisms') featuring an apparently indestructible evening dress coat, which is systematically shot at, torn and eventually set on fire, beating even Thornhill's indestructible suit in *North by Northwest*, Charles Laughton plays Charles Smith, an aspiring composer and musician down on his luck.[19] Given the chance to audition for the great impresario Arturo Bellini, he is granted the opportunity of a lifetime to conduct the premiere of his 'Bacchanale Moderne'. Evening dress being a stipulation of the performance, he is forced to wear the magical tail coat that his wife has procured for him from a pawnshop but Smith is portly and the coat far too small. Nevertheless, he wears it only to split it with a loud ripping sound as his conducting becomes more energetic and he is forced to remove the coat altogether, but by now the auditorium has been reduced to howls of laughter, and it appears that Smith's extremely brief career is over (see illus. p. 231). Bellini comes to his aid, however, and removes his coat, also forcing the other male audience members to follow suit and Smith ends the performance as the new rising star of contemporary classical music. The obvious comedic value of Smith's ripping the seams of his too-small jacket is part of the same section of the negative cinematic wardrobe that reserves room for too-tight shoes, asphyxiating ties and mislaid bags.

The frequent ripping of men's clothing can be understood as an attack on male sartorial hegemony, whereby a man's dignity and authority is stripped away, an especially potent assault in films such as *Charade*, *Bringing Up Baby* and *The Seven Year Itch* because this attack is carried out by women. These rips are for the most part accidental or part of restorative, wound-dressing scenarios. However, the intentional slashing of clothes by women is surprisingly rarer given the frequency with which this activity is reported to be carried out in reality by spurned, angry or otherwise dissatisfied female spouses.

Such is the significance of this direct sartorial attack on male authority that when they do feature in film, they are characterised as symptomatic of the obsessively and possibly psychologically disturbed lover, the act of the stalker. 'Just dropped by to hack up your wardrobe and your cleaning lady, is that what you're trying to tell me?' This question is asked by the police superintendant investigating the scene of destruction at the home of the disc jockey Dave Garver (Clint Eastwood) in Eastwood's directorial debut, *Play Misty for Me* (1971).[20] Rejected by Garver after a brief sexual affair, the obsessive fan and romantic fantasist Evelyn Draper (Jessica Walter) attempts suicide, sabotages Garver's career prospects and then, after spying on him with another woman, lets herself into his house while he is away and sets about demolishing his possessions. Draper is discovered by Garver's astonished maid crouching in his closet systematically ripping apart and slashing at his clothes with a large knife, revelling in her vestimentary carnage which she then turns on Garver's cleaner, slashing at her with equal pleasure.

Representations of this direct sartorial reprisal for real or imagined acts of betrayal are few, as stated previously, and the example included in 'Hush . . . Hush, Sweet Charlotte' (1964) even rarer, given that the clothes-slashing enacted in this film is perpetrated by one woman against another or, more accurately, by a woman on her own clothing.[21] The film's central item of dysfunctional clothing, the blood-stained dress, will be discussed in detail in the following section, but as part of Miriam Deering's (Olivia de Havilland) plot to convince people of Charlotte Hollis's (Bette Davis) insanity and to have her committed, Miriam, Charlotte's poor cousin, 'discovers' her chiffon evening dress destroyed on the eve of her first night staying at the Hollis mansion. The door of her wardrobe slowly swings open to reveal the garment slashed to ribbons: 'My dress . . . someone's slashed my dress!' she declares, turning in a bravura performance of shocked bewilderment.[22] This incident is revealed later as one of many attempts to persuade the authorities of Charlotte's insanity and the necessity for her institutionalisation, leaving Miriam free to gain her inheritance and possession of the mansion. Her act of vestimentary auto-mutilation seems to gain especial significance given that, apart from her general envy of Charlotte's familial economic and social superiority, clothing seems to have been a particular cause of resentment, as the cousins revealed when earlier Charlotte pointed out that her father was always good to Miriam, even buying her a whole new wardrobe, to which Miriam counters that it was from a store that Charlotte 'wouldn't have set foot in'.[23]

Such serious assaults must inevitably impact on the actual film narrative and usher in a layer of meta-cinematic references that question the authority of the film's narrative. Not so with the typical instances of the ripping of women's clothing, however, which owing to its clear signalling of sexual violence, no matter how comedic these references may be, is comfortably positioned within the patriarchal narratives of mainstream film. Returning to *Bringing Up Baby*, for example, although Cary Grant's ripped evening coat is the icing on his cake of sartorial embarrassment that began with his crushed top hat (referred to in Part Three's 'One size fits all?'), it is the exposure of Katharine Hepburn's underwear and bare legs once the back of her dress is torn off that provides the conventionally titillating comedy focus for this scene. To save her humiliation, Grant claps his crushed top hat over her exposed posterior, which of course Hepburn misconstrues as an inappropriate and unexpected sexual advance. However, once she discovers her revelation, she panics, resulting in the pair of them famously exiting the restaurant with Grant's body pressed close to her rear.

It is interesting that while men's clothes are often intentionally ripped by women, whether with malice or from amorous or other activity, the tearing of women's clothes is constructed as partly accidental and partly by the action of the woman herself. For example, it is the action of Susan Vance walking away from David Huxley in *Bringing Up Baby* that brings about the ripping of the back of her dress, caught unwittingly under Huxley's foot, while a similar act of dress-ripping opens the 1934 musical *The Gay Divorce*. Mimi Glossop (Ginger Rogers)

'HUSH . . . HUSH, SWEET CHARLOTTE'
1964, dir. Robert Aldrich.
[top] The ripper ripped.

BRINGING UP BABY
1938, dir. Howard Hawks.
[bottom] The exposing rip.

meets her Aunt Hortense as she docks in London and helps her repack her trunks. Unwittingly, Hortense traps the hem of Mimi's dress in a drawer, locks the trunk and then proceeds to the customs office leaving Mimi trapped, her dress hitched up to expose her legs. The dancer Guy Holden (Fred Astaire) hears Mimi calling for a porter and goes over to help. Suggesting that he can sort the matter out, he manages to free Mimi but only by ripping the back of her dress. To make amends, Guy offers the embarrassed and angry Mimi his raincoat to cover herself up. Yet even this masculine cover-up operation fails, for as Mimi storms away the raincoat is caught in a gate and pulled to the ground, exposing the backs of her legs through her torn dress. This act of repeated exposure will typify the course of the couple's dysfunctional relationship, fraught with mis-understandings and false accusations, until finally resolved in the film's musical finale, 'Night and Day'. When not occurring in 1930s musicals or screwball comedies, accidentally ripped dresses in film remained a favourite device to add scenes of momentary titillation and ritual humiliation. In the British comedy *The Wrong Arm of the Law* (1963), a gang of crooks including Pearly Gates (Peter Sellers), who operates under the cover of being a famous French couturier, and his rival Nervous O'Toole (Bernard Cribbens) join forces to stop the activities of a rival gang who have started to 'muscle in' on their territory.[24] In order to plan their next operation, O'Toole pays a visit to Gates's fashion house, causing chaos when he appears backstage at one of the fashion shows. The fashionably dressed O'Toole, complete with straw pork-pie hat, 'bum freezer' jacket and Slim Jim tie – a sort of Ivy League London mod – asks one of the models where he can find Gates and, as she motions to the showroom and walks away, the train of her dress is torn off, accompanied by a loud ripping sound and the profuse apologies of O'Toole who, just like Huxley in *Bringing Up Baby*, has been standing on the hem of her dress. O'Toole runs on stage in place of the model whose dress he has ruined and proceeds to tear further at the delicate fabric of fashionable Mayfair, introducing an unexpected glimpse of male 'street'

fashions to the genteel patrons who laugh nervously at his entrance. Gates attempts to explain O'Toole by announcing: 'As you can see, ladies and gentlemen, I too have entered the realms of men's apparel, like the great Hardy Amies, and I've called this . . . I've called this, erm, Cary Grant in Charing Cross Road, commissioned by no less a combine than The Fifty Shilling Tailors.' As the audience laugh at his pronouncement, Gates bundles him off stage with O'Toole protesting: 'Cost me 75 quid!'[25]

This dismantling of the world of fashion and its depiction as a scam run by a bunch of crooks, literally in the case of *The Wrong Arm of the Law*, is deeply embedded in popular culture. Both fictional and real-life representations of the fashion industry revel in its failings and yet, like Pearly Gates's swift cover-up of O'Toole's interruption, it also celebrates its enter-prise and ingenuity. Remaining with the theme of the torn dress, but leaving momentarily the fictional world of fashion on screen, we can find a similar ambivalence in the media coverage of a real-life fashionable sartorial mishap, in the journalistic frenzy surrounding Kate Moss and her ripped couture. The model was attending the gala dinner to celebrate the opening of the 'Golden Age of Couture' exhibition at the Victoria and Albert Museum in London in 2007, wearing a 'priceless', according to one account, '£650' to another, vintage gold satin Christian Dior couture gown (see illus. p. 236).[26] Her glamorous entrance was soon dismantled, however, as Courtney Love, also attending, stepped on the train of Moss's dress, causing a tear that quickly grew so that 'At one point her naked bottom was exposed, with further tears to her armpit and back'. So far so embarrassing, adding to the speculation that the dress's damage was in direct proportion to the intoxication of Moss, the accident 'following another booze filled evening'.[27] With a mix of prurience and sycophancy typical of the world of fashion, the tabloid press's disapprobation swiftly turned to admiration as Moss was reported to have ingeniously hitched up the damaged skirt and knotted it on one side, transforming it into a mini-dress, this remarkable design serendipity being immediately hailed as a sign of her true fashion instincts: 'Who knows? With Miss Moss's fashion savvy (she has her own range for Top-Shop) the look could be the Next Big Thing in the High Street.'[28] Not since Naomi Campbell fell off Vivienne Westwood's purple platforms while modelling her Autumn/ Winter 1993/94 'Anglomania' collection has the spectacularly dysfunctional been so swiftly and completely transformed into the functional. Campbell's relaxed amusement at her predicament was seen as the perfect response to Westwood's iconoclastic attitude to fashion, making the pair of shoes into an instant museum-piece as well as commercially successful.[29] Moss's ripping ingenuity re-enacted a similar fashionable nonchalance that is an essential component of the marketing of British style, simultaneously irreverent and soigné. No such ingenuity comes to the rescue of either Mimi Glossop or Susan Vance, however, who are forced to wear their tears with shame.

Fictional fashion mavens, however, are generally chastised for their inventiveness and industry, and their torn clothing often acts as a portent of the distress in store for them in the fickle world of fashion. Lucy Gallant, as has been seen, is enterprising, successful and smart, and yet her fashionable career is never quite satisfying enough, her achievements always ultimately found wanting compared to the love of a good man. On the eve of the opening of her first store, Casey tempts her out to his ranch for lunch and afterwards she notices a newly born calf with its mother. Stopping to admire them, Lucy leans on the barbed wire fence while Casey informs her: 'that's her fifth calf', to which Lucy responds: 'she's a real homebody huh?'[30] The note of pastoral fecundity prompts Lucy to suggest to Casey: 'With a ranch full of happily married cows having babies left and right . . . you've got it made', to which he pointedly responds: 'Not quite, Lucy'.[31] This none too subtle advance makes Lucy move away but she catches the cuff of her blouse on the barbed wire and begins to tear it in her haste to get away. Casey helps her, providing the opportunity for a moment of intimate contact between the couple before Lucy disentangles herself both from the barbed wire and Casey's

THE GAY DIVORCE
1934, dir. Mark Sandrich.
[top] Mimi is caught up at customs.

THE WRONG ARM OF THE LAW
1961, dir. Cliff Owen.
[bottom] Nervous O'Toole makes some
last minute alterations backstage.

emotional advances, with a hurried 'Casey, I really do have to go now.'[32]

This fleeting moment of sartorial dysfunction occurring a quarter of the way into the film should have been a warning to both Lucy and Casey of the ultimately dysfunctional quality of the fashion industry, for no matter how successful Lucy becomes she remains fundamentally unfulfilled. Even when she chooses an alternative male partner to Casey, her general manager from New York, whom she thinks will support her career, he is revealed to be only interested in gaining the controlling share in her fashion empire. Meanwhile, Casey, who has been secretly backing Lucy's business ventures since striking oil on his ranch, goes on a European tour to try to forget his emotional attachment to Lucy; he swiftly becomes engaged to a Paris fashion model but just as swiftly extricates himself from the alliance by paying his fiancée off. In the climax to the film, Casey comes to Lucy's financial rescue once again and reinstates her as the head of her company but Lucy, it appears, has finally realised the error of her proto-feminist ways. She asks Casey: 'Will you still back me in whatever I want to do from now, including being Mrs Casey Cole?' to which Casey enquires: 'Who'll mind the store?' and, deciding to tear up her career in fashion and remain 'caught' in Casey's construction of unfashionable domestic bliss, she responds: 'What store?'[33]

[facing] Kate Moss rips the train of her dress while attending the opening of the 'Golden Age of Couture' exhibition, Victoria and Albert Museum, London, 2007 (James Curley/Rex Features).

LUCY GALLANT
1955, dir. Robert Parrish.
[above] Caught between fashion and fulfilment.

PART 6

I'd like to add his initials to my monogram
Tell me, where is the shepherd for this lost lamb?[1]

In Mel Brooks's 1977 film *High Anxiety* (a spoof on Hitchcock's *Vertigo*), Madeline Khan plays Victoria Brisbane, the neurotic daughter of the wealthy industrialist forcibly incarcerated in the asylum recently taken charge of by Dr Robert Thorndyke.[2] Having arranged to meet Thorndyke, played by Brooks himself, Victoria arrives for their assignation in a customised limousine. The car is decked out in a version of Louis Vuitton's famous brown and gold livery, only the usual LV motif has been replaced by the letters VB, the initials of Victoria Brisbane. Not only is the car clad in this ironic visual pastiche of the luxury brand but also, on her getting out of the car, we see that Brisbane herself is likewise branded, wearing a trouser suit of a similar pattern and carrying a clutch bag all in the same VB-monogrammed material. Obviously distressed, she launches into a diatribe concerning her confused mental state, declaring to Thorndyke at one point: 'Oh Richard, Richard! The world has gone crazy; I mean nothing makes any sense any more. I don't know what to believe and what not to believe. My life is just all . . . topsy-turvey'.[3] This construction of self as luxury brand is a visual gag typically pushed to the limit by Brooks, so that later the audience observes Brisbane accessorised with the obligatory mono-grammed bag and playing with a VB teddy bear in a spoof phone-sex scene. While the scene is played for laughs, Brisbane's neurotic state and her absorption into the brand of VB befits the pseudo-psychological theme of the film and its parody of the most extreme examples of Hitchcock's psychologically motivated suspense films. The psychologist Thorndyke struggles throughout the film to free himself from a morass of multiple and mistaken identities, whereas Brisbane asserts her identity in the most explicit manner possible, by branding herself publically via her dress and possessions. This comedic fragment seems both scathingly perceptive and prophetic if viewed from the contem-porary landscape of luxury-brand saturation.

The relationship between the consumer and the brand is currently much under scrutiny: our apparently insatiable desire

HIGH ANXIETY
1977, dir. Mel Brooks.
[facing] The 'sign of me' (Photofest);
[above] Victoria retreats into her brandscape.

for luxury-branded items has been seen as representative of society's increasingly ostentatious, materialistic and celebrity-driven means of affirmation – in short, the fully developed expression of Veblen's notion of conspicuous consumption. Brisbane's branding can be understood as symptomatic of the contemporary consumer for whom the appeal of brands and their acquisition is fundamental and where 'The product is promoted as a 'sign of me' – a signal to others of our status, aspiration or personal values.'[4] In terms of contemporary manufacture and marketing, a brand's primary function is to create a set of associations and therefore desirability for a product in the consumer's mind. This is done through a variety of means, most typically advertising campaigns. Branding in order to be successful must differentiate the products it represents forcefully enough for consumers to be able to distinguish them from others. It must also encourage loyalty, whereby a customer

will continue to purchase the brand thus ensuring its continued economic success within its given marketplace.

In Roland Barthes's *Mythologies* he warns us not to 'forget that an object is the best messenger of a world above that of nature: one can easily see in an object at once a perfection and an absence of origin'.[5] This supernatural quality of perfection, of something that exists without prior knowledge of its making, of just being, is the crux of how branding functions. For all the pedigree and manufacturing heritage that luxury brands invoke in their campaigns, their products' ability just to be, or 'just do it', to borrow Nike's famous slogan, allows the consumer to project and participate in any number of fantasies that purchasing the object will bring. Whether that be beauty, admiration, sexual desirability, sophistication, taste, the list of illusions is endless and can be altered to fit the latest shift in public desire. 'In such a world,' Fredric Jameson suggested, 'material needs are sublimated into more symbolic satisfactions; the initial desire is not the solution of a material problem, but the style and symbolic connotations of the product to be possessed.'[6] So, if branding serves to manufacture and sell the impossible and unreal, its other function to individuate and set apart from the rest is perhaps easier to comprehend. In a simpler era, luxury goods meant just that, goods that were affordable by a few, and therefore signified economic superiority, familiarity with and understanding of the brand's 'values', such as craftsmanship, quality, permanence. Such values made Louis Vuitton, for example, the luggage of choice for Audrey Hepburn (dressed by Givenchy, of course) playing the recently widowed Regina Lampert in *Charade*.[7] On returning from her skiing trip, Regina, replete with a full set of Vuitton luggage, finds her apartment emptied of all possessions by her errant, deceased husband. The luggage takes centre stage in the bare apartment as she declares to Peter Joshua (Cary Grant) who enquires where everything else is: 'Charles sold it all at auction – this is all I have left!'[8] The viewer is reminded that perhaps all a lady of Regina/Hepburn's taste and status needs in life is Vuitton luggage stuffed with Givenchy: although the only possessions she has left are what is contained in the luggage, she manages to appear throughout the film in a seemingly endless supply of couture outfits. Is this a testament to the Tardis-like capacity and magical bounties a brand such as Vuitton can bestow? Or perhaps we can understand this scene in the context of early luxury-brand product placement, from a time when the 'brand message' was both more direct and uncomplicated and all you needed in life was a set of Vuitton bags.

The level of complexity that characterises the contemporary understanding of branding seems at variance with the relatively straightforward act of displaying one's identity or sense of self by wearing initialled or monogrammed clothing and accessories. Here the brand or rather monogram appears to be merely a sign of the wearer, their name abbreviated to initials and then used to 'brand' possessions as personal belongings. The use of initials and monograms in film, while often merely a reflection

HIGH ANXIETY
[facing] 1977, dir. Mel Brooks.
Brand saturation.

CHARADE
1963, dir. Stanley Donen.
[top] 'This is all I have left!'

BRINGING UP BABY
1938, dir. Howard Hawks.
[bottom] Hepburn monogrammed
on screen . . . and [following spread verso] off:
Katharine Hepburn, 1943 (SNAP/Rex Features).

THE SCARLET LETTER
[following spread recto] 1926, dir. Victor Sjöström.
The mark of shame
(Everett Collection/Rex Features).

of the fashionable popularity of these additions to clothing and accessories, can also been seen in certain productions as subverting the monogram's normal function to proclaim the identity of the wearer and instead embellish and demarcate the body as the terrain of *false* identity. Such aspirations and desires encouraged in the consumer of luxury brands made explicit in contemporary advertising are, on film, veiled, camouflaged and used almost as a form of cinematic vestimentary sleight of hand, where the viewer's recognition of the 'brand', in this case the character on screen, is misdirected. In the discussion of the films *Leave Her to Heaven*, *Whirlpool* and *Rebecca* that follows, mid-twentieth-century cinematic branding in the guise of monogrammed costumes and accessories constructs 'a sign of me' but one that is rarely singular and is often finally revealed as bogus, signalling instead the absence of self.[9]

Adding initials or monograms to clothing is an immediate, simple and relatively inexpensive way of individualising clothing, bestowing a certain level of prestige and exclusivity, and making a standard garment one's own. Of course, this is not far removed from classic definitions of the function of branding. The fashionable shift from what had long been a utilitarian embellishment, individuating garments and accessories from others, preventing their loss and demarcating individual ownership (the embroidered handkerchief a simple example of this), reached its peak in women's fashion in the 1930s and 40s. Increasingly elaborate monograms, ciphers and other arrangements of initials made their appearance on accessories and clothing alike, and movie stars sported outfits embellished with the initials of the characters they played on screen as well as their own when making public appearances or in publicity shots. The desire for marking and establishing the self via monogrammed clothing and accessories was built on a legacy of personalised possessions as the sign of aspirational intent, derived from the aristocratic tradition of displaying coats of arms and similar devices on everything from buildings to clothing.[10] For example, images of Katharine Hepburn in a variety of monogrammed outfits both on and off screen seem

entirely appropriate for the wealthy Connecticut-born actress noted for her patrician persona; as such, this suited fashions that referred to aristocratic insignia. In the previously discussed *Bringing Up Baby*, while many of Hepburn's outfits seem stylishly dysfunctional, the bathrobe that she wears in a number of scenes is emblazoned on the left arm with a striking sv monogram, standing for her character Susan Vance, while a publicity shot of her taken a few years later in 1942 shows her wearing a blouse whose collar is embroidered with khh for Katharine Houghton Hepburn (see illus. p. 244).

Why the need to establish and display identity became so prevalent in the films under discussion can perhaps be partly explained by the general feeling of insecurity sweeping Europe and North America during this period. The Second World War had the effect of erasing identities, as the general awareness of global instability increased in the 1930s, and then during and immediately after the conflict ceased, as established socio-economic divisions were transformed, the old understanding of one's position in society and sense of self could no longer be taken as fixed and unchanging. As is well known, fashions in clothing often reflect major socio-cultural and economic shifts, and the use of monograms as a way of reasserting a sense of personal identity in times of war can clearly be placed in the context of this phenomenon.

In certain films from this period, cinema's use of the monogram is closer to the historical understanding of the verb 'to brand', which is to mark indelibly the flesh, most typically with a hot iron, as the property of another. In *Leave Her to Heaven* (1945), Gene Tierney plays the father-obsessed, pathologically jealous Ellen Berent, whose abnormal behaviour has already been manifested in her construction of the shoe as 'false evidence' (discussed in Part Three's 'Criminal Accessories'). Throughout the film, Ellen's precarious mental condition, extreme possessiveness and violent mood-swings are hidden by the startlingly fashionable wardrobe Kay Nelson designed for the film.[11] Her designs reflect and incorporate many of the elements of American post-war fashion: immaculate tailoring,

LEAVE HER TO HEAVEN
1945, dir. John M. Stahl.
Ellen's intention to be a Harland is
discernible in the nascent 'H' of her monogram.

padded shoulders, trouser or play suits and the aforementioned emphasis on monogrammed clothing and accessories. After accidentally meeting her future husband Richard Harland (Cornel Wilde), Ellen finds that he is also staying at the same ranch in New Mexico where she and her family are vacationing. Ellen's extreme personality is swiftly established as we learn of her unhealthy adoration for her recently deceased father: she attempts to justify her sudden and impulsive attraction to Harland because (she thinks) he uncannily resembles the deceased Dr Berent. Given Ellen's excessive sense of filial devotion, it is unsurprising that one of the first outfits the viewer sees her wearing is a white play or lounge suit embellished with the initials EB across her throat and chest. On closer observation, the cutwork monogram appears to consist of the letters E and

B for Ellen Berent, flanking a smaller, somewhat indistinct H. This could merely be coincidental and formed as a result of the supporting areas of fabric necessary for the whole monogram to maintain its shape, but this nascent H can also be construed as being increasingly prophetic and revelatory as the film's narrative unfolds.

Ellen wears this outfit in the scene where she casually jilts her long-term fiancé and dramatically, without warning or consultation with Harland, announces her engagement and intention to marry him instead. The extent of Ellen's ruthlessness and determination to have what she wants is revealed in its true form for the first time in this scene: it is ironic that it is while her pedigree is emblazoned, or branded, across her chest, that her true intent to become Mrs Harland is signalled. While

she purports to be the grieving Berent daughter, her actual desire to be Mrs Harland is inadvertently presaged by this indeterminate monogram and, like Hester Prynne's adulterous letter A in Nathaniel Hawthorne's celebrated novel *The Scarlet Letter* (1850), Ellen's scheming nature is betrayed by this fashionable 1940s device. Further evidence of Ellen's overweening and threatening character is discovered later when, still wearing the prophetic monogram, and after giving Harland a passionate kiss, she vows: 'And I'll never let you go, never . . . never . . . never' – as the contemporary consumer understands, the embrace of the brand is hard to resist.[12]

We next see the monogrammed Ellen some time later in the film; she is now Mrs Harland and dressed in initialled silk satin pyjamas, and reveals to her new husband the true extent of her pathological jealousy, specifically as it is directed towards her adopted sister Ruth. On being accused of being in love with Ruth, Harland asks: 'What's happened to you? You're deliberately whipping yourself into a fit of hysterics', at which he sees her mood abruptly change from petulance to contrition and, breaking down, she sobs into his lap: 'I don't know! I don't know!' Moments later as he raises her up, the viewer's attention is directed towards the monogram on her breast, as her mood changes yet again into the seductive Ellen defined by her obsession for Harland; while passionately embracing him she declares: 'Darling, forgive me! I'm sorry, it's only because I love you so! I love you so I can't bear to share you with anybody!'[13]

The monogram on Ellen's pyjamas in this scene follows the conventional layout of traditional monograms: the person's first name on the left, their maiden name (in the case of a woman) on the right, and central and larger the new married family name, in this case H for Harland. Ellen's new marital status supplants her old familial name but in both cases Ellen is defined monogramatically by men – her father and husband – an embroidered veneer of conformity suitable to a dutiful daughter and wife. However, as the viewer is seeing ever more clearly, these identities are extremely fragile and Ellen is constituted by a number of other, more problematic personalities

that periodically break through this exterior of familial and matrimonial correctness.

Once again, Ellen is 'branded' for one of the most crucial scenes of the entire film, in which she wears a remarkable camel and white dressing-gown, with puritanical collar and neck-bow. The 1940s vogue for elaborate necklines on clothing is here used to good effect, transforming Ellen into a form of domestic, feminised Pilgrim Father, a contrast to her possibly Satanic intentions. Her outfit, while styled for sanctity, betrays her true nature via the attention placed on yet another embroidered monogram positioned centrally on the front of the robe's bodice. However, this time the monogram is distorted and more schematic, the individual letters EHB harder to make out and suggesting when viewed in its entirety a large B. The monogram acts as a sign of Ellen's increasingly fragile grip on reality and her growing self-destructive tendencies. Now pregnant, robed and confined, Ellen regards her unborn child as a potential threat to her complete possession of Harland's love and cannot contain the revulsion she feels for her condition, shocking the angelic Ruth when she says: 'Look at me! . . . I hate the little beast! I wish I would die!' With the camera closing in on Ellen, the monogram is placed centre screen as she continues: 'Richard and I never needed anything else.'[14]

Ellen's Salem-inspired outfit is worn as she plots her 'accidental' fall down the stairs, resulting in the loss of the baby and her miraculous survival apparently unscathed. The indecipherability of the monogram she wears on her gown is an indication of the incomprehensibility of her actions, the apparent ascendancy of the letter B a re-branding of her as the virginal daughter once more. These signs of her regression from adulthood, and by implication motherhood, to a child-like state, befit the majority of her screen appearances once she has married Harland. What Ellen's monograms signify is necessarily complex and runs counter to her easy consumption as a 'brand': at any given time she is perceived as unhealthily father-obsessed, pathologically jealous, child-like, seductive, deadly, self-destructive, sadistic – the list seems endless. Her costuming for these various personae becomes hard to decipher conventionally and the viewer is left in a similar state of bewilderment to that expressed by the narrator of *The Scarlet Letter* when he makes his discovery of the curious letter A at the beginning of the novel: 'It had been intended, there could be no doubt, as an ornamental article of dress; but how it was to be worn, or what rank, honour and dignity in by-past times were signified by it, was a riddle which (so evanescent are the fashions of the world in these particulars) I saw little hope of solving.'[15]

For the final scenes of *Leave Her to Heaven* Ellen reappears in the pyjamas she has worn previously for what is to be her ultimate act of calculated destruction, the plotting of her own poisoning and the planting of evidence so that Ruth and Richard are blamed and erroneously brought to justice for her death. The viewer witnesses her clad in the pyjamas that mark her as the dutiful, loving wife writing to her jilted fiancée, now the district attorney, of her suspicions, selecting poison from the stock of her father's laboratory and, most significantly for this exploration of psychological branding, planting the poison in Ruth's bathroom. It is in this scene that the audience is shown the full extent of Ellen's dysfunctional affinity for monograms: clad in the pyjamas, she plots not only her own destruction but also that of her husband and Ruth, substituting Ruth's bath salts for the poison that she will knowingly ingest. As Ellen switches the contents of the jars, the camera shot includes in the background a pair of towels clearly embroidered with the name 'Ruth'. The image acts as a lesson in positive branding, contrasting the hopelessly chaotic initials and negative branding of Ellen, with the clear and straightforward display of 'Ruth' as the brand that means clarity, straight-forwardness, honesty and, most of all, autonomy signalled by the use of her first name independent of family name (as noted before, Ruth is adopted and therefore belongs to no one and is nameless in that sense). Ruth is a complete person, unlike the multiple personalities of Ellen that ultimately are never united and lead to the eradication of the self and to non-existence, the antithesis of branding's primary function.

LEAVE HER TO HEAVEN
1945, dir. John M. Stahl.
RUTH, the 'honest' brand.

Just four years later Gene Tierney appeared as another branded, psychologically unbalanced heroine, in *Whirlpool*.[16] Directed in 1949 by Otto Preminger, it tells the story of Ann Sutton, who (as discussed in Part Two's 'Talismans') is seen at the beginning of the film stealing a brooch from a department store. Her kleptomania, the viewer quickly realises, is just one facet of her overall mental instability but, unlike Ellen in *Leave Her to Heaven*, she dispenses with initials and projects her identity more directly, using her first name Ann to brand her clothing. After the initial theft scene, Ann appears in a towelling robe embroidered with her name, an apparently straightforward assertion of her sense of self, but it is while wearing this robe that she receives a telephone call from the quack hypnotherapist who came to her aid when accused of shoplifting. The cleanliness and psychological security suggested by the embroidered bathrobe is immediately called into question as she swiftly realises that the therapist, Korvo (José Ferrer), is attempting to blackmail her: the compartmentalisation of her different personae including that of the kleptomaniac is about to stain her unblemished character as the beautiful wife of a successful psychiatrist. Korvo attempts to incriminate Ann by planting the brooch and a monogrammed scarf at the scene of his crime and, as noted earlier, she is at a loss to explain how these identifying marks, which constitute Ann Sutton, came to be found next to the murder victim.

The visual equivalence between outward cleanliness and inner pollution signified by Ann's marked bathrobe was reworked in the notorious 'biopic' of another famous 1940s film star, Joan Crawford, who frequently appeared in monogrammed outfits both in her on-screen roles and in her private life, and did much to popularise the fashion among her adoring fans. In the 1981 film *Mommie Dearest*, Faye Dunaway plays Joan Crawford and the film takes great delight in depicting the star's obsession with personal appearance and her punishing cleansing and beauty regime, during which she appears in a towelling robe embroidered with JC.[17] As is well known and caricatured in the film, Crawford's pristine, fashionable exterior hid a

WHIRLPOOL
1949, dir. Otto Preminger.
[top] The stability of the brand is questioned;
[bottom] the incriminating brand.

decidedly cold and ruthless persona; initials are used as opposed to her full name in this instance for a film that is determined to cast its central character in the role of a sadistic monster. The apparent innocence of displaying one's complete first name, as on Ann Sutton's robe in *Whirlpool*, is reserved it seems for characters who, although possibly psychologically unstable, are victims as opposed to aggressors. Yet, cinematic psychological characterisation via the use of personalised, branded clothing is as complex as the motivations that inspire contemporary devotees of luxury branding. Can we be certain that the JC on Dunaway/Crawford's robe is the sign of the movie star, the fiction created by the studio system? After all, Crawford changed her name from Lucille Fay LeSueur to that chosen by readers of *Movie Weekly*, and as such was a complete construct both on and off the screen. Therefore, if JC represents a sadistic

child-beating monster in *Mommie Dearest* (and, according to the autobiography written by her adopted daughter Christina, also in real life), it is surely just another persona – a persona as convincing but as easily assumed as JC the proto-feminist, self-promoting actress who knew how to play the studio system at its own male-dominated game. Alternatively, is it the JC that represents the long-suffering heroine of what could be argued was her most successful film, *Mildred Pierce* (1945)? There, she is accused of squandering the profits of her successful restaurant chain on Monte Beragon (Zachary Scott), her profligate lover and second husband, by her long-time business partner and friend Wally Fay (Jack Carson) when he declares: 'Keeping Monte Beragon in monogrammed shirts is not my idea of business'.[18] In this case the reference to monograms is reminiscent of the kept man whose wardrobe is chosen by a woman (as discussed in Part Four's 'Well, as long as the lady's paying . . .') and the branding here of Monte by Mildred is implicitly related to ownership and by extension the buying of sexual availability with expensive items of dress. Branding is after all about the assumption of identity, the wrapping of an individual psyche in the collective recognition (or in the case of Ann Sutton in *Whirlpool*, hypnosis), brought on by the sight of Chanel's interlinked CS or Vuitton's overlapping LS and VS. Hollywood film, particularly of the mid-twentieth century and its reflection of the then current vogue for personalised clothing and accessories, provides a rich and intricate visual dictionary with which to decode our contemporary brand- and celebrity-infatuated zeitgeist.

A monogrammed robe as a present for the male object of desire features in *Desk Set* (referred to in Part Three's 'Gift-wrapped'). After being stood up by her fiancé Mike Cutler (Gig Young), the researcher Bunny Watson (Katharine Hepburn) invites the efficiency expert Richard Sumner (Spencer Tracy) to her apartment to dry off after getting caught in the rain. Inviting him to stay for dinner, Bunny offers Sumner the robe that she has bought and personally embroidered with the initials MC as a Christmas present for Cutler. The latter arrives at her apartment unexpectedly and interrupts the cosy domestic scene with Sumner occupying both his role as suitor and his personalised robe. Bunny, embarrassed and angered, hopes that Cutler likes the robe as she cannot take it back since she has embroidered 'those initials myself'.[19] Her work colleague Peg (Joan Blondell) arrives and is surprised to see Sumner sitting in the robe having dinner; she declares accusingly: 'I don't know what you're supposed to be!' and, though her speech is rhetorical, Sumner is in fact what Cutler should be – an attentive male dining with his fiancée, the monogram conferring this status on him while the actual owner of these initials fails to conform to the standard required of the MC brand.[20] This scene, in which Bunny finally realises that MC is not the brand for her, is brought to a conclusion by Bunny asking Peg if she knows anyone who would like to buy a man's robe with the initials MC, 'really cheap'.

MOMMIE DEAREST
1981, Frank Perry.
[facing] JC the superbrand.

DESK SET
1957, dir. Walter Lang.
[above] The MC standard.

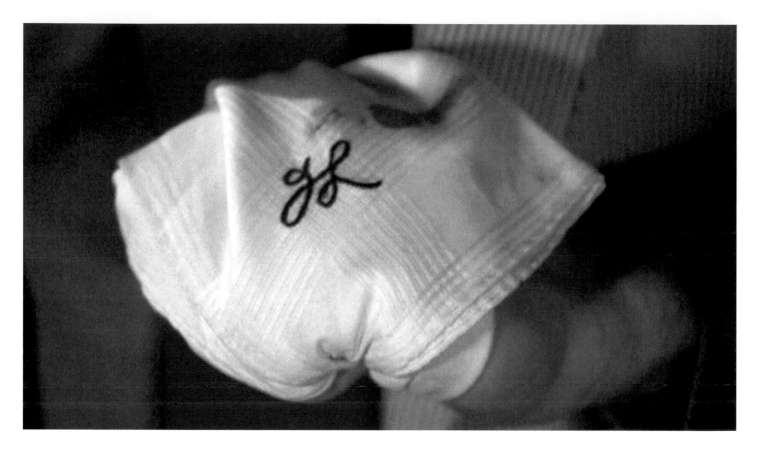

The obsession with branding that typifies much contemporary fashion consumption often borders on the psychologically dysfunctional: the desire to cloak original identities while constructing commercially promoted ones has become commonplace and the obsessive brand-hunter displays many of the same characteristics as the obsessive fan or stalker. This dysfunctional similarity is neatly crystallised in the opening scenes from *The King of Comedy* (1983) in which Rupert Pupkin (Robert De Niro) constructs a fantasy life based on an imaginary relationship with a talk-show host and comedian, Jerry Langford (Jerry Lewis), whom he idolises and attempts to emulate.[21] His obsession with Langford, the successful and aspirational comedy 'brand', nourishes Pupkin's delusions of becoming a stand-up comedian and, much like the purchase of branded items, offers the mirage of a fantasy luxury lifestyle. After a struggle in a group of crazed, adoring fans all trying to get close to Langford (the visual connection between the crazed fans and hysterical shoppers scrambling for the latest luxury branded bag is irresistible), Pupkin manages to throw himself into Langford's car and points out that he has cut himself while trying to protect Langford from the crowd. Reluctantly, Langford offers Pupkin his handkerchief to bandage his hand, which Pupkin gladly takes asking: 'Is that your initials?'[22] As Pupkin attempts to inveigle Langford into considering his request for a slot on his show, he glances regularly at his hand encased in Langford's handkerchief and, on leaving him at the steps to his apartment, looks down at the stained handkerchief, Langford's initials now nourished by Pupkin's blood. This image of sanguinary comingling acts as a catalyst for Pupkin's fantasies in which a now supplicant Langford pleads with Pupkin to take over his show for six weeks and an adoring fan approaches meekly to ask for Pupkin's, not Langford's, autograph. The sudden proximity to the sign of Langford induces visions of a fantasy lifestyle, an analogous operation whether the catalyst is a simple, initialled handkerchief or the latest branded designer accessory. As Jameson again illuminates, 'Fewer and fewer people are involved with objects as tools, with natural objects as raw materials; more and more are involved with objects as semi-ideas, busy marketing and consuming objects which they never really apprehend as pure materiality'.[23]

An ability to signal, or misdirect, the decipherer of initials provides fertile narrative opportunities for cases of mistaken identity, indeed mistaken motivation, encouraging the audience into attaching certain behaviours or possible psychological motivation to characters by means of ciphers and monograms. These guessing games can range from the straightforward as when Don Birnam in *The Lost Weekend* (discussed in Part One's 'Exchange Mechanisms') attempts to decipher the initials HST.J on the label inside the leopard-skin coat that he is given by mistake at the Metropolitan Opera's cloakroom. Incorrectly guessing Hilda or Harriet, St John or St Joseph, the true identity of the coat's owner, Helen St James, is revealed later and this instance of mistaken identity sparks the relationship that will eventually save Don from alcoholism. Inappropriate initials, however, are what eventually reveal to young Charlie (Teresa Wright) her Uncle Charlie's (Joseph Cotton) true murderous identity in *Shadow of a Doubt* (1943).[24] Given as a gift from uncle to niece, the ring becomes, once the initials engraved inside it are revealed to belong to one of Uncle Charlie's victims, a device or code that splits the two Charlies. The 'wrong' initials redefine Uncle Charlie as a murderer instead of idolised relation, and niece Charlie from doting 'soul mate' into disillusioned sleuth: passed back and forth between the two, the ring becomes a restless object that will not 'fit' either, its initials incriminating one and disabusing the other.[25]

SHADOW OF A DOUBT
1943, dir. Alfred Hitchcock.
[top] Dysfunctional inscription.

DEAD RECKONING
1947, dir. John Cromwell.
[middle] Reminder of the true self;
[bottom] transformed but still recognisable,
Johnny's 'brand' is tested by fire.'

Male monogrammed or otherwise nominated jewellery, aside from the ubiquitous identity bracelet, is rare in film; *Dead Reckoning*, made in 1947, is almost unique in the attention placed on such an item.[26] Told in flashback, *Dead Reckoning* follows 'Rip' Murdock (Humphrey Bogart) as he tries to unravel the mystery surrounding his army pal Johnny Drake's (William Prince) false identity, disappearance and death. While on a train to Washington D.C. where Drake is to receive the Congressional Medal of Honor, Murdock tries to convince Johnny to forget the woman who has broken his heart before joining the army. He goes on to make fun of Johnny's obsession with his fraternity pin, and his habit of wearing it at all times on his vest hidden beneath his army uniform. We see Johnny take off his army shirt and vest, carefully remove the pin and put it between his teeth while he washes. As their commanding officer, Lt. Col. Simpson enters their compartment to give them their itinerary, Johnny attempts to speak to him with the pin still in his mouth. Simpson asks what is wrong with him and what is in his mouth, (see illus. p. 255) to which Murdock replies: 'Top personal secret, never lets go of it. Six to even he swallows it. His senior sorority pin.'[27] Johnny becomes increasingly nervous as he learns that the press will be covering the ceremony and in his haste to get dressed drops the pin out of his mouth. Murdock picks it up and returns it Johnny who pins it back on his vest as before, but not before Murdock looks at the pin: a close-up shot reveals Drake's true identity as 'John Joseph Preston, Yale [class of 19]40'. Shortly afterwards Drake/Preston absconds and the rest of the film's action is taken up with Murdock trying to establish what his friend was escaping from and his attempt to clear his name. The convolutions of the unfolding plot include Johnny's lover, Dusty (Lizabeth Scott), as the femme fatale whose husband Johnny is supposed to have murdered, Murdock's relationship with Dusty, embezzlement, bigamy and murder. Murdock eventually tracks Johnny down but too late, for he has been killed in a planned car 'accident', his body so badly burnt – 'Like a lump of charcoal' – that the only thing that enables Murdock to identify the charred remains in the morgue is his friend's sorority pin, melted but still recognisable, as Murdock notes: 'Black enamel and gold. Johnny's senior society pin' (see illus. p. 255).[28]

Johnny's pin is the key to his true identity, an identity that he chooses to hide, so the pin is never worn to be seen but rather as a personal reminder of his true self. His personality remains hidden until its revelation at the moment when Murdock reads the inscription on the pin, at which point Johnny disappears, never to return to the film as a living character, with the pin remaining as the only surviving trace of his former self. In *Strangers on a Train* (1951), Hitchcock uses an item of personalised jewellery but, characteristically, overturns the convention concerning the use of monograms or initials to signify an untrustworthy character, such as Ellen in *Leave Her to Heaven*, or full names to identify innocent characters such as Ann in *Whirlpool*.[29] When the tennis-playing hero Guy Haines (Farley Granger) first encounters the psychotic Bruno Antony (Robert Walker) on the train, the audience could be forgiven for understanding Bruno's rather outré tie-clip spelling out his name as an ill-advised piece of personal accessorising which, along with his Surrealist-inspired lobster-print tie, constructs Bruno as flashy, loud and somewhat outmoded. The film was released in 1951 when the vogue for personalised details and the florid textiles Bruno favours were giving way to more reserved menswear that would usher in the Ivy League style of the late 1950s and 60s, presaged by Guy's clean-cut, sporty wardrobe. However, Bruno is a fully fledged sociopath and nascent serial killer and his style signals this, as obsessed by his imagined friendship with Guy as Ellen is for her father and husband in *Leave Her to Heaven*, both characters more than ready to kill to prove their love.

With Bruno there is no hiding behind the initials of a family name (after all, he despises his father), so one could argue that his tie-clip bearing just the name Bruno signals his denial of paternity and announces the bipolar 'brand' that is Bruno.[30] In *Dead Reckoning* Johnny keeps his name hidden even from his closest friend, his real identity being only a source of pain, unrequited love and ultimately unsustainable, whereas the megalomaniac Bruno wears his name for the world to see. Blatant promotion of the Bruno brand is too distinctive for his most sociopathic acts – the killing of Guy's wife or attempted framing and destruction of Guy at the fairground dénouement of the film – so the clip is absent from these scenes. Instead, the conspicuous Bruno clip is used to instil apprehension and imply menace, as when Guy's fiancée first sees him at the tennis club and then later at the Washington Museum. It is in fact not Bruno's tie-clip that becomes the central identifying male accessory in *Strangers on a Train* but Guy's lighter, decorated with a motif of tennis rackets and the initials 'A to G', a gift from Guy's fiancée Ann. Guy's identity, constructed by the lighter, signalling his profession as a tennis player, is pocketed by Bruno and becomes the binding object between them, used to coerce Guy into carrying out his half of the bargain and kill Bruno's father. Guy's image of sporting fair play schematically signified on his lighter is re-branded in Bruno's grip, the tennis-racket logo now 'read' as 'foul play', a perversion of the original brand message.

The fashion for personalised clothing and accessories provided Hitchcock with the perfect vehicle for the visual setpieces that condense complex narrative into images and which characterise his films of the 1940s and 50s; no discussion of initialisation would be complete without the branding tour de force that is *Rebecca*.[31] Its plot and character developments are signalled by a visual underscoring of the importance of initials and monograms as the signs of absence and aspirational distance. If Ellen's branding as loving wife and dutiful daughter in *Leave Her to Heaven* is ultimately unsuccessful or, more accurately, unstable, the brand that is Rebecca is so powerful that it can be likened to today's superbrands. The Rebecca brand, as with a Vuitton, Chanel or Hermès, is so established that its consumers are indelibly marked and thus identified with it, leaving no room for self-expression or interpretation beyond the brand's universally acknowledged significance and established image. In the film, the sudden appointment of the nameless young girl

STRANGERS ON A TRAIN
1951, dir. Alfred Hitchcock.
[top] Bi-polar branding;
[bottom] Foul play?

played by Joan Fontaine as the 'new face' of Rebecca the brand, social hostess of Manderley and wife of Maxim de Winter (Laurence Olivier), breaks all the laws of branding, alienates 'customers' and is in danger of making the brand itself meaningless. Her attempts to 'wear' the brand are doomed to failure since she has neither the social standing nor sophistication or maturity to make it her own, and any attempts to do so are met with condescending amusement or incomprehension. Of course, in the contemporary arena, luxury superbrands target all social and economic strata of society and the aspirational myths promulgated by a brand often find unlikely consumers. Indeed, no brand today, however exclusive in terms of price, can afford to ignore its customers wherever they might hail from socially. In the fictitious class-ridden world of 1940s England, though, seen through the lens of Hollywood, no such democratic customer-base is to be found and the function of brands such as Rebecca, to paraphrase Bourdieu's statement concerning cultural institutions, 'is to reinforce for some the feeling of belonging and for others the feeling of exclusion.'[32] For the unnamed, unbranded girl who comes to Manderley as the new Mrs de Winter, the feeling of exclusion is essential for the development of the plot, and the unattainable status of Rebecca renders the brand ultimately dysfunctional and doomed to obsolescence.

From the opening credits of *Rebecca* the viewer is made aware that Rebecca is a concept, rather than a flesh and blood character. The name signifies style, breeding, sophistication, individuality and so forth, the very qualities most contemporary luxury brands attempt to promote themselves as enshrining; like today's brands, Rebecca itself has an indispensable graphic identity. We are presented with her signature as the opening title-frame but this is no conventional signature: both the first and last letters are capitalised − R and A − and, as we witness later in the film, this graphic device is carried forward onto her married name, de Winter with a capital W and R. With Rebecca's own handwriting transformed into a graphic device for the brand, there follows in quick succession once the action moves

REBECCA
1940, dir. Alfred Hitchcock.
[top] The unobtainable brand;
[bottom] the brand's annihilation.

to Manderley an array of graphic variations on the house style. From conventional monograms to singular RS, the brand demarcates the physical and psychological territories of Manderley and its inhabitants to saturation point. The display of the more intimate of Rebecca's branded possessions is played out in the celebrated scenes where Mrs Danvers (Judith Anderson) shows the girl Rebecca's bed and dressing rooms and her personal artefacts. As Danvers forces the new Mrs de Winter into physical contact with Rebecca's things – rubbing her cheek against the fur coat Maxim gave her as a Christmas present, displaying Rebecca's underwear, 'Made especially for her by the nuns of the Convent of St Clare' and so on – the housekeeper takes on the role of a *vendeuse* from a fashion house (her demure black dress with white collar and cuffs is not unlike the typical uniform of a Parisian saleswoman), 'pushing' the brand onto her next potential client.[33] Danvers leaves the pièce de résistance to last, proudly declaring: 'I embroidered this case for her myself' as she opens the monogrammed container and displays Rebecca's diaphanous negligee, seductively asking the girl: 'Did you ever see anything so delicate?'[34] This presentation of the brand and the impossible standards it sets proves too much for the girl, who flees Rebecca's bedroom, or perhaps we can regard it as a 'saleroom', distraught.

This impossible, unobtainable brand that is Rebecca has nevertheless broken the cardinal rule of branding and made itself so exclusive that it has alienated its potential consumers and developed that most unforgivable of brand attributes, undesirability. Brands that can no longer maintain their market position are doomed to obsolescence and therefore the final scenes of *Rebecca* are reserved for the annihilation of the brand, as the viewer witnesses the monogrammed dressing case engulfed by flames. With the new Mrs de Winter finally 'brandless', the audience is left to speculate whether she will eventually find the same comfort as Hester Prynne in Hawthorne's novel, as she tears the scarlet letter from her breast: 'The stigma gone, Hester heaved a long deep sigh, in which the burden of shame and anguish departed from her spirit. O exquisite relief! She had not known the weight until she felt the freedom!'[35]

15 STUBBORN STAINS

At the most fundamental level, stained or soiled dress negates one of clothing's primary functions, which is to confer self-respect and dignity on the wearer. When this occurs in film, its negative aspects are heightened and made even more problematic than the everyday reality of clothes becoming marked and dirty. The presence of a stain on an article of clothing can register simply as evidence of the wearer's lack of care and attention or a purposeful flouting of accepted conventions concerning dress and propriety. Additionally, soiled, stained and shabby clothing is often used cinematically to signify poverty and disadvantage. Whether from untidy eating habits, occupational soiling in the workplace or the simple factor of only being able to afford one set of clothes, we understand the context and origin of these stains. However, in the cinematic negative wardrobe there are certain stains and certain circumstances that refuse to be so easily rationalised. It is these unconventional, often shocking and ultimately deceptive, incidences of stained clothing that will be discussed in this section, which in turn allow access to a visual discourse concerned with clothing's relationship to displacement and the spectacle of pollution.

The cinematic wardrobe is most often used to confer glamour and status on the wearer, or to assist in character development via a consensual understanding on the part of film-maker and audience of the psychological and emotional states that clothing can expose. Whether obvious or more subliminal, these visual cues make up a generally accepted cinematic vestimentary code and, in the majority of instances, clothing remains relatively spotless and stain-free. Therefore, when film deliberately draws the viewer's attention to clothing that is less than pristine, it presents an opportunity for dress to be perceived differently from its conventional cinematic function and, if only for a brief duration, become something other — an element of the film's discourse that demands consideration from a different critical perspective. The often comic, sometimes humiliating and frequently incriminating appearance of stained clothing acts as a form of visual caesura, its entrance invariably shocking and spectacular. Stains and stained clothing often enter a scene

STAGE FRIGHT
1950, dir. Alfred Hitchcock.
The bloodstained Dior.

suddenly and spectacularly, literally imposing themselves on the garment and by extension the wearer of that garment. In addition, these marks direct the viewer's attention to the garment with an uncharacteristic urgency that disrupts the seamless flow of images of clothing that is typically never less than perfect, functional and pristine.

These spectacular interventions expose the artifice of cinema itself: the viewer is suddenly made aware of the impossible cleanliness of cinematic clothing; realising that the stain has been artificially produced by the wardrobe supervisor, we refer to our own experiences of stained clothing and are encouraged to speculate on a stain's significance in the film's narrative. This conscious return or re-suturing back into the diegetic space of the film from the mundane world of stains and damaged clothing reminds the viewer of the essentially fictive nature of film. It is apparent that stained clothing on screen becomes problematic only when the origin of the stain is unclear or when its appearance cannot be rationally explained by circumstances such as carelessness, poverty or the wearer's occupation. Mary Douglas observed that the cultural response to dirt is based on its being understood as 'matter out of place', and it is this concept of displacement that is central to an understanding of the significance of stained clothing in the cinematic dysfunctional wardrobe:

> If we can abstract pathogenicity and hygiene from our notion of dirt, we are left with the old definition of dirt as matter out of place. This is a very suggestive approach. It implies two conditions: a set of ordered relations and a contravention of that order. Dirt then, is never a unique, isolated event. Where there is dirt there is system. Dirt is the by-product of a systematic ordering and classification of matter, in so far as ordering involves rejecting inappropriate elements. This idea of dirt takes us straight into the field of symbolism and promises a link-up with more obviously symbolic systems of purity.[1]

The representation of stains and the narrative attention they receive is proportionate to the extent of their displacement or inexcusability, so the appearance of a mechanic, for example, in oil-stained work clothes in a scene set in a garage seems entirely apposite. In fact it is often the lack of 'realism' in such scenes where workers sport permanently spotless overalls that seems the most remarkable. In contrast, wearing a paint-splattered vest for a job interview with a leading stockbroker, as the character Chris Gardner (Will Smith) does in *The Pursuit of Happyness* (2006) is both inappropriate and painful to watch.[2] Here the paint splashes on his vest and jacket are a result of his decorating and not necessarily out of place when an understandable by-product of this task, but it is the fact that these stained items are now present in a Manhattan boardroom that makes it and its dirt 'matter out of place'. So noteworthy is his unsuitable attire that his interviewer asks how he would justify giving the job to someone dressed in a similar manner, to which Gardner replies: 'He musta had on some really nice pants!' – a dialogic corrective to his dysfunctional attire by reference to a mythical pair of trousers so striking that they have the power to overcome the inappropriateness of other elements of his ensemble.[3]

Gardner's use of humour to deflect the tension created by the attention to his stained clothing is typical of the reactions of a number of soiled cinematic characters. The visual shock produced by a stained entrance, or its detection by others, is alleviated by humour, much in the same way as laughter is a common reaction to fear, most typically seen in audience reactions to horror films. To the sartorially spotless, any blemish however small is a diminishment of their identity and must be treated with derision. The fastidious and vain Shelby Carpenter's (Vincent Price) first meeting with Laura, in Preminger's 1944 film of the same name, takes place at a party, and entering the kitchen dabbing the lapel of his otherwise immaculate dinner jacket asks the housekeeper for assistance, quipping: 'Say, in the meantime, darlin', you think you could get this spot out for me? I can afford a blemish on my character, but not on my clothes!'[4]

Hamilton Bartholomew's preoccupation with his stained tie and the dry cleaning discourse it inspires in *Charade* has already been discussed and a similar interest in dry cleaning motivates the characters in *The Dark Corner* (1946). After interrogating and roughing up the white-suited Stauffer (William Bendix), a hit man working for the crooked lawyer Tony Jardine (who as noted in Part Four's 'Cutting a Dash' thinks he is 'class on a stick'), the private detective Bradford Galt (Mark Stevens) allows him to collect his belongings from Galt's desk. Reaching for his wallet, Stauffer knocks over a bottle of ink, spilling some onto Galt's hands. Galt then proceeds to wipe them clean on Stauffer's white jacket, smearing it with black ink. Throwing him a dollar bill, Galt suggests that he 'get the suit cleaned, Jardine's particular about neatness.'[5] This instance of spectacular staining takes on greater significance later in the film when, trying to track down Stauffer, Galt and his assistant (Lucille Ball) hit on the idea of ringing round all the local dry cleaners to see which one remembered cleaning ink stains from the unseasonably white suit ('bit early in the season for white suits' is the response from one establishment). The plan is successful and the suit 'no, not a seersucker, a white linen suit', is traced and Stauffer's true identity and address ascertained.[6] *The Dark Corner* is an interesting example of the incriminating stain and its cleansing as a form of forensic homing device, its memorable defilement ultimately inseparable from its bearer.

Typically, stains and dirt appearing where they ought not to be is the province of the crime film, where any number of incriminatingly displaced stains can be discovered. Long before the forensic fantasies of films and television series, which delight in revealing stains invisible to the naked eye, clothing stained with a variety of substances from ink to brake fluid have implicated the guilty wearer in plain sight, such as the oil-stained gloves in *The House on Telegraph Hill* (discussed in Part Three's 'One size fits all?').[7] The stains that will be investigated in this

THE PURSUIT OF HAPPYNESS
2006, dir. Gabriele Muccino.
[top] Matter out of place.

THE DARK CORNER
1946, dir. Henry Hathaway.
[bottom] 'Jardine's particular
about neatness'.

section, however, are bloodstains, arguably the most spectacular and most displaced of all cinematic staining. In order to understand how blood, rather than other stains, functions in the dysfunctional wardrobe, the bloodstained dresses in *Stage Fright* (1950) and '*Hush . . . Hush, Sweet Charlotte*' (1964) will be the primary focus of this discussion.[8]

A shot of impeccably turned ankles, a coat opening to let Christian Dior's accordion-pleated silk chiffon billow out, revealing the full extent of the stain soaking into the bottom of Charlotte Inwood's (Marlene Dietrich) gown, is the viewer's first encounter with the bloodstained dress, the pivotal object in *Stage Fright*. Bloodstained clothing, particularly dresses, figure large in the negative wardrobe of dysfunctional cinematic fashion, which suggests that the more feminine the garment the more impact the defilement of a bloodstain will have on audiences. Inwood's bloodstained Dior is the quintessential item of incriminating evidence; it functions both diegetically in typically Hitchcockian self-referential form and discursively to fashion and film history. While much of the plot of *Stage Fright* is driven by this particular garment, including its effect on the audience, on the characters, its disposal and replacement, this first encounter is revealed at the film's climax to be fictional. A 'flashback' narrated by Jonathan Cooper (Richard Todd), Inwood's lover, featuring the bloodstained dress is a fabrication. The significance the viewer has been encouraged to place on this dress throughout the film is revealed as both misdirected (it is not proof of Inwood's guilt but Cooper's) and misunderstood (the stain is not Inwood's murdered husband's blood but constructed after the fact by Cooper smearing his own blood on the dress). It is in fact a prime example of Hitchcock's formulation of the McGuffin.[9] The complex layering of references to the dress, where it resides, how the stain got there, its 'indestructibility' and its replication in miniature form, continues throughout the film and drives the action forward. Yet there is a further layering that surrounds this particular bloodstained garment concerning its designer

and its significance to fashion history as a whole. In fact, so self-referential and multi-faceted is the bloodstained dress as a signifier that its meaning as part of the plot becomes unstable and slides between fact and fiction, film and fashion.

At the beginning of the film in the false flashback, Inwood the society entertainer appears in her bloodstained dress at the apartment of her lover Cooper; the pleats of the dress fan out to reveal the extent of the stain, then fall back as she walks into his arms. Pleats have an ability to reveal and hide pattern, volume and colour, and are by their very nature and construction deceptive, a textile technique of artifice which in *Stage Fright* (the audience will eventually realise) mirrors the fictional origin of the stain itself.[10] However, this stain is too defiling, too obvious to be contained within the pleats of the dress and remains as an accusatory symbol on Inwood's body throughout the scene. Deciding that she must carry on with her performance that evening, Inwood, lifting the hem of the dress, drops it again declaring: 'But my dress, there's blood on it! I must go back and change.'[11] Rather than Inwood returning to the supposed scene of the crime, the murder of her husband, she sends Cooper back to get her another dress: 'There's a blue dress just like this in the big cupboard next to the window, in the bedroom'.[12] On his return, we see that the replacement dress is an exact copy of the bloodstained one, but in a darker shade, and the appearance of this second dress raises a series of conjectures centred on the idea of the original. As a character within the film, Inwood, we understand, is a performer, someone used to the idea of assuming different roles and dressing accordingly, yet multiples of the same garment feature prominently in her wardrobe, forcing the audience to question her integrity in this scene.

This characterisation is logical enough but is pushed beyond the limits of the film's narrative by the audience's identification with, and knowledge of, Marlene Dietrich playing Charlotte Inwood. Dietrich's construction as an iconic film star is entirely based on a remarkable understanding and complete control of her screen image. In particular, the films she made at Paramount directed by Josef von Sternberg and costumed by Travis Banton resulted in a succession of glamorous cinematic images that have become indelibly associated with the so-called 'golden age' of Hollywood.[13] Dietrich's and Charlotte Inwood's personae as performers are increasingly conflated as the film's action progresses, all pretence at emotion gone as she concentrates on her image when changing from her bloodstained dress, or veiled and wreathed in cigarette smoke imagining a more décolleté neckline to her widow's weeds.

The doubling of the fictional dress not only suggests a duplicity associated with its fictional wearer but also seems to provide a commentary on couture fashion, which promises and promotes exclusivity and originality and yet, in order to survive, will alter and manufacture copies of so-called exclusive designs. This analogy may seem somewhat fanciful but it is known that Dietrich demanded to be costumed exclusively by Christian Dior, that Dior insisted on a screen credit and that Paramount in turn demanded and received a twenty-five per cent discount off the price of his designs, all of which suggests a tellingly pragmatic sensibility on the part of fashion and film industry alike.[14] As Alexandra Palmer observes in *Couture and Commerce*: 'A disparity between the mythology and the reality of haute couture exclusivity was inherent in the system, and it became more exaggerated during the 1950s. Even though haute couture was marketed as unique and special, everyone knew that this was no longer true.'[15]

If *Stage Fright's* bloodstained dress appears to offer a commentary on notions of originality within the fashion industry, does its actual defilement, its ruination by wilful (as it is ultimately revealed) staining say something about Dior's reputation in Britain as a designer? *Stage Fright* was released in 1950, three years after Christian Dior unveiled his 'New Look'. This was characterised by an extravagant use of luxurious fabrics and a silhouette achieved by corsetry that was seen by many as both economically profligate and politically retrograde fol-

lowing the liberation of women's clothing that occurred during the Second World War. Dietrich/Inwood's appearance in a Dior dress consisting of yards of silk chiffon contrasts resolutely with the unglamorous, utility-style clothing of many of the characters populating Hitchcock's mise-en-scène of post-war, ration-book Britain. The spoiling of the Dior dress, rendered unwearable and ugly by the bloodstain seeping into its delicate folds, makes this dysfunctional garment an appropriate comment on Dior's New Look. Seen by many in Britain at the time as unpatriotic and irresponsible, the New Look enraged British fashion manufacturers so strongly that, as Angela Partington noted, 'on 17th March 1948, a delegation representing three hundred dress firms went to Harold Wilson (then head of the Board of trade) and asked for a ban on long hemlines. The new style was not in their interests because it meant less product for their investment of materials and labour.'[16]

So, if there are no originals, only multiple copies, it makes sense that the bloodstained dress remains somehow indestructible throughout the film. Cooper decides against throwing the offending item onto the fire and instead takes it with him to the house of Commodore Gill (Alastair Sim), who refers to the 'sanguinary garment' as a fake constructed to persuade Cooper to help Charlotte Inwood.[17] Cooper in anger then throws the dress on the fire, which paradoxically marks the beginning of the alternative 'life' of the dress as a complete fiction. For example, after watching Inwood perform, Cooper tells her that in fact he has not destroyed the dress after all or, in a crucial scene, Commodore Gill tries to shock Inwood into confessing her guilt by confronting her with a replica dress at the theatrical garden party. At the party, Gill 'sees' two spectral reconstitutions of the stain, firstly superimposed on the white dress of a passing guest and then at the shooting gallery on the dress of one of the prize dolls. These specular stains suggest to Gill a means with which to confront Inwood with her crime; so he proceeds to cut himself, smear one of the dolls' dresses with his own blood and produce a miniature version of the original offending item,

with which he then persuades a boy scout to walk slowly towards Inwood, carrying the 'relic' of her crime as if in a solemn religious procession.

The variants of the bloodstained Dior encountered at the beginning of the film suggest that, once rendered dysfunctional by the staining, it can assume a mythical status, its actual existence unverifiable, and any notion of the original lost under much conjecture and imitation. Even after the deployment of the bloodstained doll's dress at the garden party, the 'original' lives on, as Inwood is tricked into believing that it still exists and attempts to get it back by offering payment in kind, in the form of jewels and furs. In due course, the stained dress seen at the beginning is revealed as a fake that Cooper has constructed: he confesses that the dress was only a little stained, so he made it worse (presumably with his own blood) in order to convince people of Inwood's guilt. Stains, particularly bloodstained dresses, it seems, have the power to deceive even the deceiver, such is the spectacularly distracting nature of their appearance.

Once stained and unwearable, the dress becomes a conduit for a variety of narrative and discursive interpretation, 'the *stain* which precipitates a gaze and so brings about a fiction'.[18] Bloodstains on a dress are most spectacularly 'matter out of place': blood should be inside the body and not visible, and when made manifest it signifies violence, sickness and death. This rationale is useful up to a point but does not account for the often extraordinary emphasis and subsequent narrative complexity following the entry of bloodstained clothing on film. As with the concept of matter out of place, Douglas can again assist with the interrogation of cinematic bloodstains when she proposes that

> all margins are dangerous. If they are pulled this way or that the shape of the fundamental experience is altered. Any structure of ideas is vulnerable at its margins. We should expect the orifices of the body to symbolise its specially vulnerable points. Matter arising from them is marginal stuff of the most obvious kind. Spittle, blood, milk, urine, faeces or tears by simply issuing forth have traversed the boundary

[facing] Christian Dior's 'New Look', 1947 (Lipnitski/Roger-Viollet/Rex Features).

STAGE FRIGHT
1950, dir. Alfred Hitchcock.
[top] Spectral staining;
[bottom] processing the relic.

of the body . . . The mistake is to treat bodily margins in isolation from all other margins.[19]

While Douglas is concerned with the natural issue of blood (among other bodily fluids), rather than due to violence acted on the body, her suggestion that its appearance signifies a collapse of the margins or boundaries which govern the body and society is crucial. This collapse is what acts as the catalyst on film for the sudden rush of instability and disorder that follows the appearance of bloodstained dresses. These items from the cinematic negative wardrobe are evidence of something that has traversed the margins of the body, and as such is both dangerous and incomprehensible; it disrupts the natural order of things and attacks the rational. As Kristeva put it, they move us 'toward the place where meaning collapses'.[20] Just such a collapse of meaning follows the appearance of the bloodstained Dior in *Stage Fright*. Does it actually exist or not, is it a copy, whose blood is on the dress, or is it a mixture of Cooper's and Inwood's husband's blood, rendering it doubly defiled, and does it presage further bloodletting, as with Gill's construction of the bloodstained doll? The questions pile up and meaning collapses.

As has been discussed throughout this work, the items in the negative cinematic wardrobe have a potential that far outstrips the usual function of clothing; in the case of the blood-soaked dress they signify disorder, deception and chaos. Robert Aldrich's gothic horror '*Hush . . . Hush, Sweet Charlotte'* places another problematic blood-soaked dress centre stage. As with *Stage Fright,* the incriminating dress is first seen in flashback as we learn the grim story of Charlotte Hollis (Bette Davis), an ageing Southern belle living as a recluse in her mansion. Forty years earlier, Charlotte's married lover John Mayhew was found decapitated and mutilated during a ball being given at the Hollis mansion. Charlotte makes a spectacular entrance among the guests in a white dress drenched in blood, the stain filling the screen and demanding the attention of the viewer, torn between averting the gaze and seeking an explanation. She enters from the direction of the summer-house where the body is discovered and this, in addition to the knowledge that Mayhew was about to end his affair with her, leads to her being accused of his murder. Charlotte, completely traumatised by the grisly discovery, is rendered speechless and, even though her guilt was never proven, her silence and apparent descent into madness means she is subsequently regarded as the most likely perpetrator of the crime. Unlike *Stage Fright*'s, this flashback is genuine but, as with the former film, we do not see how the stain originated and instead are focused on its spectacular nature and the effect it has on the guests. Once again, the bloodstain is, if not entirely fabricated, a reason for false accusation, and is the primary cause of Charlotte's seclusion and reputation as the crazed, jilted axe-murderer. Towards the conclusion of the film, Charlotte has another flashback, or perhaps dream, in which she is once again at the ball but this time in an unstained dress. Although this vision points to Charlotte's true innocence, it is contextualised as the hallucinations of someone rapidly descending into madness and therefore its veracity is cast into doubt.

It seems that in film, dramatic, attention-grabbing bloodstains are often faked and it is their intrinsically show-stopping spectacular nature that misdirects the fictional viewer and cinema audience alike into a unified condemnation of the bearer of the stain. Guy Debord's critique of media-saturated culture suggests that

> the spectacle presents itself simultaneously as all of society, as part of society, and as instrument of unification. As a part of society it is specifically the sector which concentrates all gazing and all consciousness. Due to the very fact that this sector is separate, it is the common ground of the deceived gaze and of false consciousness, and the unification it achieves is nothing but an official language of generalized separation.[21]

As cinema-goers we visit one of the primary sites of Debord's 'society of the spectacle', ostensibly gathered together in the communal act of watching a film but in reality isolated from our fellow viewers in darkness, caught up in our individual responses to the film narrative, subjects of the 'deceived gaze'. Watching films such as *Stage Fright* or '*Hush . . . Hush, Sweet Charlotte*', like the actors on screen, we too are seduced by the spectacle of violence, the excess of visual information provided by the bloody defilement, and reach the same incorrect conclusions as the protagonists.

The bloodstained dresses function as the primary conduit for this seductive doubling of the power of spectacle, offering themselves as gratifying 'clues' that unify the viewer in a fantasy of forensic truth. However, not only are the wearers of these offending items of clothing invariably revealed to be innocent of crime, but also the stains they display are often not even the victim's blood and, in certain cases, such as in Brian De Palma's *Carrie* (1976), not even of human origin.[22] In perhaps the most extreme example of the blood-soaked dress, what is taken to be human blood by the prom guests looking on at the drenched Carrie (Sissy Spacek), is in fact pig's blood, surely one of the more disturbing examples of Douglas's concept of 'matter out of place'. This steeping of Carrie's dress has a powerful anthropological and prohibitive significance, given the strictures surrounding the proximity to both animal (particularly pig's) blood and menstrual blood. As is portrayed in the film's opening shower scene, the sudden onset of menstruation acts as a catalyst for the discovery of Carrie's supernatural powers and, following the terrifying prom-night sequence, she is seen once again showering off blood and discarding her bloody, destructive dress, her symbolic livery of maturity both sexual and annihilating.

Blood seen on a dress, the impact heightened by the contrast between red/dark and white/light ground of the dresses, allows no room for doubt or any other possible explanation for the stain on the part of the spectator. As discussed in Part Five's 'Seeing Red', the resonance of the 'idea' of red, even when occurring in black and white films, as are both *Stage Fright* and '*Hush . . . Hush, Sweet Charlotte*', is irresistible. The blood has indelibly marked both the dress and character of the wearer and, therefore, they must carry the stigma of the murderer or transgressor. Of course, the level and intensity of the deception

'HUSH . . . HUSH, SWEET CHARLOTTE'
1964, dir. Robert Aldrich.
[top] Spectacular staining.

CARRIE
1976, dir. Brian De Palma.
[bottom] More matter out of place
(Everett Collection/Rex Features).

is variable according to the scenario in which it is inserted: mass deception in the case of *Carrie* and *'Hush . . . Hush, Sweet Charlotte'*, a more intimate, one-to-one deception in *Stage Fright*. Yet, however large or small the audience, its fraudulent status is an abiding characteristic of the cinematic bloodstained dress. These stained garments are so excessive, so demanding of the viewer's attention and so overloaded with significance and contingent reference or, as Slavoj Žižek suggests, 'permeated with an excessive libidinal investment', that ultimately they have to be revealed as false.[23]

The bloodstained dress in the narratives of films such as *Stage Fright* and *'Hush . . . Hush, Sweet Charlotte'* are examples of the multi-valency of dysfunctional fashion; at the simplest level they can no longer function as wearable clothing (the automatic reaction to a bloodstain on one's clothing is either to remove the offending article or at least, if comparatively small, to try to wash the stain out). We now understand the article as abject in the Kristevan sense of the term, something that must be expelled and kept at a safe distance from the body, for fear of the contamination that the proximity to the blood of others might produce (one's own bloodstained clothing is a different matter, of course). As Peter Wollen has observed concerning crime scenes generally, these dysfunctional dresses allow us as cinema viewers to

share in the sadomasochistic enjoyment that the onlooker secretly imagines that both the perpetrator and the victim may have experienced the site of guilty fantasy. Finally there is the mesmerizing anxiety produced by contact with the abject and the uncanny, the awareness of a scene, haunted by degradation and terror, which is insistently fascinating, which suspends time and freezes the spectator into immobility yet, in the final analysis, remains safely removed from reality.[24]

So far this section has considered substantial bloodstaining, the stain that cannot be ignored or overlooked. However, owing to the formal construction and conventions of the cinematic image, the minimal and almost negligible stain can have an equally spectacular presence on screen. The close-up of a few drops of blood descending on a pale ground is loaded with as much significance as a garment dripping with blood. These spots and speckles of blood are generally divinatory, signs and portents of significant bloodletting to come. This can be almost instantaneous, as in the case of the private view held in the Chicago Natural History Museum that provides the setting for *The Relic* (1997).[25] A guest at the opening night of the museum's latest exhibition, entitled 'Superstition', fails to notice the spots of blood that fall from above onto the shoulder of her cream jacket. These stains swiftly usher in the full-scale destruction that follows, wrought by the supernatural slayer, the Kathoga, a mythical beast that feeds on the brains of its victims and which has been brought to life in the museum. The initial drops signify the beginning of the bloody rampage about to engulf the museum and its privileged guests, which soon turns into a tidal wave of blood drenching its ordered spaces. The swiftness with which these scenes of destruction follow the initial appearance of the drops of blood is perhaps due to the supernatural nature of the carnage, an equal alacrity observed in *Carrie*'s orgy of supernatural retribution following her preliminary soaking.[26] When the ensuing violence is of a mortal nature, however, there is a longer period between preliminary staining and final saturation. The viewer registers the spoiling of the clothing and only subsequently realises the full significance of this foreshadowing when witnessing the magnification of blood-letting later in the film. This delay between the first marking and bloody amplification is evident in *L.A. Confidential* (1997) where Kevin Spacey playing the corrupt cop Jack Vincennes is involved in a fight at a jail during which his tie and pale jacket become marked with blood.[27] The spoiling of the fastidious Vincennes's wardrobe is a miniaturisation of the more shocking blood-loss that soaks the carpet in the motel room where his lover is discovered later in the film with his throat cut, the stain that spreads from the wound in his lover's neck echoing that on Vincennes's previously stained neckwear.

THE RELIC
1997, dir. Peter Hyams.
[facing] Institutionalised blood-letting.

L.A. CONFIDENTIAL
1997, dir. Curtis Hanson.
[above] First blood.

Dropping blood onto white or pale cloth is a powerfully resonant sign. As long as there are sufficient textual and visual cues, the viewer will register these stains as blood even if they are not blood at all but a symbolic substitute. This act of cinematic substitution can be seen in a number of films where a red stain, most commonly caused by red wine, acts as a microcosmic indicator of the blood that will flow later in the film. Substituting wine for blood inevitably invokes Christian symbolism, specifically the act of transubstantiation where wine becomes the blood of Christ, and *The Deer Hunter* (1978) contains a powerful example of this act of symbolic substitution.[28] At the reception following the Orthodox wedding ceremony at the beginning of the film, the bride and groom, Steven and Angela (John Savage and Rutanya Alda), are required to drain a double wedding cup and 'will have good luck all their lives'

if they do not spill a drop.[29] The viewer's attention is directed to two drops of red wine that fall unnoticed by the bride and groom onto the bodice of her wedding dress. This symbolic, almost imperceptible bloodshed is a presentiment of the bloodbath that will follow, as the wedding takes place on the eve of Steven and his friends' departure for their tour of duty in Vietnam and which the rest of the film will detail in full. The spilt wine acts as a clearly discernible omen that connects the religious ritual of the wedding ceremony to the wholesale slaughter and ritual enactment of suicide in the game of Russian roulette that Steven and his comrades are forced to play in the jungle.

There are many other instances, however, where the symbolism of a few drops of blood functions on a more personal but no less ominous register. These portentous stains act as clues to other events but, unlike the conventional clues found at the scene of a crime that offer the detective a means of reconstructing what must have happened earlier, these cinematic clues function both prognostically and occasionally retroactively, as with the drops of red ink that Marnie (Tippi Hedren) spills on her white blouse and which act as an uncontainable cathexis hurtling her towards future criminal acts and away from the blood-red remembrance of her repressed childhood trauma. These stains transform the viewer into clairvoyant and detective who must decipher the signs and predict both future and past events, aided by devices such as foreshadowing and flashbacks. Carlo Ginzburg made this process explicit in his distinction between hunters and diviners: 'Both require minute examination of the real, however trivial, to uncover traces of events which the observer cannot directly experience . . . divination pointed towards the future, while the hunters' deciphering was of what had actually happened, even if very recently.'[30]

Bloodstained clothing in the dysfunctional cinematic wardrobe acts as a set of vestimentary signs of what has happened and what will happen. Rather more than a few drops of blood stain the shirt of Carter Chambers (Morgan Freeman) in *The Bucket List* (2007) and can be understood as both a reminder of past events and a prognostication of future trauma.[31] Meeting in the cancer ward of a hospital for the terminally ill, the mechanic Carter and the billionaire Edward Cole (Jack Nicholson) form an unlikely relationship; they decide to discharge themselves and fulfil a list of things they wish to do before they 'kick the bucket'. Part of that list comprises travelling the world and they start their experience by dining at the exclusive French Riviera restaurant La Chèvre d'Or. Leaving the dinner table suddenly, Carter is followed by Edward to the cloakroom where he discovers him dabbing at a large bloodstain seeping from his chest and staining his shirt. 'Jesus Christ!' declares the shocked Edward. 'It's all right! It's OK. The top of the catheter just came loose, that's all . . . it's all right, look it's all been stopped, see', replies Carter. 'Yeah, looks wonderful!' is Edward's mocking reply.[32] The sudden letting of Carter's blood acts as a shockingly

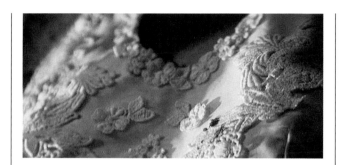

MARNIE
1964, dir. Alfred Hitchcock.
[facing] Catalytic staining.

THE DEER HUNTER
1978, dir. Michael Cimino.
[above] Transubstantiation.

sanguinary reminder of his mortality and, occurring roughly half way through the film, marks the beginning of his journey towards his death on the operating table.

The gradual degradation of Joe Buck's spectacular cowboy outfits in *Midnight Cowboy* has been discussed previously, but symbolic and real bloodstains play a distinctly prophetic role alongside his general decline into sartorial shabbiness. After his initially unsuccessful attempts as a hustler, which end up with him giving his female client money, he drops tomato ketchup on his pale grey trousers, causing a large red stain in his genital area. This soiling of his appearance accompanies a similar descent into sexual degradation as he next consents to receiving oral sex from a teenage boy only to find, once again, that he has been tricked and the boy has no money to pay him. Later, at the climax to the film, after a series of unsuccessful encounters and with his companion Rizzo's health in decline, they decide to take the bus to Florida, financed by one last sorry encounter that ends with Joe punching his guilt-wracked client in the mouth, during which Joe's jacket gets stained with blood. On the bus Rizzo notices the stain and asks 'You didn't kill him, did ya? You got blood on your jacket'. Joe replies: 'I don't wanna talk about it' but it is not the client's death that the stain attests: rather, it predicts Rizzo's, who dies during the trip and ends up cradled in Joe's arms as they travel to Miami.[33]

Larger stains such as those on the dresses in *Stage Fright* and *'Hush . . . Hush, Sweet Charlotte'* are unreliable indicators, as discussed, and what is thought to have happened is invariably an incorrect deduction. They are similarly unreliable concerning the wearer's future demise. As a sign of what will happen, smaller bloodstains are more reliable, it seems; the bloodstained handkerchief, for example, resonates throughout literature and onto the screen as a more dependable indicator. The soiled handkerchief dysfunctionally accessorises a cast of cinematic consumptives, haemophiliacs and the terminally ill who, along with the viewer, all too swiftly realise the portentous nature of bloodstained linen. From Alexei (Roderic Noble), the scion of the Romanovs in *Nicholas and Alexandra* (1971),[34] to the prostitute

THE BUCKET LIST
2007, dir. Rob Reiner.
[top] Mortal staining.

MIDNIGHT COWBOY
1969, dir. John Schlesinger.
[bottom] Defiling moment.

Satine (Nicole Kidman) in *Moulin Rouge!* (2001),[35] bloodspots are the inescapable portents of these characters' ultimate demise. These marks are not the spectacularly incriminating stains of the murderer but the marks of shame – of the sickly victim, stains that need to be hidden, quickly palmed or covered up from the view of lovers, parents and friends. They are caught sight of momentarily and then hastily removed from view. In the audience, our privileged sight of these tell-tale signs of sickness make us complicit with the sufferer. The brief, shameful glimpses of unexpected bodily fluids are registered and then put aside, with the memory of their appearance permanently 'staining' the viewer's perception of the victim. These unexpected stains usher in a wealth of disturbing associations in the viewer that are easily understood in the context of the fear of contagion. The revulsion that is triggered by the unannounced and displaced appearance of blood on screen becomes a component in films that have disease as part of their textual discourse. Bearing a similarity to the soiled clothing that results from the wearer's occupation discussed at the beginning of this section, these bloodstained vestments are also caused by the wearer's activity but the primary profession in this instance is as the diseased rather than the manual labourer. The stains are of the wearers' own making yet no longer signs of honest toil but soiling of the most humiliating and revelatory order.

Whether the barely discernible stained linen of the sick, or the spectacularly incriminating blood-drenched dress, these unbidden stains have a more lasting resonance than those that we more typically see on film. As visually arresting as the blood-spattered clothing of slasher, war or gangster movies may be, it is the less explicable, less abundant and often more spectacular stained garments that are the concern of this study. Staining as a direct result of one character harming another is an easily understood visual narrative, with the letting of blood acting as a full stop at the end of a violent sentence. We understand how this blood has been spilt, where it is and why. Bloodstains whose origin and cause is concealed or lied about must resonate more strongly for audiences who are accustomed to the sight of blood as a direct result of violence. Viewers understand these more conventional stains as the result of a breaching of the boundary wall, the skin, between internal physiognomy and external world. The cause of this breach, while possibly distressing, is conceivable when a film constructs a logical chain of events that explain the blood's entrance. However, if this visual narrative is incomplete, viewers have to supply the missing imagery. So in *'Hush . . . Hush, Sweet Charlotte'* we assume that Charlotte has dispatched her lover in the summer-house because of her subsequent appearance in the bloodstained party dress, and it this act of individual reconstruction that bestows an unlimited potential not only on this particular garment but on the dysfunctional, negative wardrobe of film clothing as a whole.

POSTSCRIPT

what is decisive in collecting is that the object is detached from all its original functions in order to enter the closest conceivable relation to things of the same kind.[1]

The catalysts for this study were three indelible cinematic memories: of a shimmering pale satin mule with its toe wedged under a fraying carpet, a close-up of the stained fingertips of a man's pigskin driving glove and the delicate pleats of a Dior afternoon dress billowing out to reveal a shocking bloodstain. These fragments from *Leave Her to Heaven*, *The House on Telegraph Hill* and *Stage Fright* have fascinated me from the moment I first encountered them. Long after the details of their narrative significance and relevance to the plot of the films in which they appear have become hazy and conjectural, they linger, their unrelenting visual excess a testament to the power of cinematic imagery. In their remembered, isolated condition they exude a surfeit of possibilities that gesture to spaces beyond the dramatic frames they inhabit on screen, of other possibilities, other dysfunctionalities. Having detached the items of clothing and accessories featured in *Dressing Dangerously* from their original function as elements within the film's narrative, what is left? Are they merely fragments that may haphazardly be grouped into potentially meaningful arrangements and just as quickly be dispersed? Is it unreasonable to think that these unsettling and unsettled shoes, gloves and dresses can also act as 'clues' to deeper, universally experienced responses to the clothes we wear? Why are these images so insistent, so beautiful, so 'too much'? Is it possible that their only function is to act as evidence of criminal activity?

It would not be unreasonable to imagine that when discussing clothing on film, especially when many of those films conform to the loose term of crime film, that items of dress play significant roles in the solving and revelation of criminal activity. The idea that an object, in this case an article of dress, can function as a trace of its owner, as a clue that charts the course of a prior event, the crime, is permanently rooted in criminal narrative. Thus Agent Purvis firmly believes that the blue wool overcoat will lead him directly to its owner, John Dillinger. When an object's relevance and its owner are unknown, however, a more analytical method of deduction is required, where the object becomes a clue to be 'read' as providing vital evidence of a past event or to 'profile' those present at the scene of the crime. Possibly one of the more unexpected conclusions emerging from this study is that even though many of my memories of cinematic clothing, such as the three just mentioned, suggest an evidential function, when these fragments are regrouped in 'relation to things of the same kind' these sequences of vestimentary dysfunctionality resist their assumed forensic potential and instead usher in the dysfunctionality of the false clue and the misleading piece of evidence.[2]

This forensic method is perhaps most famously manifested in Arthur Conan Doyle's creation Sherlock Holmes, whose study of 'tiny details provide the key to a deeper reality, inaccessible by other methods'.[3] Holmes's 'reading' of an abandoned hat in 'The Adventure of the Blue Carbuncle' (1892) is a case in point. Dr Watson on seeing Holmes studying the hat suggests: 'I suppose . . . that, homely as it looks, this thing has some deadly story linked on to it – that it is the clue which will guide you in the solution of some mystery, and the punishment of some crime.'[4] Holmes then proceeds to astound Watson by proposing that the hat's owner is highly intellectual (its size suggests a large head, therefore a large brain), has had his hair recently cut at a barber's and uses pomade (scissor-cut ends of hair stuck together and caught in the hat's lining), has fallen on hard times recently (it is a good-quality but old-fashioned style of hat), is unloved by his wife (it has not been recently brushed), rarely goes out of the house (the dust caught in the hat band is of a domestic fluffy variety rather than grittier street dirt) and probably does not have a gas supply in his house (candle-wax stains suggest the use of candles for illumination rather than gas jets). Holmes's almost supernatural ability to materialise bodies and actions from the tiniest of details made him the pre-eminent fictional detective of the nineteenth century.[5] Accessories in detective stories such as the

Sherlock Holmes cases act as parts for the missing whole and readily offer up their owner's secrets under the omniscient gaze of the detective. In crime film, however, they tend to function differently.

Accessories in many crime films conform more closely to the description of objects that the art critic Ralph Rugoff gives in his essay accompanying the forensics-inspired exhibition 'Scene of the Crime' (1997):

> We have already seen how the same artefact – whether a tire or a performance relic – can appear at once to be utterly mundane and yet charged with a surplus meaning that eludes our visual inspection and so seems vaguely uncanny . . . We may learn about a thing's meaning, in other words, only by understanding its place in a larger symbolic structure. Consideration of the crime scene leads us, in this way, to a 'postmodern' understanding in which the same object can shift between opposing categories, functioning 'successively as a disgusting reject and as a sublime charismatic apparition'.[6]

It is this 'surplus meaning' that persists in my memory of the aforementioned shoe, glove and dress: their possibly incriminating potential is understood but their power is greater than that, closer to 'sublime charismatic apparitions'. If Holmes and Dupin, Edgar Allan Poe's prototype detective, can be thought of as pre-cinematic sleuths, the creations of writers such as Raymond Chandler, Dashiell Hammett and James M. Cain are indelibly associated with their cinematic incarnations: these detectives are flawed, often deceived and laid low by their emotions, the antithesis of the rational, dispassionate Holmes, and their encounters with evidence or clues equally ambiguous, inconclusive and meandering.[7] The events that unfold during their investigations are the drivers of the plot, not the successful retelling of past events through the traces left behind. In the case of accessories, these are as likely to be red herrings, emotional triggers or devices that raise more questions than answers. 'Chandler shows his readers just how little they learn from the results of such neat interpretation and what depths of mystery the process of interpretation can reveal.'[8] This understanding of the fluid and expanded meaning of an object, its position within a larger 'symbolic structure', is closer to the dysfunctional items that are the subject of this work, which undergo necessary processes of transformation thereby enabling additional or alternative uses, meaning and indeed emotional resonance to be established between the objects on screen and the viewer.

These cinematic shards, splinters of ideal structures, such as forensic efficacy or sartorial supremacy, circulate within popular consciousness, perforating personal and public memories of scenes already seen, forgotten or yet to be seen. Their dysfunctionality is the agent of their dispersal and liberation from their original narratives, facilitating their flow from film to popular consciousness and personal reverie and back again, as Victor Burgin persuasively points out: 'associations lead not only to roots in personal history. In selectively incorporating fragments from the image environment they also branch out to weave private and public into a unitary network of meanings . . . Our forgotten answers to distant questions may reverberate down history to shatter remembered films. But what concerns us most is what we make of the fragments.'[9]

NOTES

INTRODUCTION

1 Walter Benjamin, 'N [On the Theory of Knowledge, Theory of Progress]', in *The Arcades Project*, trans. Howard Eiland and Kevin McLaughlin, Cambridge, Mass., 1999, p. 461.

2 Slavoj Žižek, 'The Hitchcockian Blot', in R. Allen and S. Ishii-Gonzalès, eds, *Alfred Hitchcock Centenary Essays*, London, 1999, p. 123.

3 Jean Baudrillard, *The System of Objects*, trans. J. Benedict, London, 1999, p. 85.

4 Jean-Pierre Oudart, 'Cinema and Suture', in *Screen*, vol. 18 no. 4, 1977, pp. 35–47.

5 Quentin Bell, *On Human Finery*, London, 1992, pp. 34–7.

6 See Lou Taylor, *Establishing Dress History*, Manchester, 2004, for a full and detailed account of Doris Langley Moore's seminal position in the establishment of British dress history.

7 *Sense and Nonsense in Fashion*, BBC Television, first broadcast 1957, part of the series *Men, Women and Clothes*. Pertinent to this study is the fact that as well as Langley Moore's reputation as a costume historian and collector, she regularly used famous actors of the day to model the outfits both in her BBC television series and for her books on costume. She also designed the costumes for Katherine Hepburn in the 1951 film **The African Queen** and another film directed by John Huston, **Freud,** in 1962.

8 Thorstein Veblen, *The Theory of the Leisure Class* (1899), New York, 1994.

9 Victor Burgin, *The Remembered Film*, London, 2004, p. 59.

10 This quotation is taken from one of the more recent publications on clothing in mainstream film: D. Nadoolman Landis, ed., *Hollywood Costume*, London, 2012, p. 42. It accompanied the exhibition of the same name held at the Victoria and Albert Museum, London, 2012–13, and is organised into four main sections that with a few notable exceptions echo the well known edicts of celebrated costume designers such as Edith Head, who maintained that film costume was principally about establishing character and that at its most effective was often unnoticeable.

11 While it is not within the remit of this work to discuss the diverging fields of dress studies and fashion theory, it is perhaps worth noting that the apparent dichotomy between the former term, which could be understood reductively as the study of the material objects of clothing, while fashion theory is concerned with the industrialisation, mediation and socio-cultural significance of 'fashion', is indicative of the discipline having arrived at a crossroads. This crossroads is increasingly congested with a number of studies waiting on one 'side' or the other of this junction but few, it appears, are willing to follow an interdisciplinary route and cross over into each other's territories.

12 Geoffrey Batchen, 'The Art of Archiving', in *Deep Storage: Collecting, Storing, and Archiving in Art*, Munich, 1998, p. 46.

13 While there have been important and noticeable studies of clothing in film that have transcended or expanded the critical parameters listed here, clothing's relationship to character development remains the overriding research dynamic in this field.

14 Jean Dubuffet, *Asphyxiating Culture*, New York, 1988, p. 13.

15 Gaston Bachelard, 'Drawers, Chests and Wardrobes', in *The Poetics of Space*, Boston, Mass., 1994, p. 79.

16 A few examples of Australian and Canadian co-productions also are included.

17 Susan Hayward, *Key Concepts in Cinema Studies*, London, 1996, pp. 75–6.

18 Certain films set in a period other than the time in which they were made, for example **Public Enemies** discussed in 'Cloaking Devices' and **Gaslight** in 'Trophies' here, are included as variations on a particular theme.

19 Anne Hollander, *Seeing Through Clothes*, Berkeley, Calif., 1993, pp. 296–7.

20 Pam Cook, *Fashioning the Nation: Costume and Identity in British Cinema*, London, 1996.

21 Raphael Samuel, *Theatres of Memory*, London, 1994.

22 Burgin, *Remembered Film*, pp. 67–8.

23 Ibid., p. 8.

24 Raymond Bellour, 'A Bit of History', in C. Penley, ed., *The Analysis of Film*, Indianapolis, 2000, p. 4.

25 A notable exception is **Rebecca** if one discounts Rebecca's accidental death after falling and hitting her head and Mrs Danvers's arson.

26 Slavoj Žižek, 'Hitchcockian *Sinthoms*', in S. Žižek, ed, *Everything You Always Wanted to Know About Lacan But Were Afraid to Ask Hitchcock*, London, 2010, p. 125.

27 Edith Head quoted in Edith Head and Paddy Calistro, *Edith Head's Hollywood*, Santa Monica, Calif., 2008, p. 194.

28 Žižek, 'Hitchcockian *Sinthoms*', p. 126.

29 Michel Foucault, *The Archaeology of Knowledge*, trans. A. M. Sheridan Smith, London, 1992, p. 5.

30 Edgar Allan Poe, *The Gold Bug*, in *The Fall of the House of Usher and Other Writings*, ed. D. Galloway, London, 1986, p. 309.

1 CLOAKING DEVICES

1 Lyrics from *Button Up your Overcoat*, 1929, Ray Henderson, Lew Brown and B. G. DeSylva.

2 This of course does not apply to period costume film or specific genres such as the western or war film where vestimentary convention dictates the use of items of dress such as the full-length duster coat or army greatcoat.

3 I am referring to European and North American conventions and this will be the case for all the subsequent items of dress considered in this book. My study is limited to cinema from North America and Britain and, therefore, both world cinema and dress is beyond its scope.

4 There are many exceptions to this, especially in the period under discussion: e.g., in the 1960s the wearing of full-length military greatcoats became popular among a newly politicised, left-wing younger generation and was perceived as a form of sartorial irony and anti-militarism.

5 **Barefoot in the Park**, 1967, dir. Gene Saks, cost. Edith Head.

6 **The Odd Couple**, 1968, dir. Gene Saks, cost. Jack Bear.

7 **Victim**, 1961, dir. Basil Dearden, cost. uncredited.

8 Although this situation remained unchanged until the Sexual Offences Act was passed in 1967, many believe that **Victim** helped to promote a more liberal attitude to homosexuality and hastened the passing of the act.

9 **Victim** warrants further study as a film not only for its groundbreaking subject matter but also as a perfect visualisation of the pivotal shifts occurring in British menswear at the beginning of the 1960s, when elegantly tailored new 'Edwardians' such as Farr rubbed shoulders with their more conservatively dressed colleagues, while the revolution in menswear that would take place during the decade is signalled by the more outré outfits worn by the film's younger, primarily, homosexual characters.

10 **Being There**, 1979, dir. Hal Ashby, cost. Mary Routh.

11 Perhaps one of the most celebrated examples of this vestimentary subterfuge can be found in Preston Sturges's 1941 comedy **Sullivan's Travels** (cost. Edith Head) which features an idealistic film director John L. Sullivan (Joel McCrea) purposely dressing as a tramp so that he can research what it is like to live as a vagrant and to lend authenticity to his next film project. Sullivan's subterfuge fails to convince until, not unlike Chance, he is unable to explain himself, due in this case to memory loss brought on after being knocked unconscious; unlike Chance, his attire lands him in prison, whence he struggles to establish his true identity.

12 Nikolai Gogol, *The Overcoat and Other Short Stories*, trans. Isabel F. Hapgood, New York, 1992, p. 91.

13 In this dysfunctional respect, coats function more like accessories, such as gloves, hats and items of jewellery. These are notable cinematically for their propensity to be lost, stolen or mislaid. Their function in the cinematic wardrobe is one of absence, and their singularity and importance to a number of film narratives is heralded by their dislocation.

14 **Witness for the Prosecution**, 1957, dir. Billy Wilder, cost. Edith Head (Marlene Dietrich), Joe King, Adele Parmenter. **D.O.A.**, 1950, dir. Rudolph Maté, cost. Maria Donovan.

15 See my *Tartan*, Oxford, 2008, esp. the chapter 'Tartan Toffs' for a detailed examination of the relationship between boldly checked cloth and exhibitionism.

16 Dialogue from **The Heartbreak Kid**, 1972, dir. Elaine May, cost. Anthea Sylbert.

17 'Clothes make the man', the popular phrase, has been attributed to Mark Twain, the complete text being: 'Clothes make the man. Naked people have little or no influence on society'.

18 'A Cup of Cold Water' was first published in 1899 as part of Wharton's earliest collection of published short fiction entitled *The Greater Inclination*.

19 Edith Wharton, 'A Cup of Cold Water', in *The New York Stories of Edith Wharton*, New York, 2007, p. 60. Henry Poole and Co. are a gentleman's bespoke tailor now situated at 15 Savile Row, London. Established in 1806, Poole and Co. are recognised as the founders of Savile Row and as such epitomised English tailoring of the highest quality and cut, an understanding of which would be essential for New York socialites such as Woburn.

20 Ibid., p. 63.

21 Peter Stallybrass, 'Marx's Coat', in P. Spyer, ed., *Border Fetishisms: Material Objects in Unstable Spaces*, London, 1998, p. 184. Wharton, 'Cup of Cold Water', p. 60.

22 Stallybrass, 'Marx's Coat', p. 183.

23 **Public Enemies**, 2009, dir. Michael Mann, cost. Colleen Atwood.

24 Dialogue from **Public Enemies**.

25 Ibid.

26 From the website of St Luke's, 'London's longest running independent creative agency', quoted in J. Chapman, *Emotionally Durable Design*, London, 2009, p. 113.

27 **Frenzy**, 1972, dir. Alfred Hitchcock, cost. Julie Harris.

28 Dialogue from **Frenzy**.

29 Dialogue from **Public Enemies**.

30 Ibid.

31 See Veblen's construction and analysis of the concept of 'conspicuous consumption' in his *Theory of the Leisure Class*. Part 2 of my book contains a more detailed exploration of the regularity with which fur coats act as catalysts for cinematic narrative.

32 **Bridget Jones: The Edge of Reason**, 2004, dir. Beeban Kidron, cost. Jany Temime.

33 **Desperately Seeking Susan**, 1985, dir. Susan Seidelman, cost. Santo Loquasto. **Pillow Talk**, 1959, dir. Michael Gordon, cost. Bill Thomas.

34 **Angel Face**, 1952, dir. Otto Preminger, cost. Michael Woulfe.

35 Diane Tremayne demonstrates a fateful and cursed relationship with clothing throughout the film, the gloves she lends her stepmother, discussed in Chapter 6, being another example.

36 **Drag Me to Hell**, 2009, dir. Sam Raimi, cost. Isis Mussenden.

37 The cursed object that must be passed on within a certain time is a

popular motif in the literature of horror, perhaps one of the more chilling examples being M. R. James's short story 'Casting the Runes', which was adapted by Jacques Tourneur in his equally chilling 1957 film **The Night of the Demon**, the cursed object being a slip of paper rather than an item of dress, but the principle remains the same.

38 Dialogue from **Beware, My Lovely**, 1952, dir. Harry Horner, cost. Michael Woulfe.

39 G. Bachelard, *The Poetics of Space*, trans. Maria Jolas, Boston, Mass., 1994, pp. 78–9.

40 **Seven Days to Noon**, 1950, dir. Roy and John Boulting, cost. Honoria Plesch. This film will be considered in further detail in the following chapter which addresses the production's deployment of the jettisoned mackintosh.

41 Dialogue from **Beware, My Lovely**.

42 Ibid.

2 EXCHANGE MECHANISMS

1 Nick Foulkes, *The Trench Book*, New York, 2007, p. 9.

2 Raymond Chandler, *Farewell, My Lovely* (1940), London, 2005, p. 248.

3 Trench coats have also been made from other non-waterproofed materials, notably black leather as worn by German officers and members of the ss during the Second World War. More recently, cinema has played a significant role in popularising the black leather or oil-cloth coat favoured by sub-cultural groups such as Goths, a significant influence being the character Neo's long black trench coat worn in **The Matrix** (1999, dir. Andy and Lana Wachowski, cost. Kym Barrett). However, the term trench for these styles is somewhat of a misnomer, since they are in fact closer in cut and length to the duster coats originally worn by horsemen to protect them from trail dust, and then with the advent of motoring providing a similar protection from dirt and dust for both men and women motorists. Duster coats were typically made from light-coloured canvas or linen.

4 **The Maltese Falcon**, 1941, dir. John Huston, cost. Burrell King (men's), Cora Lobb (women's). **Casablanca**, 1942, dir. Michael Curtiz, cost. Orry-Kelly. **The Big Sleep**, 1946, dir. Howard Hawks, cost. Leah Rhodes.

5 **Farewell, My Lovely**, 1944, dir. Edward Dmytryk, cost. Edward Stevenson (gowns). **Cornered**, 1945, dir. Edward Dmytryk, cost. Renié (gowns). **The Glass Key**, 1942, dir. Stuart Heisler, cost. Edith Head. **The Blue Dahlia**, 1946, dir. George Marshall, cost. Edith Head. **This Gun for Hire**, 1942, dir. Frank Tuttle, cost. Edith Head. **Fallen Angel**, 1945, dir. Otto Preminger, cost. Bonnie Cashin. **Laura**, 1944, dir. Otto Preminger, cost. Bonnie Cashin. **Foreign Intrigue**, 1956, dir. Sheldon Reynolds, cost. Pierre Balmain (gowns), Marie-Claude Fouquet. **The Big Steal**, 1949, dir. Don Siegel, cost. Edward Stevenson. **Out of the Past**, 1947, dir Jacques Tourneur, cost. Edward Stevenson.

6 **Farewell, My Lovely**, 1975, dir. Dick Richards, cost. Sandra Berke, Tony and Silvio Scarano. **Gumshoe**, 1971, dir. Stephen Frears, cost. Daphne Dare. **Play it Again Sam**, 1972, dir. Herbert Ross, cost. Anna Hill Johnstone. **Dead Men Don't Wear Plaid**, 1982, dir. Carl Reiner, cost. Edith Head.

7 Dialogue from **The Pink Panther**, 1963, dir. Blake Edwards, cost. Annalisa Nasali-Rocca, William Ware Theiss, Yves Saint Laurent (for Capucine and Claudia Cardinale).

8 **The Ipcress File**, 1965, dir. Sidney J. Furie, cost. Muriel Dickson. **Funeral in Berlin**, 1966, dir. Guy Hamilton, cost. Barbara Gillett, Brian Owen Smith. **Billion Dollar Brain**, 1967, dir. Ken Russell, cost. John Brady, Shirley Russell.

9 From the 1960s onwards, European screen actresses in particular, such as Brigitte Bardot and Catherine Deneuve, made memorable appearances wearing classic trench coats, e.g. **The Umbrellas of Cherbourg**, 1964, and **A Ravishing Idiot**, 1963, which can perhaps be partly contextualised by the influence of Hollywood film noir on French cinema during this period. That is not to deny that many American stars continued to give memorable trench-coated performances: Meryl Streep's appearance in **Kramer vs. Kramer**, 1979, must surely rank high in the catalogue of post-noir trench iconography. **Breakfast at Tiffany's**, 1961, dir. Blake Edwards, cost. Hubert de Givenchy (Audrey Hepburn), Pauline Trigere (Patricia Neal), Edith Head.

10 **Young and Innocent**, 1937, dir. Alfred Hitchcock, cost. Marianne. **Dial M for Murder**, 1954, dir. Alfred Hitchcock, cost. Moss Mabry, Jack Delaney (men's), Lillian House (women's).

11 Michael Walker, 'The Stolen Raincoat and the Bloodstained Dress', in Allen and Ishii Gonzalès, *Alfred Hitchcock Centenary Essays*, p. 199.

12 **Orphans of the Storm**, 1921, dir. D. W. Griffith, cost. Herman Patrick Tappe.

13 **Séance on a Wet Afternoon**, 1964, dir. Bryan Forbes, cost. Laurel Staffell.

14 Dialogue from **Young and Innocent**.

15 As will be discussed in 'Criminal Accessories', the bags, or at least Margot's bag, perform some of these same functions, as means of transport for the key, but with the additional dysfunction of insecurity.

16 Backtelling, the supposition, retracing, or re-staging of the sequence of events via a series of clues and actions leading back to the original crime, is a device common to the detective genre whether in literature or film and beloved of Hitchcock.

17 Karl Marx, *Capital: A Critique of Political Economy*, vol. 1, trans. Ben Fowkes, London, 1990,

18 Stallybrass, 'Marx's Coat', in Spyer, *Border Fetishisms*, p. 184.

19 **The Gay Divorcee**, 1934, dir. Mark Sandrich, cost. Walter Plunkett.

20 Dialogue from **Seven Days to Noon**.

21 This juxtaposition of textile and technology in the form of modes of transport will be played out in a much more violent manner, but at an equally significant moment, in the film **Drag Me to Hell** (discussed in 'Gift Wrapped'), made some sixty years later than **Seven Days to Noon** but which signals the same process of transformation of the films' central characters.

22 Dialogue from **Seven Days to Noon**.

23 See Stallybrass, 'Marx's Coat', pp. 187–9.

24 Dialogue from **Young and Innocent**.

25 **Tales of Manhattan**, 1942, dir. Julien Duvivier, cost. Dolly Tree, Bernard Newman, Gwen Wakeling, Irene, Oleg Cassini.

26 Dialogue from **Tales of Manhattan**.
27 **The Lost Weekend**, 1945, dir. Billy Wilder, cost. Edith Head.
28 Dialogue from **Lost Weekend**.
29 Jean Baudrillard, 'The System of Collecting' (1968), trans. Roger Cardinal, in J. Elsner and Roger Cardinal, eds, *The Cultures of Collecting*, London, 1994, p. 7.

3   TROPHIES

1   Lyrics from 'Gee Baby Ain't I Good to You', 1929, Andy Razaf and Don Redman.
2   **The Big Heat**, 1953, dir. Fritz Lang, cost. Jean Louis (gowns).
3   **Gentlemen Prefer Blondes**, 1953, dir. Howard Hawks, cost. Travilla, jeweller Joan Joseff.
4   Hollander, *Seeing Through Clothes*, pp. 343–4.
5   Travis Banton was the chief costume designer at Paramount Pictures and is widely regarded as one of the most innovative and influential costume designers of the 1930s. His designs for Marlene Dietrich, among the numerous stars he dressed, were arguably as intrinsic a part of the construction of her screen image as Von Sternberg's lighting and direction.
6   **Possessed**, 1931, dir. Clarence Brown, cost. Adrian, jeweller Eugene Joseff.
7   **Possessed** was the first production that brought the two married stars together on screen and saw the start of their thirty-year on/off love affair.
8   Nancy Cunard, the shipping heiress, was famously photographed by Man Ray in 1926 wearing her collection of African bangles from wrist to elbow. Crawford's growing armful of bangles recalls Cunard's distinctive look but, in **Possessed**, bone, ivory and wood are replaced by more conventional Art Deco-style diamond-set bangles, an essential element of the wealthy style-conscious woman of the 1920s and 30s. Crawford's bangles were created by Eugene Joseff, the undisputed king of Hollywood costume jewellery, responsible for many of the iconic pieces worn in Hollywood productions from the 1930s through to the 1950s. On Eugene's death the company continued under the direction of his wife, Joan, who designed the jewels featured in **Gentlemen Prefer Blondes**, including those used in the famous 'Diamonds Are a Girl's Best Friend' sequence.
9   Veblen, *Theory of the Leisure Class*.
10 Ibid., p. 104.
11 James Laver, *Taste and Fashion: From the French Revolution to the Present Day* (1937), London, 1948, p. 170.
12 **The Lady Wants Mink**, 1953, dir. William A. Seiter, cost. Adele Palmer.
13 Dialogue from **The Lady Wants Mink**.
14 Ibid.
15 Ibid.
16 Ibid.
17 Veblen, *Theory of the Leisure Class*, p. 16.
18 **Caught**, 1949, dir. Max Ophüls, cost. Orry-Kelly (for Bel Geddes), Louise Wilson. **The Reckless Moment**, 1949, dir. Max Ophüls, cost. Jean Louis.
19 Dialogue from **Caught**.
20 An interesting if somewhat disturbing variation on the mink coat as sign of familial ownership is to be found in **Sweet Smell of Success** (1957, dir. Alexander Mackendrick, cost. Mary Grant) where the overbearing, sadistic journalist J. J. Hunsecker (Burt Lancaster) uses a mink coat not as the vestimentary shackle for a wife but for his sister, Susie. The implications of unhealthy and possibly incestuous overprotectiveness are unmistakeable, as the resolute bachelor Hunsecker traps his sister in a mink-clad sense of family honour, seeing off any and every suitor he deems unworthy of her.
21 Dialogue from **The Lady Wants Mink**.
22 I refer of course to Leopold von Sacher-Masoch's novella of 1870, *Venus in Furs*, and Freud's theories concerning the fetish contained in his *Three Essays on the Theory of Sexuality*, first published in 1905, and *Fetishism* in 1927.
23 Dialogue from **The Lady Wants Mink**.
24 **Charlie's Angels: Full Throttle**, 2003, dir. McG, cost. Joseph G. Aulisi.
25 **Guys and Dolls**, 1955, dir. Joseph L. Mankiewicz, cost. Irene Sharaff.
26 Song lyrics from **Guys and Dolls**.
27 For detailed examinations of the mediation of fur's sexualisation, both Chantal Nadeau's *Fur Nation: From the Beaver to Brigitte Bardot*, London, 2001, and Julia V. Emberley's *Venus and Furs: The Cultural Politics of Fur*, London, 1998, contain much valuable information.
28 **Rebecca**, 1940, dir. Alfred Hitchcock, cost. uncredited. **One Million Years B.C.**, 1966, dir. Don Chaffey, cost. Carl Toms.
29 The campaigns mounted by various anti-fur organisations, which can be credited with significantly altering public opinion against the use of fur in the fashion industry, reached a high point in the 1980s and 90s. The campaigns of organisations such as Lynx in the UK and PETA (People for the Ethical Treatment of Animals) in the US, effectively deployed a number of celebrities, including many film stars, to endorse their message. However, more recently there has been a shift in public tolerance which has seen fur becoming fashionable again, worn by contemporary style icons such as Kate Moss, Jennifer Lopez and Keira Knightley, and featured in collections by many leading designers. This regression can be most clearly demonstrated by the volte face made by the supermodels Naomi Campbell, Elle Macpherson, Cindy Crawford and Claudia Schiffer, who all featured in the first of PETA's long-running 'I'd Rather Go Naked Than Wear Fur' campaign in 1994, and who have all (Christy Turlington being the only other model featured in the campaign who has stayed true to her word) since publically worn and endorsed fur. Further indications of this shift in opinion can be gauged by the highly popular television series and subsequent cinematic productions of **Sex and the City**, where in the first film, for example, after attending a show at New York Fashion Week in Bryant Park, Samantha has paint thrown at her fur coat by such a grotesquely caricatured group of rabid anti-fur campaigners that audience members are left in no doubt as to where their sympathies should lie.
30 **Lady in the Dark**, 1944, dir. Mitchell Leisen, cost. Raoul Penc du Bois, Edith Head, Mitchell Leisen.
31 Lyrics from 'The Saga of Jenny', 1941, Ira Gershwin and Kurt Weill.

32   For further information on this notorious costume see Head and Calistro, *Edith Head's Hollywood*, pp. 95–7, and Jay Jorgensen, *Edith Head: The Fifty-Year Career of Hollywood's Greatest Costume Designer*, Philadelphia, 2010, pp. 104, 110–11.

33   **Mildred Pierce**, 1945, dir. Michael Curtiz, cost. Milo Anderson.

34   **Lucy Gallant**, 1955, dir. Robert Parrish, cost. Edith Head.

35   **The Pink Panther**, 1963, dir. Blake Edwards, cost. Annalisa Nasali-Rocca, William Ware Theiss, Yves Saint Laurent (for Capucine and Claudia Cardinale).

36   Dialogue from **The Pink Panther**.

37   Cited in Ephraim Burford, *The 'Orrible Synne': A Look at London Lechery from Roman to Cromwellian Times*, London, 1973, quoted in Alan Hunt, *Governance of the Consuming Passions: A History of Sumptuary Law*, New York, 1996, p. 243.

38   Ibid., p. 126.

39   Dialogue from **The Big Heat**.

40   Petra Dominková, 'I Want that Mink! *Film Noir* and Fashion', in M. Uhlirova, ed., *If Looks Could Kill: Cinema's Images of Fashion, Crime and Violence*, London, 2008, p. 138.

41   **They Drive by Night**, 1940, dir. Raoul Walsh, cost. Milo Anderson. **White Heat**, 1949, dir. Raoul Walsh, cost. Leah Rhodes. **Whistle Stop**, 1946, dir. Léonide Moguy, cost. uncredited. **Quicksand**, 1950, dir. Irving Pichel, cost. uncredited. **Brute Force**, 1947, dir. Jules Dassin, cost. Rosemary Odell.

42   **Goodfellas**, 1990, dir. Martin Scorsese, cost. Richard Bruno.

43   Dialogue from **Goodfellas**.

44   **BUtterfield 8**, 1960, dir. Daniel Mann, cost. Helen Rose.

45   See Hunt, *Governance of the Consuming Passions*, p. 243.

46   **Imitation of Life**, 1959, dir. Douglas Sirk, cost. Jean Louis (Lana Turner), Bill Thomas, jewels Laykin et Cie. (for Turner).

47   Dialogue from **Imitation of Life**.

48   **Laura**, 1944, dir. Otto Preminger, cost. Bonnie Cashin. While the scope of this book will not permit it, an investigation into the frequency of other types of fur in popular cinema would reveal interesting evidence as to the valorisation and social prohibitions surrounding other skins such as leopard, fox and sable in popular culture.

49   Dialogue from **Laura**.

50   **Party Girl**, 1958, dir. Nicholas Ray, cost. Helen Rose. **All About Eve**, 1950, dir. Joseph L. Mankiewicz, cost. Charles Le Maire, Edith Head (Bette Davis).

51   Dialogue from **All About Eve**.

52   Ibid.

53   **That Touch of Mink**, 1962, dir. Delbert Mann, cost. Rosemary Odell, Norman Norell 'for special gowns'.

54   This is an interesting example of the concept of matter out of place (in this case mud etc. on Day's clothing), in the form of stained clothing acting as a narrative catalyst (see 'Stubborn Stains' below), initiating further contact between Timberlake and Shayne when she goes to ask for compensation for her ruined clothing.

55   This can be understood as an echo of the same desire for respectability that Joan Crawford craves from Clark Gable and the previously discussed presents of jewellery in **Possessed**.

56   Dialogue from **That Touch of Mink**. Bergdorf Goodman, the famous Manhattan department store, is heavily promoted throughout the film, most notably in the fashion-show sequence and in the closing credits which read: 'Our special thanks to Norman Norell for special fashions, Leo Ritter for Miss Day's furs, Cardinal Clothes for Cary Grant's suits, and Bergdorf Goodman for being Bergdorf Goodman.' This credit acknowledges the store's status as an American institution and Bergdorf Goodman featured frequently in films especially those from the 1950s and 60s, a period that saw the store's expansion under Andrew Goodman, the son of Erwin, the founder. Among many other enterprises, Andrew developed Bergdorf Goodman's famous fur salon and a number of films including **That Touch of Mink** and **How to Marry a Millionaire** directly endorsed Bergdorf's clothes and furs. The symbiotic relationship between fashion retailing and film, of which this is an early example, is commonplace today but Bergdorf's reputation has continued with films such as **Sex and the City 2**, for which the store provided a location; indeed, throughout the television series Bergdorf's was regularly cited by its fan Carrie Bradshaw. Perhaps only Saks of Fifth Avenue has a comparable presence in Hollywood film as the venue and reference point for all things fashionable for New York-set films. A surprising example of Saks's status can be seen in the last of the recent Batman trilogy of films, **The Dark Knight Rises** (dir. Christopher Nolan), where towards the end, as Batman and his allies chase down a nuclear weapon hurtling through the streets of a besieged, war-torn, mob-ruled Gotham (New York), the most prominent, unscathed and iconic retail outlet still standing proud amid the rubble is Saks of Fifth Avenue.

57   **Roberta**, 1935, dir. William A. Seiter, cost. Bernard Newman.

58   Although there are some mink-trimmed outfits in **Roberta**, the film's predilection for sable and white fox complement both Irene Dunne's character as the émigrée White Russian designer and the film's Art Deco splendour (which predates the period of mink's cinematic ascendancy). In the Art Deco period white fox especially was used to spectacular black and white effect.

59   Now in the collection of the Cristóbal Balenciaga Museum, Getaria, Spain.

60   Dialogue from **That Touch of Mink**.

61   Ibid.

62   **Make Mine Mink**, 1960, dir. Robert Asher, cost. Anthony Mendleson.

63   References from **Make Mine Mink**.

64   Laver, *Taste and Fashion*, pp. 169–70.

65   **Lifeboat**, 1944, dir. Alfred Hitchcock, cost. René Hubert.

66   Dialogue from **Lifeboat**.

4   TALISMANS

1   Roland Barthes, 'From Gemstones to Jewellery' (1961), in *The Language of Fashion*, trans. A. Stafford, ed. A. Stafford and M. Carter, Oxford, 2006, pp. 59–60.

2   I am referring here to ground-breaking American works such as Molly Haskell's *From Reverence to Rape: The Treatment of Women in the Movies*, London, first published 1974.

3 E. Ann Kaplan's 1990 edited collection, *Psychoanalysis and Cinema*, London, is an invaluable guide to how psychoanalysis has been incorporated into film theory, as is Annette Kuhn's *Women's Pictures: Feminism and Cinema*, London, 1982, which is one of the early comprehensive assessments of the relationship between feminism and film theory.

4 Scopophilia, literally 'the desire to see'. See Laura Mulvey, 'Visual Pleasure and Narrative Cinema', *Screen*, vol. 16 no. 3, Autumn 1975, pp. 6–18.

5 **The Locket**, 1946, dir. John Brahm, cost. Michael Woulfe (Laraine Day), jeweller Eugene Joseff. **Whirlpool**, 1949, dir. Otto Preminger, cost. Charles Le Maire, Oleg Cassini (Gene Tierney). **Conflict**, 1945, dir. Curtis Bernhardt, cost. Milo Anderson, Orry-Kelly (gowns). **Black Angel**, 1946, dir. Roy William Neil, cost. Vera West (gowns). **Madonna of the Seven Moons**, 1945, dir. Arthur Crabtree, cost. Elizabeth Haffenden. As explained in the Introduction, so-called costume films (which include both the UK and US versions of **Gaslight**, and **Madonna of the Seven Moons)** are not within my remit but, as examples of 1940s films that use the desire for precious stones as motives for psychological torture, or jewellery as items of emotional transference, it seems unnecessarily restrictive not to include them here.

6 In addition to Kaplan's *Psychoanalysis and Cinema*, Marlisa Santos's 2011 *The Dark Mirror: Psychiatry and Film Noir*, Lanham, Md., is informative about this specific period and Krin and Glen O. Gabbard's *Psychiatry and the Cinema*, Washington, D.C., 1999, provides a clinician's view and takes the subject beyond the classic period of psychoanalytically influenced melodrama of the 1940 and 50s.

7 Dialogue from **Whirlpool**.

8 Ibid.

9 Dialogue from **The Locket**.

10 Susan Stewart, *On Longing*, Durham, N.C., 1993, p. 127.

11 Dialogue from **The Locket**.

12 **Golden Earrings**, 1947, dir. Mitchell Leisen, cost. Mary Kay Dodson.

13 **My Favourite Blonde**, 1942, dir. Sidney Lanfield, cost. Edith Head.

14 **Desire**, 1936, dir. Frank Borzage, cost. Travis Banton.

15 **French Kiss**, 1995, dir. Lawrence Kasdan, cost. Joanna Johnston.

16 Barthes, *Language of Fashion*, p. 60.

17 **Dressed to Kill**, 1980, dir. Brian De Palma, cost. Ann Roth, Gary Jones.

18 Barthes, *Language of Fashion*, p. 59.

19 **Peeping Tom**, 1960, dir. Michael Powell, cost. Dickie Richardson, Polly Peck (Anna Massey), John Tullis of Horrockses (Moira Shearer).

20 Isaiah 3: 17–21, *The Holy Bible* (Revised Standard Version), London, 1952.

21 W. Winward (1968), 'Stick With Me, Kid, and You'll Wear Diamonds', in H. van Thal, ed., *The Ninth Pan Book of Horror Stories*, London, 1974, p. 86.

22 **Marathon Man**, 1976, dir. John Schlesinger, cost. Robert De Mora.

23 **Lantana**, 2001, dir. Ray Lawrence, cost. Margot Wilson.

24 **Gaslight** (UK), 1940, dir. Thorold Dickinson, cost. uncredited. **Gaslight** (USA), 1944, dir. George Cukor, cost. Irene, jeweller Eugene Joseff.

25 Stewart, *On Longing*, p. 61.

26 **Beautiful Stranger**, 1954, dir. David Miller, cost. Victor Stiebel at Jacqmar.

27 **You'll Never Get Rich**, 1941, dir. Sidney Lanfield, cost. Irene, Robert Kalloch.

28 **Love Actually**, 2003, dir. Richard Curtis, cost. Joanna Johnstone.

29 Dialogue from **Love Actually**.

30 Hunt, *Governance of the Consuming Passions*, p. 71.

31 **Casino**, 1995, dir. Martin Scorsese, cost. Rita Ryack and John Dunn, jewellery by Bulgari, furs by Anna Nateece.

32 Dialogue from **Casino**.

33 Ibid.

34 Barthes, *Language of Fashion*, p. 60.

35 Dialogue from **Casino**.

36 Frank Norris, *McTeague* (1899), Harmondsworth, 1982, p. 308.

37 Dialogue from **Casino**.

38 Gustave Flaubert, *The Dictionary of Received Ideas* (1913; assembled and published posthumously), trans. Robert Baldick, London, 1976, p. 301.

39 Dialogue from **Lifeboat**.

40 Ibid.

41 Barthes, *Language of Fashion*, p. 59.

42 Dialogue from **Lifeboat.**

43 Barthes, *Language of Fashion*, p. 59.

5 CRIMINAL ACCESSORIES

1 Lyrics from 'Concentratin' on You', Fats Waller and Andy Razaf, 1931.

2 Dialogue from **Serial Mom**, 1994, dir. John Waters, cost. Van Smith.

3 Not wearing white shoes after Labor Day can be seen on one level as practical advice, given that Labor Day falls on 1 September when the impracticality of wearing white shoes in possibly inclement weather seems to justify this advice. However, Waters's employment of this stricture as a motive for murder typifies the numerous petty rules of etiquette that dominated American middle-class, suburban society in the 1950s and 60s, and which he caricatures as masking an underlying moral corruption. Waters himself, though, not entirely tongue in cheek, recalls a salutary sartorial moment: 'Once on a plane, I was deeply offended by a passenger seated near me who was guilty of the ultimate fashion violation – wearing summer white after Labor Day and before Memorial Day.' Quoted in A. van Gaalen, ed., *Never Leave the House Naked*, Amsterdam, 2009, p. 69.

4 **Single White Female**, 1992, dir. Barbet Schroeder, cost. Jacqueline De La Fontaine, Elisabetta Beraldo, Andrea Wallace.

5 Peter Wollen, 'Strike a Pose', *Sight and Sound*, March 1995, pp. 10–15. **Now Voyager**, 1942, dir. Irving Rapper, cost. Orry-Kelly.

6 There are ever more websites that allow customers to upload images of themselves and then play 'dress-up' digitally with the labels' current collections, as well as an increasing use of virtual wardrobes in stores, where the physical changing room is replaced by a virtual one that allows clients to 'try on' an infinite number of looks.

7 **Leave Her to Heaven**, 1945, dir. John M. Stahl, cost. Kay Nelson.

8   **The Haunted House of Horror**, 1969, dir. Michael Armstrong, cost. Hilda Geerdts, Kathleen Moore.

9   **Niagara**, 1953, dir. Henry Hathaway, cost. Dorothy Jeakins.

10   **Angel**, 1982, dir. Neil Jordan, cost. Janet O'Leary.

11   **Marnie**, 1964, dir. Alfred Hitchcock, cost. Vincent Dee, Edith Head (Tippi Hedren and Diane Baker), James Linn, Rita Riggs.

12   **Walk Softly, Stranger**, 1950, dir. Robert Stevenson, cost. Edward Stevenson.

13   Georges Bataille, 'The Big Toe' (1929), in *Vision of Excess: Selected Writings, 1927–1939*, trans. Allan Stoekl, Minneapolis, 1985, p. 20.

14   **Feet First**, 1930, dir. Clyde Bruckman, cost. uncredited.

15   **The Devil and Miss Jones**, 1941, dir. Sam Wood, cost. Irene (for Jean Arthur).

16   **Brazil**, 1985, dir. Terry Gilliam, cost. James Acheson.

17   A notable exception to the unsuccessful cinematic shoemaker is the figure of Will Mossop, the oppressed and innocent but gifted boot-maker in the celebrated British film version of the popular stage play **Hobson's Choice** (1954, dir. David Lean, cost. John Armstrong), who achieves recognition, love and commercial success with the aid of Maggie, the determined and independent daughter his former employer Henry Hobson.

18   **Kinky Boots**, 2005, dir. Julian Jarrold, cost. Sammy Sheldon. **Elizabethtown**, 2005, dir. Cameron Crowe, cost. Nancy Steiner.

19   **Holes**, 2003, dir. Andrew Davis, cost. Aggie Rodgers.

20   **Knock Off**, 1998, dir. Hark Tsui, cost. William Fung, Mabel Kwan, Ben Luk.

21   **The Out of Towners**, 1970, dir. Arthur Hiller, cost. Forrest T. Butler, Grace Harris.

22   **The Clock**, 1945, dir. Vincente Minnelli, cost. Irene.

23   Dialogue from **Young and Innocent**.

24   **In Her Shoes**, 2005, dir. Curtis Hanson, cost. Sophie De Rakoff.

25   **The Man With One Red Shoe**, 1985, dir. Stan Dragoti, cost. William Ware Theiss.

26   **Accidental Hero**, 1992, dir. Stephen Frears, cost. Richard Hornung.

27   **The Shawshank Redemption**, 1994, dir. Frank Darabont, cost. Elizabeth McBride.

28   Narration from **Shawshank Redemption**.

29   **The Red Shoes**, 1948, dir. Michael Powell and Emeric Pressburger, cost. Hein Heckroth.

30   Dialogue from **Candyman 2: Farewell to the Flesh**, 1995, dir. Bill Condon, cost. Bruce Finlayson.

31   **Big Fish**, 2003, dir. Tim Burton, cost. Colleen Atwood. An additional explanation of this practice is that shoes flung over wires denote the location of 'crack houses' or heroin dealers, the symbolism being that once addicted a person will never be able to 'leave', hence there will be no need for shoes. This appears to be a possible reference for the scenes in **Big Fish** set in Spectre.

32   **P.S. I Love You**, 2007, dir. Richard LaGravenese, cost. Cindy Evans.

33   Dialogue from **The Red Shoes**.

34   Oscar Wilde, 'The Importance of Being Earnest', Act IV, in *Complete Works of Oscar Wilde*, London, 1971, p. 379.

35   Dialogue from **Dial M for Murder**.

36   Ibid.

37   Ibid.

6   ONE SIZE FITS ALL?

1   Klinger's remarkable series of ten etchings dating from 1881 tells the story of an unrequited love affair triggered by the dropping of a lady's glove at an ice rink. The series develops with the glove taking centre stage, a fetishised object signifying not only its wearer but also a series of fantasies acted out by the glove as the symbolic object of desire. The erotic force of the glove as representative of the organ of touch became a primary term in the visual lexicon of Surrealism. From the 1914 metaphysical painting *The Song of Love* by Giorgio de Chirico, pre-dating and influencing Surrealism with its limp and lonely over-sized glove, to the full-blown Surrealism of Meret Oppenheim's *Fur Gloves with Wooden Fingers* of 1936, or her 'Arterial' gloves made of kid decorated with embroidered veins and arteries in red of 1942, the glove retains its odour of Surrealism: witness Tim Walkers's recent photograph of a model supported by a towering glove used to adver-tise the Victoria & Albert Museum's 'Ballgowns: British Glamour Since 1950' exhibition of 2012 in London.

2   Philippe Perrot, *Fashioning the Bourgeoisie: A History of Clothing in the Nineteenth Century*, Princeton, N.J., 1994, p. 120.

3   **Blackmail**, 1929, dir. Alfred Hitchcock, cost. uncredited.

4   Perrot, *Fashioning the Bourgeoisie*, pp. 120–21.

5   **The House on Telegraph Hill**, 1951, dir. Robert Wise, cost. Charles Le Maire, Renié.

6   **A Nightmare on Elm Street**, 1984, dir. Wes Craven, cost. Dana Lyman.

7   **Gangs of New York**, 2002, dir. Martin Scorsese, cost. Sandy Powell.

8   **The Glove**, 1979, dir. Ross Hagen, cost. Rafael Arrazola, Janet Kusnick.

9   **The Mask of Fu Manchu**, 1932, dir. Charles Brabin, cost. Adrian. **Son of Frankenstein**, 1939, dir. Rowland V. Lee, cost. Vera West. **Mad Love**, 1935, dir. Karl Freund, cost. Dolly Tree. **Dr. No**, 1962, dir. Terence Young, cost. Tessa Prendergast.

10   Lyrics from 'Stronger', 2007, Kanye West. 'Stronger' marks what could be understood as the lyrical zenith of West's fascination with the world of fashion: not only is the song littered with fashionable refer-ences but also its accompanying video was partly shot in the Japanese outlets of the fashionable clothing brands A Bathing Ape and Billionaire Boys Club, the artwork for the track was designed by the artist and Vuitton collaborator Takashi Murakami and the video saw West sporting for the first time his trademark Alain Mikli-designed 'shutter shades' sunglasses.

11   For some of the most hyperbolic journalism covering the trial see Richard Price and Jonathan T. Lovitt's various articles for *USA Today* throughout 1997. Nicole Brown Simpson allegedly bought two pairs of Isotoner Lights for Simpson, available exclusively from Bloomingdales in New York. Only 300 pairs of the gloves with their distinctive stitching and v-shaped decoration were sold.

12   Lyrics from 'They Can't Take That Away From Me', 1937, George and Ira Gershwin.

13   Rosa Klebb's poisoned-tipped dagger shoe is another example of the Bond films' 'cutting edge' accessories that made its appearance in **From Russia with Love** (1963, dir. Terence Young, cost. Jocelyn Rickards). However, Klebb's dagger shoe impedes her to such an extent that Bond is able to pinion her with a chair and avoid her deadly kicking foot, while the double agent Romanova shoots her; Dr. No's prosthetic hands, referred to earlier, disable him at the climax to the film so that he is unable to grasp the railing surrounding the nuclear reactor's cooling tank and falls to his death.

14   Dialogue from **Ninotchka**, 1939, dir. Ernst Lubitsch, cost. Adrian. In the loose remake of **Ninotchka**, **The Iron Petticoat**, 1956, dir. Ralph Thomas, cost. Yvonne Caffin, the object of Western sartorial capitalism that entrances Captain Vinka Kovelenko (Katherine Hepburn) is a black-lace, red ribbon-trimmed lingerie set, rather than a hat.

15   Dialogue from **Witness for the Prosecution**.

16   Bataille, *Vision of Excess*, p. 20.

17   **Bringing Up Baby**, 1938, dir. Howard Hawks, cost. Howard Greer.

18   This iconic scene of dysfunctional clothing will be revisited in the chapter on the torn garment, 'Wear and Tear'.

19   **Bell, Book and Candle**, 1958, dir. Richard Quine, cost. Jean Louis.

20   Dialogue from **Bell, Book and Candle**. The famous pioneering photographic images of the Flatiron Building were taken on a wintry morning by Alfred Stieglitz in 1903 and of the same building at dusk in the fog by Edward Steichen in 1904.

21   **Miller's Crossing**, 1990, dir. Joel and Ethan Coen, cost. Richard Hornung.

22   Stella Bruzzi, *Undressing Cinema: Clothing and Identity in the Movies*, London, 1997, p. 79.

23   Perrot, *Fashioning the Bourgeoisie*, p. 118.

24   Antigone in Sophocles's tragedy hangs herself with her own scarf (or girdle, according to some translations), after being imprisoned by Creon for disobeying his command and burying her dead brother Polyneices. Isadora Duncan's bizarre death caused by her signature flowing scarf getting caught in the spoked wheels and rear axle of the speeding Amilcar in which she was a passenger reportedly prompted Gertrude Stein to declare that 'affectations can be dangerous'. One of the more grisly details to emerge from the testimony of Dennis Nilsen, the serial killer and necrophiliac, who murdered (usually by strangling) fifteen young men between 1978 and 1983 was that he fabricated a special ligature made of a tie attached to a piece of rough twine in order to asphyxiate some of his victims.

25   See the first chapter, 'Cloaking Devices', for a comparison between the descriptions of Blaney's jacket worn in **Frenzy** and Dillinger's overcoat in **Public Enemies**.

26   Dialogue from **Frenzy**. Hitchcock revisits the opening scenes of **Young and Innocent**, previously discussed, for the opening of **Frenzy**, both featuring the strangled body of a woman recovered from water.

27   H. Le Blanc cited in Sarah Gibbings, *The Tie: Trends and Traditions*, London, 1990, pp. 53–4.

28   Dialogue from **Frenzy**.

29   Ibid.

30   **The Boston Strangler**, 1968, dir. Richard Fleischer, cost. Travilla.

31   **The Talented Mr. Ripley**, 1999, dir. Anthony Minghella, cost. Ann Roth and Gary Jones.

32   **Holiday**, 1938, dir. George Cukor, cost. Robert Kalloch (gowns).

33   Dialogue from **Holiday**.

34   **Holiday** is the third in the films that partnered Katharine Hepburn with Cary Grant, and all are notable for their specific attention to clothing as a catalyst for confusion, embarrassment and misunderstanding. **Sylvia Scarlett** (1935) was their first paring and featured Hepburn cutting her hair and dressing like a boy for most of the film; then in 1938, prior to making **Holiday**, the two stars appeared in **Bringing Up Baby** (discussed in further detail in 'Wear and Tear'), which is a tour de force of inappropriate dressing and mayhem-inducing fashions. **Holiday** (also 1938) saw Hepburn reprise her character from **Baby**, playing once again a carefree, liberated wealthy heiress. This was followed in 1940 by **The Philadelphia Story** which uses Hepburn's glacially stylish gowns designed by Adrian and Grant's appropriately louche, man-about-town relaxed attitude to dressing to symbolise their erotic incompatibility. Grant, always immaculately dressed on and off screen, famously had his jackets tailored in Savile Row and his trousers cut in New York, and by the 1950s had it written into his contract that he would be allowed to keep any of the suits worn in his films (including the famous Savile Row Kilgour suit worn in **North by Northwest**). Hepburn's athletic poise provided the perfect body for late 1930s figure-hugging silhouettes, as well as her own highly idiosyncratic personal dress sense, making the pair perhaps the most fashionably dysfunctional coupling from Hollywood's golden era.

35   Dialogue from **Holiday**.

36   Ibid.

37   **Pick Up on South Street**, 1953, dir. Samuel Fuller, cost. Travilla and Charles Le Maire.

38   **L.A. Confidential**, 1997, dir. Curtis Hanson, cost. Ruth Myers.

39   **Charade**, 1963, dir. Stanley Donen, cost. Hubert de Givenchy (Audrey Hepburn).

40   Dialogue from **Charade**.

7   GIFT-WRAPPED

1   As will be discussed more fully in the last chapter of this book , 'Stubborn Stains', Hitchcock delights in the destruction by fire of articles of dress that can be understood as dysfunctional.

2   **Bucket of Blood**, 1959, dir. Roger Corman, cost. Marjorie Corso.

3   Perrot, *Fashioning the Bourgeoisie*, p. 7.

4   Jean Baudrillard, 'The System of Collecting', in Elsner and Cardinal, *Cultures of Collecting*, p. 8.

5   **Killer's Kiss**, 1955, dir. Stanley Kubrick, cost. uncredited.

6   **Breakfast at Tiffany's**, 1961, dir. Blake Edwards, cost. Edith Head, Hubert de Givenchy (Audrey Hepburn), Pauline Trigère (Patricia Neal). Hepburn's promotion of Givenchy's designs throughout her

film career (particularly what might be considered the 'holy trinity' of **Sabrina** of 1954, **Funny Face** of 1957 and **Breakfast at Tiffany's**) must surely be one of the more researched and fertile areas for fashion and film theorists. The 2010 biography of Head, Jorgensen's *Edith Head*, casts much-needed light on the complex question of design authorship of the clothes worn by Hepburn in these films, while Rachel Mosely's work on Hepburn's image production in her *Growing Up with Audrey Hepburn: Text, Audience, Resonance*, Manchester, 2002, and her essay 'Dress, Class and Audrey Hepburn: The Significance of the Cinderella Story' in her *Fashioning Film Stars: Dress, Culture and Identity*, London, 2005, pp. 109–20, are equally useful. Jayne Sheridan's 'Audrey Hepburn and Breakfast at Givenchy's' in her *Fashion Media Promotion: The New Black Magic*, Chichester, W. Sussex, 2010, pp. 69–104, explores how the Hepburn Givenchy vehicles can be thought of as the cinematic mother-lode of film-inspired fashion marketing. Finally, Alexandra Palmer's indispensable *Couture and Commerce: The Transatlantic Fashion Trade in the 1950s*, Vancouver, 2001, explores how the work of Givenchy, among other Parisian designers, was disseminated to the American consumer, so that by the time **Breakfast at Tiffany's** was released the label was firmly established as a leading influence on American fashion.

7   Dialogue from **Breakfast at Tiffany's**.

8   'Hangover chic' is how Hepburn's title sequence appearance is described by Pamela Clarke Keogh in her *Audrey Style*, London, 1999.

9   John Webster, *The Duchess of Malfi* (1612–13), New Mermaids Edition, London, 1983, p. 76.

10   Erwin Blumenfeld (1897–1969), the German-born photographer, most widely remembered for his fashion photography, repeatedly explored imagery of the veiled female form in his commercial fashion and personal work.

11   Truman Capote, interviewed by Eric Norden for *Playboy*, March 1968, pp. 51–3, 56, 58–62, 160–62, 164–70, was asked to explain the character and profession of Holly Golightly. In reply he said he thought of her as an American geisha, who provided company for wealthy men and expected to receive gifts in return.

12   **Desk Set**, 1957, dir. Walter Lang, cost. Charles Le Maire.

13   Dialogue from **Desk Set**.

14   The silk scarf as a 'work of art' is central to the reputation and continuing economic viability of luxury fashion accessories houses such as Hermès, famous for their silk squares, but can also be understood as fundamental to a series of fruitful partnerships between artists and textile manufacturers that resulted in striking scarves, especially in the mid-twentieth century. Partnerships included the textile company Ascher Ltd. in the UK, whose exhibition of silk squares at the Lefevre Gallery in London in 1947 included designs by Matisse, Moore, Derain, Sutherland and Cocteau. In the US, companies such as Wesley Simpson Custom Fabrics Inc. established highly successful partnerships with artists such as Marcel Vertes and Salvador Dalí. A recent and informative study of artists' textiles can be found in Geoffrey Rayner, Richard Chamberlain and Annamarie Stapleton's *Artists' Textiles 1940–1976*, Woodbridge, Suffolk, 2012.

15   **Far From Heaven**, 2002, dir. Todd Haynes, cost. Sandy Powell.

Haynes's film is most clearly inspired by Douglas Sirk's 1955 **All That Heaven Allows** which stars Jane Wyman as the widowed Cary Scott who falls in love with her gardener played by Rock Hudson. For Haynes's twenty-first-century update, homosexuality is substituted for death (Cathy's husband might as well be dead in that once his sexuality is made public he no longer exists in her conventional world) and Haysbert's race is as unthinkable as Wyman's attraction to a 'tradesman' in the earlier film.

16   Dialogue from **Far From Heaven**.

17   Dialogue from **Bell, Book and Candle**.

18   **The Devil Wears Prada**, 2006, dir. David Frankel, cost. Patricia Field.

19   **Portrait of Jennie**, 1948, dir William Dieterle, cost. Lucinda Ballard.

20   Dialogue from **Portrait of Jennie**.

21   **Blithe Spirit**, 1945, dir. David Lean, cost. Rahvis.

22   **DodgeBall**, 2004, dir. Rawson Marshall Thurber, cost. Carol Ramsey.

23   Georges Bataille, 'Formless' definition in 'Critical Dictionary', in *Encyclopaedia Acephalica*, trans. Iain White, London, 1995, pp. 51–2.

24   Georges Didi-Huberman, 'The Index of the Absent Wound (Monograph on a Stain)', trans. Thomas Repensek, *October*, vol. 29, Summer 1984, p. 65.

25   Matthew 27:51, King James Bible (Authorised Version).

8   CUTTING A DASH

1   Lyrics from 'He's the Greatest Dancer', 1979, Bernard Edwards and Nile Rogers.

2   **Scarface**, 1932, dir. Howard Hawks and Richard Rosson, cost. uncredited.

3   **The Public Enemy**, 1931, dir. William A. Wellman, cost. Edward Stevenson. **Little Caesar**, 1931, dir. Mervyn LeRoy, cost. Earl Luick.

4   This symbiosis among the media, journalism and cinema and the actual construction of the gangster as a stylish and popular 'man of the people' is the central theme of Michael Mann's **Public Enemies**, discussed above in 'Cloaking Devices'.

5   'Clothes on the Screen', *The Tailor and Cutter*, 3 July 1936, p. 835.

6   William Hazlitt, 'On the Clerical Character', in *Political Essays*, London, 1819, quoted in L. Svendsen, *Fashion: A Philosophy*, London, 2006, p. 137.

7   Baldassare Castiglione, *The Book of the Courtier* (1528), London, 1975, p. 39.

8   Bruzzi, *Undressing Cinema*, 1997, p. 69.

9   Veblen, *Theory of the Leisure Class*, p. 105.

10   **Scarface**, 1983, dir. Brian De Palma, cost. Patricia Norris.

11   **Scarface: Origins of a Hip Hop Classic**, 2003, dir. Benny Boom.

12   William Jelani Cobb, *To the Break of Dawn: A Freestyle on the Hip Hop Aesthetic*, New York, 2007, p. 115.

13   Guy Debord, 'Separation Perfected no. 12', in *The Society of the Spectacle*, trans. Fredy Perlman and John Supak, Detroit, 1983, n.p.

14   Dialogue from **Scarface**, 1983.

15   See the website http://rapgenius.com for more on West's lyrics both to this and other fashion-related tracks.

16 The defence of his fashion career informs West's 2012 release *Theraflu*, which has references to the 'six thousand dollar shoes' (Giuseppe Zanotti designed the shoes for his debut collection), his progression from 'the projects' to *Project Runway*, mixing with US *Vogue*'s editor Anna Wintour and challenging PETA for his right to afford and wear mink.

17 Pierre Bourdieu, *Distinction: A Social Critique of the Judgement of Taste*, trans. Richard Nice, Cambridge, 1984, p. 226.

18 Debord, 'Separation Perfected no. 12'.

19 David Kuchta, *The Three-Piece Suit and Modern Masculinity*, Berkeley, 2002, p. 15.

20 **Brighton Rock**, 1947, dir. John Boulting, cost. Honoria Plesch.

21 Dialogue from **Brighton Rock**.

22 Raymond Chandler, *Farewell, My Lovely* (1940), London, 2005, pp. 1–2.

23 **Gideon's Day**, 1958, dir. John Ford, cost. Jack Dalmayne.

24 **The Wrong Arm of the Law**, 1961, dir. Cliff Owen, cost. Jimmy Smith.

25 Dialogue from **Wrong Arm of the Law**.

26 **J. Edgar**, 2009, dir. Clint Eastwood, cost. Deborah Hopper.

27 Dialogue from **J. Edgar**.

28 **The Tailor of Panama**, 2001, dir. John Boorman, cost. Maeve Patterson.

29 Phrase from **Tailor of Panama**.

30 Ibid.

31 Dialogue from **The Dark Corner**, 1946, dir. Henry Hathaway, cost. Kay Nelson.

32 **Shaft**, 2000 dir. John Singleton, cost. Ruth Carter.

33 Dialogue from **Shaft**.

34 Dialogue from **The Great Gatsby**, 1974, dir. Jack Clayton, cost. Theoni V. Aldredge.

35 'Spivvy' is derived from the English term 'spiv', denoting a flashily dressed petty crook dealing in stolen goods, who typically operated during and immediately after the Second World War in Britain when goods and clothing were rationed.

36 Dialogue from **Brighton Rock**.

37 **Villain**, 1971, dir. Michael Tuchner, cost. uncredited. David Bailey included his famous photograph of the Kray twins in *Box of Pin-Ups*, a set of poster-sized images of people from the worlds of fashion, art, pop music and film, released in 1965.

38 Veblen, *Theory of the Leisure Class*, p. 105.

39 Edward Bulwer-Lytton, *Pelham, or the Adventures of a Gentleman*, London, 1828, p. 44, Maxim VII.

40 Dialogue from **Villain**.

41 Kuchta, *Three-Piece Suit and Modern Masculinity*, p. 7.

42 Dialogue from **The Nutty Professor**, 1963, dir. Jerry Lewis, cost. Edith Head, men's wardrobe Sy Devore, Nat Wise.

43 **Reservoir Dogs**, 1992, dir. Quentin Tarantino, cost. Jacqueline Aronson.

44 John Harvey, *Men in Black*, London, 1995.

45 **American Psycho**, 2000, dir. Mary Harron, cost. Isis Mussenden.

46 Bret Easton Ellis, *American Psycho* (1991), London, 2011, p. 78.

47 **The Silence of the Lambs**, 1991, dir. Jonathan Demme, cost. Colleen Atwood.

9 'WELL, AS LONG AS THE LADY'S PAYING . . .'

1 Dialogue from **Sunset Boulevard**, 1950, dir. Billy Wilder, cost. Edith Head.

2 **Someone to Watch Over Me**, 1987, dir. Ridley Scott, cost. Colleen Atwood.

3 See the discussion of ties in 'One size fits all?', above.

4 Dialogue from **Someone to Watch Over Me**.

5 John Harvey, 'Showing and Hiding: Equivocation in the Relations of Body and Dress', *Fashion Theory*, vol. 11 issue 1, 2007, pp. 65–94.

6 **Mona Lisa**, 1986, dir. Neil Jordan, cost. Louise Frogley.

7 Dialogue from **Mona Lisa**.

8 Tommy Nutter, the avant-garde celebrity tailor to stars such as Mick Jagger, Elton John and the Beatles, was perhaps most famous for creating a distinctive broad, padded-shouldered silhouette, with jackets typically made from bold checked and patterned tweeds, with exaggeratedly wide lapels, in short a 1960s and 70s re-imagining of the classic 1930s movie-star gangster. By the time **Mona Lisa** was made, Nutter's star was on the wane and presumably the interior depicted is that of his ready-to-wear outlet at 19 Savile Row.

9 Dialogue from **Mona Lisa**.

10 Dialogue from **Sunset Boulevard**.

11 Ibid.

12 Ibid.

13 See Claire Pajaczkowska and Barry Curtis, 'Looking Sharp', in Uhlirova, *If Looks Could Kill*, pp. 64–6 for more on this and other themes related to Joe's clothing in **Sunset Boulevard**.

14 Dialogue from **Sunset Boulevard**.

15 **The Sheik**, 1921, dir. George Melford, cost. uncredited. Meta-cinematic references abound in **Sunset Boulevard**, and the rather conspicuous reference to Adolphe Menjou is perhaps a barb from Wilder, a leading liberal and one of the members of the Committee for the First Amendment. The Committee was formed to support the so-called 'unfriendly witnesses' called to testify at the House Committee on Un-American Activities, with which Menjou co-operated. He was also a leading member of the Motion Picture Alliance for the Preservation of American Ideals. Given that screen-writers were the primary target of the Committee and most directly affected by the publication of the Hollywood blacklist of supposed Communist sympathisers following the hearings held in 1947 (at the time that the script for **Sunset Boulevard**, released in 1950, would have been written), it is perhaps especially appropriate that Menjou is singled out for ridicule in the film.

16 **Curly Sue**, 1991, dir. James Hughes, cost. Michael Kaplan.

17 Dialogue from **Curly Sue**.

18 **Vertigo**, 1958, dir. Alfred Hitchcock, cost. Edith Head. **Laura**, 1944, dir. Otto Preminger, cost. Bonnie Cashin. Dialogue from **Laura**.

19 **Pretty Woman**, 1990, dir. Garry Marshall, cost. Marilyn Vance. See Bruzzi, *Undressing Cinema*, pp. 14–18. **Sabrina**, 1954, dir. Billy Wilder, cost. Edith Head, Hubert de Givenchy (Audrey Hepburn)..

20 Tamar Jeffers McDonald, *Hollywood Catwalk: Exploring Costume and Transformation in American Film*, London, 2010.

21   See ibid., conclusion, where the author discusses the male re-dressings in **A Place in the Sun** and **Come Blow Your Horn**.

22   **Casino Royale**, 2006, dir. Martin Campbell, cost. Lindy Hemming (dinner jacket for Daniel Craig made by Brioni).

23   Dialogue from ibid.

24   Ibid.

25   There has been much published about the importance of Bond's tailoring, especially his evening wear – how it functions not only as a sign of his ultra-masculinity but also as an essential part of the Bond 'brand', where his quintessential Britishness is crystallised via his tailoring. As such, the Bond 'franchise' acts as an important cinematic ambassador for British tailoring, especially Savile Row where many of Bond's on-screen clothes have been produced. McInerney's edited volume, *Dressed to Kill: James Bond the Suited Hero*, published in 1996 to coincide with Pierce Brosnan's first incarnation as Bond, and therefore missing his subsequent films as well as the most recent portrayal of Bond by Daniel Craig, remains indispensable, containing essays on Bond's wardrobe as well as those of his arch-enemies. For more contemporary assessments and meticulous detail about individual Bond garments, the website www.thesuitsofjamesbond.com is invaluable. The association between the closed, esoteric world of Savile Row tailoring and espionage is a subject that warrants further research; a number of both literary and cinematic examples suggest the dedication needed to dress impeccably and, more importantly, that the dedication needed to tailor immaculate clothes is akin to that for a life of spying, John le Carré's novel *The Tailor of Panama* being the notable example. In the film version, discussed previously, there are a number of Bond-related meta-cinematic jokes: Pierce Brosnan, famous for his characterisation of Bond in a total of four films, is the star. In the opening scenes which introduce Geoffrey Rush as the bogus Savile Row tailor now running a business in Panama, we see him draping a length of cloth over a client's shoulders while flattering him by declaring it to be 'Mr Connery's choice'. **The Good Shepherd**, 2006, dir. Robert De Niro, cost. Ann Roth, is a more recent example of film conflating the arcane worlds of tailoring and the secret service, as Matt Damon, playing Edward Wilson, the head of the CIA, recalls his fledgling spying career in London.

26   From the foreword to Hardy Amies, *A B C of Men's Fashion*, London, 2008.

27   Roland Barthes, 'Dandyism and Fashion' (1962), in *Language of Fashion*, p. 67.

28   Dialogue from **J. Edgar**.

29   Harvey, 'Showing and Hiding', p. 77.

30   At the end of the Second World War all servicemen returning home were issued with this full set of 'civvies'. Many were produced by the men's outfitters Burton's, based in Leeds, who had supplied many of the British army's uniforms. This important government commission meant that for a considerable period Burton's became the high-street men's outfitters that dictated the look of the average post-war British male.

31   Christopher Sladen's *The Conscription of Fashion: Utility Cloth, Clothing and Footwear 1941–1952*, Aldershot, 1995, p. 43 notes: 'The combination of Utility cloth and austerity restrictions resulted in suits in familiar materials but with slightly shorter jackets, lacking waist pleats, breast pocket or buttons on the cuffs. Buckles disappeared from waistcoats and trousers. Trousers narrowed slightly, and of course, had no turn-ups. Apart from that last deprivation, the average male customer would probably have found it difficult to spot significant differences between utility suits and the styles which preceded them.'

32   J. B. Priestley, *Three Men in New Suits*, London, 1945, p. 2.

10   WHITE LIES AND THE TAILORING OF EVIL

1   Richard Dyer, 'White', in *The Matter of Images: Essays on Representation*, London, 1993, p. 142.

2   **Saturday Night Fever**, 1977, dir. John Badham, cost. Patrizia von Brandenstein.

3   **Midnight Cowboy**, 1969, dir. John Schlesinger, cost. Ann Roth.

4   **The Man in the White Suit**, 1951, dir. Alexander Mackendrick, cost. Anthony Mendleson.

5   **Meet Dave**, 2008, dir. Brian Robbins, cost. Ruth E. Carter.

6   Ricardo Montalban played the mysterious overseer of Fantasy Island, Mr Roarke, in the popular television series of the same name which ran from 1978 to 1984. Apparently ageless and indestructible, Roarke would be a logical character for the aliens to choose as a model for their human-formed spacecraft. Roarke's sidekick Tattoo (Hervé Villechaize) was similarly attired in an all-white suit and black tie, providing a possible explanation for the aliens' understanding that all white was a common uniform for the inhabitants of Earth.

7   Dialogue from **Meet Dave**.

8   Bruzzi, *Undressing Cinema*, p. 72, quoting Farid Chenoune, *A History of Men's Fashion*, Paris, 1993

9   **Each Dawn I Die**, 1939, dir. William Keighley, cost. Howard Shoup. **Dr. No**, 1962, dir. Terence Young, cost. Tessa Prendergast.

10   **The Man with the Golden Gun**, 1974, dir. Guy Hamilton, cost. Elsa Fennel.

11   **Thunderball**, 1965, dir. Terence Young, cost. John Brady, Anthony Mendleson.

12   **Transporter 2**, 2005, dir. Louis Leterrier, cost. Bobbie Read.

13   Dialogue from **DodgeBall**.

14   **The Untouchables**, 1987, dir. Brian De Palma, cost. Giorgio Armani and Dan Lester. **The Boys from Brazil**, 1978, dir. Franklin J. Schaffner, cost. Anthony Mendleson. **The Intruder**, 1961, dir. Roger Corman, cost. Dorothy Watson.

15   Jean Baudrillard, *Simulations*, trans. Paul Foss, Paul Patton and Philip Beitchman, New York, 1983, p. 37.

16   John Gage, *Colour and Culture*, London, 1993, p. 60.

17   Bachelard, *Poetics of Space*, pp. 40–41.

18   See Gage, *Colour and Culture*, p. 60.

19   Dialogue from **The Intruder**.

20   Mark Wigley, *White Walls, Designer Dresses*, Cambridge, 2001, p. 177.

21   Origen quoted in Gage, *Colour and Culture*, p. 60.

22   Harvey, 'Showing and Hiding', pp. 65–94.

23   Dialogue from **The Intruder**.

11 SEEING RED

1   Lyrics from 'Hi-Heel Sneakers', 1963, Tommy Tucker.

2   **Jezebel**, 1938, dir. William Wyler, cost. Orry-Kelly. **The Bride Wore Red**, 1937, dir. Dorothy Arzner, cost. Adrian.

3   Dyer, *Matter of Images*, p. 154.

4   Ibid.

5   Dialogue from **The Bride Wore Red**.

6   Jane M. Gaines, 'Wanting to Wear Seeing: Gilbert Adrian at MGM', in Adrienne Munich, ed., *Fashion in Film*, Bloomington, Ind., 2011, p. 150.

7   In fact, 'The infamous scarlet dress was actually bronze-colored [sic], which photographed better in black and white', according to Richard Schickel and George Perry, *Bette Davis: Larger than Life*, Philadelphia, Penn., 2009, p. 121.

8   **The Band Wagon**, 1953, dir. Vincent Minnelli, cost. Mary Ann Nyberg. **All That Heaven Allows**, 1955, dir. Douglas Sirk, cost. Bill Thomas. **Pretty Woman**, 1990, dir. Garry Marhsall, cost. Marilyn Vance.

9   Bruzzi, *Undressing Cinema*, p. 15.

10 Much has been written about Head's insistence that film costume was not fashion, due in part to her realisation that designs for film could appear outmoded if by the time of a film's release there had been a significant change in sartorial trends. This applied especially at the beginning of her career when American fashion was still much influenced by innovations coming from Parisian designers. For more on this subject see Head and Calistro, *Edith Head's Hollywood*, and Jorgensen, *Edith Head*.

11 Along with Gilbert Adrian, Travis Banton produced distinctive and memorable film costumes in the 1930s including Claudette Colbert's for **Cleopatra** (1934) and the trio of Marlene Dietrich films featuring some of his more extravagant creations: **Shanghai Express** (1932), **The Scarlet Empress** (1934) and **The Devil is a Woman** (1935). It was suggested that Head, who started her career as Banton's assistant, was instrumental in getting him dismissed from his post as chief designer at Paramount in 1938, because of his increasing alcoholism, but this was probably a rumour embellished by the Hollywood gossip columnist Hedda Hopper.

12 Gaines, 'Wanting to Wear Seeing', p. 149. Bruzzi, *Undressing Cinema*, pp. 3–34, 'Cinema and Haute Couture'.

13 **The House of Mirth**, 2000, dir. Terence Davies, cost. Monica Howe.

14 Edith Wharton, *The House of Mirth* (1905), London, 1986, p. 116.

15 Dialogue from **Pubic Enemies**.

16 **Last Holiday**, 2006, dir. Wayne Wang, cost. Daniel Orlandi.

17 Dialogue from **Last Holiday**.

18 **My Stepmother is an Alien**, 1988, dir. Richard Benjamin, cost. Aggie Guerard Rodgers.

19 **Don't Look Now**, 1973, dir. Nicolas Roeg, cost. Marit Lieberson.

20 **Fargo**, 1996, dir. Joel and Ethan Coen, cost. Mary Zophres.

21 The cinematic contrast provided by red on a white background is explored further in the last chapter below, 'Stubborn Stains'.

22 **The Honeymooners**, 2005, dir. John Schultz, cost. Joan Bergin.

23 For more on this particular component of Jewish costume, the entry for 'Badge' in the *Encyclopaedia Judaica*, Jerusalem, 1972, provides a thorough historical account of this proscription.

24 **Bridget Jones: The Edge of Reason**, 2004, dir. Beeban Kidron, cost. Jany Temime.

25 Dialogue from **Bridget Jones: The Edge of Reason**.

12 IT'S FROM PARIS!

1   Lyrics from 'Buttons and Bows', 1947, Jay Livingstone and Ray Evans.

2   **Now, Voyager**, 1942, dir. Irving Rapper, cost. Orry-Kelly.

3   Text from the labels pinned to Charlotte Vale's outfits in **Now, Voyager**.

4   Georg Simmel, 'Fashion' (1904), in *Georg Simmel: On Individuality and Social Forms*, trans. and ed. Donald N. Levine, Chicago, 1971, p. 300.

5   From **Roberta** made in 1935 to **The Devil Wears Prada** of 2006, by way of **Funny Face** released in 1957, mainstream film has revelled in inserting the outsider (symbolising rationality) into the world of fashion (symbolising irrationality). Much work still needs to be done on the representation of the fashion industry in film and the persistence of this particular cinematic construction.

6   **The Strange Affair of Uncle Harry**, 1945, dir. Robert Siodmak, cost. Travis Banton.

7   Dialogue from **The Strange Affair of Uncle Harry**.

8   **Sweet Home Alalabama**, 2002, dir. Andy Tennant, cost. Sophie de Rakoff Carbonell.

9   Simmel, 'Fashion', p. 299. **Raising Helen**, 2004, dir. Garry Marshall, cost. Gary Jones.

10 Dialogue from **Raising Helen**.

11 **National Lampoon's European Vacation**, 1985, dir. Amy Heckerling, cost. Graham Williams.

12 **Lucy Gallant**, 1955, dir. Robert Parrish, cost. Edith Head.

13 Dialogue from **Lucy Gallant**.

14 Jorgensen, *Edith Head*, p. 64.

15 Dialogue from **Lucy Gallant.**

16 Ibid. See 'Trophies', above, for a fuller discussion of Lucy's mink coats.

17 Simmel, *On Individuality*, p. 300.

18 Ibid., p. 298.

19 **Roberta**, 1935, dir. William A. Seiter, cost. Bernard Newman.

20 Dialogue from **Roberta**.

21 Ibid.

22 Ibid.

23 Ibid.

24 Bourdieu, *Distinction*, p. 6.

25 **Rebecca**, 1940, dir. Alfred Hitchcock, cost. uncredited.

26 Dialogue from **Rebecca**.

27 Ibid.

28 Ibid.

29 **Legally Blonde**, 2001, dir. Robert Luketic, cost. Sophie Carbonell.

30 Charles Dickens, *Great Expectations* (1861), London, 2008, p. 212.

31 **Shaft**, 2000, dir. John Singleton, cost. Ruth Carter.

32 Dialogue from **Shaft**.

33 **The Omen**, 1976, dir. Richard Donner, cost. Tiny Nicholls.

34 This particular scene from **Leave Her to Heaven** (1945, dir. John M. Stahl, cost. Kay Nelson) represents a pinnacle of sartorial dysfunctionality: the satin mules she wears have already been discussed in 'Criminal Accessories', above, and the remarkable use of monograms throughout the film will be looked at in detail in 'The Mark of the Beast'.

35 Mary Douglas, *Purity and Danger* (1966), London, 2002, p. 48.

36 Douglas's concept of matter out of place defined in *Purity and Danger* will be revisited in 'Stubborn Stains', below. **Coogan's Bluff**, 1968, dir. Don Siegel, cost. Helen Colvig. **Midnight Cowboy**, 1969, dir. John Schlesinger, cost. Ann Roth. **Blazing Saddles**, 1974, dir. Mel Brooks, cost. Tom Dawson, Nino Novarese.

37 **Coogan's Bluff** followed Eastwood's successful trilogy of 'spaghetti westerns' directed by Sergio Leone and marked the beginning of his fruitful partnership with the director Don Siegel with whom Eastwood went on to make **Dirty Harry**, playing Harry Callahan. Coogan's characterisation as the urban cowboy also formed the basis for the successful American television series **McCloud** (1970–77) in which Dennis Weaver plays the cowboy detective Sam McCloud as a fish out of water in the big city, but who always gets his man.

38 Dialogue from **Blazing Saddles**.

39 Douglas, *Purity and Danger*, p. 48.

40 Dialogue from **Blazing Saddles**.

13 WEAR AND TEAR

1 Lyrics from 'The Israelites', 1969, Desmond Dekker and Leslie Kong.

2 See Angus Patterson, *Fashion and Armour in Renaissance Europe: Proud Looks and Brave Attire*, London, 2009, for a detailed discussion of the relationship between fashionable display in Renaissance men's clothing and its reinterpretation in armour.

3 **North by Northwest**, 1959, dir. Alfred Hitchcock, cost. Harry Kress.

4 Ulrich Lehmann, 'The Language of the PurSuit: Cary Grant's Clothes in Alfred Hitchcock's "North by Northwest"', *Fashion Theory*, vol. 4 issue 4, 2000, pp. 467–86.

5 Ibid., pp. 469–71.

6 Ibid., p. 469.

7 Ibid., p. 477. Deuteronomy 8:4, King James Bible (Authorised Version).

8 **Charade**, 1963, dir. Stanley Donen, cost. Hubert de Givenchy (Audrey Hepburn). David Thomson, *A Biographical Dictionary of the Cinema*, London, 1980, p. 157.

9 Grant was acutely aware of the age-gap between himself and Hepburn in **Charade** and reports show that he requested additional dialogue referring to this difference be scripted into the film. Since he was only too aware that his screen success was to a large degree based on his debonair appearance, Grant presumably realised that his age would soon preclude or at least stretch the credibility of the roles that had been his stock in trade.

10 Dialogue from **Charade**.

11 Ibid.

12 With 'un-suturing' I am referring to the more expanded definition of suture, beyond the shot/reverse-angle shot method of 'stitching' the spectator into the film's action, so including all the devices associated with the construction of mainstream film narrative, among them continuity editing. Therefore, un-suturing in this instance is a device that wilfully 'unstitches' the viewer from the action, as well as forces apart the apparent seamlessness of Cary Grant and Peter Joshua.

13 Dialogue from **Bringing Up Baby**.

14 Although there are early highlights in Grant's career that predate the release of **Bringing Up Baby** in 1938, such as **Blonde Venus** (1932) and **Sylvia Scarlett** (1935), his appearance in both these films is eclipsed by the performances of their respective leading ladies (Dietrich and Hepburn). It is with **The Awful Truth**, released a year before **Bringing Up Baby**, in 1937, that Grant perfected his suave, comic persona. Following **Charade**, he made **Mother Goose** (1964), which sees him uncharacteristically unkempt and shabby, and he ended his career with **Walk, Don't Run** (1966), playing an older, admittedly still elegant, matchmaker to the film's younger romantic leads. The films made between the two under discussion therefore mark Grant's sophisticated sovereignty.

15 *Verfremdungseffekt*, or alienation, distancing or estrangement effect, was introduced by Bertolt Brecht in 1936 to describe 'playing in such a way that the audience was hindered from simply identifying itself with characters in the play. Acceptance or rejection of their actions and utterances was meant to take place on a conscious plane, instead of, as hitherto, in the audience's subconscious.' See John Willett, ed., *Brecht on Theatre* (1964), trans. John Willett, London, 1974, p. 91.

16 **The Seven Year Itch**, 1953, dir. Billy Wilder, cost. Charles le Maire and Travilla.

17 Dialogue from **The Seven Year Itch**.

18 Ibid.

19 **Tales of Manhattan**, 1942, dir. Julien Duvivier, cost. Dolly Tree, Bernard Newman, Gwen Wakeling, Irene, Oleg Cassini.

20 Dialogue from **Play Misty for Me**, 1971, dir. Clint Eastwood, cost. Helen Colvig.

21 '**Hush . . . Hush, Sweet Charlotte**', 1964, dir. Robert Aldrich, cost. Norma Koch.

22 Dialogue from '**Hush . . . Hush, Sweet Charlotte**'.

23 Ibid.

24 **The Wrong Arm of the Law**, 1963, dir. Cliff Owen, cost. James Smith.

25 Dialogue from **The Wrong Arm of the Law**.

26 'The Golden Age of Couture: Paris and London 1947–1957', Victoria & Albert Museum, London, 22 September 2007 – 6 January 2008. Andrei Harmsworth, 'Kate Moss has a ripper of a night', *Metro*, 19 September 2007, http://www.metro.co.uk/showbiz/66708-kate-moss-has-a-ripper-of-a-night. Clemmie Moodie, 'The ripping yarn of Kate and Courtney out partying', *The Daily Mail*, 19 September 2007, http://www.dailymail.co.uk/tvshowbiz/article-482524/The-ripping-yarn-Kate-Courtney-partying.html.

27 Harmsworth, 'Kate Moss'.

28 Moodie, 'Ripping yarn'.

29 The particular pair of shoes worn by Campbell were immediately

acquired by the Victoria & Albert Museum and have since been used in a number of marketing campaigns for the museum.

30 Dialogue from **Lucy Gallant**.

31 Ibid.

32 Ibid.

33 Ibid.

14 THE MARK OF THE BEAST

1   Lyrics from 'Someone to Watch Over Me', 1926, George and Ira Gershwin.

2   **High Anxiety**, 1977, dir. Mel Brooks, cost. Patricia Norris.

3   Dialogue from **High Anxiety**.

4   Jane Pavitt, ed., *Brand.new*, London, 2002, p. 44.

5   Roland Barthes, 'The New Citroën', in *Mythologies*, trans. Annette Lavers, London, 1973, p. 95.

6   Fredric Jameson, 'On Raymond Chandler' (1970), in G. W. Most and W. W. Stowe, eds, *The Poetics of Murder: Detective Fiction and Literary Theory*, San Diego, Calif., 1983, p. 137.

7   **Charade**, 1963, dir. Stanley Donen, cost. Hubert de Givenchy (Audrey Hepburn).

8   Dialogue from **Charade**.

9   Pavitt, *Brand.new*, pp. 18–52.

10 Louis Vuitton's interlinked L and V and the other symbols that make up its distinctive brown and gold livery are derived from just such an ancient armorial system: the Japanese *mon*, similar to the European heraldic tradition.

11 **Leave Her to Heaven**, 1945, dir. John M. Stahl, cost. Kay Nelson.

12 Dialogue from **Leave Her to Heaven**.

13 Ibid.

14 Ibid.

15 Nathaniel Hawthorne, *The Scarlet Letter* (1850), London, 2010, p. 25.

16 **Whirlpool**, 1949, dir. Otto Preminger, cost. Oleg Cassini (Gene Tierney).

17 **Mommie Dearest**, 1981, dir. Frank Perry, cost. Irene Sharaff.

18 Dialogue from **Mildred Pierce**, 1945, dir. Michael Curtiz, cost. Milo Anderson.

19 Dialogue from **Desk Set**, 1957, dir. Walter Lang, cost. Charles Le Maire.

20 Ibid.

21 **The King of Comedy**, 1983, dir. Martin Scorsese, cost. Richard Bruno.

22 Dialogue from **The King of Comedy**.

23 Jameson, 'On Raymond Chandler', p. 137.

24 **Shadow of a Doubt**, 1943, dir. Alfred Hitchcock, cost. Vera West.

25 For a detailed exploration of the significance of the ring in **Shadow of a Doubt** see Mladen Dolar, 'Hitchcock's Objects', in Žižek, *Everything You Always Wanted to Know*, pp. 31–46.

26 **Dead Reckoning**, 1947, dir. John Cromwell, cost. Jean Louis (gowns).

27 Dialogue from **Dead Reckoning**.

28 Ibid.

29 **Strangers on a Train**, 1951, dir. Alfred Hitchcock, cost. Leah Rhodes.

30 Hitchcock redeployed the tie-pin as the signature item of jewellery for the psychopath in **Frenzy**, where Barry Foster as the neck-tie murderer loses his signature stick-pin while strangling one of his victims and is later depicted in grizzly detail wrenching it free from the dead woman's stiffened fingers.

31 **Rebecca**, 1940, dir. Alfred Hitchcock, cost. uncredited.

32 Pierre Bourdieu and Alain Darbel, *The Love of Art: European Art Museums and Their Public*, trans. Caroline Beattie and Nick Merriman, Cambridge, 1991, p. 112.

33 Dialogue from **Rebecca**.

34 Ibid.

35 Hawthorne, *Scarlet Letter*, p. 152.

15 STUBBORN STAINS

1   Douglas, *Purity and Danger*, p. 44.

2   **The Pursuit of Happyness**, 2006, dir. Gabriele Muccino, cost. Sharen Davis.

3   Dialogue from **The Pursuit of Happyness**.

4   Dialogue from **Laura**.

5   Dialogue from **The Dark Corner**.

6   Ibid.

7   I am referring to productions such as the popular and long running **C.S.I.** television series which have had a profound effect on the popular understanding of criminology, especially forensics, and indeed have fostered the creation of the 'forensic aesthetic' that pervades much contemporary visual media.

8   **Stage Fright**, 1950, dir. Alfred Hitchcock, cost. Christian Dior (Marlene Dietrich), Milo Anderson. **'Hush . . . Hush, Sweet Charlotte'**, 1964, dir. Robert Aldrich, cost. Norma Koch. See Kitty Hauser's illuminating 'Stained Clothing, Guilty Hearts', in Uhlirova, *If Looks Could Kill*, pp. 68–75, for an examination of these two films and the function and reception of the faked and real bloodstain.

9   See 'Exchange Mechanisms', above, for an explanation of the function of the McGuffin in relation to the raincoat in **Young and Innocent**.

10 A perfect demonstration of this ability is to be found in the kilt which, according to whether it is pleated to sett or stripe, can hide whole blocks of colour within its pleats, radically altering the appearance of the back of the kilt from the front, though both are made from exactly the same patterned cloth.

11 Dialogue from **Stage Fright**.

12 Ibid.

13 It is well documented how Dietrich and von Sternberg experimented with every lighting possibility that would produce the most alluring effect, finally settling on a simple key light above and slightly in front of her head, which cast the shadows that sculpted her face on screen, producing the Dietrich image familiar to movie goers. Dietrich, realising the power of her image, insisted that this lighting technique be used in all her subsequent films where possible.

14 As has been noted in Part Five's 'It's from Paris!', the custom for leading actresses to demand Parisian fashion to wear on screen can

be traced back to Hollywood's infancy; Dietrich's insistence on Dior is a continuation of this tradition.

15 Palmer, *Couture and Commerce*, p. 78.

16 Angela Partington, 'Popular Fashion and Working-Class Affluence', in E. Wilson and J. Ash, eds, *Chic Thrills: A Fashion Reader*, London, 1992, p. 154.

17 Dialogue from **Stage Fright**.

18 Pascal Bonitzer, 'Hitchcockian Suspense', in Žižek, *Everything You Always Wanted to Know*, p. 20.

19 Douglas, *Purity and Danger*, p. 150.

20 Julia Kristeva, *Powers of Horror: An Essay on Abjection*, trans. Leon S. Roudiez, New York, 1982, p. 2.

21 Guy Debord, 'Separation Perfected', Ch. 1 paragraph 3, in *Society of the Spectacle*, n.p.

22 **Carrie**, 1976, dir. Brian De Palma, cost. Rosanna Norton.

23 Žižek, *Everything You Always Wanted to Know*, p. x.

24 Peter Wollen, 'Vectors of Melancholy', in R. Rugoff, ed., *Scene of the Crime*, Cambridge, Mass., 1997, p. 24.

25 **The Relic**, 1997, dir. Peter Hyams, cost. Daniel J. Lester.

26 The most striking example of spilt blood hastening supernatural carnage is to be found in the numerous cinematic versions of Dracula. Perhaps the most extreme is that of **Dracula Prince of Darkness** (1966, dir. Terence Fisher, cost. Rosemary Burrows) where Dracula's dust is reconstituted by the stream of blood flowing from the neck of the hapless traveller stabbed and then suspended above his sarcophagus.

27 **L.A. Confidential**, 1997, dir. Curtis Hanson, cost. Ruth Myers.

28 **The Deer Hunter**, 1978, dir. Michael Cimino, cost. Sandy Berke Jordan, Laurie Riley, Eric Seelig.

29 Dialogue from **The Deer Hunter**.

30 Carlo Ginzburg, 'Morelli, Freud and Sherlock Holmes: Clues and Scientific Method', *History Workshop Journal*, vol. 9, 1980, p. 13.

31 **The Bucket List**, 2007, dir. Rob Reiner, cost. Molly Maginnis.

32 Dialogue from **The Bucket List**.

33 Dialogue from **Midnight Cowboy**.

34 **Nicholas and Alexandra**, 1971, dir. Franklin D. Schaffner, cost. Yvonne Blake.

35 **Moulin Rouge**, 2001, dir. Baz Luhrmann, cost. Catherine Martin and Angus Strathie.

POSTSCRIPT

1 Benjamin, *Arcades Project*, p. 204, 'H [The Collector]'.

2 This rejection of forensic utility is relevant to the films discussed in *Dressing Dangerously* but it would of course be possible to assemble another set of images, from different films, that conforms to the concept of incriminating evidence. However, whether functional or dysfunctional, the pivotal role that clothing plays in crime film is undeniable and offers stimulating opportunities for further research.

3 Ginzburg, 'Morelli, Freud and Sherlock Holmes', p. 11.

4 Arthur Conan Doyle, 'The Adventure of the Blue Carbuncle', in *The New Annotated Sherlock Holmes*, ed. L. S. Klinger, New York, 2005, p. 198.

5 There are other rivals to Holmes's crown, most notably Edgar Allan Poe's character Dupin, who featured in the short stories *The Murders in the Rue Morgue* and *The Purloined Letter*, but Conan Doyle's Holmes retains the universal popularity he achieved on first appearing in *The Strand* in 1891.

6 Rugoff, *Scene of the Crime*, p. 82, quoting Slajov Žižek, 'Looking Awry: An Introduction to Jacques Lacan through Popular Culture', Cambridge, 1992.

7 Cinematic versions of these three writers' stories comprise some of the celebrated film noir and detective films of the 1940s: **Farewell, My Lovely**, **The Blue Dahlia**, **The Big Sleep** and **Lady in the Lake** all based on stories by Raymond Chandler; **The Maltese Falcon**, **The Thin Man** (although the original film was released in 1934, and therefore dates from an earlier period than the rest of the films cited here, so successful was the original film that five sequels were made stretching into the 1940s) and **The Glass Key** by Dashiel Hammett; and **The Postman Always Rings Twice**, **Double Indemnity** and **Mildred Pierce** by James M. Cain.

8 William W. Stowe, 'From Semiotics to Hermeneutics: Modes of Detection in Doyle and Chandler', in Most and Stowe, *Poetics of Murder*, p. 382.

9 Burgin, *Remembered Film*, p. 72.

BIBLIOGRAPHY

Allen, R., and S. Ishii Gonzalès, eds., *Alfred Hitchcock Centenary Essays*, London, 1999

Amies, H., *A B C of Men's Fashion*, London, 2008

Arnold, J., *The American Look: Fashion and the Image of Women in 1930s and 1940s New York*, London, 2008

Bachelard, G., *The Poetics of Space*, trans. Maria Jolas, Boston, Mass., 1994

Barthes, R., *Image Music Text*, trans. Stephen Heath, London, 1977

—, *The Language of Fashion* (1961), trans. Andy Stafford, ed. A. Stafford and M. Carter, Oxford, 2006

—, *Mythologies*, trans. Annette Lavers, London, 1973

Bataille, G., *Encyclopaedia Acephalica*, trans. Iain White, London, 1995

—, *Vision of Excess: Selected Writings, 1927–1939*, trans. Allan Stoekl, Minneapolis, 1985

Baudrillard, J., *Simulations*, trans. Paul Foss, Paul Patton and Philip Beitchman, New York, 1983

—, *The System of Objects*, trans. J. Benedict, London, 1999

Bell, Q., *On Human Finery*, London, 1992

Benjamin, W., *The Arcades Project*, trans. Howard Eiland and Kevin McLaughlin, Cambridge, Mass., 1999

Bourdieu, P., *Distinction: A Social Critique of the Judgement of Taste*, trans. Richard Nice, Cambridge, 1984

— and A. Darbel, *The Love of Art: European Art Museums and Their Public*, trans. Caroline Beattie and Nick Merriman, Cambridge, 1991

Bruzzi, S., *Undressing Cinema: Clothing and Identity in the Movies*, London, 1997

Bulwer-Lytton, E., *Pelham, or the Adventures of a Gentleman*, London, 1828

Burgin, V., *The Remembered Film*, London, 2004

Castiglione, B., *The Book of the Courtier* (1528), London, 1975

Chandler, R., *Farewell My Lovely* (1940), London, 2005

Chapman, J., *Emotionally Durable Design,* London, 2009

Clarke Keogh, P., *Audrey Style*, London, 1999

Cobb, W. J., *To the Break of Dawn: A Freestyle on the Hip Hop Aesthetic*, New York, 2007

Cohn, N., *Today There Are No Gentlemen*, London, 1971

Conan Doyle, A., *The New Annotated Sherlock Holmes*, ed. L. S. Klinger, New York, 2005

Cook, P., *Fashioning the Nation: Costume and Identity in British Cinema*, London, 1996

Debord, G., *The Society of the Spectacle*, trans. Fredy Perlman and John Supak, Detroit, 1983

Delpierre, M., et al., *French Elegance in the Cinema*, Paris, 1988

Dickens, C., *Great Expectations* (1861), London, 2008

Douglas, M., *Purity and Danger* (1966), London, 2002

Dubuffet, J., *Asphyxiating Culture*, New York, 1988

Dyer, R., *The Matter of Images: Essays on Representation*, London, 1993

Ellis, B. E., *American Psycho* (1991), London, 2011

Elsner, J, and Cardinal, R. eds., *The Cultures of Collecting*, London, 1994

Emberley, J. V., *Venus and Furs: The Cultural Politics of Fur*, London, 1998

Encyclopaedia Judaica, Jerusalem, 1972

Engelmeier, R. and P. W., eds., *Fashion in Film*, Munich, 1990

Esquevin, C., *Adrian: Silver Screen to Custom Label*, New York, 2008

Faiers, J., *Tartan*, Oxford, 2008

Fashion/Cinema, Milan, 1998

Flaubert, G., *The Dictionary of Received Ideas* (1913; assembled and published posthumously), trans. Robert Baldick, London, 1976

Foucault, M., *The Archaeology of Knowledge* (1969), trans. A. M. Sheridan Smith, London, 1992

Foulkes, N., *The Trench Book*, New York, 2007

Fulco, E., ed., *Cinema Wears a Hat, Borsalino and Other Stories*, Mantua, 2011

Gaalen, A. van, ed., *Never Leave the House Naked*, Amsterdam, 2009

Gabbard, K. and G. O., *Psychiatry and the Cinema,* Washington, D.C., 1999

Gage, J., *Colour and Culture*, London, 1993

Galloway D., ed., *The Fall of the House of Usher and Other Writings*, London, 1986

Gibbings, S., *The Tie: Trends and Traditions*, London, 1990

Gogol, N., *The Overcoat and Other Short Stories*, trans. Isabel F. Hapgood, New York, 1992

Harvey, J., *Men in Black*, London, 1995

Haskell, M., *From Reverence to Rape: The Treatment of Women in the Movies*, London, 1974

Hawthorne, N., *The Scarlet Letter* (1850), London, 2010

Hayward, S., *Key Concepts in Cinema Studies*, London, 1996

Head, E., and P. Calistro, *Edith Head's Hollywood*, Santa Monica, Cal., 2008

Herzog, C., and J. M. Gaines, eds, *Fabrications: Costume and the Female Body*, London, 1991

Hollander, A., *Seeing Through Clothes*, Berkeley, Cal., 1993

Hunt, A., *Governance of the Consuming Passions: A History of Sumptuary Law*, New York, 1996

James, M. R., 'Casting the Runes' (1911), in *The Collected Ghost Stories of M. R. James*, London, 1931

Jeffers McDonald, T., *Hollywood Catwalk: Exploring Costume and Transformation in American Film*, London, 2010

Jorgensen, J., *Edith Head: The Fifty-Year Career of Hollywood's Greatest Costume Designer*, Philadelphia, 2010

Kaplan, E. A., ed., *Psychoanalysis and Cinema*, London, 1990

King James Bible, The Authorised Version, Oxford, 2008

Kristeva, J., *Powers of Horror: An Essay on Abjection*, trans. Leon S. Roudiez, New York, 1982

Kuchta, D., *The Three-Piece Suit and Modern Masculinity*, Berkeley, Cal., 2002

Kuhn, A., *Women's Pictures: Feminism and Cinema*, London, 1982

Laver, J., *Taste and Fashion: From the French Revolution to the Present Day*, London, 1948

Leese, E., *Costume Design in the Movies*, New York, 1991

Marx, K., *Capital: A Critique of Political Economy*, vol. 1, trans. Ben Fowkes, London, 1990

McInerney, J., et al., *Dressed to Kill: James Bond the Suited Hero*, Paris, 1996

Mears, P., *American Beauty: Aesthetics and Innovation in Fashion*, New Haven, Conn., 2009

Mosely, R., *Fashioning Film Stars: Dress, Culture and Identity*, London, 2005

—, *Growing Up with Audrey Hepburn: Text, Audience, Resonance*, Manchester, 2002

Most, G. W., and W. W. Stowe, eds., *The Poetics of Murder: Detective Fiction and Literary Theory*, San Diego, Cal., 1983

Munich, A.,ed., *Fashion in Film*, Bloomington, Ind., 2011

Nadeau, C., *Fur Nation: From the Beaver to Brigitte Bardot*, London, 2001

Nadoolman Landis, D., ed., *Hollywood Costume*, London, 2012

Norris, F., *McTeague* (1899), Harmondsworth, 1982

Palmer, A., *Couture and Commerce: The Transatlantic Fashion Trade in the 1950s*, Vancouver, 2001

Patterson, A., *Fashion and Armour in Renaissance Europe: Proud Lookes and Brave Attire*, London, 2009

Pavitt, J. ed., *Brand.new*, London, 2002

Penley, C. ed., *The Analysis of Film*, Indianapolis, 2000

Perrot, P., *Fashioning the Bourgeoisie: A History of Clothing in the Nineteenth Century*, Princeton, N.J., 1994

Potvin, J. ed., *The Places and Spaces of Fashion, 1800–2007*, London, 2009

Priestley, J. B., *Three Men in New Suits*, London, 1945

Rayner, G., R. Chamberlain and A. Stapleton, *Artists' Textiles 1940–1976*, Woodbridge, Suffolk, 2012

Rugoff, R., ed., *Scene of the Crime*, Cambridge, Mass., 1997

Samuel, R., *Theatres of Memory*, London, 1994

Santos, M., *The Dark Mirror: Psychiatry and Film Noir*, Lanham, Md., 2010

Schaffner, I., and M. Winzen, eds, *Deep Storage: Collecting, Storing, and Archiving in Art*, Munich, 1998

Schickel, R., and G. Perry, *Bette Davis: Larger than Life*, Philadelphia, Penn., 2009

Sheridan, J., *Fashion Media Promotion: The New Black Magic*, Chichester, W. Sussex, 2010

Simmel, G., *Georg Simmel: On Individuality and Social Forms*, trans. and ed. D. N. Levine, Chicago, 1971

Sladen, C., *The Conscription of Fashion: Utility Cloth, Clothing and Footwear 1941–1952*, Aldershot, 1995

Spyer, P., ed., *Border Fetishisms: Material Objects in Unstable Spaces*, London, 1998

Stafford, A., and M. Carter, eds, *Roland Barthes: The Language of Fashion*, Oxford, 2006

Stewart, S., *On Longing*, Durham, N.C., 1993

Svendsen, L., *Fashion: A Philosophy*, London, 2006

Taylor, L., *Establishing Dress History*, Manchester, 2004

Thal, H. van, *The Ninth Pan Book of Horror Stories*, London, 1974

Thomson, D., *A Biographical Dictionary of the Cinema*, London, 1980

Uhlirova, M., ed., *If Looks Could Kill: Cinema's Images of Fashion, Crime and Violence*, London, 2008

Veblen, T., *The Theory of the Leisure Class* (1899), New York, 1994

Webster, J., *The Duchess of Malfi* (1612–13), London, 1983

Wharton, E., *The House of Mirth* (1905), London, 1986

—, *The New York Stories of Edith Wharton*, New York, 2007

Wigley, M., *White Walls, Designer Dresses*, Cambridge, 2001

Wilde, O., *Complete Works of Oscar Wilde*, London, 1971

Willett, J., ed., *Brecht on Theatre* (1964), trans. J. Willett, London, 1974

Wilson, E., *Adorned in Dreams: Fashion and Modernity*, London, 2007

—, and J. Ash, eds, *Chic Thrills: A Fashion Reader*, London, 1992

Žižek, S., ed., *Everything You Always Wanted to Know About Lacan But Were Afraid to Ask Hitchcock*, London, 2010

JOURNAL ARTICLES

'Clothes on the Screen', *The Tailor and Cutter*, 7 March 1936

Didi-Huberman, G., 'The Index of the Absent Wound (Monograph on a Stain)', *October*, vol. 29, Summer 1984, pp. 63–81

Ginzburg, C., 'Morelli, Freud and Sherlock Holmes: Clues and Scientific Method', *History Workshop Journal*, vol. 9, 1980, pp. 5–36

Harvey, J., 'Showing and Hiding: Equivocation in the Relations of Body and Dress', *Fashion Theory*, vol. 11 issue 1, 2007, pp. 65–94

Lehmann, U., 'The Language of the PurSuit: Cary Grant's Clothes in Alfred Hitchcock's "North by Northwest"', *Fashion Theory*, vol. 4 issue 4, 2000, pp. 467–86

Mulvey, L., 'Visual Pleasure and Narrative Cinema', *Screen*, vol. 16 no. 3, 1975, pp. 6–18

Oudart, J. P., 'Cinema and Suture', *Screen*, vol. 18 no. 4, 1977, pp. 35–47

Perkins, V. F., 'Moments of Choice', *The Movie*, no. 58, 1981 (repr. in A. Loyd, ed., *Movie Book of the Fifties*, London, 1982), republished online by the Australian film journal *Rouge* (issue 9, 2006) http://www.rouge.com.au/9/moments_choice.html

Sorkin, J., 'Stain: On Cloth, Stigma, and Shame', *Third Text*, 53, Winter 2000–01, pp. 77–80

Warner, H., 'Tracing Patterns: Critical Approaches to On-Screen Fashion', *Film, Fashion & Consumption*, vol. 1 no. 1, 2012, pp. 121–32

Wilson, E., and L. Francke, 'Gamine Against the Grain', *Sight and Sound*, vol. 3 no. 3 1993, pp. 30–32

Wollen, P., 'Strike a Pose', *Sight and Sound*, March 1995, pp. 10–15

WEBSITES

British Film Institute http://www.bfi.org.uk/

Internet Movie Database, The http://www.imdb.com/

Rap Genius http://rapgenius.com

Suits of James Bond, The www.thesuitsofjamesbond.com

Turner Classic Movies http://www.tcm.com/

ACKNOWLEDGEMENTS

Firstly, I would like to thank Gillian Malpass at Yale University Press for her initial enthusiasm and continued and unwavering support for the project.

Many friends and colleagues have been extremely generous in giving their encouragement and sharing their expertise with me while I have been working on *Dressing Dangerously*, and the following list represents only a small proportion of those who have been of invaluable help in bringing the work to completion: Stephen Atkinson at Rex Features; Dilys Blum and the Philadelphia Museum of Art; Mirren Arzalluz and Aberri Olaskoaga and the Fundación Cristóbal Balenciaga; Eric Musgrave; Katharine Ridler; Sandy Chapman; Paul Sloman; Jane Horton; Claire Pajaczkowska; August Davis and Adrian Baxter at Winchester School of Art; Ron Mandelbaum at Photofest.

I am especially thankful for the support of the Winchester Centre for Global Futures in Art, Design & Media.

Finally my deepest gratitude goes to Dell and Inez who had to live with a partner and father often unable to watch a film without turning to notebook and 'losing the plot' – my love to you as always.

INDEX